Fine Lines and Distinctions

Murder, Manslaughter and the
Unlawful Taking of Human Life

Terence Morris and Louis Blom-Cooper

Fine Lines and Distinctions
Murder, Manslaughter and the Unlawful Taking of Human Life
Terence Morris and Louis Blom-Cooper

ISBN 978-1-904380-66-5 (Hardback)   **ISBN** 978-1-906534-99-8 (E-book)

Published 2011 by
Waterside Press Ltd.
Sherfield Gables
Sherfield on Loddon
Hook, Hampshire
United Kingdom RG27 0JG

Telephone +44(0)1256 882250
Low cost UK landline calls 0845 2300 733
E-mail enquiries@watersidepress.co.uk
Online catalogue WatersidePress.co.uk

UK distributor Gardners Books, 1 Whittle Drive, Eastbourne, East Sussex, BN23 6QH. Tel: +44 (0)1323 521777; sales@gardners.com; www.gardners.com

North American distributor International Specialized Book Services (ISBS), 920 NE 58th Ave, Suite 300, Portland, Oregon, 97213-3786, USA. Tel: 1 800 944 6190 Fax 1 503 280 8832; orders@isbs.com; www.isbs.com

Cover design © 2011 Waterside Press. Front cover photograph copyright of the Metropolitan Police Service (full description given in plate section of this work). Design by www.gibgob.com

Cataloguing-In-Publication Data A catalogue record for this book can be obtained from the British Library.

e-book *Fine Lines and Distinctions* is available as an ebook (ISBN 978-1-906534-99-8) and also to subscribers of Myilibrary and Dawsonera.

Printed by MPG Books Group, Bodmin and King's Lynn.

Fine Lines and Distinctions

Murder, Manslaughter and the
Unlawful Taking of Human Life

Terence Morris and Louis Blom-Cooper

Foreword by Lord Judge

☒ WATERSIDE PRESS

Contents

Acknowledgements

The gestatory period of this book has been a long one. Indeed, when some-one inquired how long it had taken to write he received the jocular answer, "About fifty years!" In one sense that is true, since our work together on the penalty for homicide began in the late 1950s, at the time of the final campaign for the abolition of the death penalty. For that reason it is right to record our gratitude for the support of those no longer alive, but who gave us generously of their time and frequently re-charged our enthusiasm. They include David Astor who, when Editor of the *Observer*, published our first study of murders in England and Wales in the period from the passing of the Homicide Act 1957 to the end of 1959 as a pamphlet entitled 'Murder in Microcosm'. In 1979 the *Observer* published another pamphlet for us, 'Murder in England and Wales since 1957', at a time when calls for the re-introduction of the death penalty were becoming increasingly vocal. During the 1980s when the Thatcher Government was in office, numerous unsuccessful attempts—we estimate about 14—were made to 'piggyback' a limited provision for the death penalty on to various Criminal Justice Bills. In the meantime, our book *A Calendar of Murder* had appeared in 1964. An extension of the format of our first pamphlet, it comprehensively covered the 764 cases of indictments for murder from 1957 to the end of 1962. In this and in our later research (generously funded by the Rowntree Founda-tion) we had the warm encouragement—and on occasion the very welcome practical assistance—of Gerald Gardiner whose distinguished career at the Bar was to be followed by his elevation to the office of Lord Chancellor. That we were able to circulate copies of an interim report on this research to members of both Houses when Parliament finally affirmed abolition in 1969 was a result of his personal initiative.

Others too have helped us at various times along the way. Sir Fred Law-ton who, though when on the Bench, had firmly admonished us for some of the shortcomings of our youthful journalism, nevertheless warmly offered us much helpful advice in his retirement years. Nor can we fail to mention Lord Lane, a most distinguished holder of the office of Lord Chief Justice from 1980 to 1992. We were privileged to work with him on the independ-ent inquiry into the mandatory life sentence for murder commissioned by the Prison Reform Trust that reported in 1993. His was an inspiring example of perseverance in his opposition to the mandatory penalty of life imprisonment for murder.

Among those presently very much active in the field of criminal justice we are grateful to the present Lord Chief Justice, Lord Judge, for agreeing to write a constructively critical foreword to this book.

The Law Commissioners kindly acceded to our request for documentation from the earlier period of the Commission's existence, and the Director of Public Prosecutions, Keir Starmer QC, gave us permission to view certain Crown Prosecution Service files that are not yet generally available to the public. In his office, Janet Altham took time to ensure the process was smooth and patiently answered our various queries.

Last, but by no means least, without the exceptionally patient and able assistance of Mr Ian Aitkenhead, it must be said that the task would not only have been more protracted but more difficult. Moreover, his skill and enterprise as a researcher have materially contributed to the book.

Writing this book, at a time of movements in legislation and case law, and radical proposals for change emanating from the Law Commission, has been not unlike attempting a steady aim on a moving target. If it is discovered that not all in this book is up to date when the reader has it, we can only say that we have done our best to ensure the contrary.

Terence Morris   **Louis Blom-Cooper**

March 2011

About the authors

Terence Morris is Emeritus Professor of Criminology and Criminal Justice in the University of London and from 1955 to 1995 taught at the London School of Economics. In the course of his career he has been a visiting Professor at the University of California at Berkeley and the University of Manitoba. Originally a student of social anthropology, his interest in crime and justice began in his schooldays, stimulated by learning from his father the story of the trial and subsequent hangings of Edith Thompson and Frederick Bywaters and discovering a copy of Hobhouse and Brockway's *English Prisons Today.* His first contact with convicted murderers was as a visitor to men reprieved from the gallows and serving life sentences in Wormwood Scrubs. This inspired his anthropological study of an English prison, in preparation for which he spent six weeks living in one and working in its laundry. During the 1960s he served as an adviser to the Commonwealth and Colonial Office, reporting on the state of crime and justice systems in the Caribbean and Western Pacific territories. His extensive travels enabled him to visit many prisons in North America and view, *inter alia,* their varieties of execution apparatus. His broader interests (aside from bicycles and old motor cars) are in the histories of criminal justice policy and the criminal law, and were for long balanced by practical involvement in the form of service as a lay magistrate in London for more than 30 years.

Sir Louis Blom-Cooper QC practised at the English Bar from 1952 until 2004, mainly as a civil law practitioner with no experience of criminal justice until he took silk in 1970, after which for a number of years he appeared as counsel in a various criminal trials at the Old Bailey. On two occasions in the 1980s he appeared as counsel in appeals to the House of Lords in murder cases, *R v Cunningham* (1982) and *R v Moloney* (1985). Apart from his extracurricular activity in the campaign for the abolition of capital punishment from 1956-1983, he taught criminology and penology to social science students at Bedford College, University of London from 1961-1981. He has honorary doctorates from Loughborough University, the University of East Anglia and Ulster University, Coleraine, Northern Ireland. He is a Fellow of King's College, London. From 1992-2000 he was the Independent Commissioner for the Holding Centres in Northern Ireland.

The author of the Foreword

Lord Judge (Baron Judge of Draycote) is Lord Chief Justice of England and Wales, head of the judiciary and head of criminal justice. He was formerly President of the Queen's Bench Division of the High Court of Justice before becoming a Lord Justice of Appeal.

Foreword

By Lord Judge
Lord Chief Justice of England and Wales

This is a thought provoking and, I suspect, intentionally provocative book about a complex aspect of the criminal law, which applies to an area of extreme public sensitivity. The law relating to homicide, that is the unlawful cutting short of the life of another human being, before it comes to its natural end, arises in an almost infinite variety of situations.

It applies to the terrorists who deliberately plan to and do blow up a train, or an aeroplane, or a building, or a crowded nightclub, with catastrophic indiscriminate consequences, and to armed criminals who use weapons to remove the inconvenient guard or police officer who, in the course of duty, stands between the criminals and the objective of their crime, and a ready escape from arrest or detention. It also applies to devoted spouses who, after years of mutual love and devotion, and perceiving their actions as the final demonstration of that love, finally agree to heed the pleas of their beloved to bring unbearable suffering to an end by hastening death by a few weeks. It covers the idiot who, after consuming a vast amount of alcohol, inexcusably drives his car dangerously and causes death, and to the driver who, after leading a blameless life, enriching the community by the contribution he or she has made to it, and who, as we all do from time to time, while at the wheel of the car, makes a minor error of judgment which has catastrophic and unintended consequences for another motorist or pedestrian.

The term 'homicide' and the epithet 'killer' are applied equally to each of them, yet no-one would suggest an equivalence of moral culpability. Nevertheless, each has unlawfully caused death, and in doing so will, save exceptionally where the deceased has left no-one to mourn for him or her, have caused profound distress and grief, and an unassuagable sense of loss to the family of the deceased. For them the loss is life scarring, but again, the individual attitudes to the crime which has scarred their lives are also infinitely variable. Some will demand justice and others will be understanding of mercy. Sometimes members of the same family will want different outcomes to the criminal justice process. Yet nothing in that process can restore the lost life or fill the lifelong gap caused by the death.

These are some of the complexities which the modern law of homicide is required to address. They do not stop there. One issue which constantly arises is the difficult question of the state of mind required before guilt can be established. Should the defendant who causes death intend injury (if so, how serious?) or death? Should foresight, or recklessness, of injury or death suffice? Are the defences to homicide to be seen as providing a justification for the actions which produced death, or simply a lawful excuse for those actions? There are no easy answers. Indeed the authors themselves underline that if the analysis contained in these pages is correct, or nearly so, their ambition is to encourage 'a root-and-branch reform of the law of homicide', an ambition which they readily acknowledge does not yet command Parliamentary support which, because the reforms they seek must depend on legislation rather than law-making by judges, makes the prospects 'bleak'. The critical word in that last sentence is 'yet'. With what some would regard as huge optimism, the authors hope that the validity of their analysis of the problems will be acknowledged and the complexities surrounding the law of homicide addressed and resolved.

I doubt whether any reader of this book will agree with everything in it. And I readily admit that, although happy to write the *Foreword* to such a stimulating and important work, I do not. To take but one example, I have difficulty with the proposition that *mens rea* should only be relevant to the assessment of the sentence, after conviction when 'the moral culpability of the offender must be assessed'. And I can hardly express my agreement with some of the criticisms made by the authors of passages in one of my own judgments. Indeed, I cannot comment on them at all. However, it was not a pre-condition to my agreement to write this foreword that the authors should agree with me, and equally, they did not suggest that I should disqualify myself from writing it if, having read the book, I found that I disagreed with some of its contents.

As the authors demonstrate in a wide-ranging historical analysis, the issues which they address have been the subject of discussion over very many years, indeed, they would say, for far too many years now. They explain their views in trenchant and unequivocal terms. They do not use language which obscures their meaning. Their ideas will undoubtedly stimulate and contribute to the continuing public debate about the nature and ingredients of the crime of homicide, the defences to it, and the appropriate punishment for those convicted of unlawful killings.

CHAPTER 1

PROLOGUE

In the Beginning

The Murder (Abolition of Death Penalty) Bill came before the House of Lords at the committee stage in July 1965. It had been introduced into that House (following its passage in the House of Commons over the first half of 1965) by Baroness Wootton of Abinger[1] and, although not a Government Bill in the strictest sense, it enjoyed every support and facility the Government could provide. In the course of the debate she had said:

> As a layman, I have always been accustomed to believe that the law drew fine dis-
> tinctions, sometimes distinctions that were so fine that they were not always easily
> intelligible to the man and woman in the street.[2]

The Lord Chief Justice, Lord Parker, was presciently aware that the transition from one mandatory penalty to another, that of death to life imprisonment, needed further consideration and it was he who attempted, by means of two successive amendments, to provide for an element of judicial discretion in the determination of just how long a 'life' sentence should be. In the course of the debate he followed up on Lady Wootton's shrewd observation in a seminal comment:

---

1. For a biography of Barbara Wootton, see *A Critical Woman: Barbara Wootton, Social Science and Public Policy in the Twentieth Century* by Professor Ann Oakley (Bloomsbury, 2011).
2. *Hansard* HL Vol 268 Col 1232 (27 July 1965).

The noble Lord, Lord Stonham[3] held up his hands in horror at the fact that I was tending and intending to merge manslaughter and murder. Let me make it clear. Of course, as a matter of law, murder is a separate offence and it is, equally, perhaps the most serious offence. But, equally, like the noble Baroness, I dislike fine lines and technical distinctions.

I think that there is one offence of homicide, varying from the lowest degree of manslaughter up to the most deliberate and calculated true murder. Therefore, I think my argument is based on the anomaly [the mandatory sentence of life imprisonment] which has been produced by the abolition of the death penalty.[4]

The title of this book derives directly from the words of both Lady Wootton and Lord Parker in the course of that historic Parliamentary debate. The former attained her great legislative objective — the abolition of the death penalty for murder — while Lord Parker achieved only limited success in establishing a role for the judiciary, that of doing no more than recommending the period of the life sentence to be served before release on licence. It is the 'fine lines and distinctions' that, while they may be attractive to some academic lawyers and practitioners, seem never to cease to baffle the 'man and woman in the street'. It is not just that the definitional niceties of the criminal law with respect to unlawful killing — this being murder while that is manslaughter; one being causing death by dangerous driving and another causing death by careless driving — appear at times to defy both logic and understanding; it is the very opacity of the reasoning behind such categorisation that serves only to reinforce the layman's belief that the law is an impenetrable thicket of arbitrariness. Nor does the problem cease when the layman learns that a conviction for murder can rest upon proof, not only of an intention to kill, but simply a resolve to do serious harm from which death unhappily results. The partial defences to murder in the Homicide Act 1957 serve further to promote a perception of arbitrariness.

---

3.   Minister of State at the Home Office.
4.   *Hansard* HL Vol 268 Col 1241 (27 July 1965).

The Received Wisdom

It was James (later Lord) Callaghan in his role as Home Secretary who, in March 1970, gave the Criminal Law Revision Committee (CLRC) the task of a review of offences against the person. Its terms of reference were clear and straightforward:

> To review the law relating to, and the penalties for, offences against the person, including homicide, in the light of, and subject to, the recent decision of Parliament to make permanent the statutory provisions abolishing the death penalty for murder.

The CLRC concluded that the mandatory sentence of life imprisonment could be safely left undisturbed. It presented an interim report to Parliament restricted to the penalty for murder[5] to his Conservative successor, Mr Robert Carr (later Lord Carr of Hadley).

The report, which had taken the 14 members of the committee almost three years to produce, was, in the event, a concise document of no more than 24 pages containing some 43 paragraphs and one appendix comprising three tables of data on life sentence prisoners. The signatories to the report, with one exception, set out what has become the orthodox view on the penalty for murder, namely that it should be visited by the mandatory penalty of imprisonment for life. The sole dissenting voice was that of Professor Glanville Williams, who was opposed to the mandatory sentence in principle on the ground that the judge is thereby deprived of the power, which he possessed in all other cases, to distinguish between murders of different gravity by the sentences he imposes and since he cannot take into account any matters of mitigation.

---

5. Criminal Law Revision Committee, Twelfth Report, *Penalty for Murder*, Cmnd 5184 (HMSO, January 1973), p.10, para 13. The CLRC had been charged with a broader remit than that of the committee set up by the Secretary of State for Scotland in September 1970, chaired by Lord Emslie, and which reported ahead of its English counterpart, in November 1972 (*Penalties for Homicide*, Scottish Home and Health Department, Cmnd 5137). Its terms of reference were: 'To review the law relating to the penalties for homicide in the light of the statutory abolition of capital punishment for murder and to report on the considerations that should govern any proposal for a change in that law'. The Emslie Committee recommended that the courts should uniformly indicate a minimum period that a murderer should serve.

The exception to the mandatory sentence identified by the committee related to what were considered to be

certain tragic cases of murder to which special considerations apply. Examples we have in mind are those in which a killing was done deliberately from motives of compassion...where a mother killed her deformed child or a husband terminated the agonies of his dying wife.[6]

In these instances the recommendation was that the trial judge should be able to make a hospital order, a probation order with a condition of psychiatric treatment, or order a conditional discharge where the sentencer was satisfied that it would be contrary to the interests of justice for the accused to serve any sentence of imprisonment. But this was no more than a sensitive, liberal suggestion for moderating the effect of the law, which would seem to bear down—unjustly—upon those least deserving of public obloquy. At the core of the conclusions of the CLRC was a simple statement that the mandatory life sentence for murder should be retained, that the life sentence represented a greater deterrent than a determinate sentence, together with the implication that, since murder should remain a separate offence distinct from manslaughter, this should be reflected by a wholly different and more serious penalty. The committee's argument on this point is worth stating in full:

We first considered whether there should continue to be a separate offence of murder and, if so, whether the existing definition of murder at common law was satisfactory. It is sufficient for present purposes to say that, although it might be argued that by reason of the abolition of the death penalty for murder there was no longer the same need to draw a distinction in cases of homicide between murder and manslaughter, we are of the opinion that there should be a separate offence of murder. We believe that the stigma which, in the public's mind, attaches to a conviction of murder rightly emphasises the seriousness of the offence and may have a significant deterrent value.[7]

---

6.   *Ibid.* para 42.
7.   *Ibid.* para 6.

This is a clear expression of the orthodoxy that has been rehearsed on every subsequent occasion when either the logic or the utility of the mandatory life sentence has been the subject of challenge.

When the CLRC set out its final conclusions in its Fourteenth Report on Offences Against the Person it had shifted its stance on its previous position of favouring retention of the mandatory penalty, having particular regard to a number of factors, including two official reports recommending the abolition of the mandatory penalty.[8] It concluded:

> Our re-examination of this important matter has involved long and anxious discussion. In the result we are deeply and almost evenly divided. We cannot and do not claim that our experience gives our views special weight. At most they can be said to be those of members of the public whose working lives bring them closer to the administration of justice than most. As we are so evenly divided, we have thought it right to set out in some detail the arguments for and against the mandatory penalty for murder.[9]

Thereafter, from 1980 onwards, almost all official and unofficial reports have opted in favour of abolition. What is of significance in this seemingly abrupt resiling from the negative response of 1973 is an unpublished memorandum of February 1978 presented by the Law Commission in response to a restricted questionnaire from the CLRC, in which the former law reform body favoured the ending of the mandatory penalty.[10]

An 'Evidence-Based' Challenge

In 1975, two years after the interim view of the CLRC, a distinct echo of Lord Parker's words that 'there is one offence of homicide, varying from the lowest degree of manslaughter up to the most deliberate and calculated true

---

8. The Butler Committee on Mentally Abnormal Offenders, Cmnd 6244, paras 19.14-19.16 and the Advisory Council on the Penal System on *Sentences of Imprisonment: A review of maximum penalties* (June 1978) para 236.

9. Cmnd 7844 (March 1980) para 42.

10. With the permission of the chairman of the Law Commission, Sir Terence Etherton, we publish in Appendix 5 to this work the first 20 pages of the 31-page document.

murder' was to be heard in the case of *Hyam*[11] in the House of Lords when Lord Kilbrandon (a Scots Law Lord) observed (in a dissenting judgment):

> It is not so easy to feel satisfaction at the doubts and difficulties which seem to surround the crime of murder and the distinguishing from it of the crime of manslaughter. There is something wrong when crimes of such gravity ... call for the display of so formidable a degree of forensic and judicial learning as the present case has given rise to. I believe this to show that a more radical look at the problem is called for, and was called for immediately upon the passing of the Murder (Abolition of Death Penalty) Act 1965 ... Since no homicides are now punishable with death, these many hours and days have been occupied in trying to adjust a definition of that which has no content. *There does not appear to be any good reason why the crimes of murder and manslaughter should not be both abolished, and the single crime of unlawful homicide substituted* [present authors' italics]; one case will differ from another in gravity, and that can be taken care of by variation of sentences downwards from life imprisonment. It is no longer true, if it was ever true, to say that murder as we now define it is necessarily the most heinous example of unlawful homicide.[12]

That judicial entreaty was ignored, both politically and legislatively, as was a similar plea twenty years later when Lord Mustill observed:[13]

> Murder is widely thought to be the gravest of crimes. One could expect a developed system to embody a law of murder clear enough to yield an unequivocal result on a given set of facts, a result which conforms with apparent justice and has a sound intellectual base. This is not so in England, where the law of homicide is permeated by anomaly, fiction, misnomer and obsolete reasoning. One conspicuous anomaly is the rule which deals with 'malice aforethought' (a doubly misleading expression) required for the crime of murder not only with a conscious intention to kill but also with an intention to cause grievous bodily harm. It is, therefore, possible to commit a murder not only without wishing the death of the victim but without the least

---

11. *Hyam v DPP* [1975] AC 55.
12. *Ibid.* at p.98. The Law Commission in its memorandum of February 1978, in answer to a specific question about Lord Kilbrandon's remarks, totally supported that powerful judicial statement.
13. *Attorney-General's Reference No 3 of 1994* [1998] AC 245.

thought that this might be the result of the assault. Many would doubt the justice of this rule, which is not the popular conception of murder and (as I shall suggest) no longer rests on any intellectual foundation. The law of Scotland does very well without it, and England could perhaps do the same.

In the last 30 years no fewer than 12 appeals dealing with the distinction between murder and manslaughter had to be decided by the House of Lords[14] which was authorised to entertain criminal appeals only if the Court of Appeal (Criminal Division) certified that the case raised a point of law and an issue of general public importance and leave was granted either by that court or the Law Lords themselves. The indecisive case of *Hyam* was upset in 1985,[15] since when all shades of culpability and fine distinctions have peppered the judgments by our senior judiciary, to the point where the law of homicide became demonstrably in desperate need of Parliamentary attention. It is only the popular and widely misunderstood view of murder as more serious than manslaughter that might be thought to stand in the way of its replacement by a simple offence of criminal homicide. The simplistic assertion that murder is, invariably, the most wicked of all crimes, and that it must be sharply distinguished both in its character and its penal consequences from all other forms of unlawful homicide, ought now to be thoroughly discredited.

While murder is, indeed, widely considered to be the gravest of crimes, yet it is a word often employed as a synonym for a variety of forms of unlawful and frequently violent death which are better subsumed under the general term of homicide. Irrespective of how the idea is expressed, it is impossible to escape from the fact that for society at large, no less than for the individuals who are affected directly by it, the unlawful killing of one human being by another, in whatever circumstances, is an awesomely dreadful happening.

One might not, therefore, unreasonably expect the law to provide 'apparent justice' founded upon a 'sound intellectual base'. Is such a thing so much to ask? Clearly, it is otherwise. This being so, this book attempts to consider how things have reached this point after a long traverse of the centuries since the times of de Bracton, Fleta,[16] Coke, Blackstone and those

---

14. Now the Supreme Court.
15. In *Moloney* [1985] AC 905.
16. Fleta, the title of a late 13th century dissertation on the laws of England, is the commonly used

other legal luminaries who have contributed to the development of the law of homicide. It will quickly become clear to the reader that central to this book is the contention that the time for further amending the law of murder in a fragmentary, *ad hoc*, fashion is over and that the time has come for fundamental reform: in short, the authors' case is that the offence presently identified as murder, together with all the various species of manslaughter, be consolidated into a single offence of criminal homicide.

A Unitary Offence of Criminal Homicide and the Problem of 'Labelling'

The concept of 'fair' labelling has a distinguished academic pedigree—it finds no place in the criminal law or in the case law of the criminal courts. Its progenitor was Professor Andrew Ashworth who, in a notable paper in 1981,[17] had termed it 'representative' labelling. The adjective 'fair' was later suggested as a substitute by Professor Glanville Williams.[18] While Ashworth appears to concentrate on the issue of how the labelling of offences may fairly reflect the nature and magnitude of the lawbreaking itself, Glanville Williams focuses more sharply upon the forensic aspects of the problem. Thus:

> I understand this ['representative labelling'] to mean not merely that the name of the abstract offence but the particulars stated in the conviction should convey the degree of the offender's moral guilt, or at least should not be positively misleading as to that guilt, the chief reason being that on a later occasion the conviction may be on the back of the indictment before the judge or be read out in court and thus affect the future sentence.

While it is important to bear in mind that the concept of 'fair labelling' is seen as applicable across the whole spectrum of criminal offences and is not confined to those of homicide, Ashworth nevertheless makes some important

---

Latin pen name of its anonymous author.

17. 'The Elasticity of Mens Rea' in C F H Tapper (ed.), *Crime, Proof and Punishment: Essays in Memory of Sir Rupert Cross*, London (Butterworth, 1981).

18. 'Convictions and Fair Labelling' (1983) 42 CLJ 85.

assertions. In his *Principles of Criminal Law*,[19] he argues that there is a need to differentiate cases within the range of homicide offences by affixing their labels, specifically reducing the label of murder to manslaughter 'because of extenuating circumstances'. The extenuating circumstances include the circumstances in which the killing took place and other matters having a bearing on the culpability of the killer. If, however, the simple offence of criminal homicide constitutes the offender's criminal responsibility, leaving consideration of the nature and degree of culpability to discretionary sentencing, there would be no need for 'fair labelling': every unlawful killing bears its own peculiar features in the homicidal event.

Both he and others[20] argue the case for 'fair labelling' (a task primarily that of the legislature) for the purpose of criminal justice and of informing the public, if only for sustaining the principle of proportionality in fixing maximum (and, possibly, minimum) penalties. We doubt whether, apart from assessing the substantive law and the penalty in individual statutory provisions, labelling does anything more than assist those engaged in the administration of the criminal justice system. Professor Ashworth explains it as

> assisting the law's educative or declaratory function in sustaining and reinforcing social standards. Fairness demands that offenders be labelled and punished in proportion to their wrongdoing; the label is important both for public communication and, within the criminal justice system, for deciding on appropriate maximum penalties, for evaluating previous convictions, for classification in prison, and so on.[21]

The Law Commission's recommendation of 2006 that the current crime of murder be divided into Murder 1, Murder 2 and Manslaughter, Professor Ashworth says, 'may appear to be a triumph for fair labelling', but, ironically, he notes that provoked killings are classified not as manslaughter (as at present), 'but as murder in the second degree—which some [including

---

19. Oxford (OUP, 6th edition, 2009) pp.78-80 and 249-250.
20. Glanville Williams, 'Convictions and Fair Labelling' (1983) 42 CLJ 85; Horder, 'Re-thinking Non-fatal Offences Against the Person' (1994) OJLS 335; Barry Mitchell, 'Multiple Wrong-doing and Offence Structure: a plea for consistency and fair labelling' (2000) 64 MLR 393; Chalmers and Leverick, 'Fair Labelling in Criminal Law' (2008) 71 MLR 217 at 246.
21. *Principles of Criminal Law.* (6th ed.) at p.78.

the authors of this work] might regard as a misuse of the ultimate label'. That is not the only misuse. To suggest that the public perceives the crime of murder as synonymous with the definition—essentially a precise term of art—recognised in the criminal law is not merely a mismatch of 'fair labelling' but the existence of total confusion in the state of the law. And the Law Commission may be forgiven for perpetuating the murder/manslaughter dichotomy, since its terms of reference precluded consideration of any alternative form of homicide law.

Any form of 'fair labelling' appears necessary when the body of the criminal law is to be found in a plethora of statutes, not to mention the additional archaism of judge-made law in the case of the law of murder: it is quite astonishing that in the 21st century the serious offence of unlawful killing is still part of the common law of England. In 1985 a team of four academic lawyers under the outstanding leadership of Professor Sir John Smith QC prepared—at the instigation of the Law Commission—a report on the general principles of the criminal law. A codification of the criminal law, to pick up the threads of the project, with an explanatory memorandum for the ordinary citizen, would render 'fair labelling' as a concept no longer having any practical purpose. Will the Law Commission in its Eleventh Programme, shortly to be published, take that task on board?

None of the arguments that have been advanced for retaining the current categories of unlawful killing—and certainly none of those for the introduction of Murder 1 and Murder 2 whilst retaining the offence of manslaughter—has dissuaded us from thinking that the most rational change would be to adopt an essentially consolidated offence of criminal homicide. All the functions of fair labelling would be assured in the process of sentencing in which, unlike the present situation whereby judges are not merely guided but constrained by the provisions of Schedule 21 of the Criminal Justice Act 2003, the nature and gravity of the particular offence would be marked by a sentence specific and appropriate to it. In giving the judiciary the power to fit the penalty to the crime it would be possible to reflect in sober and measured form the moral sentiments of society while moderating the extremes of ill-informed and emotionally driven opinion. The bespoke approach to sentencing has not only justice but also logic and functionality to recommend it. In contrast, both the 'one size fits all' character of the mandatory sentence and the correspondingly 'small, medium and large' philosophy that is reflected in the proposed co-existence of Murder 1, Murder 2 and Manslaughter serve only further to confound an already confused situation that, far from promoting a clarity readily appreciated by laymen, constantly baffled by those all but impenetrable intellectual thickets of the present law, renders it ever more remote from their comprehension. Given the establishment of a single offence of unlawful killing, consolidating all the present array of offences comprising the various manifestations of criminal homicide what would the prosecution need to prove before a judge and jury?

- First, it would need to be proved that the defendant had committed the act that had caused the death of the deceased.

- Second, that the defendant knew and must have realised that he or she was performing the act that resulted in the death of the deceased.

- Third, that at the time of committing the act the defendant possessed the requisite foresight of the consequences of the act, namely, the serious possibility that death would ensue. In short, the defendant must be shown to have foreseen that he was endangering the life of the deceased.

Many of the confusions that exist in the public mind relate to the way in which certain partial defences, if accepted, can result in a verdict, not of murder, but of manslaughter. That to prove murder it is only necessary to prove an intent to do serious harm is a fact that runs counter to the widely held belief that the proof of murder is the establishment of a deliberate intention to kill. It is our view that a single offence of unlawful killing would not only clarify matters in the mind of the general public but also, by permitting judges the discretion of sentencing at large, persuade it that there was adequate provision in the law for the penalty to fit the homicidal event. While this might encompass sentences of considerable severity it would also enable courts to be merciful in cases characterised not by a pitiless disregard for the victim but a tragic, if misguided, belief that what was being done was for a good purpose. These are so-called 'mercy killings' — unambiguously unlawful though they may be — in which the ideal of justice is best served by the passing of a merciful sentence.

The Demise of the Mandatory Penalty

It cannot escape the attention of even the most casual observer that every change, enacted or merely proposed, to the law of murder since 1957 has been directed not towards a rational definition of unlawful killing, designed to meet the needs and beliefs of a modern society rather than anachronistically reflective of the interests of the ruling élite of Jacobean England, but to ways of limiting the penalty of what is termed murder. The sole purpose of the provision of a category of non-capital murder in the Homicide Act 1957 was to limit the application of capital punishment and certainly not to provide an arcanely devised list of types of homicide thereby considered less heinous than others. In similar fashion, the Law Commission, its remit of July 2005 deliberately limited by Government to exclude consideration of the mandatory life sentence for murder, proposed a second category of murder to which it would not apply. If both the draftsmen of the 1957 Act and the Law Commission deserve recognition for good intent in their respective desires to limit the penalties of mandatory death and 'life' it must, at the same time, be recognised that in seeking to devise exclusions by inventing new labels for certain types of murder they strained to attain the wrong prize. The lock so securely fastened against rational change is set not upon the crime but the penalty. Rid the law of a mandatory penalty, be it death or life, and the *ignis fatuus* of labelling is extinguished or, to borrow the phrase of Sir Ernest Gowers, Chairman of the Royal Commission on Capital Punishment 1949-53, the hunt for the Chimæra[22] can at last cease.

---

22. Used by him in a conversation with the authors in 1963. The Report of the Royal Commission concluded: 'We began our inquiry with the determination to make every effort to see whether we could succeed where so many have failed, and discover some effective method of classifying murders...we conclude with regret that the object of our quest is chimærical and that it must be abandoned'. (p.189, para 534). The Chimæra was a fabulous monster in Greek mythology, described by Homer as having a goat's body, a lion's head and a dragon's tail. It was eventually slain by Bellerophon, riding the winged horse Pegasus.

Pressing on with Change

Our proposal for a single homicidal offence is not, we would emphasise, an idea original to ourselves. Rather, we would claim that it may be clearly identified in the thinking of such distinguished members of the judiciary as Lord Parker, Lord Kilbrandon and Lord Mustill. What holds back the tide of change is the apparent determination of so many politicians to retain the concept of 'murder' as a way of describing what they frequently maintain to be the most heinous of all criminal offences. By references to a mythical 'pact' at the time of abolition they argue that the public would not want the crime of murder to be in some way diminished in its importance by the abolition of the mandatory penalty of life imprisonment. In fact, as the most recent research by Professors Barry Mitchell and Julian Roberts has demonstrated,[23] the public is by no means firmly attached to the notion of a mandatory 'one size fits all' penalty.

What the Mitchell and Roberts study demonstrates, among other things, is support for a finding in earlier research by Professor Mitchell that there is a belief that the different circumstances of homicidal events warrant different sentences. More ominously, this latest research confirms a significant degree of public ignorance, most believing that murder has increased over the past decade, or at best stayed the same (whereas over the last decade it has shown some slight decline). A large proportion of those surveyed underestimated the length of time that most murderers spend in prison before being released on life licence. One is inevitably led to question how far public perception of the nature and incidence of murder and the penal experience of those sentenced to life imprisonment is shaped by the way in which these issues are portrayed in the mass media of communication.

The portrayal of this area of crime and criminal justice frequently leaves much to be desired. Not least has been the comparatively recent practice in the media of referring to tariffs set in pursuance of Schedule 21 of the Criminal Justice Act 2003 as if they were determinate sentences. Thus the offender is frequently described as having been sentenced to serve 25 years,

---

23. Barry Mitchell and Julian Roberts, *Public Opinion and Sentencing for Murder: An empirical investigation of public knowledge and attitudes in England and Wales* (The Nuffield Foundation, October 2010).

when the 25 years refers not to the maximum time he must *serve* in custody, but the minimum period that must *elapse* before he may apply for parole without — and this is seldom publicly appreciated — any guarantee that his application would be granted. Nor is it underscored that even should parole be granted, his freedom will remain conditional and his liability to be returned to prison, should the circumstances so warrant, is indeed lifelong.

Among the most useful improvements to the law of homicide would be the potential saving in both time and cost of trials. While no one would wish to return to the days in which a defendant could plead to the indictment in the morning and be swinging on the gallows by late afternoon, it is an essential requirement of justice that it be administered with reasonable dispatch, a specific safeguard under Article 6 of the European Convention on Human Rights. Time expended, therefore, in ensuring a fair trial within an efficient and effective mode of trial is reflected in the costs, not only to the public purse but also to the parties. Quite apart from the fact that many of the procedures of jury trial are time-consuming and trials are often burdened by prolixity, it is our impression, gained in half a century of study,[24] that trials are taking longer and longer to conclude. We cannot, of course, assess precisely what savings in the trial process might be made if our proposals were to be enacted in the future, assuming the full retention of the lay jury system. From our discussions with criminal law practitioners, we gauge that contemporary murder trials overwhelmingly focus on two principal issues — the intention (*mens rea* for murder) of the accused and the partial defence of provocation (since October 2010 re-framed under the rubric of loss of self-control). The volume of evidential material that has currently to be placed before the jury, mostly by way of oral testimony, relates to these indisputably important issues which we would consign to the sentencing stage of the trial. Once the material relevant to these matters, and to the other partial defence of diminished responsibility, is so consigned, we believe that a considerable shortening of homicide trials could be safely achieved. One countervailing factor that we can discern would be the time required to consider specialist evidence from expert witnesses, both on the cause of

---

24. Our first major study of murder trials related to the 762 cases of persons indicted for murder in England and Wales from 1957 to 1962): *A Calendar of Murder*, London (Michael Joseph, 1961). See also our *Murder in Microcosm*, London (*The Observer*, 1961).

death and mental responsibility, that might prolong the sentencing stage. There is also the possibility, though its likely impact is not easy to assess, that there could be a greater requirement for Newton hearings.[25]

There is another reason why, in our in view, murder trials are becoming more protracted, perhaps even more than during the last days of capital punishment when courts would be highly sensitive of the need to ensure that every avenue of defence remaining open to the accused might be explored. Much of this lengthening we think is due to the complexities of scientific and technological evidence (the cases of child deaths at the hands of parents and carers are a prime example). But we must emphasise that it is only our impression that the time actually taken up in adducing the evidential material is lengthening. Our firm recommendation is that a study be undertaken in a sample of Crown Court centres (including, specifically, the Central Criminal Court) to assess the length of murder trials over the last 20 years.[26] The study should identify the various issues which occupy the time of the court in adducing and testing by examination and cross-examination of oral testimony.

It is also worth observing that if the jury were to be relieved of considering the partial defences, the saving of time might assist in judging the procedural safeguards required under Article 6 of ECHR, in the light of what the *Taxquet* judgment of 16 November 2010 from the Court of Strasbourg has now imposed on trials involving a lay jury.[27]

A Government Initiative

Despite several official and unofficial reports in recent years which pointed overwhelmingly in favour of a discretionary life sentence for murder, from the 1990s onwards Ministers, both New Labour and Conservative, have, without convincing argument to the contrary, declined to yield to professional

---

25. When a defendant, having pleaded guilty to an offence, disputes the facts of the prosecution case, the court will have to hold a hearing to determine the facts. It is conducted without a jury in order to determine a basis for sentencing: *R v Newton* (1983) 77 Cr App R 13.

26. A similar study was conducted by the Roskill Committee on Fraud Trials in 1986 (HMSO, 10 January 1986) paras 10.13 and 10.14, pp.177-8.

27. See *Chapter 14* of this work, *A Matter for the Jury*.

and other opinion in Parliamentary debates. Opposition to the penalty has been invariably brushed aside. Yet of the penological unsoundness of the mandatory penalty there can be no doubt. A withering attack on the concept was mounted by no less a commanding figure than Lord Bingham of Cornhill (then Lord Chief Justice of England and Wales) when delivering the Newsam Memorial Lecture on 13 March 1998 at the Police Staff College.[28] The higher judiciary thereafter, albeit privately, retained the same objection to the fettering of their traditional sentencing discretion. This coincided with the declaration by the European Court of Human Rights that the factors of deterrence and punishment, reflected in the tariff element of the penalty, had to be exercised judicially, in the courtroom, and not secretly in the corridors of executive Government. The New Labour Government responded legislatively and in its Criminal Justice Act 2003 established a classification of murders, with 'starting points' graded to reflect their assumed seriousness.

In December 2010 the Ministry of Justice in the newly installed Conservative-led Government published a Green Paper entitled *Breaking the Cycle: Effective Punishment, Rehabilitation and Sentencing of Offenders.*[29] These generalised proposals for an overhaul of the current sentencing framework, the majority of which are directed towards the penalties for crimes other than murder, envisage only the most modest shift towards adjusting the penalty for that offence.[30]

The mandatory life sentence itself would remain as deep-rooted as ever, as would the general run of minimum terms of imprisonment; the only proposed candidate for the axe is the categorisation of murders, with its respective 'starting points' in Schedule 21 of the Criminal Justice Act 2003. The Green Paper echoes our own critical assessment[31] of the statutory guid-

---

28. The lecture is reproduced in Lord Bingham's selected essays and lectures, *The Business of Judging* (Oxford University Press, 2000) at pp 329-343: *The Mandatory Life Sentence for Murder.*
29. CM 7972 of 7 December 2010 presented to Parliament.
30. *Ibid*, para 170, pp 50-51.
31. See *Chapter 16.* Paragraph 170 of the Green Paper is unambiguously direct, stating: 'A key part of simplification will involve Schedule 21 to the Criminal Justice Act 2003. It is essential that we preserve Parliament's role in setting the sentencing framework for murder. We have no intention of abolishing the mandatory life sentence or of prompting any general reduction in minimum terms imposed for murder. However, Schedule 21 is based on ill-thought out and overly prescriptive policy. It seeks to analyse in extraordinary detail each and every type of murder. The result is guidance that is incoherent and unnecessarily complex, and is badly in

ance on tariff-fixing of the minimum term in prison for murderers by trial judges, declaring it to be 'incoherent and unnecessarily complex and ... badly in need of reform so that justice can be done properly in each case'.

Exactly what the reform should consist of is a matter on which the document is deafeningly silent. What would appear most likely would be a reversion to what Parliament intended as long ago as 1965 in the form of the minimum recommendation to be found in section 1(2) Murder (Abolition of Death Penalty) Act (and repealed in the 2003 Act), with the difference being that the recommendation would in future have legal effect and not be restricted, as the case-law determined,[32] to the more 'serious' murders: 'mercy killings' might thus attract a low minimum tariff.[33] All this is speculation and notwithstanding a consultation exercise the likelihood, at the time of writing,[34] would seem to be that while it is currently on the back burner of proposals for new legislation it may well be taken off the stove altogether as other more politically pressing issues engage the mind of Government. If the demonstrable urge to simplify the sentencing system is as good as could be expected, the angularity of the Government's approach towards the mandatory sentence of life imprisonment is only marginally softened. It is hardly the stuff of penal reform. For the time being at least the iron equation between crime and punishment remains.

A Question in the House of Lords

On 24 January 2011 a Question was asked by Lord Lloyd of Berwick:[35]

---

need of reform so that justice can be done properly in each case'.

32. *R v Flemming* (1973) 57 Cr App Rep 524. It is important to note that the part of the judgment stating that any recommendation should be for not less than 12 years was strictly *obiter* although it subsequently became case law; the reason being that the point at issue was whether a minimum recommendation could be applied in the case of a juvenile sentenced not for murder under section 1(2) Murder (Abolition of Death Penalty) Act 1965 but on conviction for manslaughter and sentence under section 53(2) Children and Young Persons Act 1933.

33. This was hinted at by the Lord Chief Justice in *R v Inglis* [2010] EWCA Crim 2637.

34. February 2011.

35. *Hansard* HL Vol 724 Col 675.

To ask Her Majesty's Government whether they plan to reconsider their decision, announced in the Ministry of Justice Green Paper *Breaking the Cycle: Effective Punishment, Rehabilitation and the Sentencing of Offenders*, not to abolish the mandatory life sentence for murder.

The Minister of State, Ministry of Justice, Lord McNally, replied:

My Lords, the government have no plans to abolish the mandatory life sentence for murder.

Lord Lloyd of Berwick responded to

thank the noble Lord for that Answer. Is he aware of recent research that shows that the public are not in favour of a life sentence in every case of murder, as is so often thought, especially not in cases where the conviction has been of a mercy killing? Seventy nine per cent of those consulted in face to face interviews last May said that they thought that nine years or less would be sufficient in such cases which corresponds almost exactly with a recent decision in the Court of Appeal that reduced the minimum term from nine to five years. Against that background, why do the government continue to think that a life sentence is necessary in every case of murder? Why not leave it to the judge to decide on the facts of the particular case? Why not at least consult the public on this in the consultation exercise that is currently taking place?

Others of their Lordships joined in the discussion, including Lord Thomas of Gresford, Lord Borrie, Lord Walton of Detchant, and Lord Hamilton of Epsom. In his various replies, the Minister omitted to mention that the terms of reference of the Law Commission that had recently reported specifically excluded any consideration of the mandatory penalty and maintained, three times, that 'the time was not right to take forward such a substantial reform of our criminal law'.[36]

When there is such a body of evidence to suggest that considerable, never mind root and branch, reform of the law is needed, why the time is

---

36. This sounds remarkably like the words of the Bellman in the *Hunting of the Snark*: 'What I tell you three times is true'.

still 'not right' remains an unanswered question that demands an answer, not least in the light of the findings of the researches of Professors Mitchell and Roberts. This last assertion, that the time was 'not right', scarcely constitutes a reasoned argument in defence of the mandatory penalty, however firmly it may affirm a belief that the mandatory nature of the 'life' sentence (whatever meaning may be put upon it) is, and somehow ought to remain, essentially immutable.

In regard to 'mercy killings', an issue raised by Lord Walton, a distinguished member of the medical establishment and a former president of the British Medical Association,[37] Lord McNally referred to:

> when the plea is on grounds of a mercy killing or a related defence, successive Governments have taken the view that this is a matter for Parliament rather than the Government of the day. Within their broad decision not to attempt a major reform of the law at the moment, the Government are trying to look at the guidance so that it may be simplified and to trust the judgment of the judges in these matters.

On indictment for murder there is, of course, no such plea available as that of 'mercy killing'. The Minister was, no doubt, referring in a form of verbal shorthand to the *partial* defence of diminished responsibility that has been increasingly, and in our view improperly, used in many such cases in an attempt to arrive at a verdict of manslaughter with its sentence being determined according to the circumstances by the judges. Should the defendant be convicted of murder, then the judicial function at the stage of sentence is to determine such a tariff for a mandatory life sentence as is legally possible within the labyrinthine restrictions embodied in Schedule 21 of the Criminal Justice Act 2003. Might then the phrase 'trying to look at the guidance so that it might be simplified' refer to possible changes to Schedule 21?

One can well understand the reasoning behind the use of diminished responsibility as a partial defence, since it is the only means of avoiding the harsh inflexibility of the mandatory life sentence in circumstances where jus-

---

37. Lord Walton had been chairman of the House of Lords Select Committee on Medical Ethics that in its Report in 1993 had expressed the opinion that the mandatory sentence should be abolished.

tice so frequently demands not retributive punishment but compassionate understanding.

But what precisely did the Minster imply when he said that 'successive Governments had taken the view that this was a matter for Parliament rather than the Government of the day'?

All such changes in the law, whether originating in Government or Private Member's Bills, are subject to the final will of Parliament. If what he meant was that successive Governments have declined to introduce legislation designed to remedy this and the other many shortcomings that presently afflict the law of homicide, then of course he is quite correct. But does it therefore follow that an initiative from a Private Member would be appropriate or desirable or even effectual? Sydney Silverman's attempt to achieve the abolition of capital punishment came by way of an amendment to the Criminal Justice Bill introduced by the Attlee Government in 1947 but had no Government support. In contrast, the Murder (Abolition of Death Penalty) Bill of 1965 was a Government Bill in all but name, since without such support it would never have had adequate Parliamentary time. Private Members' Bills, as the *Hansards* for so many Fridays testify, are fortunate if they do not immediately fail for lack of time.

The case for the retention of the mandatory life sentence for murder after almost two decades of criticism remains intellectually threadbare. All criticisms of it have for the last twenty years been resolutely dismissed by a succession of ministers of both Conservative and New Labour Governments while the current Conservative-led administration, as Lord McNally's answer to Lord Lloyd of Berwick clearly demonstrates, would appear to have not the least intention of changing the law.

But if there has been a surge of criticism against the rock-like mandatory penalty over the last two decades, it is not perhaps without some significance that there has been, at the same time, another current moving in the opposite direction, directed towards ensuring that the time served by prisoners so sentenced shall not only be longer but more circumscribed in its determination. The process began with the statement by the Home Secretary Leon (later Lord) Brittan in 1983 when he announced a series of changes that brought executive decision-making on the length of time to be served much closer to a sentencing exercise. By 1991 the Home Office Minister of State, Dame

Angela Rumbold, was advancing a controversial interpretation of the meaning of the mandatory life sentence for murder, maintaining *inter alia* that:

> According to the judicial process, the offender has committed a crime of such gravity that he forfeits his liberty for life without the necessity for judicial intervention. The presumption is, therefore, that the offender should remain in custody until and unless the Home Secretary concludes that the public interest would be better served by the prisoner's release than by his continued detention. In exercising his continued discretion in that respect the Home Secretary must take account, not just of the question of risk, but of how society as a whole viewed the prisoner's release at that juncture.[38]

Leaving aside what construction might be placed upon the somewhat delphic phrase 'necessity for judicial intervention', further questions arise of how the view of 'society as a whole' might be assessed and whether it is desirable that the penal experience of an offender should be influenced by populist sentiment rather than determined by judicial authority. In 1991, the view of the then Government at least was plain: the final decision should be that of the Home Secretary. By 1994, another Home Secretary, Michael (now Lord) Howard was reported in *The Times*[39] as intending to impose 'whole life' tariffs on some 20 notorious killers. The pressures for executive supremacy in determining the tariff proportion of the life sentence were eventually overcome by a series of legal challenges both domestically and in the European Court of Human Rights at Strasbourg, requiring the process to be judicialised. But by 2003 the New Labour Government was able, by means of Schedule 21 of the Criminal Justice Act 2003, to ensure statutory authority for a tariff system that ensured the limits that would henceforth be the legal norm, specific to different types of murder, would now be defined with elephantine precision. In a most unsatisfactory way, it has ensured that any available element of flexibility in what is, by definition, primarily an inflexible sentence is severely circumscribed by the terms of Schedule 21.

It was in 1995, shortly after the executive decisions to raise the tariffs of certain prisoners to 'whole life', that the myth,[40] whereby abolition of the

---

38. *Hansard* HC Vol 193 Cols 311-312 (16 July 1991).
39. 4 April 1994.
40. We discuss its various manifestations such as a 'Pact with Parliament' or 'Pact with the People'

death penalty had been achieved by means of a 'pact' between abolitionists and retentionists—death being exchanged for mandatory life—emerged as a justification for the *status quo*.

The departure of a Conservative Government and its replacement by the New Labour administrations, first of Tony Blair and then of Gordon Brown, demonstrated that on the issue of the mandatory penalty there was an ironfast bi-partisan approach. Never mind the arguments, it was, and would remain, here to stay. Though the party political pendulum has swung once more, it would seem to have altered nothing.

Uncoupling the Welded Chain

It is an irony in the history of criminal justice that the penalty of death was never without the possibility of mitigation through the exercise of the prerogative of mercy. Even such a recommendation from a jury, though it had no status in law, was nevertheless indicative of a belief that the ultimate outcome ought not to be inflexibly shackled by the mandatory nature of the sentence of the court. The same cannot be said of the mandatory sentence of life imprisonment for though the tariff followed by conditional licence is a realistic probability for all save a tiny minority of those sentenced, the sentence itself cannot be ameliorated. It consists of a liability to imprisonment that is life-long, ultimately determinable by death itself.

As far as the penalty for our proposed offence of criminal homicide is concerned, it follows that the mandatory sentence of life imprisonment for murder would disappear with the crime of murder itself. Consolidation aside, we are unequivocally of the view that mandatory penalties without any possibility of mitigation have always been, and remain, wholly without merit, whether they relate to death or imprisonment for life, or are inflicted as a penalty for a particular category of offence irrespective of the individual circumstances of the criminal event. No army could effectively march if its

---

in *Chapter 7* of this book. The article in which we believe we demonstrated that no such pact or compact was ever made has never been rebutted in the 15 years since its was publication. See Terence Morris and Louis Blom-Cooper, 'The Penalty for Murder: A Myth Exploded' (1996) Crim LR 707-717.

soldiers' boots were issued on the principle of 'one size fits all'; any system of criminal justice employing such a maxim is similarly hobbled.

Mandatory sentences are, to put it simply, a negation of the very concept of judgment, for as an intellectual exercise they are more like a non-negotiable price for an essential commodity: the purchaser can only identify the price, and take it or leave it. Neither judgment nor discretion is involved.

The quality of criminal justice is contingent upon balance in more than one dimension: between responsibility and harm done, and between the interests of society and the rights of those accused of crime, including consideration of matters in mitigation. A consequence of this, which follows from our proposal for a single offence of criminal homicide, is that those defences which currently function as a means for reducing the crime of murder to that of manslaughter would cease to have any forensic purpose, becoming matters to be put in mitigation. Since each criminal event must be individually assessed, the proper place for such assessment is certainly not the bear pit of politics, often echoing with calls for rhadamanthine punishments to be inflicted whether they fit or not, but the ordered atmosphere of the courtroom. Politicians are nothing if not ephemeral and the immediate attention span of the media seldom exceeds 24 hours. While historically there was a time when judges were prone to do the will of their political masters no less eagerly than some of them took bribes, those days are long gone. While there are occasions when we may not approve of their judgment, there is never a time when their reasoning is so arbitrary or opaque that it cannot be subjected to critical analysis conducted with intellectual rigour and immune from contempt of court or scandalising the judiciary. And, in the absence of a written constitution, a judiciary whose probity is above reproach can alone be the ultimate guarantor of individual liberty. Indeed, if we cannot trust the judges, not least in imposing sentence at a time when the intellectual quality and independence of thought characterising the higher judiciary approaches an excellence hitherto unknown, we can trust no one.

It is more than 35 years since Lord Kilbrandon's observations in *Hyam* and more than 16 since Lord Mustill's no less trenchant comments in which he identified the law of homicide as characterised by 'anomaly, misnomer and obsolete reasoning'.

About the time of the conclusion of the work of the Committee on the Penalty for Homicide, set up by the Prison Reform Trust in 1993 and chaired by Lord Lane, the then recently-retired Lord Chief Justice of England and Wales, one of us[41] received a letter from him, written on House of Lords notepaper and dated 'Guy Fawkes night [November 5] 1993'. Accompanying the letter was a draft article by Lord Lane (which is included herewith in an appendix to this chapter). The article was never submitted to any newspaper or journal that might have been contemplated by Lord Lane. We suspect that it was overtaken by the forthcoming publication of the Prison Reform Trust's report which was largely written by Lord Lane himself. The report is a model of clarity and comprehensiveness. It bears reading nearly 20 years on.

Again and again, with every attempt to introduce order and clarity into the substantive law, one is faced with the mandatory penalty as the primary impediment to change. Those who share our view, that the time for reform is not only right but long overdue, must recognise that what at times appears to be a dialogue with the deaf can be a dispiriting experience. But so too, in many respects, was the long struggle for the abolition of capital punishment, a task that took virtually a century to accomplish.

While we would not expect to succeed in persuading every reader to our viewpoint, our hope is to promote discussion not only about the ethical considerations that must apply to the law of homicide but also about the practical nature of the penalties that are imposed. The former is an issue for moral debate; the latter for public policy.

---

41. Louis Blom-Cooper.

ANNEX TO CHAPTER 1

ARTICLE BY LORD LANE [42]

The task of a sentencing judge is to punish the offender and so far as possible to try to protect the public from future harm by deterring the offender and others.

Whether the conviction has resulted from the verdict of a jury or from a plea of guilty the judge must have heard in detail the facts of the offence and the history of the offender together with any mitigation, all in open court. He is then in as good a position as anyone can be to decide what the proper sentence should be.

But in murder cases all to no avail. Whatever the circumstances of the offence or of the offender, whatever the mitigating factors, the judge has no option but to order him or her to suffer imprisonment for life, however inappropriate such a sentence may be.

The definition of murder means, broadly speaking, that anyone who is proved to have unlawfully caused the death of another with the intention that the other should suffer serious injury (though not necessarily death) is guilty of murder. It scarcely needs pointing out that that definition embraces a wide range of conduct and, perhaps more important, a wide range of intentions. Whether the crime is murder or whether it is manslaughter (in which the life sentence is the maximum but not the mandatory penalty) may depend largely on chance or the availability of medical help. It may depend upon the fine distinction between an intent to do serious harm and an intent to inflict a lesser degree of injury.

The offender may be a caring husband whose only wish has been to put an end to the agony his dying wife is suffering. It may be a wife, no longer

---

42. The covering note, on House of Lords notepaper and dated 'Guy Fawkes night 1993', reads: Dear Louis, Herewith a B— attempt at a Times article for you to eviscerate. Please do. I'm not happy with much of it—particularly the final paragraph. With any luck no one will print it anyway!

able to tolerate the behaviour of a bullying husband, who, after years of suffering, kills him in circumstances which fall outside the strict (some say too strict) rules of provocation.

At the other end of the scale it may be an armed robber trying to shoot his way out of trouble or a terrorist blowing up an aircraft in flight and killing hundreds in the process. The judge must sentence all alike to imprisonment for life. The robber and the terrorist are clearly proper subjects of a life sentence—and will remain so. The others equally clearly are not.

Who decides how long each of these offenders must spend in prison? Not the trial judge, though his views will be sought—and often overruled. Not anyone who has heard the proceedings at the trial. That decision is taken behind closed doors by a Minister at the Home Office, no doubt acting on the advice of civil servants in the department. It has none of the safeguards of a judicial decision; there is no public hearing; no system of appeal.

How did this state of affairs come about? Hanging as punishment for murder was abolished in 1965. That result was reached only after highly charged debates about the morality and expediency of the death penalty. It is understandable that in that atmosphere too little attention was paid to what punishment should replace the death penalty in future. In the upshot the legislation simply replaced one fixed penalty—death—with another, life imprisonment. It is to be noted that Lord Parker, the Lord Chief Justice at the time, was strongly in favour of the judges being free to decide the length of imprisonment.

> I dislike a fixed sentence, and now it is proposed to abolish the fixed sentence of the death penalty, I do not wish to see another fixed penalty in its place. In a fixed sentence there is no room for any mitigation...

Subsequent experience has shown, at least to those concerned with trying to administer the 'lifer' system, how unwise it was to depart from the fundamental principle that sentencing is a judicial function and not one to be entrusted to politicians however eminent or to civil servants however experienced.

The present system has resulted in our having in our prisons at the moment over 3,000 lifers, more, we are told, than are to be found in all the other prisons in Western Europe put together. 80% of the 3,000 are mandatory lifers, that is to say convicted of murder. That involves a heavy administrative load. It involves great expense. It is unsatisfactory to the families of victims who, generally speaking, have no idea when the offender is likely to be released or what the real sentence upon him is. It has given rise to a number of side-effects (incomprehensible to the victim's family) whereby a conviction for manslaughter rather than for murder has resulted, thus absolving the judge from the obligation to impose a life sentence in circumstances where such a course would be abhorrent.

That is why an independent committee, set up by the Prison Reform Trust under my chairmanship, is advocating that there should be a reassertion of the basic principle that sentencing is a function of the courts and that life imprisonment should be the maximum but not the mandatory penalty for murder. If our recommendations are accepted, life imprisonment will be reserved for those murderers whose crime really is so heinous that no lesser penalty would be adequate and for those who would represent a danger to the public if released, the extent of that danger in terms of years being difficult to predict.

It is the horrifying murders which, inevitably, occupy the headlines. Research shows that they represent only a small proportion of the total. The great majority of unlawful killings are the result of domestic strife, of sudden bouts of temper, of drunken brawls and so on, where a fixed term of imprisonment would be adequate by way of punishment and deterrence.

Some argue that to remove the mandatory nature of the life sentence would be a display of weakness — 'going soft on the killer' and such-like expressions. It seems to the Committee that the opposite is the case. At the moment the life sentence means, not what it says, but simply that the length of time the offender spends in prison will be decided not by the judge but by a politician.

If our recommendations are accepted, the life sentence will start to have a serious meaning. It will indicate that the particular offence is so appalling and/or the offender is so dangerous that it is impossible to fix an appropriate term of years. It will be a sentence to be feared and no longer an empty phrase, as everyone knows, it is at present.

There are of course a number of grave offences in which the offender may at the discretion of the judge be sentenced to life imprisonment. These include manslaughter and attempted murder. It is not generally appreciated that in order to bring home a charge of attempted murder the prosecution must prove an actual intent to kill. Proof of an intent to do serious harm is not, unlike in the case of murder, enough. Thus attempted murder may often be, in terms of wickedness, a much more reprehensible crime than murder. Yet the judge has a wide discretion as to the penalty he should impose in the case of the attempt.

One seeks the reason for the persistent refusal by the Home Office to consider any alteration of the system, despite the strong recommendation of the Nathan Committee and others. The official line was expressed by the present Home Secretary, Michael Howard, last month as follows:

> The nature of the mandatory sentence is different. The element of risk is not the decisive factor in the imposition of a life sentence; in such a case, the offender has committed a crime of such gravity that he is required to forfeit his liberty to the State for the rest of his life. The presumption is that the offender should remain in custody unless and until I, or the Home Secretary of the day, concludes not only that the imprisonment served is sufficient to serve the interests of retribution and deterrence and that it is safe for the prisoner to be released but also that the public interest would be better served by the prisoner's release than by his continued detention…[A]ccount has to be taken not just of punishment and risk, but of how society as a whole would view the prisoner's release at the juncture.[43]

There are two obvious comments to be made on that statement. First, it suggests that all murders are equally heinous and so grave that the offender should forfeit his liberty for the rest of his life. That is demonstrably false. Second, the proposition that the length of a prison sentence should be determined by the views of society as a whole is startling, to say the least, coming from any source, let alone from the Home Secretary himself. Any assertion

---

43. Although Lord Lane does not say so, we believe this quotation is from a communication from Howard to Lane in response to the Report of the Committee on the Penalty for Homicide published by the Prison Reform Trust and which had just been published.

by a politician that he is acting according to the dictates of public opinion should be examined with meticulous care, cynics might say with suspicion.[44]

---

44. The following alternative ending was composed by Louis Blom-Cooper at the time: The assumption that every murder is equally heinous, and that every murderer must automatically forfeit liberty for the rest of his or her life is patently absurd. Murderers range from the most wicked to those deserving of sympathy, and every degree of criminal responsibility in between. The idea that the length of the prison sentence should be determined other than by a court of law is alarming. To say that it is a politician's task to determine how long a murderer should be kept in prison is nakedly to usurp the function properly allocated by the public to the judges.

CHAPTER 2

A JACOBEAN LEGACY: THE CREATIVITY OF COKE

Murder is when a man of sound memory, and of the age of discretion, unlawfully killeth within any county of the realm any reasonable creature in rerum natura under the King's peace, with malice aforethought, either expressed by the party or implied by law, so as the party wounded, or hurt, etc. die of the wound or hurt, etc. within a year and a day after the same.[1]

By these words, Sir Edward Coke[2] produced the definition of murder that has served the English common law for more than four centuries. When the Victorians determined that the criminal law with respect to offences against the person needed statutory authority[3] the basic ingredients of the crime of murder were conspicuously absent.

Outwith the law the term 'murder' occupies a place in demotic language, serving as a synonym for those unlawful killings which are held in the greatest opprobrium. Homicide, by contrast, covers a wider range of actions resulting in death and by no means visited with the same degree of social revulsion. That term 'homicide' derives from the Latin *homicida*; a conjunction of *homo* (a man or human being) and *caedo* (to cut, cut down, strike or beat). This etymology is simply descriptive and in no way addresses the subjective issues of circumstance or intention that are essential to the process whereby the law distinguishes between different categories of unlawful killing and those accidental killings to which no criminal penalty attaches. Homicide is not, however, a word used with great frequency in common

---

1. Sir Edward Coke, *Institutes of the Lawes of England* 1628-34, paragraph 3.47. ('Coke' was the contemporary spelling of Cook).
2. 1552–1634.
3. Offences Against the Person Act 1861.

speech.[4] When the body of a person who has clearly suffered a violent and unnatural death is discovered in circumstances suggesting that the victim has suffered a fatal assault at the hands of some other person, the reports in the public media almost invariably refer to a 'murder' having taken place. But whereas homicide is an objective description of the criminal event, murder is essentially a term of art. More precisely, it is a legal definition of a criminal event that can be applied only at the conclusion of a trial, initially in the court in which the evidence is put to a jury and, finally, should there be an appeal, in a superior court. And while a conviction for murder may sometimes be quashed and a verdict of manslaughter substituted, though rare, it has not been unknown for a verdict to alter between the Court of Appeal and the House of Lords.[5]

The term 'homicide' is inclusive of several legally discrete categories of unlawful killing, including not only murder and manslaughter, but also infanticide and those parts of road traffic law which relate to causing death by drunken, dangerous or careless driving. Each of these categories of homicide is subject to particular definition but this does not exclude alleged offences from overlapping. Certain partial defences to murder may reduce the offence to one of manslaughter, though, while a death resulting from a road traffic event can result in conviction for manslaughter at common law, the usual choice of the prosecution is to proceed on a charge of causing death by dangerous or careless driving.[6]

The killing of one human being by another, not least when victim and assailant are unevenly matched or when the killing is accompanied by apparently gratuitous cruelty, is regarded by society at large as repellent. While there are individuals at the margins of society whose behaviour indicates otherwise, for the majority, killing other people without lawful excuse is simply wrong. It is important at the outset, however, to consider the sources

---

4. While police forces in the United States have 'homicide' departments or squads, in England and Wales the term 'murder' is used to describe such specialist units.

5. As in *DPP v Smith* [1961] AC 290.

6. It was because of the widespread (and not infrequently perverse) refusal of juries to convict drivers at common law, with its attendant maximum sentence of life imprisonment, that Parliament was persuaded in 1956 to identify a separate statutory offence of causing death by dangerous driving for which the maximum penalty was five years' imprisonment (recently raised to ten years). See further *Chapter 10* of this work, *Homicide on the Road*.

of the beliefs that inscribe the moral labels that are attached to human conduct. Most of the world's great religions present their followers with a code of conduct in which each prohibition is characterised by a notion of wrong that is generally coterminous with the idea of sin. It is undoubtedly the case that the common law, like Roman law, has incorporated by a process of social osmosis many of the beliefs and assertions of Western Christianity, itself in debt to the traditions of Judaism; yet it is in no way based upon Christianity (as perhaps some would believe and others might prefer it to be).[7]

The essentially secular qualities of the English law which disengaged itself—though not without difficulty—from the ecclesiastical jurisdiction during the 16th century are demonstrated by the fact that its proscriptions are essentially *social* as distinct from 'other-worldly' constructs. The matter can be summed up simply: the law is concerned with those things which men[8] living in society have deemed to be of such importance that they should be subject to rules of conduct that are non-negotiable. Likewise, they stand to be applied without distinction of wealth, rank or social origin. Moreover, attaching to the rules are sanctions, characterised by varying degrees of coercion, whose object it is to deter or to ensure compliance and to visit with a penalty, should that not be forthcoming. Additionally, the penalties attaching to the infringement of certain rules may be intended or perceived to reflect the social opprobrium with which such rule-breaking is thought to be properly regarded. The import of all this is that the categories of behaviour identified by the law as meriting a criminal sanction derive from the way legislators, and those who influence them, think about the world in which they live. Yet the very inclusivity of the criminal law—the fact that it applies without social distinction to those within its jurisdiction and that it is 'non-negotiable'—eclipses, for most of the time, two important considerations.

The first is that the laws and the precepts which they embody are derived from the values and beliefs current at the time of their conception;[9] the sec-

---

7. See *Bowman v National Secular Society Ltd* [1917] AC 406. With regard to the Old Testament prohibition of homicide in the Commandments see our comments in *Chapter 9*.

8. Throughout this work the terms 'man', 'men', 'him', etc. imply both men and women unless otherwise stated.

9. The ecclesiastical courts of the Middle Ages provided the death penalty for witches, a task assumed by secular authority by the Witchcraft Acts of 1541 and 1603. A Georgian Witchcraft Act of 1735 remained on the statute book until repealed by the Fraudulent Mediums Act in

ond is that the provision of new law is not infrequently a response to the demands of particular interest groups—and this was especially true in the past—rather than the expressed priorities of society as a whole. This is a point forcefully made by Dicey[10] and which can readily explain such social inequities as the capital penalties suffered by country labourers convicted of poaching in the 18th century, as well as the Enclosure Acts which limited the possibilities of subsistence husbandry for the rural poor. It is perhaps the first of these considerations that had the greatest bearing upon the development of the law of homicide: principally, the idea that wrongdoing, whatever the offender might have had in mind, once embarked upon would be sufficient to establish his guilt for the outcome of other consequences, however unintended. It is in relation to these issues that the genesis and importance of Sir Edward Coke's thought and expression needs to be understood.

In the Beginning: Laws for Less Orderly Times

Although there is a temptation to think that, until Coke, there had been little by way of comparable attention given to the crime of murder, the legal history of those centuries termed the Middle Ages discloses much that has contemporary significance. The mediaeval jurists were as much concerned with homicide in general as with artificially discrete categories of unlawful killing.

In the England of the period immediately before the Norman Conquest, the establishment of centralised monarchy was a comparatively recent phenomenon and the institutions of feudalism, with clearly defined rights and obligations based upon land tenure, were the dominant source of effective social and political control. Criminal justice was but one constituent element of the system and was given to being rudimentary in both concept and execution. The coming of the Norman kings and their Angevin successors energised social and political change from which the law was not exempt. While this is not the place in which to rehearse the history of the

---

1953.

10. A V Dicey, *Lectures on the Relation between Law and Opinion in the Nineteenth Century*, London (Macmillan, 1905).

process whereby the powers of the feudal nobility were finally tamed by the Crown, not least by the establishment of royal courts of justice and the introduction of itinerant Justiciars offerering a superior service to that of the manorial lords, these institutional changes had an important bearing upon conceptions of crime and the penalties applicable to particular offences. The terms 'felon' and 'felony', coming from the Old French into Middle English,[11] originally denoted a breach of fidelity in the feudal relationship embodied in homage, but over time came to have a different currency in England from that in mainland Europe, becoming synonymous with the most serious offenders and their crimes. These still contained the same essential ingredient, namely a breach of trust or obligation. Thus the mediaeval law of treason[12] contained what might seem odd nowadays, in that in addition to such things as compassing or imagining the death of the king or his family, violating his womenfolk, levying war against him in his realm, or such assorted mischiefs as slaying the Treasurer, Chancellor or judges sitting in court—the so-called 'High Treasons'—there were also 'petty treasons' which included the slaying of a master by a servant, of a husband by his wife or a prelate by his subject (secular or religious). These 'petty treasons' were not finally subsumed within the common law of murder until 1828. The term 'treason'[13] essentially implies a breach of trust on the part of the offender: the loyalty of the subject to the sovereign, of the servant to his master, of a wife to her husband or of a lesser cleric or layman to a prince of the church. Implicit in this concept of trust is the obligation on the part of the inferior party to the superior.

The term 'murder' has a no less interesting history, not least since the word from which it derives referred not only to an offence but also to a penalty imposed by the Norman conquerors of Saxon England. Earlier, in Anglo-Saxon times, when a man was killed (whether wilfully or by accident made no matter) the offender was required to bear the feud, or else hand over a sum of money amounting to the worth of the dead man (the *wergild*), normally calculable in terms of the deceased's feudal obligations. This form of compensatory justice has parallels in the social systems of other

11. In use *circa* 1200-1500.
12. Statute of Treasons 1352 (25 Edw. III, st. 5, c. 2).
13. From the Norman French *treisoun* (*trahison* in modern-day French) meaning 'betrayal'.

non-industrial civilisations in which cattle or childbearing women are given by way of compensation to the kin of the dead person.[14] While this suggests a comparatively restrained approach to violent death in the England of long ago, it must be acknowledged that the circumstances of the political economy lent themselves perhaps more readily to what later ages have been able to do by means of civil process: namely, to distinguish liability in tort from criminal guilt and to attempt some degree of restorative justice. But the law could take a firmer line when circumstances demanded. Certainly, in Saxon England, the law had made provision for killings done by way of ambush (*foresteal*)—yet another manifestation of serious breach of obligation or trust—and in the period after the Norman Conquest this notion appears to have become the basis of a more complex jurisprudence with regard to premeditated crimes classified in the Norman French as assault *prepensé* or the Latin as *assultus premeditatus*. It is at this period that the term *malitia excogitata*[15] first appears, emerging eventually into the world of Tudor and Jacobean lawyers as 'malice aforethought'.

The term 'murder' derives from the concept of *murdrum*, used in Saxon times to describe what was regarded as an especially heinous crime, that of killing another in secret. After the Conquest, disgruntled Saxons engaged so frequently in deadly ambush attacks on their Norman conquerors that William I enacted that if the perpetrator of such a killing were not found, then the inhabitants of the hundred in which the death had occurred should be required to pay a fine known as the *murdrum*, the crime and the punishment described by a single word. This provision for collective punishment in the event of unsolved homicides was abolished in 1340.[16]

It is the presumption of malice in the homicidal event, as distinct from negligence or plain accident, which complicates the law of murder in this early period still further, since it was linked to the offender's entitlement to a pardon, depending upon the circumstances. It has been suggested that

---

14. See: Isaac Schapera, *A Handbook of Tswana Law and Custom* (2nd ed.) London (Cassell, 1955). Bohannan notes a similar practice among the Tiv of Central Nigeria: Paul Bohannan (ed.) *African Homicide and Suicide*, Princeton, NJ. (Princeton University Press, 1960).

15. Coke uses the term *malitia præcogitata*.

16. 14 Edw. III, st. Ch.4.

pardons were not uncommon.[17] By 1390[18] the statute distinguished pardons sought in respect of such events as self-defence or misadventure from those for murders done in await, assault or malice *prepensé*. It is here that we can observe the origins of the distinctions between various kinds of homicide on the basis of the imputed moral qualities of the act, which were at this time expressed in terms of a hierarchy of sinfulness, an important concern to mediaeval theologians and clerical jurists.

The concept of *sin* was predicated upon the notion of a wrongful act, prohibited by divine injunction, having been freely willed by the sinner, an evil intention having been translated into a physical deed. Thus the knights who had murdered Thomas à Becket in his cathedral were first and foremost guilty of the sin of sacrilege, never mind what might later have been identified as a murder done in malice *prepensé*, and were required by the Church to do penance. Henry II, thought to have inspired the deed by his incautious expression of exasperation with the Archbishop, was required to undergo a penitential (if somewhat notional) flogging by the monks of Canterbury. Sin and 'wilful murder'[19] could be readily elided in terms of culpability; not so in the case of those homicides in which, although a degree of fault might be identified, it did not amount to an unambiguous intention of bringing about the victim's death. This was at a time when the ability of the agents of the State to protect citizens from robbery, burglary or assault was rudimentary and self-help in such situations was recognised as often the only means whereby the citizen could protect his person or his goods.

What appears to have brought matters to a head in the early Tudor period was the vexed issue of 'benefit of clergy' and for a brief explanation we need to return to the essence of the quarrel between Henry II and Becket.[20] Henry was keen to centralise the power of the Crown by various means, including the extension of royal jurisdiction over all who were deemed to be subjects within the feudal polity. These included clerics, the most powerful of whom

---

17. See: Theodore Plucknett, *A Concise History of the Common Law* (4th ed.) London (Butterworth & Co, 1948).
18. 13 Rich. II, st. 2 ch. 1.
19. A term which first appears in statute in 1532 (23 Hen. VIII, Ch.1).
20. Ironically, it was Henry who had leaned heavily on his old companion Thomas of London, (*aka* Thomas à Becket) to become Archbishop of Canterbury. See: David Knowles, *Thomas Becket*, London (Adam and Charles Black, 1970).

(the bishops and abbots) were ranked as peers among the nobility, the 'clerk' being defined as one who was in holy orders, however lowly. Becket, on the contrary, was determined to preserve what he understood to be the liberties of the church for which there was scriptural authority.[21] The Constitutions of Clarendon in 1164 claimed to re-state an earlier arrangement whereby a 'criminous clerk' was to be charged in the King's court, sent to the ecclesiastical court for trial and, if 'unfrocked', then returned to the secular court for sentence. This might, of course, be death. Becket's murder in 1170 set back this movement towards bringing all offenders within the ambit of the royal justice for several centuries. The situation nevertheless moved towards that conclusion; those who sought benefit of clergy claimed it through their ability to recite in Latin the opening verses of Psalm 50.[22] Clerks were, on conviction, supposed to be exempt from the death penalty but subjected to branding[23] (to ensure that they could not claim benefit of clergy again) but there is reason to think that the system was far from reliable in preventing 'clerks convict' from being hanged as a result of sentence in the royal courts. While Tudor legislation developed to make the most serious crimes 'non-clergyable', the system did not finally disappear until 1827.

From this time on it seems clear that what had been the old felony of murder was now divided into those offences which were 'wilful and of malice aforethought', not clergyable and consequently capital, and those which, being neither in self-defence nor as a result of misadventure, nevertheless bore culpability.[24] This would seem to have been the result of enthusiasm on the part of the Tudor legislators to limit the unacceptable lenity of the provision whereby those successfully claiming benefit of clergy were able to escape the death penalty for otherwise heinous instances of homicide. The effect was to drive a great wedge into the law of homicide, splitting off the discrete crime of murder from those other killings which were to become known as manslaughter. The analytical task of distinguishing between mur-

---

21. Notably the passage in 1 Chronicles 16:22 — 'Touch not mine anointed and do my prophets no harm'.

22. *Miserere mei Deus secundum magnam misericordiam tuam.* (Have mercy upon me, O God, according to the greatness of thy mercy.), numbered Psalm 50 in the Latin Vulgate but 51 in the Hebrew and King James versions. This became known as the 'neck verse'.

23. After 1490 (4.Hen. VII, Ch.13).

24. See Plucknett. *op.cit.*

der and manslaughter was increasingly to rest upon the interpretation of the concept of 'malice' and/or the establishment of its presence. The notion of 'malice', if it were not, in its most abstract form, already fraught with problems of definition and identification, was to be subdivided in the ensuing period into categories productive of further complexity.

A Forceful Man of Law; of Many Parts and Great Learning

It is at this point that we need to return to the contribution of Coke, acknowledged to be one of the greatest common lawyers and a jurist whose influence was to be immense, in that his definition of murder was to survive largely untouched for almost 400 years. But to understand Coke, not least in respect of his promotion of the doctrine of constructive malice, it is important to consider the man himself, his view of the world in which he lived and his highly partisan involvement in its affairs of State.

Born in 1552 into the minor gentry of rural Norfolk, he lived an unusually long life through the reigns of Elizabeth, James I and Charles I, to the age of 82. From his stratum of society were to emerge many of the socially mobile figures of late Tudor and Jacobean England, and he was no exception. By the late-1590s he had become excessively rich and had risen to prominence in the worlds of politics and the law. His career would, by today's standards, be nothing short of extraordinary. By 1592 he had become Solicitor-General and two years later Attorney-General. Between 1606 and 1616 he held successively the offices of Chief Justice of the Common Pleas and Chief Justice of the King's Bench. Royal displeasure having cost him both the status and pecuniary benefits of judicial office, he was returned to Parliament in 1621 (having briefly been Speaker of the Commons in 1593) where he again became a thorn in the royal side. This resulted in his spending most of his seventieth year as a prisoner in the Tower. Back in Parliament he continued to be a vocal critic of the increasingly autocratic style of the King's rule. Charles I, who, succeeding to the throne in 1625, was to prove even more autocratic than his father, managed temporarily to keep him out of the Commons by appointing him Sheriff of Buckinghamshire. In 1628, at the age of 76, he retired to his home in that county at Stoke Poges to begin his great four-volume *Institutes of the Lawes of England.* Four years later, Charles I, his political ineptitude undiminished, thought it prudent to limit Coke's influence by ordering the seizure of his papers. Only one volume of the *Institutes* was published in his lifetime, the remainder appearing after the outbreak of the Civil War.

It was in the third volume of the *Institutes* that Coke dealt with the criminal law. The first attempt to provide a comprehensive view of the law since the treatise of Henry de Bracton in the mid-13th century,[25] it had an immense effect, not least on account of Coke's encyclopaedic knowledge of case law and the fact that his position went largely unchallenged. In its presentation, as with the attribution of particular judgments in his law reports[26] he was by no means always accurate. As Plucknett suggests:

> ...the seventeenth century was apt to see the mediaeval authorities only through Coke's eyes...If every lawyer had gone to the Year books for himself and read them as uncritically as Coke did, it might well be that his idea of the continuity of English law would have broken down...By a careful selection of material Coke was enabled to conceal the inconsistencies and difficulties which were inherent in his position.[27]

Professor Plucknett notes that there were shortcomings in his writing which had 'few literary graces', and that he was also given to employing 'passably good Latin maxims which had an air of antiquity about them, in spite of the fact that he himself invented them'.[28]

As Attorney-General he had prosecuted in numerous high profile cases, many of an overtly political character. He prosecuted in the treason trial of Elizabeth's erstwhile favourite, the Earl of Essex, and later Sir Walter Ralegh, whom the new King James I was anxious to have out of the way, the conspirators of the so-called 'Gunpowder Plot' in 1606 and, later, James'

---

25. Henricus de Bracton, *De Legibus et Consuetudinibus Angliæ* vols 1-4, ed. George Woodbine, New Haven, CT (Yale Historical Publications, 1915-1942). A later edition, setting the original Latin text alongside Woodbine's translation, was produced by Samuel E Thorne in association with the Selden Society, Cambridge, MS and London (Belknap Press, 1968-77). De Bracton was working on his *magnum opus* around 1254 and was therefore a contemporary of Aquinas (q.v.).

26. *Coke's Reports* (of which there are no fewer than thirteen volumes).

27. Plucknett. *op.cit.* at p.268.

28. *Ibid.* at p.267.

favourite Robert Carr, Earl of Somerset, and his wife for the murder of Sir Thomas Overbury. His forensic manner was characterised by aggression, insult towards the accused and behaviour generally which, on the part of any advocate, would simply not be tolerated by any modern judge. At the trial of Ralegh at Winchester in November 1603[29] his conduct was particularly disgraceful:

COKE   You are the most vile and execrable traitor that ever lived.

RALEGH You speak indiscreetly, uncivilly and barbarously.

COKE   I want words sufficient to express your viperous treasons.

RALEGH I think you want words indeed, for you have spoken one thing half a dozen times.

COKE   You are an odious fellow; your name is hateful to all the realm of England ... I will make it appear to the world that there never lived a viler viper on the face of the earth than you.

Sir John Popham, the Chief Justice, and his fellow judges were clearly hostile to the prisoner and failed to provide any summing up for the jury and in this environment Coke's conduct went wholly unreproved. Moreover, the judges had ruled that *examination*[30] (our italics) of the prisoner alone could provide sufficient evidence of the alleged treason (for which the death penalty applied) and no witness was required to corroborate the testimony of prosecution witnesses. Yet in the third *Institute* Coke was subsequently to advance quite the contrary opinion, notwithstanding that he had earlier been content to take advantage of this ruling in Ralegh's case.[31]

---

29. Dramatically re-enacted in Middle Temple Hall on its precise 400th anniversary on 17 November 2003 in the play *Sharp Medicine* by Anthony Arlidge QC.

30. Examination was by no means identical with confession on the part of the prisoner. Guy Fawkes and his co-conspirators were certainly 'examined' two years later—on the rack!

31. In this trial Coke was quite openly serving the interest of the King, whose approbation he was overtly seeking to gain. Master Bruce Williamson, *Lector Autumnalis* in the Middle Temple in 1935, expressed a trenchant view on the honesty of Coke's position: 'What would be thought today of a Counsel who took advantage of a ruling he believed to be erroneous to secure a conviction on a capital charge? I do not think he would long wear his Barrister's gown or be suffered to remain in any Inn of Court which had the misfortune to number him among its members'. *Sir Walter Ralegh and his Trial*, Williamson B, London (Sir Isaac Pitman and Sons, 1936), at p.29.

Nor was Coke's behaviour as a courtroom bully significantly at variance with his actions in private life. His conduct towards his extensive family (his first wife bore him seven children and his second two more) would be readily identified by any contemporary family court as intolerable. In attempting to subject one of his daughters to abduction and forcible marriage to secure political advantage, he was prepared to employ domestic violence, threatening his wife's servants with violence and ordering his own men to batter down doors for the purpose. It is hardly surprising that his second wife, on being given the news of his death in 1634, is said to have responded: 'We shall never see his like again, praise be to God!'

If Coke was at times an unprincipled and intellectually dishonest advocate whose behaviour in court was often appalling, that is not to detract from his outstanding ability as a jurist. His great work belongs to the very last years of his life and it is possible that the fire that had stoked his unattractively egocentric personality[32] for so long now burned low. Yet Coke, like many who have made a major intellectual impact well beyond their own time, was no reforming visionary but rather one who, by some process of mental osmosis, encapsulated in his writing the beliefs and sentiments of the world in which he lived.

Coke in the World of Jacobean England

Coke, it should be remembered, was not only a lawyer of great reputation and status, but also a man of property who would have naturally shared the values of that class of gentry that enjoyed substantial privilege in what was an extremely unequal society. While concerned that royal power should not limit its freedom, it was nevertheless keen to ensure that its security was in no way threatened by those lower in the social order. It is the ideological approach of this class towards those who infringed the criminal law that is reflected in Coke's writings, perhaps most strikingly in his more extreme interpretations of the concept of constructive malice. What he presents, notably in his broader interpretation of the law of homicide, is suggestive less of

---

32. Whether or not Coke was possessed of a severe personality disorder, or whether he was no more than a disagreeably arrogant bully, must be for readers of his biography to judge.

a distillation of the case law of earlier times but rather more of a statement of what Kant was to identify as a categorical imperative:[33] a statement not of what *is*, but of what *ought to be*. The categorical imperative is summed up in the Kantian injunction: 'Act only according to that maxim whereby you can at the same time will that it should become a universal law'. Coke's representation of the law of murder is characterised by precisely this approach.

The social structure of England in the late 16th and 17th centuries had changed substantially since early Tudor times. The position of the traditional aristocracy was challenged by this new class that had originally grown rich upon the loot of monastic property but was now frequently the beneficiary of enclosures and greatly expanded foreign trade.[34] Although its members might be rewarded with knighthoods and peerages, its possession of property — essentially in land — was a manifestation not of birth and position within a feudal structure, but of acquired wealth. And while in France the nobility of the *ancien régime* did not meet its nemesis until 1789, it could be argued that the corresponding date for its English counterpart was the opening of the Civil War in 1642. In the Parliament of 1628, Coke had challenged the royal despotism by resorting to what he identified as the freedoms guaranteed by the common law, culminating in the Petition of Right[35] of which he was an author. He could be properly considered one of the fathers of what was essentially a bourgeois revolution.

But the security of this new class remained politically vulnerable.[36] Above it stood the Crown,[37] as yet not displaced by the Parliamentarian Commonwealth. Beneath it were the rural poor, and an equally impoverished but potentially politically volatile element in the towns[38] besides large numbers

---

33. *Fundamental Principles of the Metaphysics of Morals* (1785) and *Critique of Practical Reason* (1788).

34. The great voyages of discovery had opened up trade routes to Africa and the Americas, stimulating, among other things, the beginnings of a highly lucrative slave trade.

35. The catalogue of the King's violation of his subjects' liberties was nothing if not impressive. It included imprisonment without cause, never mind without trial, levying taxes at will, the sale of monopolies and the arbitrary imposition of martial law.

36. As Ralegh and others among Elizabeth's favourites had learned to their cost.

37. In this instance in the persons of the petulant and unpredictable James I and his son Charles I whose continuous (and effectively suicidal) amplification of his father's assertion of the Divine Right of kings was to lead him to the scaffold in January 1649.

38. London was unsafe for Charles I at the outbreak of the Civil War in 1642.

of those made landless and destitute by a combination of enclosures and economic circumstance. The 'sturdy beggars' identified by the vagrancy laws of Elizabeth had by no means disappeared. The economic security of men like Coke was contingent upon wealth in which land was the significant element.[39] It was (and remains) *real property* as distinct from personal possessions, which in an age long before the advent of mass manufacture and the pressures of consumerism, tended to be limited in scope.[40] Moreover, while venture capital might be invested in a particular voyage or 'company' there was neither a stock market nor anything resembling a modern banking system.

The privileges of the class to which Coke belonged were, nevertheless, precariously secured; on the one hand by royal benevolence — or a tolerance born of grudging necessity — but more importantly on the other, by a system of social control of which a repressive criminal law was a dominant constituent. Unlike the great prisoners of state, petty malefactors went speedily and largely unrecorded to their deaths on public gallows.[41] Just as Charles I came to fear the power of Coke's assertions in constitutional law, so in his turn Cromwell came to fear the influence of the radical doctrines of the Diggers and Levellers. The privileges that this English Revolution sought to assert and affirm were not those of the common people but of a landowning class that would in Victorian and Edwardian England be described as 'new money'.

If we consider these aspects of the immediate social world of Sir Edward Coke, we may come closer to understanding his concerns with the concept of 'malice' particularly regarding homicides connected with property offences and those involving persons of status and authority. In the 17th century, the maintenance of property rights and social order were functionally interdependent and remained a central feature of the polity until the coming of the Industrial Revolution and the exponential growth of a contractual labour force within the new manufacturing cities.

---

39. Coke himself owned more than a hundred different properties.
40. Shakespeare, it might be recalled, made reference in his will to his 'best bed'.
41. The rapidity of the criminal trial of common people charged with capital offences persisted well into succeeding centuries and, as Alexander Pope was to observe in *The Rape of the Lock*: 'The hungry judges soon the sentence sign/and wretches hang, that jurymen may dine'. Less of a *memento mori* in the philosophical sense, the corpse of a highway robber that swung from a crossroads gibbet was more akin to a specimen displayed in a gamekeeper's larder.

The Concept of 'Malice' in its Various Guises

The idea of constructive malice, a device that patently disadvantaged the defendant on a charge of murder, does not merely offend against widely held notions of fairness but represents a kind of premium or excess penal liability upon what has been the primary criminal act. It is Coke's interpretation of the concept, presumptive of an intention that is not immediately derivative from the facts of the case, which is significant in the socio-political context we have outlined above. Intellectually, its roots were in the theology of the Middle Ages which was deeply influenced by Aristotelian philosophy, whose great exponent was Thomas Aquinas,[42] a contemporary of Bracton. In his *Summa Theologiæ*[43] he identifies what he terms voluntary homicide (*homicidium voluntarium*). This, he says, can come about in two ways, the first when a man engages in activities in which he should not have done (*rebus illicitis*) or when he does not take due care (*solicitudinem*). Where the activity is legitimate and due care has been exercised there is no guilt of homicide, but where the activity is illicit, or even when it is not, but due care is not taken, then there is guilt for any resultant homicide. Considering those unlawful homicides arising from *rebus illicitis* there is clearly discernible the kernel of the notion of a 'premium' or culpable excess. It would have been logically consistent for the Tudor lawyers to extend it and for Coke to complete the task by formalising it in the *Institutes*. By Coke's time we have a clear distinction between those homicides predicated upon deliberate intention (malice) and those which, although there is fault sufficient to generate culpability, are nevertheless exclusive of malice *prepensé*. However, it is important to recognise that Aquinas (like de Bracton) was writing in Latin and there is a certain capacity for elasticity in translation. The three words *culpa*, *delictum* and *peccatum* may all be translated as 'fault'. Aquinas, however, employs the word *culpa* to mean 'fault' and *peccatum*[44] to mean 'sin'. Aquinas is, of course, concerned here in Volume 38 of the *Summa* with injustice in the broader context of moral theology and not with the dimen-

---

42. 1225-1274.
43. Vol. 38, trans. Marcus Lefébure OP, London (Blackfriars in conjunction with Eyre and Spottiswoode, 1975).
44. Though the word can also be translated as 'mistake' he does not use it in this sense.

sions of criminal guilt, which by the end of the 16th century had acquired a definitively secular meaning.

In the *Institutes*[45] Coke distinguishes between malice aforethought that is *express* as distinct from that which is *implied*. It is express 'when one compasseth to kill, wound or beat another, and doth it *in sedato animo*. This is said in law to be malice aforethought, *prepensé, malitia praecogitata*'.

He then identifies three categories of malice implied:

1. *In respect of the manner of the deed.* Thus in the case of unprovoked killing malice is implied;

2. *In respect of the person killed.* As if a magistrate or known officer, or any other that hath lawful warrant, and doing or offering to do his office, or to execute his warrant, is slain, this is murder, by malice implied by law;

3. *In respect of the person killing.* If A assault B to rob him, and in resisting A killeth B, this is murder by malice implied, albeit he (A) never saw or knew him (B) before.

Malice, notwithstanding that it is express in the sense that the offender forms a clear intention of killing his victim, cannot, as a matter of course, presume the rationality of the act, but Coke was not concerned with defences based upon the accused's mental state; the same applies to his first category of implied malice where there is killing without provocation. It is in the second and third of his categories of implied malice that the social dimension of the 'constructive' element — the 'penal premium' — comes into focus.

Notably, it is magistrates and others concerned with the enforcement of the law who are the first to be identified, not on account of their especial vulnerability as victims *per se*, but on account of their office. Given that the law was often disadvantageous to the relatively powerless, their resort to physical violence would not be beyond the bounds of possibility — for example in the context of the enforcement of the vagrancy laws, or evictions from enclosed common lands. Nor is it without significance when

---

45. *Institutes* 3: 51–52.

Coke goes on to amplify the doctrine of constructive malice in instances of poaching. If the offender, 'shooting at a cock or a hen, or any tame fowl of another man and the arrow, by mischance kills a man', then this is murder, because the intention being to do an unlawful act, this is held sufficient to warrant the penalty for murder. This would be going a great deal further than Aquinas when he discusses a homicide committed whilst the offender is engaged in another illegal act or acts (*rebus illicitis*). The term 'mischance' cannot do other than exclude the idea of deliberation and today we would view such an event as manslaughter. But Coke's employment of the idea of constructive malice to bring the consequence within the ambit of murder is clearly indicative of his concern that the context of the event is a crime, not against the person but against *property*. This is negligence or recklessness in an otherwise neutral setting; here it is a homicide committed in the context of violating another man's property right. The penal premium, with its consequential penalty of death, is thus applied to those who challenge the social order, whether by offering violence to its agents of control or by violating the proprietorial rights of others when these actions result in the unintended consequence of death. After the passage of centuries we see these ideas echoed in the Homicide Act 1957 by which the murder of a police or prison officer, murder when resisting or avoiding arrest, and murder in the course of theft all remained capital crimes.

Coke having effectively invested the penal premium with the authority of a statement of the substantive law,[46] succeeding generations of commentators went little further than to modify some of the detail, the *corpus* of the doctrine of constructive malice remaining unaffected. Stephen[47] was of the view that it was not accepted by Hale[48] and Chief Justice Holt expressly limited it to cases of felony,[49] a view shared by Foster[50] in the mid-18th century. Even limited this far, Stephen considered it to be 'cruel and monstrous'[51]

---

46. He had enacted the Kantian injunction in acting whereby his 'maxim' of 'malice implied' is presented as being a universal law.
47. Sir James Fitzjames Stephen, *History of the Common Law* (1883).
48. Sir Matthew Hale (1609-1676) *History of the Pleas of the Crown* (1736) (i.e. posthumously).
49. *R v Keate* (1697), also *R v Plummer* (1700).
50. Sir John Foster, *op.cit.*
51. Report of the Royal Commission on Capital Punishment, 1949-53, Cmnd 8932, Appendix 7.5 at p.384.

perhaps because of the very large number of offences defined as felonies. It would appear that by the end of the 18th and in the early 19th century, courts were nevertheless becoming less confident about the automatic application of the principle in felony cases.[52] Both the cases of *Lad* and *Greenwood* had concerned instances of children who had died as a consequence of rape, anticipating some of the issues to be raised many years later in the case of *Beard*.[53] A case in 1862[54] (which bears some comparison with the modern case of *Hyam*) involved the demise of an unknown tramp who had been burned to death following the arson of a straw stack. In summing up to the jury, the trial judge, Bramwell B, had indicated:

> ...*though it may appear unreasonable* [our italics], yet as it [the doctrine of constructive malice] is laid down as law it is our duty to act upon it. The law, however, is, that a man is not answerable except for the natural and probable result of his own act; and therefore, if you should not be satisfied that the deceased was in the barn or enclosure at the time the prisoner set fire to the stack, but came in afterwards, then, as his own act intervened between the death and the act of the prisoner, his death could not be the natural result of the prisoner's act, and in that view he ought to be acquitted on the present charge.[55]

There are few homicides in which the person responsible for the death does not have some 'intention', whether formed on the spur of the moment in reaction to some stimulus, or long before what emerges as a criminal event. Since the law presumes a substantial degree of rationality, foresight and demonstrable intention on the part of the offender, the establishment of both *actus reus* and *mens rea* presents, in theory, few intellectual problems. The questions are very straightforward:

- Is what is alleged that which was actually done?

---

52. See: *R v Lad* (1773), also *R v Greenwood* (1857).
53. *Beard v DPP* [1920] AC 479.
54. *R v Horsey* [1862] 3 F&F 287, 176 ER 129.
55. Report of the Royal Commission on Capital Punishment, 1949-53. Cmnd 8932, Appendix 7.8 at p.385.

- Was it the defendant who did it?

- Did the defendant intend to do what he did?

The forensic reality, however, is often a very long way from that atmosphere of seminar-room simplicity. The history of homicide is replete with instances in which the offender, by his initial act, precipitates an avalanche of happenings over which he has decreasing, if indeed any credible control, and in which he, along with his victim, is swept to a conclusion as unintended and unwanted as it is invariably tragic. These are the crimes, which, catastrophically, 'go wrong'; in which 'intention' becomes hard to identify and 'motive' is something long lost in the often swift passage of events the precise nature and order of which are often difficult to recall with any accuracy.

The Homicide Act 1957 was little more than an unsteady stepping stone on the path to the abolition of capital punishment. Its significance in the context of Coke's doctrine of constructive malice is that the Act abolished it in the following way:

Abolition of Constructive Malice

(1) Where a person kills another in the course or furtherance of some other offence, the killing shall not amount to murder unless done with the same malice aforethought (express or implied) as is required for a killing to amount to murder when not done in the course or furtherance of another offence.

(2) For the purposes of the foregoing subsection, a killing done in the course or for the purpose of resisting an officer of justice, or of resisting or avoiding or preventing a lawful arrest, or of effecting or assisting an escape or rescue from legal custody, shall be treated as a killing in the course or furtherance of an offence.

In spite of the Act, the ghost of constructive malice continued to lurk in the shadows of forensic interpretation. There were those who suspected that the new statute had 'not killed the snake but scotched it'. No attempt had been made to attempt a similar despatch for 'express' or 'implied' malice or to make those terms more meaningful. Meanwhile, the Act re-affirmed the principle of the penal premium.

The presumption that a man intended the natural and probable consequences of his actions set out in *Horsey*[6] in 1862 was to be a central issue in *DPP v Smith*[57] in 1960, the judgment in the House of Lords being *inter alia* perhaps the most momentous, if not disastrous, re-affirmation of the doctrine of the penal premium in modern times. Following a reference to the Law Commission its recommendations[58] became the basis for section 8 Criminal Justice Act 1967. Section 8, however, only went half way towards the implementation of the proposals, being concerned only with *how* intention or foresight must be proved, not *when*.

The Legacy: What is it Worth?

The common law has among its champions those who take the view that among its central propositions are some, hitherto immutable, which ought to remain exempt from any attempt at change. The law of homicide is still essentially a creation of the common law, notwithstanding that statutes have brought about changes, notably with regard to penalties rather than substance. That in many respects it has become dysfunctional is widely recognised, but legislators are wary of the political consequences of fundamental review.

All law is the product of particular philosophical, religious and political views that have at some time been in the ascendant; it has no apocalyptic pedigree. For the most part, and certainly in centuries previous to the last, these were expressed not by any popular or democratic will, but rather by those whose power—almost always (but not invariably) a derivative of their wealth—could never be effectively challenged. Yet, since the very idea of crime is a social construct, certainly those offences which are statutory, it cannot pretend to a quality of immutability either in its substance or in the arrangements for its prosecution. Law is created by men for their own

---

56. See note 53 *supra*.
57. We discuss *Smith* in *Chapter 6* of this work.
58. *Imputed Criminal Intent: Director of Public Prosecutions v Smith*, Law Com No. 10 (1967).

purposes; as a convenient statement of contemporary morality, inevitably subject to a time lag. As Lord Devlin argued,[59] it is often a filter for social change and there is much to support that view; reforms of the law relating to such diverse topics as suicide and obscenity, prostitution and homosexuality are merely examples. Increasingly, if public confidence in criminal justice is to be maintained, its intellectual content must become more accessible. The citizen should be able to make sense of the law by perceiving it to relate to a world inhabited by real people.

But there is a dimension of that world which cannot be neglected. There are numerous opportunities for the expression of populist views about the nature of crime and its punishment, which, though sincerely held, can be based on misunderstanding or even misinformation. In an educated mature democracy it should be possible to tell the difference between public clamour and the persuasiveness of argument based upon careful assessment of all aspects of the situation. The arcane interpretations that are sometimes used to distinguish murder from other forms of homicide can often be perceived as resulting in manifest injustice. The remedy is not difficult to identify, yet, four centuries after Coke, we still lack a statutory definition of murder, never mind a coherent law of homicide that is appropriate to our times.

---

59. Sir Patrick (later Lord) Devlin, *The Enforcement of Morals* (Oxford University Press, 1965).

CHAPTER 3

THE WISDOM OF MR JUSTICE OLIVER WENDELL HOLMES JR

The Ingredients of Murder; or How to Tell One Kind of Killing From Another

Every law student is taught that the two essential ingredients of the crime of murder are the act of killing another human being and the killer's accompanying intent to kill or to cause grievous bodily (or very serious) harm — expressed by lawyers in the Latin tag, *actus non facit reum, nisi mens sit rea*.[1] That judge-made law has remained stubbornly untouched by legislation over four centuries, the only marginal changes relating to the partial defences (diminished responsibility and provocation)[2] and rules of evidence and procedure.[3] Most of the academic commentaries, reports of official bodies and practitioner problems have concentrated on the fault element in murder and manslaughter. Indeed, the main focus of the Law Commission's proposals — the categories of first and second degree murders with manslaughter as the third rung of the ladder — has been an attempt to rationalise the fault element within the present state of the law. The interplay between the act of killing (the *actus reus*) and the fault element (the *mens rea*) in the killer has not in practice caused difficulties, if only because the two ingredients of the crime address discrete issues in the criminal trial.

---

1.   An act does not make a person guilty unless the mind is guilty: *Younghusband v Luftig* [1949] 2 KB 354 at p.370.
2.   Sections 2 and 3 Homicide Act 1957 were in origin used to circumvent the death penalty for murder. See now sections 52-55 Coroners and Justice Act 2009.
3.   Section 1 Homicide Act 1957, section 1(2) Murder (Abolition of Death Penalty) Act 1965, section 8 Criminal Justice Act 1967, section 269 of and Schedule 21 to the Criminal Justice Act 2003.

But in terms of criminal responsibility their relationship is problematic, as we shall observe henceforth.

As a common law offence the ingredients of the crimes of murder and manslaughter have been adapted and worked over by the higher judiciary in an ever-expanding body of case law, interpreting, applying and re-applying the precise scope of the requirement to establish the accused's intention (the 'malice aforethought'), and explaining the increasingly uncertain scope of the two partial defences which are nowadays deployed in homicide trials predominantly to escape the mandatory penalty of life imprisonment. In recent years a plethora of cases in the appellate courts, many of them eventually reaching the House of Lords, have woven juristic patterns that have reduced the common law offence of murder to what the Law Commission has recently described as a 'mess'.[4] The common law of murder has appeared, more accurately, to be dysfunctional and lacking in clarity, never more so than when grappling with the elusive nature of the fault element. Yet, if as a civilised society we are content (as we would appear to be) to affix with criminal liability anyone who kills another as a result of gross negligence — an unintentional, unlawful killing which is identified as the crime of manslaughter, punishable by imprisonment — why are we so insistent on maintaining a fault element (an intentional act of killing or of serious harm resulting in death) where the charge is one of murder? It can only be that such other forms of unlawful killing involving what would appear to be deliberation induce in the public mind an enhanced, even exaggerated, sense of social and moral outrage that far exceeds that which is involved in deaths from 'gross negligence'. In which case we could as well dispense with consideration of the killer's state of mind in all forms of criminal homicide, and safely assign issues of individual moral culpability (if only because of the infinite variation in attitudes towards unlawful killings, ranging from relative tolerance, through strong disapproval to extreme opprobrium[5]) to the sentencing stage of criminal justice. Is it necessary or even sensible to

---

4.   The choice of such moderate language is indicative of what many would call a masterpiece of understatement. A 'moral maze' might be more decorous.

5.   Even where deliberation is not at issue, public attitudes vary widely. So-called 'mercy killings', utterly deliberate as they are often freely admitted to be, attract little opprobrium and, not infrequently, sympathy, in contrast to the brutal killings of children. The fact exposes a fundamental weakness in the proposal for a 'Murder 1' as proposed by the Law Commission.

equate criminal responsibility with moral culpability within the definition of the substantive crime?

Fair Labelling

In its proposals for reforming the law of homicide, the Law Commission thought it appropriate no longer to adhere to the two-tier level structure of murder and manslaughter. Instead it opted for a 'three-layer cake' structure which would render it possible 'to distinguish between homicidal wrongs, and hence to respect principles of fair labelling, in a more sophisticated way', and added that this 'would enable a greater measure of justice to be brought to sentencing in homicide cases'. This approach to the identification of different crimes within a category of similar offences stems from a generalised view of academic lawyers and criminal practitioners that guidance is readily obtainable from the law, both before the criminal event and afterwards, for those judging and assessing wrongdoers.

In short, the aim of the legislature is to equiparate criminal responsibility with moral culpability. If the effect of fair labelling, thus, is to impose the iron equation between the offender's crime and the individualising of the sentencing process, nothing is gained before the criminal trial and everything that humanises the penal system is, in an instant, lost. Indeed, the constant campaign in legal professional circles to abolish the mandatory life sentence for murder presupposes the widespread hostility to the equation. Why is it necessary to measure the appropriate penalty to the label? To do so, moreover, renders the 'mercy' killer on a par with the professionally contracted killer. The absurdity of such a result is at least acknowledged by the Law Commission in recommending a separate review by Government of 'mercy killings', rather than relying on juries to bring in verdicts of diminished responsibility — hardly a good example of fair labelling for those determined to assist the terminally ill to end their life.

Even assuming an appropriate linking of crime and penalty, the aim is frequently frustrated in the case of homicides committed by individual members of a group. Here the law with regard to complicity in homicide has produced a disfigurement. Broadly speaking, there are two groups of offenders:

(a) individuals engaged in non-fatal criminal activity in the course of which one of the group unlawfully kills the victim, such as to attract the crime of murder; and

(b) individuals who jointly attack a victim and one of its members inflicts the fatal injury, but it is not possible to identify which one of them did so (there is a variant on this theme, in that individual members of the group will have participated in an attack at various stages of the homicidal event and with differing degrees of the fault element).

This aspect of the law which involves the application of the doctrine of common purpose to complicity in homicide has itself been regarded as 'a mess' — or, to put it more decorously, has rendered the scope of liability for joint criminal enterprise a constant source of controversy and of practical difficulty for juries. It was only in 2008 that the House of Lords introduced some rationality into a complex area of law. The practical difficulties, however, remain. If the endeavours of the Law Lords in *R v Rahman*[6] are to provide greater concurrence between moral culpability and criminal responsibility, one asks: to what end, if the degree of culpability by the individual group member for his criminality can be readily assessed at the sentencing stage? The participant in the group killing must, in justice, receive a penalty according to the degree of personal participation. At present moral culpability in group killings is too easily trumped by the desire for criminalisation. (We deal with the difficult problem of 'joint enterprise' in a separate chapter.)

The Mental Element

As long as the penalty for murder was death, mitigated only by the exercise of the Royal Prerogative of Mercy, it is perhaps unsurprising that the

---

6.   *R v Rahman and Others* [2008] UKHL 45; on appeal from [2007] EWCA, Crim 342.

judges, in formulating the ingredients of the crime, should have sought to ensure that only exceptional blameworthiness merited that ultimate, inflexible and irreversible sanction. Forfeiture of any human life at the hands of a public executioner demanded nothing less than the most rigorous judicial exactitude in demonstrating the perpetrator's utmost wickedness. The replacement in 1965 of one inflexible penalty (the sentence of death) with another sole penalty no less inflexible (that of the mandatory sentence of life imprisonment) might have induced a Parliamentary response to scrutinise the social cost and presumptive benefit of maintaining the mental element in criminal liability for unlawful killings. After all, the establishment of an individual's liability for the criminal event amply justifies the right of the State to inflict punishment, proportionate and appropriate to the level of moral culpability it discloses.

The persistence of *mens rea* at the stage of trial is historically explicable. Coke's definition of the crime of murder,[7] incorporating the notion of malice, was extensively debated in both academic and legal professional circles during the latter part of the 19th century. In Coke's jurisprudence the 'wickedness' that constituted malice was extensive: not limited to being 'aforethought' it could be 'implied' or 'constructive'. It survives in the concept of *mens rea*. In 1863 Sir James Fitzjames Stephen stated in his *General Review of the Criminal Law of England*[8] that the state of mind required in criminal law is generally 'malice', stripped of technical accretions, meaning simply 'wickedness'. By the time that Stephen prepared his *Digest of Criminal Law*[9] he would seem, however, to have cast out *mens rea*, even in cases of murder. But by 1883, returning to the issue in his *History of the Criminal Law*,[10] Stephen expressed the view that 'as all crimes (except crimes of omission) must be voluntary actions, intention is a constituent element of all criminal acts'.

The apparent *volte-face* by Stephen, between 1863 and 1877 was noted by Oliver Wendell Holmes Jr[11] when in 1881, as a practising lawyer in Bos-

---

7. Like a kind of radioactive material, Coke's jurisprudence has undergone little by way of perceptible change in almost four centuries and remains as intellectually hazardous as it ever was.
8. London and Cambridge (Macmillan and Co, 1863).
9. London and Cambridge (Macmillan and Co, 1877).
10. London (Macmillan and Co, 1883).
11. Holmes (1841-1935) was an Associate Justice of the Massachusetts Judicial Supreme Court from 1882 until 1899 when he became Chief Justice. In 1902 he was appointed a Justice of the

ton, he wrote his classic work, *The Common Law*. Holmes' treatment of the concept of liability (in both civil and criminal law) was markedly different from the prevailing English view as expressed alternately by Stephen and his judicial contemporaries, who followed the traditional approach that argued for the law's evolution with an increasing focus on the accused's state of mind. Holmes, by contrast, argued that concerns about motives and intention were replaced in the early period of the development of the common law by external considerations, such as how the average person exercising reasonable ponderance would act; what level of care the average person would exercise in any given situation and whether the average person would have foreseen the harm produced by a particular action. The proper focus, Holmes argued, should be on the harm itself and the way in which it is effected, rather than on the mental state of the defendant whose action produced the harm. In short, Holmes was keen to rid the law of what he termed the 'baggage of morals'.[12]

Holmes' advocacy for the concept of criminal liability led him to the conclusion that

> to make an act which causes death murder, then, the actor ought, on principle, to know how, or have notice of the facts which made the act dangerous ... furthermore, on the same principle, the danger which in fact exists under the known circumstances ought to be of a class which a man of reasonable ponderance could foresee ... If a consequence cannot be foreseen, it cannot be avoided ... The question of knowledge is a question of the actual condition of the defendant's consciousness, the question of what he might have foreseen is determined by the standard of the prudent man, that is, by general experience. For it is to be remembered that the object of the law is to prevent human life being endangered or taken.[13]

Supreme Court of the United States, an office he held until his retirement in 1932. A man of wide and profound scholarship, John Morley considered that, in Holmes, America possessed the greatest judge of the English-speaking world.

12. This approach requires the determination of criminal guilt in the course of the trial by the exclusion of what are essentially concepts derived from a moral lexicon, such as 'malice'. Our reading of this does not, however, preclude such considerations being other than relevant at the stage of penalty.

13. *The Common Law* (Transaction Edition, 2005) (a facsimile of the 1881 edition) at p.47.

Holmes' espousal of the concept of liability was grounded in legal philosophy, but admitted of certain exceptional cases, such as insanity or lack of age, where he recognised that the law did require proof of an actual intent, and importantly he conceded that 'the question of knowledge is a question of the actual condition of the defendant's consciousness'.[14] Significantly, Holmes did not adopt the argument relating to the difficulty of proving the mental element, a factor that is increasingly reflected in the length of contemporary criminal trials. The question, therefore, as to whether *mens rea* remains necessary in the 21st century may properly form the basis of renewed debate on the law of homicide.

Holmes ended his thesis of criminal liability in unmistakable terms:

> The test of criminality in such cases is the degree of danger shown by experience to attend that act under those circumstances. In such cases, the *mens rea*, or actual wickedness of the party, is wholly unnecessary, and all reference to the state of his consciousness is misleading if it means anything more than that the circumstances in connection with which the tendency of his act is judged are the circumstances known to him.[15]

The rejection of Holmes' concept of liability (which has been dubbed by his opponents as 'objective', and hence objectionable), both in England and in the United States of America, and other Anglo-Saxon legal systems, has stemmed consistently from a failure to reflect the moral distinction between intentional and negligent wrongdoing. Holmes himself was aware of the rival arguments. Dealing with the crimes of murder and of manslaughter, he observed that the difference between the two would be found to lie in the degree of danger attaching to the act in the given state of facts:

> To explode a barrel of gunpowder in a crowded street, and kill people, is murder, although the actor hopes that no such harm will be done (an illustration taken from Stephen's *Digest*[16]). But to kill a man by careless riding in the same street would

---

14. *Ibid.* (1881 edition) at p.56.
15. *The Common Law* at p.61.
16. Article 223 Illustration 1.

commonly be manslaughter. Perhaps, however, a case could be put where the riding was so manifestly dangerous that it would be murder.[17] (Italics supplied).

Lawyers Play a Sort of Tennis: The Case of 'Gypsy' Jim Smith

It is necessary at this stage to revisit the notorious (to lawyers, at least) case of *DPP v Smith*.[18] At the Old Bailey on 7 April 1960, before Mr Justice Donovan and a jury, Jim Smith was convicted of the capital murder of police constable Meehan pursuant section 5(d) Homicide Act 1957, being 'any murder of a police officer acting in the execution of his duty'. He was accordingly sentenced to death.

Smith's appeal to the Court of Criminal Appeal on 18 May 1960 was allowed; a verdict of manslaughter was substituted and a sentence of ten-years' imprisonment imposed. The Director of Public Prosecutions, after the Attorney-General had granted his fiat, duly appealed to the House of Lords. The appeal was allowed and the verdict of capital murder thereby restored. Meanwhile, the Home Secretary[19] had already announced that in the event of this reversal of the manslaughter verdict, a reprieve would be granted, so that the ultimate penalty was life imprisonment.[20]

The ground of appeal to the Court of Criminal Appeal was that the trial judge had misdirected the jury as to the application of the rule that a person intends the natural and probable consequences of his acts. The main complaint was that the judge was applying what is referred to as an objective test, namely, the test of what a reasonable man would contemplate as the probable result of his acts. The defendant must, therefore, presumptively have intended to cause serious harm. The appellant Smith contended that the question for the jury should have been what he himself had intended. Smith had maintained that the death of PC Meehan was either an accident — a

---

17. *The Common Law* at p.50.
18. [1961] AC 290. We deal more fully with the political implications of this decision in *Chapter 6*.
19. R A Butler, later Lord Butler of Saffron Walden.
20. The fearsome shadow of the gallows did not, therefore, cast its dark shape over the proceedings in their Lordships' House, although abolition was still five years away.

barely plausible defence which would, if successful, have led to an acquittal — and that he never intended to cause the constable any severe injury, let alone to kill him, which would have resulted in a verdict of manslaughter.

The single judgment of the House of Lords, delivered[21] by the Lord Chancellor, Lord Kilmuir, criticised the Court of Criminal Appeal in the following way:

> They were saying that it was for the jury to decide whether they, having regard to the panic in which he said he was, the respondent [Smith] in fact at the time contemplated that grievous bodily harm would result from his actions, or indeed, whether he contemplated anything at all. Unless the jury were satisfied that he in fact had such contemplation, the necessary intent to constitute malice would not, in their view, have been proved. This purely subjective approach involves this, that if an accused said that he did not in fact think of the consequences, and the jury considered that that might well be true, he would be entitled to be acquitted of murder.

While the judgment did not, on the face of it, doubt the need for the essential element of *mens rea* (the necessary intent), the fault in the reasoning lay in the resurrection of the concept of constructive malice, supposedly abolished by section 1 Homicide Act 1957, by the import of the objective approach. The gravamen of the complaint that accompanied the ensuing torrent of critical academic and legal opinion thus focused not on the issue of *mens rea*, but on the supposed evidential rule that there is a presumption that a person intends the reasonable and probable consequences of his actions. It was precisely that evidential point that was dealt with specifically in section 8 Criminal Justice Act 1967, which was concerned not with questions of foresight *per se*, but with how a person's intention or foresight was to be proved, if required. The section also re-affirmed the wider view that the so-called 'presumption' — the idea that a person intends the natural and probable result of his actions — had always been a nonsense.[22] In a divorce

---

21. But thought to have been drafted by Lord Parker. See: Thomas Bingham, *The Old Order Changeth* 122 LQR 211-217, footnote 48. In *Chapter 6* we show how we have established that Lord Parker was the true author of the judgment delivered by the Lord Chancellor.

22. The importance of this point was re-affirmed almost 20 years later by Lord Diplock in *R v Lennon* [1979] 2 WLR 281, at 289c: 'If the law as expounded by this House in *DPP v Smith* had remained unchanged and had been treated as applicable beyond the field of homicide to

case in 1955 the House of Lords itself had indicated that the proposition that a man intends the reasonable and probable consequences of his actions is not an inference that *must* be drawn, but which may be.[23] The proposition was given its judicial *quietus* by Lord Reid in a picturesque judgment in *Gollins v Gollins*:[24]

> People often intend something quite different from what they know to be the natural and probable result of what they are doing. To take a trivial example, if I say I intend to reach the green, people will believe me, although we know that the odds are ten to one against my succeeding; and no one but a lawyer would say that I must be presumed to have intended to put my ball in the bunker because that was the natural and probable result of my shot.

On the face of its judicial reasoning, the House of Lords in *Smith* did nothing to disturb the traditional elements of the crime of murder containing the prerequisite of an intention to kill or to cause serious harm. The fascination for present purposes is the fact that, uniquely and tantalisingly, their Lordships relied on passages on the criminal law in Holmes' *Common Law* as their primary and, in this context, non-judicial authority, to support the employment of the objective test. Taking that reliance on the writings of an American lawyer, widely acknowledged as a profound legal scholar and eminent judge of the US Supreme Court, at their face value, the case might then — and even today — be construed as undermining the basis of *mens rea*, despite extra-judicial attempts to qualify the less guarded pronouncements in *DPP v Smith*.

It is hard to find in any of the criticism anything to the effect that *mens rea* was being impliedly or surreptitiously discarded as an element in the

---

other crimes which required a specific intention...blasphemous libel might well have reverted to what in effect would be an offence of strict liability'. Lord Edmund Davies observed (at 306g): 'My noble and learned friend, Lord Diplock, has rightly observed that section 8 of the Criminal Justice Act 1967 is concerned simply with how intention is to be proved *where intention is of relevance*, and says nothing about when intention is to be proved'. (present authors' italics)

23. *Lang v Lang* [1955] AC 402 at 425. This case was cited in the course of the hearing before the Court of Criminal Appeal.
24. [1964] AC 644 at 660.

crime of murder. The most notable critic, Professor Glanville Williams, in a coruscating attack on the decision, chose to entitle his article in *The Modern Law Review* 'Constructive Malice Revived'.[25] In an article of 25 pages, only one is devoted to the views of Holmes. Professor Williams wrote:

> The passage quoted (in Lord Kilmuir's judgment) laid down the sweeping and wholly unacceptable proposition that, in criminal law generally, the question of foresight is to be resolved exclusively by reference to what a man of reasonable foresight would have foreseen. It seems a pity, if an extrajudicial source is to be quoted, that care should not be taken to ascertain the movement of opinion since it appeared. Greatly as Holmes J is venerated in the United States, it is fair to say that his theory of objective responsibility in crime is now regarded, over there, as an unfortunate aberration...a strong effort is being made by legal commentators to make the criminal law more 'subjective' in its approach.

Just so, but that comment apart, the whole tenor of the criticism was that the House of Lords was improperly extending the scope of 'malice' from the 'expressed' (intent to kill) and the 'implied' (intent to cause serious harm) to a wider category of 'malice'. And, so far as we can detect, there has been no suggestion that the substantive law of murder was itself being altered.

In commenting upon Holmes as an 'extrajudicial source' Glanville Williams nevertheless went on to refer to him as 'Holmes J' notwithstanding that the passages concerned formed no part of any pronouncement of Holmes in the capacity of a judge, but were the work of Holmes the legal scholar. He should not, therefore have been so described, and in this context he is certainly neither a 'persuasive' nor a 'compelling' authority. Yet, over seventy years after his death, such remains the standing of Holmes the jurist that he cannot rightly be set lightly aside.

The House of Lords' reception of the material from Holmes' *The Common Law* in support of the objective tests for the knowledge and foresight of the consequences of the actions by the killer was unusual for a literary work. Moreover, the material had not been cited in the lower courts and, seemingly, it had never been judicially considered in earlier cases. For reasons

---

25. Vol 23 (November 1960).

that will become clear, the passage had not been referred to in the documentation presented in advance of the oral hearing in the Lords. The passages in Holmes' lectures were cited by the Attorney-General when he came to reply to Smith's counsel's address in response to his (the A-G's) opening of the appeal in which 'it is agreed (both by the Crown and the defendant) that intention is all-important in criminal cases'.[26]

The passages were directed to those advancing the test of foresight, namely, what a man of reasonable prudence would have foreseen. Since there was agreement about the necessity for intent as an ingredient in criminal trials, there was no reliance placed upon Holmes' conclusion of his liability that 'mens rea, or actual wickedness of the party, is wholly unnecessary'. Certainly, it would not have been in the interest of the appellant for counsel to have argued for such a proposition! But that should not have deflected their Lordships from Holmes' ultimate conclusion about mens rea.

A further observation concerns the context in which DPP v Smith was decided. The injection of an element of objectivity in the search for ascertaining an accused's intention was anathema to those liberal reformers deeply committed to abolition of the death penalty. That was made abundantly clear from criticism in other parts of the Commonwealth. In Australia, the High Court had always dutifully followed decisions of the House of Lords, but DPP v Smith led to the extinction of such Imperial loyalty. In 1963 Sir Owen Dixon CJ announced[27] that in future the High Court might depart from its previous attitude, so strongly did he and his fellow judges disapprove of DPP v Smith. That judicial dissociation from London was apparently prompted by a private communication to the Chief Justice from a judicial colleague, Mr Justice Fullagar, who expostulated that 'They're hanging men for manslaughter in England now'.[28]

When the House of Lords handed down its decision in Smith the movement for abolition of the death penalty was approaching its climax. The distinction between capital and non-capital murder in the Homicide Act 1957 was already attracting judicial and legal hostility. At least Lord Parker, a member of the Appellate Committee that sat to hear DPP v Smith, was

---

26. DPP v Smith [1961] AC 290 at p.320.
27. In Parker v The Queen (1963) III CLR 610 at 632.
28. P Ayres, Owen Dixon. Melbourne (The Miegunyah Press, 2003) at p.276.

soon to declare himself as wishing to see not only the abolition of capital punishment and its replacement by a maximum life sentence, but also the ending of what he termed the 'fine lines and distinctions' between murder and manslaughter.

The debate over capital punishment in the 1950s and 1960s was conducted without any serious proposal to change the substantive law of murder. Nor did the reversal of the evidential rule in *DPP v Smith* by section 8 Criminal Justice Act 1967 do anything to alter, let alone dismantle, the element of 'malice aforethought'. In the Home Secretary's remit to the Criminal Law Revision Committee in 1970 to review the law of murder, there was no hint of changing the basic elements of the crime. Not until Lord Kilbrandon in *Hyam v DPP* proposed a single offence of criminal homicide, with the penalty at large according to the merits and demerits of the individual killer's case, was there any proposal to address judicially the problem that Lord Parker had earlier identified in the legislature: his dislike of 'fine lines and distinctions' between murder and manslaughter. By implication, Lord Kilbrandon was siding with Mr Justice Holmes.

Reviewing[29] a biography of Holmes and his classic work[30] in the *New York Review of Books* in 1963, Professor H L A Hart took Holmes to task for his main argument in favour of objective liability, arguing that

> Even if the general justification of punishment is the utilitarian aim of preventing harm, and not vengeance and retribution, it is still perfectly intelligible that society should defer to principles of justice and fairness to the individual, and not to punish those who lack the capacity or fair opportunity to obey.

By imposing a standard of conduct that demanded that of the reasonably prudent actor, Hart argued that the weaker brethren in society were entitled to be spared punishment for failing to meet the standard of behaviour of their more fortunate fellow citizens. Holmes' retort to that kind of accusation would no doubt have been that it is 'precisely to those who are

---

29. Volume 1 No 4 (17 October 1963).
30. *Oliver Wendell Holmes: The Common Law*, ed. Mark De Wolfe Howe, Cambridge, MS (Harvard University Press, 1963).

most likely to err by temperament, ignorance or folly—that the threats of the law are the most dangerous'.[31]

Fairness and justice are undoubtedly due to every individual in the criminal process. Article 6 of the European Convention on Human Rights demands no less. A fair trial includes fairness at all stages of the process, from arrest and charge to conviction and sentence. Incapacities ensuing from inherent defects of the individual's mind or from those subsequently acquired are, however, highly relevant to the extent of the liability to punishment. And justice, in the sense of a verdict of the court, needs to be even-handed, the public and the individual feeling satisfied with the result. Holmes never sought, however, to address the penal consequences of a conviction on the basis of an objective liability. Fairness and justice, which are encapsulated in the notion of due process, constitute an inalienable moral standard, wholly independent of the values that underpin the mutable criteria of criminal liability and its consequent penalties.

Hart concluded his review by saying that almost everything that Holmes said in *The Common Law* 'still reverberates. This is not only a tribute to the magic and sonority in his style. It still pays handsome dividends in thinking about any subject on which Holmes touched'.

Just so. In revisiting today the wise words of Mr Justice Holmes, we would do well to review also our response to *DPP v Smith*. It deserves re-assessment, 40 years on, in the light of a law which is acknowledged to be 'in a mess'. The importunate case law that disfigures and distorts the prosecution of murder trials calls urgently for a sensible and intellectually accessible re-ordering.

The consensus of learned opinion at the time of the Lords' decision in *Smith* was undoubtedly that it was an unfortunate aberration, even if much of the criticism was directed at evidential and procedural aspects of the matter rather than the substantive law of murder. Viewed retrospectively, the decision was entirely consistent with the attachment of highly influential judges[32] in the post-war period to the belief that only maximum severity would serve to stem what was perceived to be a dangerous increase in violent crime. In addition to that pragmatism there may well have been an unrecognised

---

31. *The Common Law* at p.43.
32. Notably the Lord Chancellor, Lord Kilmuir, the former Lord Chief Justice, Lord Goddard, Lord Denning, and Lord Tucker.

inclination towards the basic tenet of the Positivist school of legal theory, as exemplified by the adoption of Holmes as a 'persuasive authority'. If that is so, it has been the tenacious attachment of the legal profession to the necessity of retaining moral criteria in the process of determining criminal guilt which ultimately accounted for the widespread hostility engendered by the decision in *Smith*. The Positivists have yet to establish a bridgehead within a modern criminal justice system.

Holmes (Finally) Before Their Lordships

In his final submissions to the Appellate Committee, counsel for Smith, Mr Edward Clarke QC, said that, applying Holmes' 'objective test', a doctor who performed a dangerous operation in the knowledge that in all probability it would bring about the death of the patient would be guilty of murder.[33] Although in 1963, in his review of Holmes' newly published edition of *The Common Law*, Professor Hart was to note that when a member of the Supreme Judicial Court of Massachusetts Holmes had applied his own doctrine of foresight in at least two murder cases,[34] counsel in *Smith v DPP* was seemingly unaware of the more important of the two[35] which happened to involve a doctor who, even by the standards of his day, had enterprised upon a decidedly unusual and, as it proved to be, fatal course of treatment for a patient. Dr Pierce prescribed for a female patient suffering from what may have been a bacterial or viral infection, that, while clothed, she should be drenched in kerosene at three-hourly intervals for two days. His theory was that the kerosene would act like a poultice on a boil, drawing out the infection. Suffering considerable distress from the consequent burns to her skin the treatment ceased; she died some seven days later and Pierce was subsequently convicted of her manslaughter.

Had counsel (and their Lordships) been aware of that decision and other judicial pronouncements from Holmes as a judge (to which we refer

---

33. [1961] AC 290 at p.323.
34. *Pierce* (1884) and *Kennedy* (1897).
35. *Commonwealth of Massachusetts v Pierce* (1884) 138 Mass 165. The bizarre nature of the treatment prescribed by the defendant is set out in detail in the indictment.

hereafter), it would have been clear that only a grossly neglectful doctor would be engaged in an unlawful killing, whether murder or manslaughter, depending upon the degree of dangerousness in the particular operation. Even if counsel had not pursued his researches as far as he might have done, one might have hoped for a more scholarly enthusiasm on the part of their Lordships to explore Holmes' reported judgments and his extra-judicial work in *The Common Law*. It would be interesting to speculate whether the House of Lords would have affirmed the early English cases that Holmes had declined to follow. Adopting the 'persuasive authority' for testing the foresight of the consequences of the accused's act, their Lordships would, we think, have been compelled intellectually to an examination of 'malice aforethought' as the basis for the mental element in murder. Coke's legacy might have been put to the test—and found wanting.

Holmes in Action

Holmes' theory of liability owed nothing to the practicalities, or specifically to the argument, advanced by some of Holmes' supporters, that the state of an accused's mind was incapable of proof in a criminal trial and should be abandoned. At the time of writing *The Common Law* in the 1870s Holmes was a practising lawyer at the Massachusetts Bar. His book had the aim of presenting a general view of the common law using tools besides logic. The maxim enshrined in its opening paragraph is that '[t]he life of the law has not been logic; it has been experience', meaning an historical view of legal development.

Surprisingly, there was a notable absence of judges putting Holmes' theory of liability into practice, the more so since Holmes spent 20 years as a judge in the Supreme Judicial Court of Massachusetts and 30 more in the United States Supreme Court. While Holmes did put it to the test in *Pierce* (described more fully above), *The Common Law* was never revised, although it went through numerous reprints (the 41st appeared in 1948) and it continues to be re-published, sometimes with an editorial introduction or annotated notes. Hence when the House of Lords in 1960 cited Holmes as the primary source for its decision it inaccurately referred to him as 'that persuasive authority', acknowledging that the author was no mere armchair academic commentator but a judicial figure of pre-eminence in the Anglo-Saxon legal world,[36] yet not citing any court decision as a judicial precedent.[37]

Holmes' judgment in *Commonwealth of Massachusetts v Pierce* is instructive. The appeal raised the question whether the existence in a physician of 'an honest purpose and intent to cure' a patient precluded the physician's having the requisite intent to be convicted of manslaughter. As Holmes put it, the question was 'whether an actual good intent and the expectation of good results are an absolute justification of acts, however foolhardy they may be if judged by the external standard'.[38] Holmes concluded that an external standard should govern; the existence of a benevolent but foolhardy intent should not constitute a justification.

He had begun his judgment by pointing out that the standard in civil cases was an external one, based on the evaluation of a defendant's conduct against that of 'a man of ordinary prudence'. He thought this standard sensible, since in civil suits it had the effect of allowing 'losses … to rest where they fall in the absence of a clear reason to the contrary' and went on to argue that 'there would seem to be at least equal reason for adopting it in the criminal law, which has for its immediate object and task to establish a general standard, or at least general negative limits of conduct for the community, in the interest of the safety of all'.[39]

Some earlier Massachusetts cases, however, following an English case,[40] had held that a physician 'who gives a person a poison without any intent of doing him any bodily hurt', was not guilty of murder or manslaughter if the remedy, 'contrary to the expectation of the physician', killed the patient'.[41]

Holmes found the English reasoning inappropriate where the physician's actions could be shown to be reckless. He concluded that 'the recklessness of the criminal no less than that of the civil law must be treated by what we have

---

36. In the report of *DPP v Smith* he is referred to as 'Holmes J'.
37. That situation changed in 1982. In *R v Cunningham* [1982] AC 566, at 569H, counsel for the Crown cited Holmes' *Common Law* (41st printing, 1948) at pp.51-68, demonstrating the Holmes reference to express and implied malice in a case concerning 'grievous bodily harm'.
38. (1884) 138 Mass 165 at p.176.
39. (1884) 138 Mass 165 at p.176.
40. 1 Hale PC 429.
41. *Commonwealth v Thompson* (1809) 6 Mass 134.

called the external standard', and that 'the question whether (a physician's) act would be reckless in a man of ordinary prudence is evidently equivalent to an inquiry into the degree of danger which known experience shows to attend the act under the circumstances known to the actor'.[42]

The phrase 'circumstances known to the actor' makes the external standard an amalgam of subjective and objective elements, although Holmes did not so elaborate on his application of the principle of objective liability. Dr Pierce was thus a member of that class of persons on whom external standards of liability in the criminal law fall the hardest—those 'most likely to err by temperament, ignorance or folly'.[43]

Holmes' use of language precisely mirrored what one finds in the chapter on the criminal law in *The Common Law*. He admitted as much in a letter to Sir Frederick Pollock[44] in early 1884 when the Pierce case was being decided. Holmes wrote that he had written opinions 'in some very interesting cases', (which included *Pierce*): 'If my opinion goes through (in that case) it will do much to confirm some theories of my book'.[45]

It did go through, but there is no indication that Holmes' judicial utterances were cited in the House of Lords in *DPP v Smith*, or elsewhere in English cases. Had that been so, the sobriquet of 'persuasive authority' would have been entirely apt. Holmes had been exercising a judicial role when, in the course of his judgment, he had examined the English and US authorities.

Holmes wrote another judgment in 1897, by which time he had become Chief Justice of Massachusetts. In *Commonwealth v Kennedy*[46] the defendant had been convicted of attempted murder as the result of his failure to kill by putting rat poison on the underside of the crossbar of a 'moustache' cup of tea. The question for the court was whether the defendant possessed the intent for murder, since his expectation that the victim would drink the tea 'may have been unfounded and unreasonable'.

---

42. At p.177.
43. *The Common Law* at p.34.
44. (1845-1937). Jurist, legal historian and lifelong correspondent with Holmes.
45. Holmes to Pollock, 2 November 1884. *Holmes-Pollock Letters* 1.26, cited in G Edward White, *Justice Oliver Wendell Holmes: Law and the Inner Self* (Oxford University Press, 1993) at p.260. There is no indication of what Pollock himself thought.
46. (1897) 170 Mass 18.

Holmes concluded that 'the act done must come pretty close to accomplishing [a prohibited] result before the court will notice it. [This was because] … the aim of the law is not to punish sins but … to prevent certain external results'.

The focus of Holmes' judgment was thus firmly on the defendant's acts, not on his state of mind. This issue again surfaced, two years later, in an opinion by Holmes in the Supreme Judicial Court of Massachusetts in the case of *Commonwealth of Massachusetts v Chance and Another.*[47]

The jury properly might have been instructed that it is possible to commit murder without any actual intent to kill or do grievous bodily harm, and that, reduced to its lowest terms, malice in murder means *knowledge* (our italics) of such circumstances that according to common experience there is a plain and strong likelihood that death will follow the contemplated act, coupled perhaps, with an implied negation of any excuse or justification.

Had Holmes' judicial pronouncements, putting into practice what he had preached in *The Common Law*, been considered by the House of Lords in *DPP v Smith*, it is interesting to speculate on the fate of the old English cases which Holmes had declined to follow. In adopting the 'persuasive authority' advanced by Holmes for testing the foresight of the consequences of the accused's acts, their Lordships would, we think, have been compelled to consider the question in the context of Holmes' major thesis that *mens rea* was, at the very least, a piece of supererogation in testing criminal liability for an unlawful killing. Coke's legacy of 'malice aforethought' might have been treated as not addressing the state of the accused's mind, except in the sense that the accused was cognisant of circumstances which rendered his conduct dangerous, which was precisely the state of Smith's knowledge and foresight of the consequence of depositing PC Meehan onto the highway in the face of oncoming traffic in an urban area.

---

47. (1899) 174 Mass 245.

Holmes Versus Stephen

Stephen probably, by implication at least, had Holmes' theory of objective liability in mind when he discussed in his *History of the Criminal Law* 'modern writers of eminence [who] have been in the habit of regarding criminal law as being entirely independent of morality'.[48] Although Stephen made no direct and systematic attempt to evaluate Holmes' Utilitarian argument, he did attack the general theory of objective liability. He pointed out, for example, that only in manslaughter and regulatory crimes was there a restricted scale of strict liability offences. And there were additional manifestations of objective liability in the partial defence of provocation and the full defence of self-defence. More interesting from our point of view, Stephen noted that it was in the scale of personal culpability that is reflected in the nature and severity of individual penalties: this, we contend, is an unnecessary confusion of criminal responsibility with moral culpability.

Stephen was contending that Holmes' error was to assume that taking account of personal mental responsibility for the commission of the offence was necessarily incompatible with the Utilitarian aim of reducing harm to the victims of homicide; and that to require some form of mental element in the actor inevitably assigned to the offence a retributive function of punishment. Precisely so, as Bentham, a century earlier, had maintained, that the mischief of an act is measured by its consequences, and that an actor's mental state is germane to the deterrent effect of punishment.[49] The contrary argument advanced by jurists of Stephen's time and throughout the 20th century has been to observe the antithesis between the rival theories, but that personal mental attributes are assignable both to criminal responsibility and moral culpability. No doubt it is arguable, even justifiable, to insist on a requirement of subjective liability throughout the criminal process on the independent grounds of fairness and justice, and at the same time to support the general objective of reducing criminal activity. So be it, but is it necessary for the promotion of Utilitarian aims to confound responsibility and culpability?

---

48. Vol II, p.79.

49. *An Introduction to the Principles of Morals and Legislation*, ed. Burns and Hart, chapters XII and XIII.

It is a curiosity of the unspoken dialogue of Holmes and Stephen that Holmes did not in his classic work of 1881 respond to Stephen's opposing account of criminal responsibility, although he did allude to general observations in the *History* in a letter of 1883 to Sir Frederick Pollock, noting that 'my opinion of him [Stephen] as a law writer does not grow higher as I read this or his former books. He knows nothing, it seems to me, of the scientific aspects of the history of law, and he is to my mind rather a model of a fine old 18th century controversialist rather than a philosopher'.[50]

K J M Smith, in his fascinating biography of Stephen, *James Fitzjames Stephen, Portrait of a Victorian Rationalist*,[51] ventures the opinion that there was a hint of hostility between the two men. He wrote that Holmes' remarks in the letter to Sir Frederick Pollock 'are distinctly less than generous'. Smith adds: 'Whether or not Holmes was in any way justified in placing Stephen's talents in the eighteenth century, and notwithstanding the later proliferation of strict liability offences, Holmes certainly lost the debate over *mens rea* to Stephen'. We disagree: in the 21st century, in our opinion, the wisdom of Holmes is the winner.

Holmes in the 21st Century

The jury in *Smith* having discounted any possibility of the death having been accidental, why then did the question of the accused's mental state remain of any conceivable importance? The event was, on any showing, an unlawful killing as a result of what the accused knew to be a dangerous activity with the high risk of death. The immense expenditure of judicial resources in appeals such as *DPP v Smith* and others over the last half century[52] have arisen precisely because the law has resolutely resisted any consolidation of the crimes of murder and manslaughter into a single offence of a homicide offence based upon liability with its inherent mix of the killer's knowledge and reasonable foresight of the consequences of his acts.

---

50. *Pollock-Holmes Letters*, ed. Mark de Wolfe Howe, Cambridge, MS (Harvard University Press, 1941).
51. (Cambridge University Press, 1988) p.65.
52. The most recent case of *Coutts* [2006] UK HL 39 is an exemplar.

The issue was clearly in play in *DPP v Smith*; it was urged by Professor Rupert Cross[53] that, by 1970, Parliament should legislate to consolidate murder and manslaughter; it was again pointed up by Lord Kilbrandon in 1974 when he complained of the time and effort that had been expended in unravelling the law of murder and manslaughter in *Hyam*.[54] In 1978 the Law Commission endorsed the Kilbrandon proposal for change and the last 30 years have witnessed the law in an increasingly confused and unsatisfactory state that its successor has identified as a 'mess'. Nor are those labours with which Lord Kilbrandon was so disenchanted limited to the appellate stage; the cost in trials of murders that could be found to be manslaughter where judges and juries may need to spend not hours but days—even weeks—in considering evidence seeking to prove or disprove the defendant's state of mind are surely no less cost ineffective.

It is perhaps absurd to suggest that it is *never* possible forensically—or indeed otherwise—to determine with certainty what it is that a man has intended, but in the majority of instances it must remain extremely difficult. As a 15th century judge, Sir Thomas Bryan,[55] observed:

> As for the other conceit, it seems to me that the plea is not good without shewing that he has certified the other of his pleasure; for it is common learning that the intent of a man cannot be tried, for the devil himself knows not the intent of a man.[56]

However, the adoption of the objective standard of liability, without imperilling the justice of any subsequent penalty, certainly renders this near impossible task redundant. But while it is manifestly clear that discovering the state of a person's mind may be, and often is a daunting task, it is one undertaken daily by juries in murder trials. It has not been better stated than by Justice Cardozo in *State of New York v Zachowitiz*[57] when he wrote:

---

53. 'Penal Reform' in 1965, Crim LR 184 (1966).
54. *Hyam v DPP* [1975] AC 35 at p.98.
55. Chief Justice of the Common Pleas 1471-1500.
56. (1478) YB 17 Ed IV Pasch f.1 pl.2. Cited *in extenso* in Cecil Herbert Stuart Fifoot, *History and Sources of the Common Law: Tort and Contract*, London (Stevens, 1949) at pp.252-254. Although this case involved an alleged trespass to goods, the principle is unaffected and must in logic be equally applicable, whether in tort or crime.
57. 254 NY 192, at 195 (1930).

With only the rough and ready tests supplied by their experience of life, the jurors must look into the workings of another's mind, and discover its capacities and disabilities, its urges and inhibitions, in moments of intense excitement, delicate enough and subtle is the inquiry, even in the most favourable conditions, with every warping influence excluded.

For a variety of reasons, cases in the Crown Court are taking longer and longer to try. Some of that is the result of prolonged evidence on the issues of intent and the partial defences, all of which Holmes declared was unnecessary in a rational law of homicide.

The Aims of the Criminal Law

From a Utilitarian standpoint, the task of the law is to control the behaviour of individuals who break, or contemplate breaking, the criminal law as it applies in a variety of situations. Others would see its object as the promotion of virtue by means of controlling vice, a task about whose chances of success one might be rightly sceptical. Difficulty, however, undoubtedly arises when the law is employed to enforce moral standards, not least when they appear to be both mutable and arbitrary, though where homicide is concerned, while there is substantial agreement in principle about its undesirability, there is much less about a hierarchy of 'seriousness'.[58] It is a characteristic of all cultures to confer moral approval or disapproval on particular actions, but differentially: a fact that cannot be ignored. What is commonly confused, not least in the public mind, is that while the process of labelling *actions* presents little difficulty, that of labelling *individuals* requires an omniscient ability to probe the mind of the individual, not least when that individual is himself uncertain of what is happening inside his head. The objective standard of criminal liability enables the law to avoid not only excursions into conjectural forensic psychology, but also the moral examination of the individual as a constituent element in the establishment of that liability. The opprobrium to be allocated to malfeasance is a task for later.

---

58. Compare the substantive law that provides penalties for killing with motor vehicles with that which governs deaths in the workplace.

Holmes, though wanting to rid the law of the 'baggage of morals', did not, however, exclude gratification or revenge from a role in the criminal law. He cited the opinion of 'two authorities[59] so great as Bishop Butler and Jeremy Bentham, and so opposed in other views' as well as quoting Stephen in stating that 'the criminal law stands to the passion of revenge in much the same relation as marriage to the sexual appetite'.[60]

Holmes, himself a wounded hero of the American Civil War, well understood the human response to the loss of human life and added:

> If the law did not help them (the victims of crime), the law has no choice but to satisfy the craving itself, and thus avoid the greater evil of private retaliation. At the same time, this passion is not one which we encourage, either as private individuals or as law-makers.

The wisdom of Holmes is to countenance society's need to punish unlawful killers at the stage of sentencing with penalties proportionate and appropriate to the individual homicidal event. *Mens rea* (if defined as a guilty mind or intention) has no place in determining criminal liability, but belongs to that stage, after conviction, at which the moral culpability of the offender must be assessed.

Indeed, it is such punishment that gives meaning to the criminal law, and it has been the uneasiness about the justice of punishment for the particular homicidal event, be it the death penalty until 1965 or the mandatory life sentence for murder since then, that has led to the refinements and subtleties, not to say absurdities of this branch of the law. Stephen in his *History of the Criminal Law* identified this functional aspect of the law in the observation that:

> The sentence of the law is the moral sentiment of the public in relation to any offences what a seal is to hot wax. It converts into a permanent final judgment what might otherwise be a transient sentiment.[61]

---

59. *The Common Law* at p.36 citing Butler, *Sermons VIII* and Bentham, *Theory of Legislation:* Principles of Penal Code (Part 2 Ch 16).
60. *General View of the Criminal Law of England*, at p.99.
61. (1883) vol II, at p.81.

Stephen himself was in little doubt as to what that moral sentiment ought to be, and he continues:

> I am ... of opinion that this close alliance between criminal law and moral sentiment is in all ways healthy and advantageous to the community. I think it highly desirable that criminals should be hated, that the punishments inflicted upon them should be so contrived as to give expression to that hatred, and to justify it so far as the provision of means for expressing it and gratifying a healthy and natural sentiment can justify and encourage it.[62]

Stephen's robust view would, no doubt, attract popular approval today when there is often a crudely expressed desire for increasingly punitive solutions to the problem of criminal behaviour. It would seem unlikely to do so among those practitioners in the criminal law who, never minding its language, would be sceptical of the value of so simplistic approach to sentencing.

Mens Rea: a Coda to Holmes?

If Sir Edward Coke was the acknowledged progenitor of the mental element in criminal law, Mr Justice Fitzjames Stephen not merely gave it increase through his scholarly writings, but by dint of his judicial prowess embedded *mens rea*[63] in the *corpus* of English criminal law, where it has remained entrenched. But what does the concept of *mens rea* entail? Any doubts that may have been entertained about the common law's insistence on *mens rea* as a vital ingredient of criminal liability was decisively dispelled 40 years ago by the decision of the House of Lords in *Sweet v Parsley*.[64] The case was concerned primarily with a statutory provision seemingly imposing strict liability in respect of certain offences connected with the use of dangerous drugs. But the case enunciated the principle, in the magisterial words of Lord

---

62. Stephen was at times given to somewhat hyperbolic language; *ibid.* at pp.81-82.
63. In *R v Tolson* (1889) 23 QBD 168 at 185, Mr Justice Stephen wrote: '*Mens rea* means in the case of murder, malice aforethought; in the case of theft, an intention to steal ...'
64. [1970] AC 132.

Reid, 'that *mens rea* is an essential ingredient of every offence unless some reason can be found for holding that it is not necessary'.[65]

The five separate judgments delivered in the House of Lords, however, did little to explain either the nature or scope of the mental element in crime, or the relationship of *mens rea* to the other main component of criminal liability, the *actus reus*.

As Professor Paul Robinson observes, in his essay 'Should the Criminal Law Abandon the *Actus Reus-Mens Rea* Distinction?',[66] the two concepts are a logical extension of the obvious empirical difference between a person's act (which is directly observable) and his intention (which is neither directly observable, nor, for that matter, easily ascertainable). Professor Robinson goes on to assert that it is natural to extend the *mens rea* required for liability beyond an intention to injure, to include knowledge, recklessness, or negligence as to injuring another. Are knowledge, recklessness or negligence qualitatively different, or merely aspects of the person's acts, objectively judged? Thus Lord Steyn in *B (a minor) v DPP*,[67] a House of Lords case that broadly followed *Sweet v Parsley*, said that in a case calling for the establishment of *mens rea* 'recklessness or indifference as to the existence of the prohibited circumstance would be sufficient for guilt'.

As things stand at present, murder is a distinctively intentional crime and it is permissible to interpret the mental element as something extending beyond an intention to cause death, to an intention to cause really serious harm. Indeed, it is upon that latter basis that the majority of convictions for murder arise. Yet, unless we admit to the survival of a variety of constructive malice — that snake originating in the work of Coke which was thought to have been legislatively killed but that may, seemingly, have only been scotched — it would appear to run counter to common sense to argue that if a man had intent to do no more than serious harm it follows that intention to do worse may be imputed to him, notwithstanding that

---

65. *Ibid*, p.148. It is not without significance that Holmes in *The Common Law* specifically states that *mens rea* was unnecessary to establish murder or manslaughter.

66. Contributed to *Action and Value in Criminal Law*, ed. Shute, Gardner and Horder, Oxford (Clarendon Press, 1993) at pp.187–211.

67. [2000] 2 AC 428, at 477A–B.

he never had such intent. The consequences of such a course embody what we earlier identified as a 'penal premium'.[68]

Sweet v Parsley did not directly call for an explanation of the fault element in crime, since the defendant did not possess even the requisite knowledge for the specific statutory offence. Stephanie Sweet, a schoolteacher, sub-let her farmhouse in Oxfordshire, which she rarely visited, to students who, unbeknown to her and without her permission, smoked cannabis on the premises. She was charged with being concerned in the management of premises used for that (illegal) purpose, namely the smoking of cannabis,[69] and convicted by the magistrates (a conviction upheld by the High Court).

Lord Wilberforce, distinctively, decided in Ms Sweet's favour in a helpfully prosaic interpretation of the provision in the Dangerous Drugs Act 1965 that contemplated some kind of purposeful management, and that Ms Sweet clearly had not been concerned in the management of a cannabis shop or a cannabis smoking den or parlour. Lord Wilberforce said specifically that he did not need to embark on a wider examination of the 'problem of absolute offences, or of guilty intention'. Other Law Lords were only marginally more expansive on these problems.

Lord Morris of Borth-y-Gest said, ambiguously, that the cardinal principle of *mens rea*, 'an evil intention or a knowledge of the wrongfulness of the act', was an essential ingredient of a criminal offence. Lord Pearce talked interchangeably of 'knowledge or *mens rea*'. Lord Diplock tantalisingly pointed out that *mens rea* lacked precision and called for closer analysis beyond what is involved by its translation into English as no more than 'an evil intention or a knowledge of the wrongfulness of the act'. Lord Diplock concluded that such a definition suggested a simple mental element common to all criminal offences, and appeared to omit thoughtlessness 'which at any rate if it amounted to reckless disregard of the nature or consequences of an act, was a sufficient mental element in some offences at common law' (particularly, we note, *not* in the main homicide offence).

---

68. See: Louis Blom-Cooper and Terence Morris, *With Malice Aforethought: A Study of the Crime and Punishment for Homicide*, Oxford (Hart Publishing, 2004) at pp.26-27.

69. As a landlord she was under no duty to ensure, still less to warrant, that the premises were not being used for an unlawful purpose. Indeed, it could be argued that her duty to ensure that her tenants had quiet enjoyment of the property might well have limited her ability for covert discovery of what was going on.

Neither has precision been conspicuously forthcoming from the courts, nor statutorily supplied, save to say that, generally speaking, *mens rea* is, in practice, translated by trial judges in their summings-up as an intentional or deliberate (not accidental) act done with the requisite intention, the mental element for the particular crime. Clarity would be provided if the courts were to recognise the difference conceptually between the guilty mind and the knowledge of wrongdoing. Knowledge of the wrongfulness of the act done and the foresight of its consequences, if judged objectively, are morally neutral conditions of the mind. Cognitiveness is observable fact. A guilty mind (or an evil intention) is morally weighted according to the culpability of the individual actor.

Our Prescription

If (as we advocate should be the case) the fault element in the crime of murder — the intention to kill or to cause serious harm — is not essential in the establishment of criminal liability, but should be a consideration assigned to the sentencing stage of the criminal trial, what then ought the law to state about the personal liability of an unlawful killer? Rather than trudging through the moral maze[70] of the existing jurisprudence on the law of homicide, we think it is imperative to formulate the principles that should underpin the legislation for determining liability for violent and unnatural deaths.

A convenient starting point is Article 2 of the European Convention on Human Rights, which provides that everyone's life shall be protected by law. It imports the obligation of the State to put in place effective provisions in criminal law to deter the commission of offences against the person, backed by law enforcement machinery for the prevention, suppression and punishment of breaches of such provisions. Article 7 of the European Convention, which prohibits any legislation that criminalises an act retrospectively, also implicitly demands that the criminal law must be clearly defined. In other words, the criminal offence must be formulated with a sufficient degree of

---

70. A euphemism for the 'mess' that is the present state of the law.

precision to enable the citizen so to understand the legal limitations upon his conduct and regulate it accordingly.

So long as the state of the law of murder remains in a 'mess', as a result of the shifting standards whereby killings are declared unlawful by decisions of the courts, and hence defies clarity in definition, there must be dissatisfaction with the law. Nevertheless, it would probably pass muster before the European Court of Human Rights. The desirability of putting the law of murder on a statutory footing is, however, intrinsically compelling. The European Convention imposes no requirement as to the content of the criminal law of any State: it would appear that it assumes that, for the protection of life, homicide law should be based on a categorical requirement to protect the life of every citizen. Nor would it appear to adopt any particular moral position other than the prevention of harm resulting in death.

The primary focus of any law of homicide must be the act or omission, which results in a (putatively) unlawful death. It is the homicidal event giving rise to potential liability, either civil or criminal, that attracts the attention of the agents of law enforcement. It is not the label that attaches to the particular criminal event that engages the legal system, unless and until someone arrested is charged with a labelled offence arising out of such an event. The motive, purpose, premeditation or intention of the killer has no relevance (save for the purpose of the prosecutor's discretion) until the criminal justice system, as opposed to any official investigatory process conducted into the criminal event, is wheeled into place and becomes the focus of authoritative scrutiny. Article 6 of the European Convention, providing for a fair trial, looks back to the time of the individual suspect undergoing criminal investigation, and may also be engaged in considering the process of examination of the dead body, but it does not concern itself with the killer-victim relationship other than in the context of criminal justice.

Our conclusion is that the criminal law should define the conduct of the killer as unlawful without necessarily requiring any view of the killer's alleged intention. It is irrelevant whether killing was the result of gross negligence, or failure to exercise a duty of care owed to another on the part of the killer, or whether it was the outcome of his or her premeditated act. None of these situations instinctively or automatically imports, of itself, any definitive estimate of moral culpability. These are not matters that need trouble the court in the determination of criminal liability: indeed, seeking to prove 'intent' rather than to be satisfied as to a defendant's knowledge (*per* Holmes) may serve to make the process more difficult. It is unjustifiable homicide that matters. That exercise should ensure that there is a conclusion that the killing was unlawful. The degree of moral culpability for the unlawful killing can be assessed only in the light of all the circumstances leading up to and resulting in the death and thus *only* after liability has been established. It may be, however, and often is the case, that such circumstances are, for evidential reasons inherent in a fair trial, necessarily excluded from the decision-making process of the trial court. Even the partial defences of provocation and diminished responsibility impose their forensic limitations that may not reflect the true nature of the homicidal event.

The structure that we propose for a reconstructed law of homicide consists of determining that a killing has been unlawful and to which the law may attach an appropriate label for the purpose of dispensing criminal justice. The verdict of the trial court, after examination of the facts of the event which, the prosecution argues, was unlawful, must be directed to that issue. No mental element in the conduct of the killer need be established, other than knowledge (a cognitive factor) of the act of killing and any foresight such as would be possessed by a reasonable person that the act was inherently dangerous to the lives of others. That process thereby establishes both criminal and civil liability. But since punishment arises only from criminal liability, any estimate of moral culpability (in which intention may well be highly germane) is relevant only at the stage of sentencing. That is what is involved in the notion of liability as advanced by Holmes in *The Common Law* in 1881: a liability which is an amalgam of the subjective (the knowledge by the killer of his act) and the objective (his reasonable foresight of its consequences).

Far from the suggestion made by the Law Commission that our proposed single offence of criminal homicide embodies 'no fault requirement of any kind'[71] our proposal is precisely fault-based. Knowledge of the act or omission with foresight of their consequences gives rise to legal liability, both criminal and civil. To determine whether the killing was unlawful in

---

71. Law Com No 304, *Murder, Manslaughter and Infanticide* (20 November 2006) 2.21 at p.22.

these terms, it will always be necessary to examine the mental condition of the defendant, but only for the purpose of determining whether he had subjective knowledge of the act or omission. Unfitness to plead and insanity (however legally defined) would negative the requisite knowledge and result in no liability. So too, accident defeats liability.

It is our contention that, liability having been established, the moral desert of the offender is a matter for judicial estimation as a preliminary stage in the allocation of an appropriate penalty. It is certainly not for juries to convict, or otherwise, on the basis of *their* estimate of what is popularly termed the wickedness of the offender.

We began this chapter with the thought that the interdependent and necessary conditions for establishing the crime of murder — *actus reus* and *mens rea* — presented a problem in their relationship. The radical form for unlawful killings devised by Holmes, based upon knowledge rather than imputed intent — rejected long ago by English jurists such as Fitzjames Stephen — does not seem readily to strike a chord with contemporary criminal lawyers, certainly if the Law Commission's outright response to our proposal for a unitary offence of criminal homicide is any test. But we would invite those disposed towards a conservative approach to what would admittedly be a profound change in the law of homicide, to consider the conclusion of Professor Hart in his classic work *Punishment and Responsibility* some 40 years ago:

> If knowledge (the constituent *par excellence* of *mens rea*) may be considered part of the *actus reus*, it seems quite senseless to insist on any distinction at all between the *actus reus* and the *mens rea*, or to develop a doctrine of criminal responsibility in terms of this distinction.[72]

Perhaps we have alighted on an unsuspected alliance between Holmes and Hart. Knowledge of the act of killing with reasonable foresight of its consequences suffices to constitute the single crime of criminal homicide. It establishes the actor's criminal responsibility and the liability to punish-

---

72. Herbert Hart, *Punishment and Responsibility* (2nd ed. with an introduction by Professor John Gardner) Oxford (Oxford University Press, 2008) at p.145.

ment. Moral culpability, on the other hand, reflects punishment and is a matter for judicial sentencing in each individual case.

What will a prosecutor (the Crown) have to prove to a jury to obtain a conviction for criminal homicide? The essential two elements of the simple offence of criminal homicide are:

(a) knowledge of the act which resulted in the killing; and

(b) foresight of the consequences of that act.

Self-defence, duress and necessity will each constitute a complete defence to the charge. And accident (a killing which occurs as a result of a non-negligent act) is the negation of any criminal liability.

The first element, namely knowledge (a modern form of *mens rea*, but distinct from motive, premeditation, or specific or general intention) of the commission of an unlawful act, is a prerequisite to the offence of criminal homicide. The second element, foresight of the consequences of such an act, complements the knowledge to constitute the concept of fault in the homicidal offence. Insanity or mental disorder of such gravity that the defendant does not have the requisite knowledge negatives the commission of the offence. All other aspects of the current homicide offence — loss of self-control and diminished responsibility — are matters of mitigation that fall within the penalty structure, which would confer an unfettered discretion on the trial judge.

The jury will be directed to bring in a verdict either of guilty or not guilty. A judge may request that the jury provides some indication of the seriousness of criminal homicide so as to inform him of the appropriate sentence. But it is optional.

CHAPTER 4

THE LAW OF HOMICIDE

Part I: THE SUBSTANTIVE LAW

Murder and Manslaughter

A Law Unreformed

On the second reading of the Bill in 1965 to establish the Law Commission, Lord Gardiner argued the case for a systematic simplification and modernisation of the criminal law. He pleaded for its reduction to an accessible form by way of a code. He referred to the famous speech on law reform by Lord Brougham in February 1828 when the latter declared himself encouraged by the comment on that speech in Lord Campbell's *Lives of the Lord Chancellors* that:

> It lasted about six hours during which long period of time notwithstanding the dryness of the subject there was seldom any serious danger of the House being counted out.

Lord Campbell had prefaced that comment by some disparaging remarks:

> Brougham's great exploit during the present session was his memorable speech on law reform, which now may be gleaned at with wonder, although I cannot say that it would be justifiable to condemn anyone actually to read it through unless as a punishment for some grave dealings.

Lord Brougham's speech did not fall on deaf ears. The concern about the state of the criminal law led in 1831 to the establishment of Her Majesty's Commissioners of Criminal Law with a view to the possibility of codifying the criminal law of England and Wales. The Commission produced its first report in 1835 and issued seven more reports over the next ten years, culminating in a Criminal Code Bill. That Bill was referred to a Select Committee, but proceeded no further. If a Criminal Law Code is still awaited, at least reform of the law of homicide is in sight.

The Fourth Report (1839) and the Seventh Report (1843) of the commissioners both dealt with the law of homicide as part of the commissioners' remit to engage in a digest of law 'touching crimes, and the trial as punishment thereof'.

Although the penalty for murder was death, there was no suggestion that the commissioners were debarred from treating the ingredients of any criminal offence as separate and distinct from the penalty. Indeed, the commissioners, while endorsing the death penalty for murder, recommended (at p. xvi) that

> it will conduce to the honour and dignity of our law, if all the additions to the simple punishment of death [the exhibition of beheading and quartering] were expressly abolished.

Might not the Law Commission in 2006 have likewise recommended the dropping of the mandatory element of Murder 1, so heartily and universally disliked by those concerned with the administration of criminal justice, even if the terms of reference precluded so bold a move? The Commission did not hesitate to drop the mandatory penalty from Murder 2.

The commissioners in their Seventh Report of 1843 alluded at the outset to the peculiar difficulties presented by the existence of the criminal law developed on a case-by-case basis by trial judges. They wrote (at p. ix):

> Our experience has proved (as was anticipated in our First Report) that the most laborious part of the undertaking is the systematic reduction of those classes of crimes which rest on common law authority. The difficulties peculiar to the Digest of Common Law Crimes (arising principally from the vague, changing and often

conflicting authorities from which the law is extracted) are far more formidable than those which attended the consolidation of statute. *This last remark particularly applies to the common law offences comprised under the general heads of homicide*... (emphasis in original).

In their Seventh Report of 1843 the commissioners, in a section dealing with offences against the person, pointed up the difficulty of determining the mischief of potential harm to life and limb which the law should seek to prevent, and said this (at p. 7):

> In respect of homicide, in particular, we laboured to reduce the important class of cases which have been said to be comprised within the notion of implied malice, to a more simple and certain test, in making such cases to depend, not as questions of law, 'upon symptoms of a heart devoid of social affective, or fatally bent upon mischief', *but on the fact of a wilful endangering of life* from which the badness of heart so figuratively described is but an inference. (Emphasis added)

Between 1844 and 1882 there were no fewer than eight occasions when attempts were made to introduce a code. In 1879 a Royal Commission did produce a code, but after 1882 there were no further attempts until the Law Commission came into being in 1965, since when efforts in that regard have been abortive. Between 1867 and 1908 no fewer than six Bills came before Parliament that sought to amend either the law of murder or the law of homicide generally, none of which was to be enacted.[1] Another 40 years were to elapse before the matter again came before the legislature. It cannot be other than a cause for reproach that since the Second World War, Parliament, while willing to debate (frequently in the 1980s) and to legislate (generally in 1957 and 1965/1969, and piecemeal in 2003[2]) for the *penalty* for murder, has (with one minor exception[3]) stubbornly declined to define the *offence*. In 1957 Parliament did, however, marginally amend the law, in

---

1. In contrast to the situation regarding other violent crimes hitherto prosecuted at common law which were to come within the provisions of the Offences Against the Person Act 1861.
2. We discuss the provisions in the Criminal Justice Act 2003 (the 'Blunkett proposals') later.
3. Section 8 Criminal Justice Act 1967 abolished the doctrine of constructive malice, revising the much-criticised decision of the House of Lords in *DPP v Smith* [1961] AC 290. The legislation to define corporate manslaughter in 2007 provides another instance.

respect of the partial defence of provocation (now under the rubric of 'loss of self-control') and by introducing the concept of diminished responsibility. Murder is nevertheless the only offence in the criminal calendar which has been left to be defined by the common law and through the extensive body of case law.

Parliament's omission to settle the arguments about the law of homicide might not be a matter of great moment, were it not for the fact that the law of homicide is a matter that has consistently occupied the persistent attention of appellate courts in a seemingly endless search for clarification and certainty. Judicial efforts to rationalise the law of murder and manslaughter, in a long succession of cases, have cried out for parliamentary intervention, to no avail. As the Lord Chief Justice exclaimed in his Birmingham University lecture on 8 March 2007, the precise circumstances of killings amounting to murder 'have received consideration in an extensive and conflicting body of jurisprudence'.

In the last 30 years no fewer than 12 appeals—an astonishing number—have had to be decided by the House of Lords, which is authorised to entertain criminal appeals only if the Court of Appeal (Criminal Division) certifies that the case raises an issue of general public importance and leave is granted either by that court or by the Law Lords (now Supreme Court Justices) themselves. The 1974 case of *Hyam*[4] was upset in 1985, since when all shades of culpability and fine distinctions have peppered the judgments of our senior judiciary, to the point where the law of homicide is in desperate need of Parliamentary attention. It is only the popular—and widely misunderstood—view of murder as more serious than manslaughter that might be thought to stand in the way of its replacement by a simple offence of criminal homicide. But not so, if the Law Commission has its way in its scholarly, if over-lawyerly, report, *Murder, Manslaughter and Infanticide*[5] recommending a three-tier hierarchy of Murder 1, Murder 2 and Manslaughter.

The mechanistically repetitive statement that murder, no matter the circumstances of the criminal event, is the most heinous of all crimes, and that it must be sharply distinguished from all other forms of unlawful homicide, is thoroughly discredited. Given the variables in homicidal events and the

4. *Hyam v DPP* [1975] AC 85.
5. Law Com No 204, HC 30, London (The Stationery Office, 28 November 2006).

moral opprobrium attaching to any one individual killer, there is no need in contemporary society to label unlawful killings other than by the rubric of a single crime. This chapter seeks to demonstrate both the variable nature of homicides and the moral responsibility for each case.

The traditional (or old) definition of the offence of murder was unlawful killing, with malice aforethought, resulting in the death of the victim within a year and a day (a time-limit that no longer applies). In modern times, the emphasis has invariably focused on the state of mind of the accused (the malice aforethought). It is a common misapprehension among non-lawyers that a person can be convicted of murder only if it is proved that the accused intended to kill; in fact only a minority of people convicted of murder possess that extreme intent. It is sufficient for the prosecution to prove an intention to cause really serious injury. If death ensues, however unexpected, unpremeditated, or lacking in intention to kill, the offence of murder is made out, and the mandatory sentence of life imprisonment must follow. It is thus possible to commit a murder not only without wishing the death of the victim but also without the least thought that this might be the result of the assault. Few people would think that this represents a notion of justice.

By contrast, where the accused is charged only with an attempt to murder, it is necessary for the prosecution to prove a specific intent to kill; an intention to cause serious injury will not suffice. The case of Dr Nigel Cox points up the absurd illogicality of the law. Dr Cox was tried and found guilty of the attempted murder of a terminally-ill patient by giving her a an injection which had lethal consequences, for which offence he received a 12-month suspended sentence. Had the prosecution been for murder, it would have been necessary only to show that he intended to cause her serious harm.[6]

The laudable aim of contemporary law-makers in the Anglo-Saxon legal system, be they legislators or judges, has been to establish a consistent moral basis for the law of homicide, and that is attainable only by an accurate assessment of the degree of culpability of the individual killer. If the general

---

6. Situations in which, though the treatment is primarily for the humane purpose of relieving suffering, a consequence is the hastening of death present the law, never mind ethics, with a difficult problem. Given the current state of homicide law such issues are far from straightforward. Indeed, the whole question of so-called 'mercy killings' presents an immediate problem for the scheme of 'Murder 1' and 'Murder 2' proposed by the Law Commission.

justification for the prosecution, conviction and punishment of offenders were to be the Utilitarian aim of preventing harm, the law might be content to apply objective standards of human conduct towards those who kill. Oliver Wendell Holmes Jr (Mr Justice Holmes of the US Supreme Court) in his classic work *The Common Law*[7] took pains to emphasise that 'the tests of liability are external, and independent of the degree of evil in the particular person's motives or intentions'.

Holmes' purpose in championing an external standard of liability was to strip the criminal law, like other legal subjects, of what might be termed the 'baggage of morals'. In particular, Holmes was fond of converting terms such as 'malice'[8] or 'intent' from subjective to objective concepts. 'Acts,' he wrote, 'should be judged by their tendency under the known circumstances, not by the actual intent which accompanies them'.[9]

A Holmesian view finds modern expression in an essay by Lord Irvine of Lairg:

It is surely not for the accused himself to decide what level of risk he is permitted to take. That must be for the law to decide. And we have to decide these perplexing questions, with a level head and an open mind, perhaps best under the shade of a coolibah tree.[10]

Apart from an occasional dalliance with such notions,[11] English law has adhered rigidly to the principle that for all serious crimes, principles of justice

---

7. Oliver Wendell Holmes Jr, *The Common Law* (1st ed. 1881) at p.50. Holmes is quoted in the judgment in *Smith* (see footnote 11 below). See also Holmes' judgment in *Commonwealth of Massachusetts v Pierce* 138 Mass 165, 168–9 (1884).

8. Although principally remembered for the 'golden thread' running through English law that places the burden of proof upon the prosecution, the judgment in *Woolmington* (delivered by the Lord Chancellor, Lord Sankey) importantly addressed in some detail the history of the term. *Woolmington v DPP* [1935] AC 462.

9. Holmes, *supra*, p.66.

10. *Human Rights: Constitutional Law and the Development of the English Legal System*, Oxford (Hart Publishing, 2003), Chapter 20: *The English and Australian Law of Criminal Culpability*, p.346.

11. *DPP v Smith* [1961] AC 290, 327–8. Citing Holmes, Lord Kilmuir LC said: 'The test of foresight is not what this very criminal foresaw, but what a man of reasonable prudence would have foreseen'. We develop the Holmesian approach in *Chapter 3: The Wisdom of Mr Justice Oliver Wendell Holmes Jr*.

and fairness apply to accused persons, thus desisting from the punishment of those who lack the capacity or fair opportunity to obey the standards of society. Moral culpability for the criminal event alone can justify the imposition of any penal sanction.

Had the Holmes doctrine of foreseeability of the known circumstances, tested by objective standards, become the established rule of the English common law, there would be no room for the concept of 'oblique' intention, that is to say an intention inferred indirectly from the individual's actual foresight of his actions and their perceived consequences. But in the development of homicide law, apart from sections 1 and 2 Homicide Act 1957, the task has fallen exclusively to the judges who have had to grapple with the complexities of the mental processes of human beings behaving in a disorderly fashion. Once the objective judgment of conduct is abandoned, what suffices to constitute the requisite intention, in contradistinction to unintentional conduct, which is treated from a moral and legal point of view as non-culpable as far as criminal responsibility is concerned? Inevitably, the courts tended to resort to indirect ('oblique') aspects of desire or foresight on the part of the accused. Any analysis of the extensive case law will demonstrate the fluid, not to say confusing, state of the law of homicide.

If jurisprudence has directed (or misdirected) the shape and form of the law relating to the question of intent to kill or cause really serious harm, the resultant case law has to be viewed in the context of the process of criminal justice in which the task of the court of trial is distributed as between the judge and jury, the distinction being that the judge rules on the law (but, *quaere*, whether that is decisive of the case at the hands of an uncontrolled jury) while the jury must decide whether its findings of fact constitute a proper inference of the criteria for concluding the requisite intention.

That important qualification to a logical analysis of the case law is manifest in the speech of Lord Scarman in *Hancock and Shankland*.[12] A year earlier, in *Moloney*,[13] the House of Lords held that judges should generally avoid using the term 'intention' beyond explaining that it does not encompass motive. Lord Bridge of Harwich, interpreting what their Lordships had variably (and unhelpfully) said a decade earlier in *Hyam* about the requisite inten-

---

12. *R v Hancock and Shankland* [1986] 1 AC 455.
13. *R v Moloney* [1985] 1 AC 905.

tion of an arsonist of a residence in which known individuals, who were the accused's former lover and her children, were killed, said: 'The probability of the consequence taken to have been foreseen must be little short of overwhelming before it will suffice to establish the necessary intent'.

Lord Bridge's observation about the 'natural consequence' flowing from an act would seem to cover the actor who has knowledge to a high degree of certainty that his or her behaviour is likely to result in death. In *Nedrick*[14] Lord Lane CJ used the language of 'virtual certainty' of death or serious harm to reflect the result of the actions of the accused and that there was appreciation that such was the case. The language of certainty is dangerous, if only because it is an absolute. In so far as in common parlance we all talk of degrees of certainty, such impression merely gives rise to differing views abut how near to certainty one must get.

The vagueness of the phrase 'natural consequence' was considered in *Hancock and Shankland* to be too misleading for the jury. Lord Scarman expressed himself as being concerned less with intent and more with the way in which a jury might go about determining intent: a jury should be aware that 'the greater the probability of a consequence, the more likely the consequence was foreseen and if that consequence was foreseen, the greater the probability is that the consequence was intended'.

This development on intent, by the process of narrowing the legal criteria, shifted the question away from the area of judicial direction and towards the jury, to find intent, or not, on the basis of the evidence. That, however, did not bring the judicial debate to an end. Another trip to the House of Lords was necessary. In *Woolin*,[15] it was held that the jury should be told that it could 'find' the requisite intention rather than 'infer' it from the circumstances of foresight, but — and it would seem a big 'but' — that it would be a misdirection to tell the jury that intention could be inferred from foresight that there would be a 'substantial risk of death or serious harm'. This blurs the dividing line between intention and recklessness, and demonstrates that the law has given more than simple accommodation to oblique intention. Recklessness may, it seems, spill over into the realm of intent.

---

14. *R v Nedrick* (1986) 83 Cr App R 267.
15. *R v Woolin* [1999] 1 AC 82.

A presently unanswered question is what a jury should understand, in terms of foresight, about an intention on the part of an accused to *endanger* life. Should the law require not merely an intention to cause really serious harm but incorporate also an intention to endanger life? A decision of the Court of Appeal in Northern Ireland, on 1 April 2003,[16] would seem to suggest an affirmative answer. Whether this extension to the established rule about what constitutes 'really serious harm' is affected by Articles 3, 6 and 7 of the European Convention on Human Rights raises the spectre of yet further uncertainty in the law. The obliqueness of intent comes in a European garb. Can the English common law resist the incoming tide of precepts in international human rights?

Judicial criticisms concerning the concept of really serious harm abound. In *Attorney-General's Reference No 3 of 1994*, a re-run of the doctrine of transferred malice, Lord Mustill stated that 'the grievous harm rule is an outcropping of old law from which the surrounding strata of ratiocinations have withered away'.[17] Again, in *Powell (Anthony)*,[18] Lord Steyn said that the rule turned 'murder into a constructive crime resulting in defendants being classified as murderers who are not in truth murderers' (precisely our point!).

The remedy — another form of obliquity — lies in the recommendation of the Select Committee of the House of Lords on Murder and Life Imprisonment[19] that a person commits murder if he causes the death of another 'intending to cause serious personal harm and being aware that he may cause death'.

If there is any room in the English common law for a concept of oblique intent, it does no more than import a theoretical underpinning of the law of homicide. It must be concluded that, willy-nilly, the law's inertia has accommodated obliquity in its endless search for a consistent moral basis by way of establishing the *mens rea* for murder. In its search for pragmatism, the judiciary has effectively consigned the statement to the archives of the criminal justice system.

---

16. *R v Anderson (Samuel)* [1986] AC 27.
17. [1998] AC 245, p.258.
18. [1999] AC 1.
19. HL Paper 78-1, Session 1988–1989, para 71.

The task of the criminal court today is to determine whether the ultimate aim of the accused, as distinct from the preceding stages of the accused's activities, is intended or unintended. The substantial and shifting body of case law reveals an unwillingness, or perhaps even an inability, to define intent and to leave to the jury the task of deciding whether the circumstances disclose intention or inattention. The result is a confused and confusing mosaic, a piecing together of judicial directions and jury verdicts.[20] 'What a muddle!' exclaimed the leading academic criminal lawyer of his day, the late Professor Sir John Smith QC. He was depressingly right.

The distinction between murder and manslaughter is not derived from the physical harm contemplated, since in both cases the proscribed harm is the same unlawful killing of a human being. What sets them apart is the moral principle that intentional wrongs are generally more heinous than unintentional ones. There's the rub. The task of identifying the killer's intention in relation to the specific victim is difficult enough for both judge and jury, the less so for the former whenever he sits alone (as in the Diplock courts in Northern Ireland) and is required to give a reasoned decision which is susceptible to challenge by way of an unqualified appeal. The comparative study of one killer's intention with that of another for the purpose of assessing appropriate penal sanction is infinitely more complicated. Since in the case of murder that exercise is not performed by the trial court, it can be gauged only by the appellate court that supervises the sentencing policy and practice, or by the post-conviction process of tariff-fixing by the judiciary and in the process of determining when the killer should eventually be discharged from prison. If the trial verdict be manslaughter, the penalty available to the court is at large; not so, for murder.

In medieval times, European legal systems gave effect to the distinction between intentional and unintentional killing at the stage of sentencing by varying the punishment in the light of the presence or absence of intention; this being done *after* liability had been determined according to the doctrine of causation, seldom an easy task in cases of homicide. In contemporary cases of mothers killing their babies, supposedly by suffocation or

---

20. The Lord Chief Justice in his Birmingham University lecture of 8 March 2007 described the efforts of the House of Lords in the frequent sorties of appellants as attempts to improve the law, but more often than not 'succeeded in making confusion more confounded'.

violent shaking, the ascertainment of causation has often been limited by the extent of medical knowledge, notably regarding those particular instances commonly referred to as 'cot deaths'.[21]

In principle, there is no reason why that same approach, considering the issue of intent at the sentencing stage, could not be adopted today. But since the Middle Ages the authors of the common law, in unintentional collusion with legislators, have long since decreed otherwise. For the last four centuries intention has been wedded to liability. By attaching greater moral turpitude to intentional killing, murderers and manslayers have been convicted of different criminal offences according to the perceived public heinousness of the criminal event, though the infliction of harm and the death of the victim have been common to both murder and manslaughter. Everything in a murder trial focuses on the alleged intention of the accused in order that the correct legal label may be affixed to the event, so vital for the imposition of the penalty: in the instance of murder, fixed and immutable, in that of manslaughter, at large. Since the nature and circumstances of the criminal event of an unlawful killing are infinitely variable, it hardly seems sensible to pigeonhole its unlawfulness into different legal compartments. One label should readily suffice, that of criminal homicide.

The weight of contemporary academic opinion[22] is that the language of risk-taking belongs to the realm of recklessness rather than to intention. This smacks of semantics rather than a reasoned method of stating the substantive law. If the dichotomy of murder and manslaughter were swept away and replaced by a single offence of criminal homicide, as Lord Parker argued for way back in 1965, any distinctions in moral culpability between a reckless disregard of a risk to human life and well-being, and deliberate intention to cause death or serious injury, could be reflected in the degree of punishment imposed. Nor would that sentencing exercise be encumbered by legal

---

21. While in a pre-scientific era the techniques of forensic pathology were rudimentary, the sophistication of modern science is no warranty that in some instances it will not prove extremely difficult to establish the facts. Expert witnesses are not infrequently at variance in their opinions as to how the evidence should be interpreted to establish the facts. See *Chapter 13, Expert Evidence on Trial.*

22. See Finbar McAuley and Paul McCutcheon, *Criminal Liability*, Dublin, 2000 (Round Hall Sweet & Maxwell, 2000) at p.300.

tests — subtle or unsubtle — of criminal responsibility; it would provide all the necessary flexibility of proportionality in graduated punishment.

Stripped of the elusive element of intention, other forms of unlawful killing are subsumed by the law under the rubric of involuntary manslaughter as risk-taking activity, such as causing death by dangerous driving, which fall short of being murder. There are, however, at least three ways in which death resulting from risk-taking can constitute manslaughter.[23]

First, where the defendant subjectively foresees a risk of death or serious injury (but the degree of foresight fails to come within the narrow confines of the test in *Woolin*, such as to constitute murder) there is liability for manslaughter. In practice, this category covers instances in which the jury rejects the verdict of murder and finds the defendant guilty of manslaughter. It is a common experience that the Crown Prosecution Service indicts for murder on the basis that the jury is the proper forum for the decision as to which side of the dividing line the case falls.[24] This unsatisfactory practice on the part of the prosecution was neatly illustrated in the case of *Moloney*. The defendant was a young soldier at home on leave, engaged in a celebration that went on late into the night. The young man killed his stepfather (with whom he was on affectionate terms) with a shotgun. He would not in any way have desired the victim's death, which occurred in the course of a contest between them to see who could be quicker on the draw. When the defendant drew first, the victim dared him to shoot. He did just that, with the fatal result. The trial judge, Mr Justice Stephen Brown (later to become President of the Family Division of the High Court) told the jurors that they were entitled to convict the defendant of murder if they were satisfied that the defendant foresaw that his actions were likely to cause serious bodily harm. The jury convicted. Ultimately the House of Lords put matters right, but it is worth tracing the course of the criminal proceedings to demonstrate the judicial conflict about the law and the public's understanding of the law of homicide.

The killing, on any view, was a human and family tragedy. The defendant had instantly given himself up to the police, and was charged with murder.

---

23. Strictly speaking, there is no separate offence of 'involuntary' manslaughter, but for convenience the three ways are so described.
24. Not infrequently, of course, the defendant will plead guilty to the lesser offence of manslaughter.

When the case came before the local magistrates, they declined to commit the defendant to the Crown Court in respect of murder, and substituted a charge of manslaughter—no doubt a sensible layman's view—and right, as it turned out to be! The prosecution, as it was entitled to do, no doubt relying on *Hyam*, restored the charge of murder to the indictment. The defendant appealed to the Court of Appeal (Criminal Division). The appeal failed miserably. The Court, however, with a display of judicial reluctance, while certifying that the case raised a point of law of general public importance, emphatically refused to give leave to take the case to the House of Lords. It was confident that the law had been correctly stated in the direction to the jury.

Leave was in fact readily granted by the Law Lords, and the appeal succeeded resoundingly.[25] That there should have been such a divergence of views among the senior judiciary in 1985 on the question of intention as the mental element in the crime of murder, and that nothing in this regard would seem to have changed,[26] is itself a sad commentary on the law's failure to declare with certainty the ingredients of a serious criminal offence.

Second, where the defendant commits a dangerous and unlawful act that results in death, manslaughter is the appropriate crime.

Third, where the defendant owes a duty of care to the victim of homicide and breaches that duty in a negligent manner causing death—the negligence is usually stated to be 'gross', but it is not clear what that adds to the negligent act—there can be liability for manslaughter. In short, the requirement of the law is that the risk of physical harm be foreseeable. This category would, in theory, catch those cases once popularly known as 'motor manslaughter' before the legislation making statutory provision for the offences of causing death by dangerous driving or causing death while driving under the influence of drink or drugs. Prosecutions are invariably brought under the road traffic legislation.[27]

---

25. [1985] AC 905. The issue was considered the following year by Lord Lane CJ in the Court of Appeal in *Nedrick* (1986) Cr App R 267.
26. See *R v Smith (Morgan)* [2001] 1 AC 146. See also Law Commission Consultation Paper No 173, *Partial Defences to Murder* (2003) paras 4.69–4.161.
27. Road traffic offences are, for the most part, subject to substantially less social opprobrium than other crimes. This is a matter of immense significance to the relatives of the victims of such crimes who are frequently at a loss to perceive either logic or justice when what they

Corporate manslaughter for public transport and industrial disasters is a rarity, but the campaign to broaden the responsibility appears to have persuaded the Government to legislate in the form of the Corporate Manslaughter and Corporate Homicide Act 2007.

The unsatisfactory state of the law of manslaughter has been comprehensively and critically reviewed by the Law Commission,[28] but its recommendations remain un-enacted. There is no need for us to rehearse the difficulties in the law on involuntary manslaughter or the possible solution. The Law Commission's review of 1996, together with the cascade of contemporary case law from the House of Lords, has, one must concede, at least made the darkness of the law less completely impenetrable, but the jurisprudence remains without clear landmarks and continues to be enveloped in a grey mist of uncertainty. Moreover, the legitimate defences, never mind the other defences which are arguably less intellectually legitimate, to a charge of murder make no contribution to answering the primary question of how, through its criminal law, a civilised society should respond to unlawful killings.

The Law Commission in its Report of 28 November 2006[29] has recommended a new Homicide Act that would divide homicide into three categories, instead of the two categories of murder and manslaughter that currently exist. We defer our comments on these proposals to a later chapter. It too remains unenacted and awaits its fate on the Statute Book.

Part II: THE DEFENCES TO A CHARGE OF MURDER

Necessity

A hundred and twenty years ago the Lord Chief Justice of the day, Lord Coleridge, in a case involving cannibalism at sea, explained why the law

---

hold to be homicides are nevertheless visited for the most part with comparatively lenient sentences within a specified maximum which falls well short of that of the discretionary life sentence available to the courts in cases of 'ordinary' manslaughter. See further *Chapter 9*.

28. Law Commission Paper No 237, *Legislating the Criminal Code: Involuntary Manslaughter* (1996).

29. *Murder, Manslaughter and Infanticide*, Law Com No 304.

provided no defence of necessity to a charge of murder. The yacht *Mignon-ette*, outward bound from Southampton for Australia, foundered off the African coast and her delivery crew took to her small dinghy. Adrift, and without food or water, the master and mate killed the cabin boy (physically the weakest, and therefore the most likely to die first if they were not rescued) and had begun to eat the body when help arrived. In his celebrated judgment Lord Coleridge observed:

> It must not be supposed that in refusing to admit temptation to be an excuse for crime it is forgotten how terrible the temptation was; how awful the suffering; how in such trials to keep the judgment straight and the conduct pure. We are often compelled to set up standards we cannot reach ourselves and to lay down rules which we could not ourselves satisfy. But a man has no right to declare temptation to be an excuse though he might himself have yielded to it, allow compassion for the criminal to change or weaken in any manner the legal definition of the crime.[30]

Lord Coleridge dismissed the claim that self-preservation was a lawful defence[31] and, holding it to be 'unworkable and dangerous in practice', continued:

---

30. *R v Dudley and Stephens* (1884) 14 QBD 273, 288. The two who were rescued were subsequently found guilty of murder and sentenced to death. Sir Henry James (the Attorney-General) and Sir Farrer Herschell (the Solicitor-General) implored Sir William Harcourt (the Home Secretary) to exercise mercy, stating that public opinion was in sympathy with the defendants. On 5 December 1884 James wrote to Harcourt: 'If you announce a commutation to penal servitude for life or even to any shorter term you will never be able to maintain such a decision and you will have to give way'; to which Harcourt replied: 'It is exactly to withstand an erroneous and perverted sentiment on such matters that we are placed in situations of very painful responsibility'. Harcourt relented to the extent that the death sentences were commuted to ones of imprisonment for six months. For a critical view of devious judges and sanctimonious Whitehall mandarins ensuring the two sailors' convictions, see A W B Simpson's *Cannibalism and the Common Law: A Victorian Yachting Tragedy* (Chicago University Press, 1984).

31. It may be argued that the necessity of preserving life, not least one's own, constitutes perhaps the most extreme form of duress. The House of Lords was, many years later, to confirm that duress did not constitute a defence to murder; even if the defendant's own life is threatened it cannot be justifiable to take another innocent life: *R v Hoe* [1987] AC 417. This issue is discussed *ex hypothesi* by Professor Andrew Ashworth in the context of a more recent maritime disaster, the sinking of the *Herald of Free Enterprise*: Andrew Ashworth, *Principles of Criminal Law* (3rd ed.), (Oxford University Press, 1999).

> Certainly I would rather be in an open boat with companions who accepted [this]
> principle than in company with lawyers who accepted necessity as a defence to murder.

Two distinguished academic lawyers have written that it would be premature to conclude that necessity can never be a defence to murder.[32] The suggestion is that where the person sacrificed has innocently imperilled the lives of others, for example, by falling over a precipice while roped to another climber who then cuts him loose to save his own life, the defence might be available. An incident that emerged from the inquest into the deaths caused by the sinking of the *Herald of Free Enterprise* at Zeebrugge in March 1987 impliedly supports such a suggestion.[33]

A remarkably eloquent instance of extra-judicial writing by Justice Benjamin Cardozo has probably best expressed the approach of the English common law:

> Where two or more are overtaken by common disaster, there is no right on the
> part of one to save the lives of some by the killing of another. There is no rule of
> human jettison. Men there will often be who, when told that their going will be
> the salvation of the remnant, will choose the nobler part and will make the plunge
> into the waters. In that supreme moment the darkness for them will be illuminated
> by the thought that those left behind will ride to safety. If none of such mould are
> [*sic*] found aboard the boat, or too few to save the others, the human freight must
> be left to meet the claims of the waters. Who shall choose in such an hour between
> the victims and the saved? Who shall know when the masts and sails of rescue may
> emerge out of the fog?[34]

The extreme caution of Justice Cardozo in entertaining a defence of the choice of the lesser evil in homicide is not the prevailing one, as the treat-

---

32. J C Smith and Brian Hogan, *Criminal Law* (8th ed.) London (Butterworths, 1996) at p.258. See also J C Smith, *Justification and Excuse in Criminal Law*, London (Sweet & Maxwell, 1989) at pp.73–79.
33. The incident allegedly involved a passenger who, in a panic no doubt born of terror, blocked an escape route to others by continuing to cling to a rope ladder. The unfortunate individual was said to have been eventually pushed off. No prosecution resulted. See also J C Smith, *ibid*.
34. Benjamin Cardozo, *Law and Literature* (1931) cited in McAuley and McCutcheon, *Criminal Liability*, Dublin (Round Hall Sweet & Maxwell, 2000) at p.800.

ment of the problem by the US Model Penal Code shows. In its commentary on the passage from Cardozo's writing, the Code states:

> It would be particularly unfortunate to exclude homicidal conduct from the scope of the defence [of choice of evils] ... Conduct that results in taking life may promote the very value sought to be protected by the law of homicide. The life of every individual must be taken ... to be of equal value and the numerical preponderance in the lives saved compared to those sacrificed surely shall establish legal justification for the act ... Although the view is not universally held that it is ethically preferable to take one innocent life than to have many lives lost, most persons probably think a net saving of lives is ethically warranted if the choice among lives to be saved is not unfair. Certainly the law should permit such a choice.[35]

Assuming that the principle of choosing the lesser evil were to become available as a defence to a charge of homicide, Dudley and Stephens, the two crew members of the *Mignonette*, might conceivably succeed today. Lord Coleridge's statement that 'it is admitted that the deliberate killing of this unoffending boy was clearly murder, unless the killing can be justified by some well recognised excuse admitted by the law' confused justification with excuse. The distinction clearly exists. One justifies causing harm to another by showing that one did it deliberately and, after due reflection, nevertheless concluded that in the circumstances it had been the right or the best thing to have done. One excuses someone from blame for the harm done to another by conceding that it was wrong to cause the harm, but that nevertheless, in the circumstances, it could not be helped and therefore one cannot really be blamed for it.

The latter might be a partial or a complete excuse. We think the law should now establish the distinction.

---

35. The Code was drafted in the late-1950s and was prepared and published by the American Law Institute, the Official Draft appearing in 1962. The Code has served as a guide for measuring possible and proposed reforms in procedural and substantive criminal law in the various jurisdictions of the United States.

Duress

Duress as a defence to murder has had a more chequered career than its counterpart, necessity, in coping with the expedient taking of human life. While duress may be raised as a defence to most non-homicidal offences, the common law has not generally accorded such status to it in respect of the crime of murder. Thirty years ago[36] the House of Lords, by a majority of three to two, did find that the defence was available in a case of attempted murder, but that was to be rejected by a unanimous House in 1987 in *Howe*[37] and again in 1992 in *Gotts*.[38] Duress can now be regarded as a plea of general application available to all crimes except murder, attempted murder and some forms of treason. In any event, the courts have been able to negative a plea of duress to a charge of murder whenever the killer was a voluntary member of an organization, thereby committing himself to an unlawful campaign; the killer was not permitted to take advantage of the pressure exercised on him by his fellow criminals. In Northern Ireland, in a case involving the Official Irish Republican Army, Lord Lowry observed that it was not possible to do so 'in order to put on, when it suits him, the breastplate of righteousness'.[39]

Speaking of the defence of duress in the *Fitzpatrick* case, Lord Lowry said that if the conscious intent to commit a crime, including logically to kill or cause really serious injury, was formed under a compulsion so strong that it could be said that the perpetrator ought not reasonably to be expected to resist it, the moral excitability erases the criminality of the guilty act. He added:

> Putting the matter thus, one can appreciate an argument for saying that duress, if proved, should merely be reflected in the severity of the punishment and not in exculpation of the crime, but it is now too late to pretend that this approach would reflect the common law.

---

36. *DPP for Northern Ireland v Lynch* [1977] AC 653.
37. [1987] AC 417.
38. *R v Gotts* [1992] 2 AC 412.
39. *R v Fitzpatrick* [1977] NI 120.

Yet it is never too late for Parliament to decide that this mitigation, too, can be appropriately assigned to the sentencing stage. Lord Mackay of Clashfern in *Howe* said:

> I have not found any satisfactory formulation of a distinction which will be sufficiently precise to be given practical effect in law and at the same time differentiate between levels of culpability, so as to produce a satisfactory demarcation between those accused of murder who should be entitled to resort to the defence of duress and those who are not.[40]

Touché. Once it is acknowledged that the killing was unlawful, claims that the killer was under duress can safely be left to the stage of sentencing. The Law Commission has recommended that duress should, if successfully pleaded, be a full defence to first degree murder, whenever the threat is one of death or life-threatening harm.[41] We prefer the option of leaving the issue of duress to the stage of sentencing.

Self-defence

Where a person kills in self-defence, the law adopts an 'all or nothing' approach. If the killer, in order to protect himself, or even his home, uses more force than is reasonable, he is liable for murder; there is no halfway house in a partial defence of excessive force. This is a time-hallowed view enunciated by Aquinas 800 years ago, who maintained that 'it is legitimate to answer force with force provided it goes no further than due defence requires'.[42]

Yet here again, in modern times, the law has tended to waver. An Australian initiative contemplated a lesser homicidal offence than murder where the killing narrowly crossed the threshold between a reasonable and an unrea-

---

40. [1987] AC 417, 453.
41. The Law Commission added a possible refinement where the defendant satisfies two conditions: (a) on a balance of probabilities and (b) the jury concludes that a sober person of reasonable fortitude in the circumstances might have committed first degree murder. Law Com 304, p.126, para 6.66. See also Paragraphs 7 and 8 in Appendix C, *Defences to Murder*.
42. *'Vim vi repellere licet cum moderamine inculpatæ tutelæ'. Summa Theologiæ*, trans. Marcus Lefébure, London (Blackfriars in conjunction with Eyre and Spottiswoode, 1975) at p.43.

sonable amount of force.[43] The Privy Council in 1971[44] rejected that idea, on the ground that the full application of self-defence could adequately favour those who used such force as they instinctively thought necessary in the circumstances.

In its Fourth Report in 1980 the Criminal Law Revision Committee disagreed, recommending that a verdict of manslaughter should be possible where the force that the killer used was reasonable in the circumstances. The High Court of Australia set the clock back in 1987 by denouncing the doctrine of excessive force as too complicated for juries.[45]

But the issue has not gone away. Private Clegg, a British soldier serving in Northern Ireland, had been convicted of murder as a result of shooting at a car that drove through an army checkpoint. The House of Lords upheld the conviction, although Lord Lloyd of Berwick, while expressing some sympathy for the soldier's dilemma, thought that the question of reform was a matter solely for the legislature.[46] The Government's response was to contend that, whatever the force of the argument for a compromise verdict of manslaughter, it was outweighed by the complexity that would ensue from a change in the law.[47]

The more recent case of the Norfolk farmer Tony Martin brought the issue of self-defence into sharp, contemporary focus and is a subject which excited a great deal of public interest. Martin was originally convicted of the murder of a teenage burglar, and sentenced accordingly to life imprisonment. Martin's subsequent appeal against his conviction for murder was, nevertheless, allowed on the grounds of evidence of diminished responsibility and he was sentenced to five years' imprisonment for manslaughter. In December 2003, BBC Radio 4's *Today* programme invited listeners to put forward suggestions for law reform; the proposal that proved most popular was for a law to permit householders to use any means to defend themselves

---

43. *R v McKay* [1957] ALR 648 and *R v Howe* (1958) 100 CLR 448.
44. *Palmer v R* [1971] AC 814 and *R v McInnes* (1971) 55 Cr App R 551.
45. *R v Zecevic* (1987) 71 ALR 641.
46. *R v Clegg* [1995] 1 AC 482, 499–500. Subsequently at a re-trial, on fresh evidence, Clegg was convicted of a lesser (non-homicidal) offence.
47. *Report of the Interdepartmental Review of the Law on the Use of Lethal Force in Self-defence or the Prevention of Crime*, London (Home Office, 1996).

or their property against criminal threat.[48] Public opinion appeared to be divided about the correctness of the jury verdict of murder. What is clear from the various responses to the outcome of the Martin case is the degree of public dissatisfaction and misunderstanding of the law. That Martin should be imprisoned for life, having killed the youth who was engaged in committing a serious crime against him, represented for some a kind of dissonance between the law and a common sense notion of what was equitable. Clearly, manslaughter was, for many people, a preferable outcome, but one cannot but retain an element of scepticism about how far that arose from an intellectual concern about the distinction between murder and manslaughter, rather than from the more practical consideration that manslaughter carries an essentially discretionary sentence, likely to result in a shorter period of incarceration. Indeed, on his successful appeal the Court of Appeal substituted a sentence of five years' imprisonment. The issue that the Martin case raises, yet which has passed with little comment, is the successful promotion of the defence of diminished responsibility, the defence of self-defence having initially failed. In recent years this statutory defence[49] has been advanced in some instances in which its legislative progenitors might well have considered it inappropriate, though it is by no means unknown for a law to be enacted for one purpose but to be used by succeeding generations for another. Diminished responsibility has been used in attempts to enlarge the scope of provocation, and in this instance appears almost to have pushed the issue of determining the nature of reasonable force in self-defence into a secondary place. Our view is that the defence of diminished responsibility, if it is to be retained, ought to be confined to demonstrating that there is, where the defendant is suffering from some form of mental impairment or disorder, insufficient evidence of the *mens rea* required for the crime of murder. The long-term view must surely be that diminished responsibility, like any other currently available defence having the effect of reducing the crime from murder to manslaughter, raises issues that can

---

48. Although scarcely likely to be a representative sample of public opinion, the poll revealed the intensity of feeling that the issue has aroused through appearing to suggest that having embarked upon a criminal enterprise, the offender should be seen as having effectively forfeited anything beyond the most vestigial consideration of his welfare. In this we might hear an echo from Coke, perhaps the most articulate advocate of the 'penal premium'.

49. Deriving from the Homicide Act 1957.

only properly be addressed at the sentencing stage, being essentially miti-gatory in character. In any event, the abolition of the distinction between murder and manslaughter, for which we would strongly argue, can be the only logical direction for the long-overdue reform of the law of homicide, and would render this axiomatic.

Defences Relating to Issues in Mental Health

Insanity

The relationship between the mental competence of a person charged with a criminal offence and the establishment of the responsibility sufficient for the proper imposition of a penal sanction is a problem that is far from new. In the 13th century the jurist Henry de Bracton devised his so-called 'wild beast' test,[50] while in the 19th century, with the problem still unresolved, the judges were exercised to produce the M'Naghten Rules. Although applicable to all crimes, the issue of the insanity defence at an early stage became entangled with the mitigation of the capital penalty. This was due, no doubt, to the fact that the offences committed by those suffering from various forms of mental illness tend to attract attention when they are of a very serious nature, such as homicides, arson and, in particular, the assassination of public figures, all crimes which in the past carried the death penalty. Add to this the aggravat-ing feature that they are often accompanied by bizarre circumstances, and anxieties concerning risk to the community at large are readily amplified. A deep-seated fear, not so much of mental illness *per se* but of mentally-ill people, has been a feature of many societies throughout history, our own contemporary world included. Indeed, Bracton's 'wild beast' has by no means become extinct in the popular lexicon within which some sexual and other violent offenders are categorised. If what might be considered a populist approach to sentencing philosophy has changed, it has been little more

---

50. Applied in 1724 by Mr Justice Tracey in *Arnold's Case* (6 State Trials 764, 765). This is unsur-prising in view of the fact that in the *Institutes* Coke, in his account of *Beverley* (1603), notes that a beast, being incapable of reason, is similarly incapable of felonious intent. For a fuller discussion of issues relating to mental incapacity and criminal responsibility see Terence Mor-ris, 'Mad, Bad or Simply Dangerous? Homicide and Mental Disorder' in Gavin Drewry and Charles Blake (eds.) *Law and the Spirit of Inquiry: Essays in Honour of Sir Louis Blom-Cooper*, London (Kluwer Law International, 1999).

than for reactions to range from a demand that such 'beasts' be put down to an insistence that they be caged securely for the rest of their natural lives.

The special verdict of 'not guilty by reason of insanity' is found in an average of only three cases a year. Since the only outcome of this verdict is that the defendant is detained in a Special Hospital[51] with the same status as a restricted patient under the Mental Health Act 1983, the defence of insanity is worth raising only when the prospect of indefinite hospital detention is thought preferable to the likely period of imprisonment for the offence, that is, life imprisonment for murder. By comparison, the verdict of guilty of manslaughter by reason of diminished responsibility (above) provides a wider and more flexible alternative, although it provides no guarantee that a defendant suffering from mental illness who advances this defence will necessarily receive treatment as part of the sentence of the court. Research conducted by the present authors into the operation of the Homicide Act 1957[52] indicated that in the first five years following its enactment there was considerable variation in the nature of disposal by the courts, including determinate sentences of imprisonment, hospital orders and periods of supervision on probation. The old 'insanity' defence for murder seems then to have become obsolescent, if not in practice obsolete, although it is still raised occasionally for cases other than murder. It is also occasionally invoked to establish unfitness to plead[53] which essentially comprises an inability, deriving from some condition of the mind, to understand the evidence before the court, to give evidence as a witness, or to give instructions to counsel.

The so-called 'M'Naghten Rules' were once famously described by the American criminologist Sheldon Glueck as having both the flexibility of the bed of Procrustes and the rigidity of an army mattress.[54] Certainly, since their original formulation in 1842, judges have provided juries with a range of interpretations, though the process was influenced by the theoretical constructs that were promoted by medical authorities in the field until comparatively recent times. It was widely held that there was a distinction to be

---

51. Or other hospital, specified currently by the Minister of Justice and prior to May 2007 by the Home Secretary.
52. Terence Morris and Louis Blom-Cooper, *A Calendar of Murder*, London (Michael Joseph, 1964).
53. See *R v Johnson* [2002] EWCA Crim 1900.
54. Sheldon Glueck, *Law and Psychiatry: Cold War or Entente Cordiale?* London (Tavistock, 1962).

drawn between the 'sane' and the 'insane', and the latter were considered to be identifiable by errors of cognition. Half a century ago it was still possible for textbooks on criminal law containing examples of hypothetical defendants unable to distinguish between cutting a woman's throat and slicing a loaf of bread, or killing under the delusion that they were breaking a jar.[55] The Victorian psychiatrist Henry Maudsley had paraphrased the two principal elements of the rules as consisting in the defendant either not knowing the nature and quality of his actions or, if he did know them, not knowing them to be wrong. The first criterion, like that of the 'wild beast' test, led to the 'all or nothing' dichotomy between sanity and insanity. The second rendered impossible the serious defence of those whose evident paranoia was nevertheless expressed in the most lucid fashion. If the first criterion applied a test of cognition, extreme to the point of such absurdity as to be useless as a test of the defendant's understanding of his actions, the second applied a test of knowledge and conformity to the law which automatically excluded the defences of those who, however articulate, were deluded by the mental disorder from which they suffered.

A problem arose when the defendant was firm in his belief that what he was doing was *right* in the sense that his concept of what was morally right was superior to any system of legal prescription. Even if the defendant were suffering from a mental illness that, for example, involved paranoid delusion, this second part of the formula would not provide a defence. The matter was dealt with in the case of *Windle*,[56] some five years before the Homicide Act 1957 provided the statutory defence of diminished responsibility. The defendant, whose wife was seriously mentally-ill and constantly speaking of suicide, was said to be suffering from a *folie à deux*. He administered her a dose of one thousand aspirins and, surrendering himself to the police, is reported to have said 'I suppose they will hang me for this'. At the trial before Devlin J, psychiatrists for both prosecution and defence were in agreement that the defendant knew what he was doing was against the law and the

---

55. Gordon Hewart, Lord Chief Justice from 1922 to 1940, reflected in an extra-judicial observation that 'The mere fact that a man thinks he is John the Baptist does not entitle him to shoot his mother'—an absence of any Oedipus complex! G. Hewart, *Not Without Prejudice*, London (Hutchinson, 1937).
56. [1952] 2 QB 286.

issue was withdrawn from the jury. When the matter came before the Court of Criminal Appeal the Lord Chief Justice, Lord Goddard re-affirmed the position established by the judges in 1842:

> Courts of law can only distinguish between that which is in accordance with the law and that which is contrary to law. The law cannot embark on the question and it would be an unfortunate thing if it were left to juries to consider whether some particular act was morally right or wrong. The test must be whether it is contrary to law.

The clarity with which the Victorian judges had pronounced was forthright:

> Notwithstanding the party accused did the act complained of with a view, under the influence of an insane delusion, or redressing or revenging some supposed grievance or injury or of producing some public benefit, he is nevertheless punishable, according to the nature of the crime committed, if he knew at the time of committing such crime that he was acting contrary to law; by which expression we understand your Lordships to mean the law of the land.

Two observations can be made at this point. The first is that Goddard, in saying what the law can and cannot do is clearly *ad idem* with Holmes: the law can only be the arbiter of *legality*, never of morals. The second is that he underscores the no less important consideration that it is the task of the jury to find facts on the basis of evidence, not to interpret them for the purpose of making moral judgments that would have an effect upon any subsequent sentence on conviction.

Notwithstanding what one might have assumed to be the unassailable position established in *Windle*, the High Court of Australia in the case of *Stapleton*[57] employed a broader interpretation as a 'failure to appreciate that the conduct was morally wrong'. This of course covers those instances in which the defendant's perception of the social world is effectively divorced from reality and some research has shown that many psychiatrists accord

---

57. *Stapleton v R* (1952) 86 CLR 353 at p.358. See also: Norval Morris, "Wrong' in the M'Naghten Rules' 1953 16 MLR 435.

with this view.[58] *Windle* was nevertheless followed by the Supreme Court of Canada over a quarter of a century later in *Schwarz*.[59]

These shortcomings relating to the 'insanity' defence have long been regarded by psychiatrists as inappropriate, in that the most disturbed person labouring under the severest delusions usually understands the nature of the act he has committed and knows that the act is regarded as morally wrong by society at large, even though he may have been driven by fear, anger or 'the voices' to override his own moral concerns. The key point is that the majority of mentally disordered offenders are still possessed of both reason and memory together with a capacity for cognition; only those with what are severe mental health problems (sometimes amplified by learning disabilities) are likely to be entirely without competence.

A modern case in the Privy Council[60] demonstrates that the question of the defendant's knowledge about 'wrong' when the homicide is undeniably the outcome of a conscious and deliberate act was by no means resolved by *Windle* half a century ago. In *Philip and John* the defendants had been convicted after a trial in the High Court of St Lucia of the murder of a Catholic priest and a nun, and sentenced to death in April 2003. Their appeals against conviction and sentence were dismissed by the Court of Appeal of the Eastern Caribbean Court of Justice (St Lucia) in May 2004. Special leave was granted for them to appeal to the Privy Council in March 2006 and written judgment was given in May 2007. The appeals were focused upon the safety of the convictions, given the mental state of the defendants and the directions given by the judge to the jury.

The facts were straightforward. On 31 December 2000 the pair went into the Catholic cathedral in Castries during early morning Mass carrying timber posts and quantities of inflammable material including petrol. They attacked members of the congregation and when the priest intervened John threw petrol over him and set him on fire. When the nun approached them John hit her three times about the head with a timber post. She died

---

58. R D McKay and G Kearns, 'More Facts About the Insanity Defence' [1999] Crim LR 714-715. See also the discussion by Andrew Ashworth in his *Principles of Criminal Law* (3rd ed.) (Oxford University Press, 1999).

59. (1979) 29 CCC (2d) 1.

60. Privy Council Appeal No 110 of 2005.

from her injuries later that day; the priest suffered severe burns and died just under four months later. The defence was one of insanity. The central issue was the question of whether they were acting under the influence of such delusions as would succeed in establishing that defence. Section 21 of the St Lucia Criminal Code deals with insanity along M'Naghten lines in that it is two-pronged, but otherwise differs in its construction. It provides an insanity defence if the defendant

(a) was prevented, by reason of idiocy, imbecility, or any mental derangement or disease affecting the mind, from knowing the nature of consequences of the act in respect of which he is accused, or if he did know it, he did not know that what he was doing was contrary to law;

(b) if he did the act in respect of which he is accused under the influence of a delusion of such nature as to render him, in the opinion of the jury or of the Court, an unfit subject for punishment of any kind in respect of such an act.

Giving the opinion of the Privy Council, Lord Carswell identified the content of section 21(a) of the St Lucia Code as corresponding to the M'Naghten test of insanity, but:

their Lordships consider that the test of insanity contained in section 21(b) is a free-standing test and the Court of Appeal [of St Lucia] was incorrect in holding that the general rule applicable to the plea of insanity applies equally to the plea based on delusion, with the result that the conditions set out in paragraph (a) would have to be satisfied before the latter plea could be made out.

The St Lucia Code goes further than the M'Naghten formulation in that while section 21(a) focuses upon knowledge and cognition on the part of the defendant of the wrongful nature of his actions, section 21(b), by reference to delusion, incorporates the presence of an influence towards persuasion or compulsion to act which is external to the defendant. The Privy Council decided that it was first necessary to prove that the defendants suffered from a delusion or delusions and second that the delusion must be of such a nature as to render him unfit for punishment of any kind. It went on to say:

> The latter in their Lordships' opinion carries the connotation of a delusion of the presence of some outside influence which operates on the defendant's mind in such a way that he is impelled or persuaded to commit acts which he knows to be forbidden. The threat of punishment would have no deterrent effect, one of its main objects. The object of retribution would be repugnant to the conscience of the ordinary citizen. Accordingly, punishing such a defendant with ordinary criminal sanctions would be both inappropriate and pointless.[61]

Statements made by the defendants to the police, and later in unsworn form from the dock, suggested a strong belief that they were acting in a noble cause at the prompting of an influence outside themselves. In their Lordship's opinion the purpose of section 21(b) was to widen the defence of insanity:

> by getting away from the defendant's knowledge of the nature and quality of his act or that it was contrary to law. If it is proved to have been under the influence of a delusion, such that he is an unfit subject for punishment, the defence is made out, even if the lack of knowledge required by section 21(a) cannot be established.[62]

In terms of the doctrine in *Windle*, it would be difficult to see how, in this case, the insanity defence could ever have had any serious hope of success but, by provision of an alternative criterion in section 21(b), the St Lucia Code made it possible to prevent the narrowest applicability of M'Naghten.

That said, it is worth noting that in a very large number of cases where the insanity defence has been pleaded, delusions, very commonly of a paranoid variety, have been at the heart of the matter. That these my be accompanied by what are techniques of neutralisation, effectively setting aside any constraint of the criminal law, cannot justify a defendant's behaviour.[63] What can, however, emerge is a basis for determining the appropriate sanction employed in the criminal justice process.

---

61. At paragraph 24.
62. At paragraph 23.
63. The point made, if more colourfully, by Gordon Hewart. See footnote 55 above.

Every now and again the insanity defence is complicated by the arguments over whether or not someone is suffering from 'insane automatism'[64] or should be totally acquitted on the grounds that the offence was committed as a result of 'non-insane automatism', a transient state produced, for example (in theory) by drugs, the post-ictal phase of focal epilepsy, hypoglycaemia,[65] sleepwalking or any organic cause of reduced consciousness.

Amnesia has also been raised as an issue, perhaps most notably in the case of Günter Podola, who was charged in 1959 with the murder by shooting of a police officer. *Podola* was a singular case in that the defence argued that, although Podola understood the charge, he had no recollection of the events to which it related. Unusually, the Home Secretary referred the case[66] to the Court of Criminal Appeal on the issue of whether the onus of proof of fitness to plead rested on the defence or the prosecution.[67]

In summary, the M'Naghten Rules are widely regarded as 'past their sell-by date' and effectively superseded by 50 years of case law since the introduction of the statutory defence of diminished responsibility. Medical knowledge has propelled the old insanity plea towards oblivion and as a forensic device its eclipse by diminished responsibility is almost complete, a situation unlamented by lawyers. Reform is unnecessary; insanity now exists only to establish fitness to plead. Nor is there any enthusiasm for the recommendations made in 1975 by the Butler Committee on Mentally Abnormal Offenders[68] that there should remain a special verdict renamed 'not guilty on evidence of mental disorder' which would include transitory abnormal mental states and apply to both mental illness and learning disability.

---

64. Though 'automatism' is a 'condition' that has no medical meaning other than to refer to the behaviour observed in the aftermath of the fit in Jacksonian (focal) epilepsy, that has not prevented arguments about it in the courts in which psychiatrists have participated.

65. It was used successfully in the Northern Ireland case of Ian Hay Gordon in 1953. See *R v Gordon* [2000] NICA 28 when in a reference by the Criminal Cases Review Commission the NI Court of Appeal quashed the verdict of 'guilty but insane'.

66. Under the terms of section 19(a) Criminal Appeal Act 1907.

67. The Court dismissed the appeal against conviction and the Attorney-General refused his *fiat* for an appeal to the House of Lords. Podola was hanged 12 days after he had been sentenced to death for capital murder.

68. Cmnd 6214. Recently, the Scottish Law Commission has produced a report on reform of the law relating to insanity: see Scot Law Com No 195.

There seems recently to have been a shift in medical thinking, at least among those leading forensic psychiatrists who now feel that if people are fit to plead they should have the right to be tried on the evidence of the facts, and that the main role of psychiatrists should be confined to the sentencing and disposal phase. Theirs may not be the opinion of the membership of the Royal College of Psychiatry as a whole, which by its nature tends to a more conservative view of any proposed change and may be less willing to see the disappearance of the verdict that is meant to absolve the 'patient defendant' from all blame or punishment. In practice, patients are not keen on being labelled as 'insane', whether or not it attaches to a 'not guilty' verdict, particularly as incarceration in a hospital on a restriction order is often regarded by those with either previous experience or good inside knowledge as substantially less preferable to a prison sentence.

Diminished Responsibility

The partial defence of diminished responsibility was introduced for the first time in England by section 2 Homicide Act 1957, with the express purpose of mitigating the effects of the death penalty for the mentally disordered. It is now the preferred and commonest route for those whose mental state is considered to be relevant to the charge of murder. Yet it is a defence which, almost half a century after its introduction, is diminishing in its applicability[69] and receives virtually universal condemnation from those psychiatrists who are called upon to give evidence. Effectively, it exists only to provide the courts with the flexibility provided by the wide range of sentencing options available following a conviction for manslaughter, in contrast to the inflexible mandatory penalty for murder. The Law Commission has recommended that the defence should reduce a charge of Murder 1 to Murder 2 but, strangely, not to Manslaughter.[70] The criterion for the defence, the accused being of 'such abnormality of mind as substantially impaired his mental responsibility for his acts or omissions in doing or being a party to the killing', is arguably wide enough to cover socially unacceptable behaviour during bouts of irritability brought on by a head cold, but the evidential proof necessary to

---

69. The partial defence is successful in fewer than 20 cases annually, compared with 70-85 cases in the 1980s.
70. Law Commission No 304, Para 5.112.

establish the defence causes profound difficulties for those forensic psychiatrists who do not feel qualified to make judgments on the moral dimension of 'responsibility'. Nevertheless, they are often invited by judges to express an opinion. There is, moreover, a temptation, to which some psychiatrists succumb, to pontificate on degrees of responsibility as if there existed a sliding scale of this essentially abstract moral phenomenon. It often comes down to 'well, how bad is this person, and how morally wrong in this instance?': terms of art having little meaning in the realms of forensic science. Thus the scene is set for a psychiatric protagonist to argue about a topic in court for which none of his colleagues would claim any expertise outside it!

Forensic psychiatrists agree that this is unseemly, bringing psychiatry into disrepute, if not ridicule. They are agreed that, if the mandatory life sentence were abolished, to be replaced by a range of penalties for murder as flexible as that for ordinary manslaughter, these sometimes farcical situations would be avoided. The types of case in which psychiatrists experience most unease are those where ascertainment of mental abnormality, either transient or chronic, is feasible, but in which lawyers, quite frequently, hope for a helpful quota of 'emotional instability' to be dug out of the psyche. How far a psychiatrist is willing to go in support of a claim of diminished responsibility may owe more to his or her own moral judgment on the imputed wickedness of the defendant than to psychiatric training or medical knowledge.

The case law on section 2 Homicide Act 1957 is, moreover, jurisprudentially unedifying. After the abolition of the death penalty in 1965/1969,[71] the *raison d'être* of this defence to murder ceased to exist, save for the desire of some to avoid the stigma of a conviction for murder and the consequent sentence of life imprisonment. If it retains an instrumental function, it is to enable avoidance of the mandatory sentence of 'life' for murder that has replaced the mandatory sentence of death. Juries might also be reluctant to convict those offenders whom they consider not to be morally reprehensible, if they did not have the option of the less stigmatising verdict of manslaughter upon which to fall back. The abused spouse, the 'mercy' killer as well as the person suffering from deluded schizophrenia—are they all to be labelled murderers? Of course, if the distinction between murder and manslaughter

---

71. The Act abolishing it in 1965 did not become permanent until 1969.

were to be abandoned and all unlawful killings subsumed within a general category of homicide, the problem of differential stigma based upon the offence of which the defendant stood convicted would be resolved.[72] In general, psychiatrists feel that the stigma attached to the verdict of murder would not be greatly lessened by any change in the court's discretion to sentence, and therefore they acknowledge the force of the argument for maintaining a lesser verdict for some cases. Their concern is to see psychiatrists removed from the forum of arguments for it.

The dissatisfaction in psychiatric circles with the partial defence of diminished responsibility is now mitigated by a revised version of section 2 Homicide Act 1957, as substituted by section 52 Coroners and Justice Act 2009 on the recommendation of the Law Commission. For the outmoded concept of an abnormality of mind, the psychiatrically acceptable notion of a 'recognised mental condition' is the replacement. This is grounded in a valid medical diagnosis linked to accepted classificatory systems, flexible enough to account for new and changed conditions. Section 52 sensibly modernises the law's attitude to mental disorders that prompt homicide, but at the same time reduces the existing flexibility in the statutory provision for diminished responsibility, adding to the clause two positive elements — first, 'substantial impairment' must relate to specified aspects of the accused's mental capacity; and second, 'abnormality' of mental functioning must provide an explanation for the accused's involvement in the killing and be a significant contributor in causing the victim's death. The section should provide, however, a clearer role for forensic psychiatrists and other medical expert witnesses. Parliament has wisely adopted the Law Commission's modernising proposals, save in one important respect.

The law on diminished responsibility makes no reference to age. Since the age of criminal responsibility is deplorably low at the age of ten, offenders under 18 can be convicted of murder. Only four percent of all homicides annually are committed by young people. Since children and adolescents may, and often do, lack the capacity either to understand the nature of their

---

72. As it is, offenders who kill children or elderly pedestrians whilst committing other road traffic offences, such as dangerous or drunken driving or driving without a licence or insurance, are regarded for the most part with greater opprobrium than those responsible for so-called 'mercy killings'.

conduct from a rational judgment or to control themselves, it was proposed that developmental immaturity should be included among those claiming diminished responsibility for unlawful killing. The official explanation for not including such a provision to safeguard the child or young person from a conviction of murder was that developmental immaturity was not a medical, but a social condition. The argument is linked to the age of criminal responsibility. So be it. That too needs to be studied in a review of homicide law. But we are of the opinion that emotional immaturity is not linked to any specific chronological age.

Infanticide

Infanticide is now used to cover cases of women who, in a wide range of situations, kill their babies as a result of circumstances that can include personality problems, difficulties in forging a relationship with the baby, failure to cope with social pressures, material and social deprivation, and poverty. It clearly covers a lot more than the effects of birth and lactation. Brenda Hoggett (now Lady Hale of Richmond) poses extra-judicially an incisive question:

> Should these amount to an excuse at all? If they should, why should they not apply to fathers? Or to other people who are driven to killing by the intolerable pressures of their surroundings, although unprovoked by the victims?[73]

An offence of criminal homicide would adequately cover the killing of children by their parents in situations of great stress, and those living under the strain of mental illness induced by the situation within the family, including mothers suffering from post-puerperal depression. Nor would there be a defence limited to killings during the first year of the child's life. The courts are able, within the existing law relating to offenders suffering from mental illness or disorder, to deal appropriately with those convicted of such criminal homicides in ways that meet both the needs of the offender for treatment by which the interests of the community are best protected. The Law Commission recommended that the offence of infanticide be retained unamended.[74]

---

73. Brenda Hoggett, *Mental Health Law* (3rd ed.) London (Sweet & Maxwell, 1990).
74. Law Com No 304, p.161, para 8.23. Section 57 Coroners and Justice Act 2009 has made a textual amendment to sub-sections 1(1) and (2) Infanticide Act 1938.

Provocation / Loss of Self-Control

The substance of the defence here is that the defendant has been provoked by the victim, thus reducing the crime of homicide from murder to manslaughter. The law, however, lays down strict preconditions before a jury can convict of the lesser offence of manslaughter. Section 3 Homicide Act 1957 restated the long-established rule of the common law, but with the addition of 'words spoken' to 'acts done'.

It is, however, unclear whether the defence of provocation (loss of self-control since 2009) is classified as a partial justification or a partial excuse. If the former, it accepts that the intentional killing (or causing of serious injury) was partially warranted. If the latter, a defence that operates as a partial excuse is based on the understanding that the killing was wrongful but that the accused was only partially to blame. The defence varies according to whether the criminal event is perceived as a partial justification, which concentrates on the deceased's wrongful action in provoking the homicide, whereas a partial excuse rests on the accused's loss of self-control. In the Northern Ireland case of *Winchester*, the observation of Lowry Lord Chief Justice that 'one has to consider in provocation cases the enormity of the crime, the gravity of the provocation (and here it was grave indeed) and the excusability of loss of control on the part of the accused'[75] would seem to endorse the defence as being a partial excuse.

What has long been regarded as the classic test of provocation was set out more than half a century ago by Devlin J in *Duffy*:

> Provocation is some act, or series of acts, done by the dead man to the accused, which would cause in the accused *a sudden and temporary loss of self-control*, (our italics) rendering the accused so subject to passion as to make him or her for the moment not master of his mind.[76]

Devlin's test, enunciated in the context of the common law, that spoke of the 'act, or series of acts, done by the dead man' was amplified by the Homicide Act 1957, section 3, by which words were to be treated as a spe-

---

75. *R v Winchester* [1978] NIJB, recited in *Lord Lowry: A Tribute, A selection of Lord Lowry's talks, lectures and judgments* (SLS Legal Publications, 2000) at p.117.
76. *R v Duffy* [1949] 1 All ER 932.

cies of 'act', recognising that a taunt or revelation, or indeed any instance of verbal aggression, can produce a reaction no less violent than a physical action: the human tongue is as aggressive as a mortal blow!

There have been critics of both the test set out in *Duffy* and of the statutory modification, particularly in those cases in which the provocation did not prompt immediate reaction, contemporaneous with a sudden and temporary loss of control. In other words, if there is a sufficient lapse in time between the provocative conduct and the passion cooling, such that the passion abates and the accused's self-control is restored, the defence is unavailable. This test barely accommodates the lapse of time between provocative behaviour and the reaction experienced by battered wives or partners. Modern authority still stresses the importance of the element of immediacy,[77] while treating persistently violent behaviour by the male, husband or father as a factor to be taken into account by the jury, rather than immediacy being itself a legal requirement. The Court of Appeal has adapted the immediacy test to accommodate 'battered woman syndrome' alone or in conjunction with a personality disorder, on the ground that the reasonable person with those characteristics might have reacted suddenly to provocative conduct although the provocation had built up over a period of time.

The test of the reasonable man has itself given rise to discussion and legal debate. The courts have generally emphasised that the objective approach is to evaluate the act of the accused by reference to a standard form of conduct. Thus in the Privy Council case of *Philips*,[78] it was held that the reaction of the accused must not exceed the reaction of a reasonable man. In much earlier cases such as *Mancini*[79] the law required an element of proportionality between the provocative act and the reaction of the accused: like should be met with like. Thus it was stated that a provocative blow could not be met by the use of a deadly weapon. Resort to a firearm was disproportionate to a blow by the fist. Subsequently this has been modified, post-1957, by holding that a reasonable retaliation is not required as a matter of law, but, as with the immediacy factor, it is to be taken into account by the jury. But the legal

77. *R v Thornton (No 1)* [1992] 1 All ER 306; *R v Thornton (No 2)* [1996] 1 WLR 1174; *R v Ahlu-walia* [1992] 4 All ER 889; *R v Savage* [1991] 3 NZLR 155.
78. *Philips v The Queen* [1969] 2 AC 130.
79. *Mancini v DPP* [1942] AC 1.

test, that the reaction of the defendant to the provocation must not exceed what would have been the reaction of the reasonable man, remains intact.

Proportionality is, therefore, the guide to the question of what is 'reasonable' retaliation. In *Philips* counsel for the appellant[80] contended that once a reasonable man loses self-control as a result of the provocative conduct of the deceased, he ceases to be a reasonable man and cannot be accountable on those terms. Lord Diplock, stating the opinion of the Privy Council, firmly rejected that argument, stating that the submission was 'based on a premise that loss of self-control is not a matter of degree but is absolute; there is no alternative between the detachment and going berserk. This is false. The average man reacts to provocation according to its degree'.

The judicial view reflects the supposed common experience of members of the judiciary alone. Loss of temper is typically moderated by the degree of provocation experienced. But is it the common experience that there is invariably proportionality? The reaction to provocative behaviour may depend on the accused having, as in cases involving battered woman syndrome, a personality disorder that prompts a disproportionate response. The excessive retaliation thereby generated should not automatically disqualify the accused from claiming an excuse. A psychological approach can have special application with regard to the reliability of eyewitness testimony and the mental state of the defendant. Medical evidence may be used to show that a witness, including of course the defendant, suffers from such disease or defect or abnormality of mind that it affects the reliability of the evidence. Such evidence is not confined to a general opinion of the unreliability of the witness but may display all the characteristics of mental ill-health, not only in the foundation and reasons for the diagnosis, but also the extent to which the credibility of the witness is affected.[81]

There is a further dimension to the issue related not to mental health but to cultural factors. Those lacking in linguistic skills may react to provocative words physically rather than verbally, such that the frustrated response to a comment that is perceived to be offensive or insulting is the instant infliction of pain by way of physical injury, rather than by means of a stinging verbal riposte. Here we are once more in the territory of the 'reasonable man' and

---

80. And co-author of this book, Louis Blom-Cooper.
81. *Toohey v Metropolitan Police Commissioner* [1965] AC 595.

all its attendant temptations to resort to cultural relativism. Ought those who more readily speak with their fists than their tongues to enjoy the potential licence which stems from it? We doubt it, notwithstanding that these are the 'weaker brethren' whom Holmes had in mind.

If the defence of provocation was to be retained — and not all commentators agreed that it should be[82] — both the statute and the case law were ripe for review. If the penalty for murder were to cease to be the mandatory sentence of life imprisonment, all cases of provocation would readily be accommodated at the sentencing stage, where partial justification and/or partial excuse for criminal homicide could be invoked. Moral innocence is as much a concern of the law as moral culpability. Lord Hoffmann in *Smith (Morgan)* thought that the abolition of the mandatory sentence would not necessarily render the defence of provocation superfluous. He said:

> It might be thought desirable to allow the jury to decide whether provocation was a reason why the killer did not deserve the degree of moral condemnation and severity of sentence associated with the crime of murder.

We profoundly disagree. A jury verdict of criminal homicide would suffice to condemn the killer morally, and the 'severity of sentence' is emphatically not a task for the jury, not even one to be shared with the trial judge.

Judges have struggled manfully, and we use that gender word advisedly, to indicate an absence of a feminist judicial approach in a topic heavily focused on domestic killings, to interpret and apply the notion of 'lost self-control' as a description of the necessary state of mind of the killer. The Homicide Act 1957 effectively made three changes to the existing law which, up to that date, had been primarily concerned with the extent to which a delay between the provocation and the loss of self-control undermined a defence of provocation. The element of immediacy or suddenness in the temporary loss of self-control, rendering the killer no longer master of his mind, hardly resembles the stored-up aggression that afflicts discord between spouses or domestic partners.

---

82. J Horder, *Provocation and Responsibility* (Oxford University Press, 1992) Ch9. See also McAuley and McCutcheon *supra* footnote 22 at p.885.

The changes that were to disfigure the already confused law of provocation (unique as a defence to murder) were that:

(a) henceforward words alone (or in combination with actions) could amount to provocation;

(b) the trial court could no longer rule that, as a matter of law, something was not capable of amounting to provocation — that issue had to be left to the jury, however implausible the claim might appear to be. Only in 2006 in *Coutts*[83] did the House of Lords finally conclude that trial judges were bound to leave the alternative verdict of manslaughter, even if the parties indicated that they were not conducting their cases on other than the basis of a verdict of murder or an acquittal; and that

(c) judges were also no longer able to dictate to the jury what were and were not the characteristics of the reasonable man.

The problem of the 'reasonable man' arose in the case of *Luc Thiet Thuan*[84] that came to the Judicial Committee of the Privy Council from Hong Kong, thereby introducing an element of confusion in the application of the doctrine of precedent (as we shall see). The 'reasonable man' test appears to provide a single objective standard against which the conduct of the defendant is to be judged. But defendants and their legal representatives were not slow in attempting to broaden out the statutory definition in order to escape the inflexibility of the mandatory life sentence.

The House of Lords in *DPP v Camplin*[85] considered the issue of provocation in the case of a defendant who was aged 15. How was the 'reasonable man' test to be applied in such circumstances? Lord Diplock said that the 'reasonable man' is 'an ordinary person of either sex, not exceptionally excitable or pugnacious, but possessed of such powers of self-control as everyone is entitled to expect that his fellow citizens will exercise in society as it is today'.

---

83. [2006] UKHL 39.
84. [1997] AC 131.
85. [1978] AC 705.

He also gave a model direction for juries, in which he indicated that trial judges should explain that the 'reasonable man' 'is a person having the power of self-control to be expected of an ordinary person of the sex and age of the accused, but in other respects sharing such of the accused's characteristics as they think would affect the gravity of the provocation to him'.

The decision in *Camplin* led, inevitably, to much argument in the course of trials as to what (alleged) characteristics of the defendant the judge should permit the jury to consider as coming within Lord Diplock's model direction. Inevitably, because each case was fact-specific, it was not easy to discern clearly what the law was.

The Privy Council considered the issue of provocation in *Luc Thiet Thuan*. At his trial for murder the defendant had relied on the defences of diminished responsibility and provocation. Medical evidence called on his behalf showed that he suffered from brain damage and was prone to respond to minor provocation by losing his self-control and acting explosively. The jury was directed by the judge that this medical evidence was not relevant to the defence of provocation. Lord Goff of Chieveley, having noted that the defendant's mental infirmity, if it had been the subject of taunts by the deceased, might be taken into account in relation to the gravity of the provocation, went on to say:

> But this is a far cry from the defendant's submission that the mental infirmity of a defendant impairing his power of self-control should, as such, be attributed to the reasonable man for the purposes of the objective test.

The majority upheld the trial judge. Lord Steyn's dissent exposed the injustice of the objective test.

The House of Lords in *Smith (Morgan)* rejected that approach by three votes to two. The view of the majority was that the standard of self-control required by the common law and by statute was not the constant standard of the person having and exercising ordinary self-control. The jury should apply a more flexible standard, that of the control to be expected of the particular individual. Accordingly, the question that the jury should ask themselves was whether the defendant 'exercised the degree of self-control to be expected of someone in his situation'. Lord Hoffmann said that the jury was 'to determine not merely whether the behaviour of the accused complied with some legal standard but could determine for themselves what the standard in the particular case should be'.

He went on to say: 'The jury must think that the circumstances are such as to make the loss of self-control sufficiently excusable to reduce the gravity of the offence from murder to manslaughter. This is entirely a question for the jury'.

That approach was clearly at odds with the decision of the Privy Council in *Luc Thiet Thuan*, which had the vigorous support in *Smith (Morgan)* of the minority of Lords Hobhouse and Millett.

Following the decision in *Smith (Morgan)*, many judges left the issue of provocation to juries in the terms to which Lord Hoffmann had referred. That meant that there was no objective standard that applied in every case: the standard would vary according to the facts of the individual case and the individual accused. But *Smith (Morgan)* came in for some fierce criticism, from both academics and practitioners.

In *Attorney-General for Jersey v Holley*,[86] nine members of the Privy Council, all serving Law Lords, sat to determine the appeal. Following a retrial, Holley, who was a chronic alcoholic, was convicted of murder. He admitted killing his girlfriend with an axe; the sole issue for the Jurats (a system of magistrates elected for life and peculiar to the Channel Islands) had been that of provocation. The Deputy Bailiff instructed the Jurats that the fact that a person is drunk or under the influence of alcohol at the time of the killing and, as a result, is provoked more easily than if he were sober, was not something that could be taken into account in his favour. In allowing Holley's appeal against his conviction for murder, the Jersey Court of Appeal held that the Deputy Bailiff had been wrong: he should have directed the Jurats that they could take into account the fact that he was suffering from chronic alcoholism when considering whether, in their opinion, having regard to the actual provocation and their view of its gravity, a person having ordinary powers of self-control would have done what Holley did.

The Board of the Privy Council was split six to three. The minority view (Lord Bingham of Cornhill, Lord Hoffmann and Lord Carswell) was that

---

86. [2005] 2 AC 580.

the law had been correctly stated in *Smith (Morgan)* and that the decision of the Jersey Court of Appeal had been correct. The judgment of the majority (Lord Nicholls of Birkenhead, Lord Hope of Craighead, Lord Scott of Foscote, Lord Rodger of Earlsferry, Lord Walker of Gestingthorpe and Baroness Hale of Richmond) was given by Lord Nicholls, and drew attention to the direct conflict between the decision of the Board in *Luc Thiet Thuan* and that of the House of Lords in *Smith (Morgan)*. The majority held that the decision in *Luc Thiet Thuan* was correct and that, accordingly, the appeal should be allowed. The majority held that the Deputy Bailiff's direction to the Jurats had been, if anything, unduly favourable to Holley. He had directed the Jurats to consider 'whether there was anything about the defendant's own particular characteristics which reduced his powers of self-control and, if there were, whether it provided a sufficient excuse for what he did'. The majority opinion in *Holley*, rejecting as erroneous the law as explained in *Smith (Morgan)*, is summarised clearly in paragraph 22 of the judgment. It reads, in part, as follows:

> But their Lordships consider that there is one compelling, overriding reason why this view [that of the majority in *Smith (Morgan)*] cannot be regarded as an accurate statement of English law. It is this. The law of homicide is a highly sensitive and highly controversial area of the criminal law. In 1957 Parliament altered the common law relating to provocation and declared what the law on this subject should thenceforth be. In these circumstances it is not open to judges now to change ('develop') the common law and thereby depart from the law as declared by Parliament. However much the contrary is asserted, the majority view [in *Smith (Morgan)*] does represent a departure from the law as declared in section 3 Homicide Act 1957. It involves a significant relaxation of the uniform, objective standard adopted by Parliament. Under the statute the sufficiency of the provocation ('whether the provocation was enough to make a reasonable man do as [the defendant] did') is to be judged by one standard, not a standard which varies from defendant to defendant. Whether the provocative act or words and the defendant's response met the 'ordinary person' standard prescribed by the statute is the question the jury must consider, not the altogether looser question of whether, having regard to all the circumstances, the jury consider the loss of self-control was sufficiently excusable. The statute does not leave

the jury free to set whatever standard they consider appropriate in the circumstances by which to judge whether the defendant's conduct is 'excusable'.

The decision in *Holley* presented a peculiar problem for courts in England and Wales. Should they adhere to the strict rules of precedent and continue to follow the House of Lords in *Smith (Morgan)*, or should they accept the judgment of the Privy Council (which made plain that the law of England and the law of Jersey were the same)? The answer was provided in *R v James, R v Karimi*[87] by a five-judge constitution of the Court of Appeal (Criminal Division), presided over by the Lord Chief Justice. Giving the reserved judgment of the Court, Lord Phillips of Worth Matravers said that there were exceptional reasons that justified the Court of Appeal (Criminal Division) following the majority decision of the Privy Council in *Holley*. And the Law Commission, in recommending a modified version of provocation, would favour the approach of the majority in *Holley*.

It is unsurprising that the topic of the defences to murder should have been on the agenda of public discussion, given the number of cases involving battered women, householders defending their premises against intruders, and the use of guns and knives. But there is generally a difference in approach, sometimes reflected in a tension between Government and politicians on the one hand, and practitioners and expert observers on the other, on the issues of reform. In this instance, Ministers are sensitive to what they perceive to be the preferences of the electorate, the 'consumers', as it were, who have a choice between political leaders and their policies no less than between different supermarkets and the goods on their shelves. The practitioners of the law, who have an interest both in its utility and in its fitness for purpose, meanwhile share some common ground with those who note its operation from a distance and may reflect upon its wider social and moral perspectives.

We would argue that the task of considering the defences to murder in isolation from the substantive law, while of great importance, is to be given the wrong brief. That is a proposition which can be demonstrated by reflecting that the distinction between murder and other unlawful homicides is essentially artificial. 'Murder' is a term used in common parlance,[88] often

---

87. [2006] QB 588.
88. Newspapers almost invariably report homicides as if they were already defined as murders.

without much discrimination, to describe incidents of violent and unnatural death to which social opprobrium is attached, notwithstanding that a court may conclude at trial (if any) that the proper verdict under the law is one of manslaughter. Labelling, either at the moment of reporting the homicidal event or before the jury's verdict, is misleading to the general public, and hence cannot be a fair procedure. 'Murder' is essentially a term of art; a social or cultural construct having its origins in the intellectual patchwork of the common law, responsive to the currents of opinion but without any overarching logic—still less philosophy—that has evolved over the centuries. In no way can it be regarded as a phenomenon *sui generis*, since the boundary between murder and manslaughter shifts as readily as the precise limits of a sand bar under the influence of wind and tide.

The defences that may be employed to identify the crime as manslaughter rather than murder are as chimærical in character as the attempts to create categories of murder to which may be attached a range of differential penalties. The question that must, therefore, be posed is whether it is profitable to expend further intellectual energy and costly resources in pursuit of the *ignis fatuus* of their perfection. Intellectual energy and fresh, complicated directions to juries will now have to be expended on provocation's successor, the partial defence of loss of self-control.

Were the mandatory penalty of life imprisonment for murder to be abolished, the incentive for defendants to persuade the courts that if they plead guilty it is to manslaughter and not to murder would cease to exist, and with it the problems of interpretation of motives and states of mind that presently demand so much forensic attention. That incentive removed, the existence of a common sentencing tariff to reflect the proportionality of penalty to the specific nature of the criminal event would make plain the underlying intellectual imperative: the establishment of a single offence of criminal homicide.

Loss of Self-Control

For years now the law of provocation, as a partial defence to a charge of murder, has exhibited a confusing mixture of judge-made law and legislative overlap, rendered more confounded where words said, in addition to things done, could be adduced as evidence that the defendant was provoked

to lose his or her self-control. By contrast to this mish-mash of human mis-
conduct and misplaced legalism (available only in the law of homicide), if
a defendant was not provoked, even though he or she killed the victim by
reason of a substantial fear or threat of violence emanating from the victim,
the courts declined to extend the defence. Both demonstrable deficiencies
in the law appear to be remedied in a fasciculus of 15 sub-sections and eight
sub-sub-sections in sections 54 and 55 Coroners and Justice Act 2009. But
will this new partial defence to murder clear up the 'mess', or is the mess
made messier? By paraphrasing the Parliamentary draftsman's handiwork,
we recognise the danger of compression and hence imprecision, not to say
inaccuracy. But if that is the right conclusion to be drawn from what we
are about to say, what price will juries have to pay for the judicial directions
they will receive?

The two sections in the Coroners and Justice Act 2009 introduce a two-
step (or should we say, two-shot) qualification for the defence of loss of
self-control. First, the loss of self-control must be fired by a 'qualifying trigger' (so says the headnote to section 55). The trigger is itself threefold in form:

(i) the loss of self-control must be attributable to fear of serious violence
(either from the victim against the defendant or another identified person); or

(ii) the loss of self-control was attributable to things done or said which constituted circumstances of an extremely grave character and caused the
defendant to have a justifiable sense of being seriously wronged;

(iii) the loss of self-control was attributable to a combination of (i) and (ii).

If the qualifying trigger applies, the defendant must have displayed a
normal degree of tolerance and self-restraint and in the defendant's circumstances, a person of the defendant's sex and age might have reacted in
the same or in a similar way to the defendant. Whoo! Reminiscent of the
interminable argument that raged over the reasonable man or woman in
Holley: at last, a Pyrrhic victory for the minority Law Lords — Bingham,
Hoffmann and Carswell.

There is a sting (perhaps three stings) in the tail of legitimising loss of self-control, ranging from justifiable anger to acts or threats of violence. First, a defendant's action must not stem from a 'considered desire for revenge'. Second, it matters not whether the loss of self-control was sudden: thus a building of accumulating circumstances of extremely grave character or a growing, justifiable sense of being seriously wronged may suffice to 'trigger' the loss of self-control. Third, bizarrely, section 55(6)(c) provides—we quote verbatim—'the fact that a thing done or said constituted sexual infidelity is to be disqualified'. A peer, during the Parliamentary passage of the Bill, described the sub-sub-section as 'outstandingly obnoxious'; he could hardly be accused of speaking hyperbolically.

What now will juries make of all this jumble of verbiage? The Judicial Studies Board will no doubt be framing specimen forms of direction for hard-pressed Crown Court judges seeking to navigate through this new legislative minefield, with the hope of clarity of expression and ease of translating legalese into simple language for weighing up the evidential material.

A tentative conclusion only can be drawn. The new defence of loss of self-control would seem designed to limit the occasions when retaliatory action by a killer of a fellow human being will reduce the crime of murder to manslaughter. Will more convictions for murder bring greater safety to potential victims? Even if it were to assume that much, is the retained complexity of the law, with the inevitable aggravation of a whole new body of case law from appellate courts, worthwhile? Even if there is an overall justice in more convictions for murder than at present, we think not. Justifiable loss of self-control, tightly drawn, should either be a complete defence or, if unjustified, the conduct can properly be a mitigation of the sentence of the court of trial, according to the circumstances of each specific case.

CHAPTER 5

SECONDARY LIABILITY IN HOMICIDE

If our proposal for a single offence of unlawful killing (or criminal homicide) is sound and is generally acceptable, what should be the liability of those who participate jointly in lethal acts by private gangs, of which the following is a recent and all too commonplace example?[1] A 16-year-old schoolboy was stabbed to death in broad daylight in a busy street in west London. Six people stood trial at the Old Bailey for his murder. One defendant was acquitted; two were convicted of murder and three of manslaughter. All of the defendants were teenagers (one of them was only 13 at the time of the killing). In prosecuting the six defendants, the Crown was unable to identify (as is a feature of group criminality) which of the defendants had inflicted the single stab wound that proved fatal. Hence the Crown had to rely on the law relating to secondary liability. If the current law of murder is a 'mess', so too, for similar reasons of legal history, is the current law of secondary liability.

The unsatisfactory state of the law is ascribed to the piecemeal development of the common law. From its earliest days our criminal law has recognised that a person may be convicted of committing a crime that has been committed by someone else. The only relevant statute is 150 years old. Section 8 Accessories and Abettors Act 1861 (as amended by the Criminal Law Act 1977) did not itself create any offence, but prescribed the procedure and punishment of secondary parties — the aiders and abettors, counsellors and procurers who were to be indicted, tried and, if convicted, punished as principal offenders. A spate of decisions in the courts in recent years — two of them from the House of Lords[2] — have done little or nothing to clarify the law or to simplify the task of juriesin joint venture homicides.[3]

---

1. *R v Yemoh and others* [2009] EWCA Crim 930 and 1775.
2. *R v Powell and English* [1999] 1 AC 1 and *R v Rahman* [2008] UKHL 45.
3. In the Serious Crime Act 2007, Parliament created certain new offences of complicity in crime. By contrast to the secondary liability for joint ventures in crime, these new offences

Thus Professor David Ormerod (a member of the Law Commission) in the 12th edition of Smith and Hogan's *Criminal Law*[4] states that 'the current law of secondary liability is unsatisfactorily complex and displays many of the characteristic weaknesses of a common law that has been allowed to develop in a pragmatic and unprincipled way'. Professor Ashworth in his *Principles of Criminal Law*[5] describes the law as 'replete with uncertainties and conflict. It betrays the worst features of the common law: what some would regard as flexibility appears here as a succession of opportunistic decisions by the courts, often extending the law, and resulting in a body of jurisprudence that has little coherence'. Other academic writers adopt a different approach, branding the criminal liability of secondary participants as a 'special case of complicitous participation and not merely a subspecies of assistance and encouragement'.[6] The condemnation of the law has not been confined to academic writers. Mr Justice Kirby, in a dissenting judgment in the High Court of Australia,[7] was no less critical. He concluded that the result of the common law in the 21st century

> is unconceptual and unduly complex. It is also unjust. It casts the net of liability for murder too widely. It is insufficiently discriminating in respect of individual responsibility. It catches potentially weak and vulnerable secondary offenders and, by a legal rule, attributes to them liability that may properly belong only to the principal offender. Effectively at the option of prosecutors, it fixes people with very serious criminal liability because they were in the wrong place at the wrong time in the wrong company.

Much of the unsatisfactory state of the current case-law stems from adherence to the murder-manslaughter dichotomy in homicide. The insistence on *mens rea* (either as intention, or as a modified form of knowledge, recklessness or gross negligence) is the basis of the joint liability. Our proposal

---

are inchoate and thus occur and are committed quite independently of whether or not the 'principal' goes on the commit the anticipated offence.

4. Ch8 p.178.
5. *Principles of Criminal Law* (6th edition, 2009).
6. A Simester and R Sullivan, *Criminal Law: Theory and Doctrine*, Hart Publishing, (2nd ed., 2003) p.221.
7. *Clayton v R* [2006] 231 ALR 500 (para 120).

to be rid of murder and manslaughter and to render *mens rea* unnecessary as an ingredient of the defendant's knowledge of the criminality leaves the question of secondary liability for unlawful killing (or criminal homicide) to be answered. These two features are the product of the law's aim to restore greater concurrence between moral culpability and criminal responsibility as much as to reduce anomalies, disparities, inconsistencies or lack of symmetry. Our aim is, of course, to split off moral culpability to the sentencing process. That is our approach to secondary liability. We are also conscious that the present law procedurally favours the prosecution. In instances involving multiple offenders acting to some extent in concert, it eases the prosecutor's path to the securing of a conviction of *all* participants in a criminal event, without the irksome task of differentiation between them, or troublesome attention to what the prosecutor has actually to prove from the acts of each of the individuals accused. An acquittal at trial is no remedy to having been faced with a criminal prosecution. While ensuring that secondary liability for unlawful killing should remain, courts should avoid any trumping of the supportive bystander card by the desire for criminalisation of gang activity.

Given our formula of stripping out the moral culpability from criminal responsibility, we have searched for a simple proposition that will fit the case of multiple participants involved in a homicidal event. We have accepted (with appropriate changes adapted to meet our formula) the clear statement of legal principle laid down by Lord Lane CJ in *R v Hyde*:[8]

> If D realises (without necessarily agreeing to such conduct) that P may unlawfully kill some other person, but nevertheless continues to participate fully with P in that venture, that will amount to sufficient criminal responsibility for D to be guilty of unlawful killing, so long as P does commit the act of unlawful killing, by whatever method, in the course or furtherance of the joint venture.

It is our view that D has in those circumstances lent himself actively to the joint venture and has thereby provided assistance and encouragement to P in carrying out the joint venture which D realises may involve an unlawful

---

8. [1991] 1 QB 134, followed by the High Court of Australia in *McAuliffe v R* (1995) HCA 37, para 18, and supported by Kirby J in *Clayton v R* [2006] 231 ALR 500 at para 126—a formula correlating 'legal responsibility and moral culpability' which we would wish to see separated.

killing. If there are circumstances arising out of the homicidal event that distinguish D from other participants in the joint venture, that can readily be reflected in the penalty to be proportionately imposed.

We are comforted in this proposal by what Lord Scott of Foscote said in a short judgment in *R v Rahman and others* (a case of joint liability):[9]

> Since the abolition of the death penalty and the introduction of specified minimum terms of imprisonment is passed [under the classification of tariff lengths in sched-ule 21 of the Criminal Justice Act 2003] *the degree of culpability and responsibility of those convicted of an unlawful killing* [our italics] can be reflected by the length of the specified minimum terms. This constitutes, in my opinion, a far more satisfactory means of dealing with those whose liability for the unlawful killing is secondary, than a rule which will exonerate them from criminal liability on the ground that they did not know or suspect that the primary party was carrying a particular weapon that delivered the blow.

Lord Scott's *obiter dicta* deserve to be put alongside the wise words of Lord Kilbrandon in *Hyam*: the route to sensible reform of the law of murder is beginning to be mapped out!

---

9.   [2008] UKHL 45, para 32.

CHAPTER 6

FIATS, FORDS AND FORESIGHT: EXCURSIONS TO THE HOUSE OF LORDS FROM WOOLMINGTON TO SMITH

Down the centuries trials of murder have been for the most part mundane affairs (particularly so since the abolition of the death penalty in 1965) and soon concluded, affecting public consciousness only briefly. Few trials for murder have any effect upon the law. The forensic process, like tranquil water, may be briefly ruffled by what is often no more than a passing interest or notoriety. Yet there are moments in the history of criminal justice when, to the surprise of many, that calm is subjected to sudden and unexpected turbulence.[1] It is as if something large and solid has been suddenly heaved into the still waters of the judicial pond.

A Country Tragedy

Among those who have stood trial for murder, generally in previous ignorance of the labyrinthine arguments that could accompany its prosecution, was Reginald Woolmington, a 22-year-old Dorset farm labourer of hitherto good character. In 1935, on no less a day for lovers than February 14, he was convicted at Bristol Assizes of the murder by shooting on 10 December 1934 of his 17-year-old wife who, having deserted him, had returned to her mother. It would seem that he had loved her dearly. The crime itself had the classic ingredients of young love, despair and death: a pastoral tragedy that might have come from the pen of Thomas Hardy. The story was to move from the

---

1.   J D Caswell KC, who defended Reginald Woolmington, wrote: 'One of the most fascinating aspects of a barrister's life is the way in which the unforeseen can suddenly shatter even the best-grounded expectations'. *A Lance for Liberty*, London (George G Harrap & Co Ltd, 1961) at p.86.

sparse surroundings of a humble cottage, and by way of two Assize courts and the Court of Criminal Appeal, to the House of Lords itself.

The name of Woolmington has been associated ever since with the image of 'one golden thread' to be seen running through the fabric of the criminal law affirming the burden of proof to lie exclusively upon the prosecution.[2] In his summing up, Mr Justice Swift had addressed the jury on the law, employing language having perhaps more in common with the King James Bible than that of the mid-1930s: 'for the law presumeth the fact to have been founded in malice, unless the contrary appeareth'.[3]

So much for Woolmington's claim that the gun had gone off by accident. Violet was dead and the gun had been discharged maliciously. Given the facts of the case and the judge's directions to the jury on the law, a conviction followed by a hanging would in its time have been seen as entirely predictable and wholly unexceptional. Save, that is, for the decision of the House of Lords that it was not for Woolmington to persuade the jury that Violet Woolmington's death had been an accident, but for the prosecutor to prove beyond reasonable doubt that it was otherwise.[4] Woolmington's acquittal was, in the circumstances, an astounding result, not least since the summing up by the trial judge, Mr Justice Swift, was impeccably in accord with what was at the time enshrined not only in the pages of *Archbold's Criminal Pleading and Practice* but in the words of Sir John Foster as 'the law of this country for all time since we had law'.[5] In that Woolmington was charged not with manslaughter but with murder, the prosecution would not have needed to be concerned with such issues as accident or recklessness, but only with dem-

---

2. The 'golden thread' has subsequently been much restricted by the increasing number of statutory provisions for strict liability in criminal cases, but not in murder. The issue of such exceptions to the presumption of innocence is discussed at length by Sir Anthony Hooper in 'The Golden Thread', Chapter 33 of *The Judicial House of Lords, 1876–2009*, ed. Blom-Cooper, Dickson and Drewry (Oxford University Press, 2009); See also: *R v Lambert* [2002] 2 AC 545.

3. Foster, 'Introduction to the Discourse on Homicide' in *Crown Law* (Clarendon Press, 1762) at p.235.

4. *Woolmington v DPP* [1935] AC 462. The Attorney's *fiat* in 1960 that allowed *Smith* to go the Lords would be the last, the requirement being abolished by the Administration of Justice Act 1960. Swift, who had tried Woolmington at Bristol, had a reputation for great experience in criminal trials. See Edgar Fay, *The Life of Mr Justice Swift*, Foreword by Viscount Sankey (Methuen, 1939).

5. Foster, *op cit.*

onstrating an intention on his part either to kill or to do his estranged wife serious harm. Given all the circumstances immediately preceding his visit to the cottage — his taking of a shotgun, sawing off the barrels and then loading it with two cartridges — it can be readily understood that a jury might well come to the not unreasonable conclusion that these actions were not what might normally be taken as indicative of uxorial tenderness but rather, the contrary. Yet there were only two witnesses of what actually took place in the room: Woolmington himself, and his wife Violet who, being dead, was not available at the trial (and even if she had survived the shooting, she might not have been able, any more than the jury, to say what was going on in Woolmington's head). What was in his mind, that is to say, what did he *intend* to achieve when he inflicted on a girl of seventeen what by any standard would have been a terrifying experience to most people, would be a matter for the Crown to prove. But at the trial the jury were directed that since he had maintained that her death was not intended but was accidental, the burden of demonstrating that lay upon him. Things did not look at all good for the prisoner in the dock. He had, for ill-measure, left a distressed but highly incriminating note speaking, among other things of having 'no more cartridges, only one for her and one for me'. His counsel went so far as to write later: 'if ever a man did his best to talk himself on to the scaffold it was Reginald Woolmington'.[6]

When Mr Casswell appeared before the Court of Criminal Appeal in March 1935 seeking leave to appeal, the court was presided over, not by the Lord Chief Justice, Lord Hewart, who was ill, but by the senior King's Bench judge, the 83-year-old Mr Justice Avory. Hewart was subsequently regarded as having been one of the most unsatisfactory incumbents of that judicial office, not least for his rude and disputatious manners in court. But any relief at his absence would have been rapidly dispelled by the presence of Avory, an equally disagreeable personality. Casswell sought to challenge the authority of *Archbold*[7] in which the passage from Foster's *Crown Law* was reproduced. In vain did he argue that the trial judge ought to have told the jury that if they entertained any reasonable doubt about the evidence they should have acquitted or convicted the defendant of manslaughter. Avory

6. Casswell. *op cit*. at p.90.
7. As a *vade mecum* for practitioners *Archbold* had long enjoyed a status of immense authority.

would have none of it, maintaining that if Mr Justice Swift had indeed given such a direction the jury would have 'inevitably' convicted him!

The Attorney-General was Sir Thomas Inskip[8] and it was he who was to grant the historic *fiat* allowing Woolmington's final appeal to the Lords. Shortly before the hearing, the Lord Chancellor, Lord Sankey, had indicated that the defence should be led by leading counsel.[9] Unlike Avory, he must have been persuaded that there was at least an argument to be heard upon its merits. The remainder of the court was comprised of the Lord Chief Justice, Lord Hewart, now back from sick leave, together with Lords Atkin, Tomlin and Wright. While it must remain speculative, it may well be that in the course of the hearing the remarks of Atkin, frequently following upon those of Hewart, suggested an element of dissent among their Lordships. In any event, the powerful judgment given by Sankey suggests that the innate hostility to defendants so often manifested in the comments of both Hewart[10] and Avory did not prevail over a rational interpretation of the law. Politics was not absent from this climate: Inskip was a member of the Government in the capacity of a law officer as was the Lord Chancellor, and Hewart, though Lord Chief Justice, was essentially a politician *manqué*.[11] Yet neither the predominantly conservative attitudes of the senior judiciary nor the fact that the profession of the law was socially insulated from the world of humbler people was to determine the eventual outcome. Woolmington's case, a triumph for justice, was ultimately a triumph of reason and critical thought over a slavish adherence to precedent.

To many, perhaps most people, then and now, Woolmington's behaviour would have appeared reckless, to say the least. Loaded sawn-off shotguns are dangerous things. However, he had been indicted not for manslaughter, but for murder, and the question of such an alternative verdict did not arise

8. Inskip was a Conservative politician who had held ministerial office until he succeeded Lord Hewart as Lord Chief Justice in 1940. He was succeeded by Lord Goddard in 1946. As Attorney he conducted the last trial of a peer in the House of Lords.

9. The choice was to light upon Terence O'Connor KC.

10. See for example the manner in which Hewart dismissed the appeal of George Stoner, also in 1935. See: Sir David Napley, *Murder at the Villa Madeira* (Weidenfeld and Nicholson, 1988). On occasion, both Hewart and Avory gave the impression that they held criminal appeals to be a complete waste of time.

11. His appointment as Lord Chief Justice was very much the outcome of a behind the scenes political deal.

either at the trial or subsequently. His defence, such as it was, was that of accident, the trial judge ruling that the burden of its proof rested upon him alone. By its resonant judgment the verdict of the House of Lords set him free in every sense of the term. Almost three decades later the Homicide Act 1957, by extending the partial defence of provocation to words as well as deeds, might have assisted him.

It may be one thing to infer criminal guilt from the behaviour of the 'reasonable man' but quite another to do so from that of the conduct of one from whose mind overpowering emotion has driven out both reason and restraint. Yet young men of twenty-one are prey to be governed at times of stress less by reason than by passion. Not least is it important to be reminded that it is impossible to infer, other than with varying degrees of confidence, what has actually transpired in those generally brief moments within which the act of homicide occurs. In the days when the hangman plied his ancient trade the law could not mitigate the penalty for one convicted of murder. Only the equally archaic device of the Royal Prerogative of Mercy could render his services redundant and allow the executive to ensure an appropriate alternative, something by no means a certainty, even when it came by way of a recommendation from the jury.

Death on Another Winter Day

On Friday 8 December 1944, the Second World War was in its concluding stages. The battle on the mainland of Europe still raged, but the City of London, though devastated by fire and bombs in the 'blitz' of 1940-41 had returned to some semblance of normality. Many of its shops were open again, including a jewellers at 23 Birchin Lane which in the early afternoon was to be the scene of a 'smash and grab' robbery in which over £2,500 worth of goods were to be stolen. That, in 1944, was a very substantial haul indeed but it was trivial matter compared with the appalling human cost of the event that was to follow. By some strange twist of fate, this crime, and its prosecution were to be mirrored, though with a different outcome, 16 years later in the famous case of *DPP v Smith*.

Around lunchtime that day a company car, a 'J' type Vauxhall saloon,[12] was taken from Arthur Street where it had been left locked, and arrived outside the shop. A group of men, probably four in number, sprang out, smashed the shop window, took the jewellery and prepared to drive off. The shopkeeper came to the door and blew a police whistle and a number of people shouted, Stop them! Stop that car!' As the car began slowly to move off, a serving naval officer, Captain Ralph Binney, stood in front of the car, putting up his hands in an attempt to get it to stop.[13] The car continued to move, and, according to witness evidence, knocked him down. It was then said to have stopped and reversed before driving forward again, trapping him beneath it. The Vauxhall, a powerful 'executive' car in its day, was then driven at speed into King William Street and across London Bridge. It was not seen to stop. By London Bridge railway station it appears to have turned into Tooley Street and continued on its way. It was subsequently discovered abandoned near Vine Lane. Captain Binney was found lying nearby in the roadway in Bermondsey Street, a distance of over a mile from Birchin Lane. He died in Guy's Hospital from his inoperable injuries some hours afterwards, unable even to make a dying declaration.[14]

It did not take long before the police had an idea of where they should begin to look for those responsible and their inquiries took them to Bermondsey and one of the local billiard saloons known to be patronised by professional criminals in the area, many of them related by blood or marriage. Eventually Ronald Hedley, aged 26, of Rotherhithe and Thomas James Jenkins, aged 24, of no fixed address were charged with Captain Binney's murder, it eventually proving impossible to pursue a viable case against others who had also been arrested and suspected of involvement. The preparation of the case against Hedley and Jenkins was uphill work for the police, since—unlike those who were witnesses at the scene—among those interviewed in the Bermondsey and Rotherhithe area some were regarded by the

---

12. The 'J' type Vauxhall had a powerful 1.7 litre six cylinder engine, advanced steering and suspension for its time and was by no means an ordinary 'family' car.

13. This, and other descriptions of events, is based upon witness statements, made for the most part by articulate, and in some cases professional, people. In all there were no fewer than 58 witness statements on file.

14. In essence a witness statement admissible in court proceedings, notwithstanding the impossibility of it being tested by cross-examination.

police as unreliable. At least eight identity parades were set up in an attempt to identify all those involved.

On 12 March 1945, Hedley and Jenkins stood trial at the Central Criminal Court presided over by Mr Justice Macnaghten. Hedley, who had originally said that he had been with a woman whom he declined to identify, put forward the plea that it was an accident and that Captain Binney did not give the driver a chance to avoid it. The same argument was advanced by his co-defendant Jenkins. Since they were engaged in a joint enterprise, that of robbery, and the prosecution alleged that Binney's death had come about in the course of their decamping from the scene with the stolen goods, they were both properly indicted for murder, notwithstanding that it was Hedley who was at the wheel of the car and Jenkins a passenger.[15] Hedley was convicted of murder and sentenced to the mandatory penalty of death. For reasons that are unlikely ever to be discovered, the jury acquitted Jenkins of murder and brought back an alternative verdict of manslaughter. In sentencing him, however, Mr Justice Macnaghten made matters very clear:

> The jury have taken a merciful view of your case. The circumstances were such that they might quite properly have found you guilty of murder.

But in the event, no matter the lenity of the jury's verdict, nor the severity of a sentence of eight years penal servitude, neither would seem to have had a deterrent effect on his younger brother, Charles Henry Jenkins, then 17 but who was to have little more life ahead of him.

On 13 April 1945, Hedley's appeal against conviction was heard in the Court of Criminal Appeal (Singleton, Wrottesley and Tucker JJ).[16] On his behalf it was argued

---

15. Perhaps the most notable case of a murder prosecution arising from an instance of joint enterprise in the post-war period was that of *R v Craig and Bentley* in which Craig (aged 16), who actually shot the police constable, though convicted of murder, was too young to be hanged while Bentley (aged 19), who was alleged to have shouted words of encouragement for him to do so, suffered the death penalty.

16. Both Wrottesley and Tucker later became Lords of Appeal in Ordinary. Mr (later Lord) Justice Tucker was to be one of the five Law Lords to hear *DPP v Smith*; Mr Byrne who had prosecuted in *Hedley and Jenkins* was (as Mr Justice Byrne) to deliver the Appeal Court judgement which the crown sought to overturn.

1. that the trial judge had failed to direct the jury on the law of murder and manslaughter;

2. that both during the trial and in the course of his summing up he had usurped the functions of the jury; and that

3. in his summing up he had failed adequately to put the defence case and had misrepresented the evidence.

One instance cited by counsel[17] for Hedley were the trial judge's words to the jury (on the plea of accident):

> That, of course, is a question of fact for you, but the evidence seemed overwhelming that there was ample opportunity for the driver to stop before he reached Captain Binney.[18]

In giving judgment[19] Mr Justice Singleton made it abundantly clear that the judge had gone on to remind them of the ancient principle that it was the function of the jury to find the facts and it is the function of the judge to tell the jury the law.[20] Mr Justice Macnaghten had given them what the appeal court thought was a very clear and unambiguous direction on the law of murder and manslaughter:

> You have got to make up your minds whether the driver, assuming Hedley to be the driver, knocked down Captain Binney intentionally. If he did, my direction to you is that by the law of England he committed the crime of murder.

> Manslaughter is the unlawful killing of a human being, and where a person by his driving of a motor vehicle, which is of course a dangerous vehicle, conducts himself so as to show a disregard of human life . . . it is open to the jury to find him guilty

---

17. He was represented by Mr Eric Neve KC and Mr H Fenton. The Crown was represented by Mr L A Byrne (who as Mr Justice Byrne appears later in this chapter).
18. The quotations from the remarks of the trial judge are taken from the judgment of the Court of Criminal Appeal.
19. [1945] 31 Cr App R 35.
20. In the time-honoured words of Sir Edward Coke: 'Ad quaestionem facti non respondent judices: ad quaestionem juris non respondent juratores'. *Coke Upon Littleton*, Institutes (1628).

of the crime of manslaughter. Of course [he] had no intention of killing Captain Binney; it would seem all he wanted to do was to get away with the stolen goods. If you think that in the excitement of the moment he did not realise that he was knocking down Captain Binney and that he did not intend to knock him down, you may find that this was a case of manslaughter.

Far from having failed adequately to put the defence case to the jury, the trial judge had, no fewer than ten times in the course of his summing up, made it clear to the jury that before they could convict the defendant of murder they must be satisfied that he had knocked down the victim intentionally when he could have stopped.

Hedley returned to the death cell from where, after the expiry of three clear Sundays, he could expect to walk to the gallows. But even at that point things were not quite over; an application was then made to the Attorney-General for his *fiat* to appeal to the House of Lords on a point of law of 'exceptional' public importance.[21] That argument was never to be set out and it is difficult to see how, given the substantive law and the clear endorsement by the appeal court of the correctness of the trial judge's statement of it, there could have been any serious prospect of success. But the tide was still running in Hedley's favour; even though on 25 April the Director of Public Prosecutions, Sir Theobald Mathew, received a letter from the Attorney-General, Sir Donald Somervell, officially informing him that Hedley's application had been refused, another letter, also dated 25 April, from the Permanent Under Secretary, Sir Frank Newsam, informed him that the Home Secretary had 'advised his Majesty to respite the capital sentence with a view to its commutation to penal servitude for life'.[22]

One can but speculate as to how the Home Secretary came to his decision. He would, of course, have been advised by the civil servants in the Home Office and it may be that the fact that the jury had returned a verdict of manslaughter rather than murder in the case of Jenkins indicated some gesture of equity. On the other hand, since it was Hedley at the wheel, Jenkins could have done little to prevent the car from being driven such that Captain

---

21. As provided by section 1(6) Criminal Appeal Act 1907.
22. Our information is that Hedley served approximately nine years of this sentence in prison and was released on life licence in 1954.

Binney was knocked down and carried beneath it, save for verbal entreaty to the driver to stop. But what is truly remarkable is that the Home Secretary was none other than Herbert Morrison. Morrison, the son of a policeman, was no convinced abolitionist. Indeed, at the time of the Criminal Justice Bill in 1947, he counselled against acceptance by the Government of the amendment put down by Sydney Silverman that would have incorporated abolition within it. He was fearful of the effect on public opinion. Does his decision in the case of Hedley identify him as being privately an abolitionist but one with a pragmatic eye to the politics of populism? Whatever the truth of the matter, Ronald Hedley would have had good cause to utter a sigh of relief when the prison governor gave him the good news. His account had been rejected by the jury and his appeal was without discernible merit. What could have been the 'exceptional' point in his case, not least since generations of criminals, before and after him, would have killed in the course of attempting to flee from scenes of crime?

The appeal court judgment in *Hedley and Jenkins* describes Captain Binney as:

> an officer in His Majesty's Navy...courageously performing a duty of a kind with which any citizen may be faced. He was seeking to stop or secure the arrest of persons who had committed a felony and were endeavouring to escape with the proceeds of their crime.

The bravery of Captain Binney is straightforwardly commemorated in the Binney Medal[23] but the case of Hedley and Jenkins is entwined, not only with respect to the forensic details and legal issues, but also with the *dramatis personæ* of *DPP v Smith*, not a case which was to change the law, save in a marginal sense,[24] but rather one which was to arouse a storm of protest at its judgment that resonated not only in England but around the Commonwealth.

---

23. Binney's naval colleagues established a trust fund in 1947 to award a medal in his name to a person, not a police officer, demonstrating exceptional courage in the cause of law and order in the areas of the Metropolitan and City of London Police Forces (as then styled).

24. Criminal Justice Act 1967, section 8.

But the criminal fraternity of Bermondsey and Rotherhithe that had been involved in the Birchin Lane robbery was to be represented in yet another crime having great similarities with it. On 29 April 1947, Charles Jenkins, in the company of Christopher Geraghty and Terence Rolt, was fleeing the scene of an armed robbery in Charlotte Street in the West End. A member of the public, Alec de Antiquis, endeavoured to stop them but was shot dead. On 28 July all three were convicted of murder and on 19 September 1947, all appeals against conviction having failed, Charles Jenkins, now aged 21, and Christopher Geraghty, aged 23, were hanged at Pentonville. Terence Rolt, being less than 18, had earlier been sentenced to be detained at His Majesty's pleasure.[25]

Murder — Manslaughter — then Murder Again: the Trials of 'Gypsy Jim' Smith

At about 7.30 in the evening of March 2 1960, Jim Smith drove his car, a Ford Prefect 100E,[26] out of Beresford Square in Woolwich, south-east London, with police constable Leslie Meehan hanging precariously on to it, only shortly to fall into the roadway and be killed by an oncoming vehicle. Following his conviction for murder a not entirely dissimilar issue from that in *Hedley and Jenkins* was to be the fulcrum upon which the interpretation of the criminal law was again to take an unexpected — and to many an unwelcome — turn.

The facts in *DPP v Smith* were uncomplicated, and the ensuing criminal process deceptively straightforward — a case of either murder or manslaughter. Smith came from gypsy stock and was of limited education. He seems

---

25. The case was cited in evidence to the Royal Commission on Capital Punishment 1949-53 by the Metropolitan Police commissioner, Sir Harold Scott: *Report*, Cmnd 8932 at pp.335-6. There is reason to believe that Charles Jenkins may well have been one of the unidentified passengers carried in the car that was used in the Birchin Lane robbery in 1944. The car used in the Charlotte Street robbery in 1947, which had earlier been stolen by Jenkins, was none other than a 'J' type Vauxhall. While clearly something of a robbers' 'vehicle of choice' at that time, its failure to start as they fled the scene was a factor in their confrontation with their victim.

26. The Prefect 100E was produced from 1953 until 1959. The vehicle driven by Smith was four years old and, unlike earlier Prefects, had no running boards.

not to have passed a driving test though the vehicle was his own. He was 26 years old, as Hedley had been in 1944. But in terms of criminality, the two were on a different plane. Smith was no robber who drove a high-powered stolen car to get away from a high value robbery. He dealt in what is known as 'dodgy gear' and knew the value of scrap metal. Nothing in his past history suggested that he was a man of violent proclivities. In the back of the car were not rings or necklaces; only sacks of scaffolding clips that had been stolen from a building site some miles away at Chiselhurst.[27] PC Meehan, a Metropolitan Police officer, known to Jim Smith, spotted the sacks and told the driver to pull into the kerb, which initially he did, while the policeman walked alongside. But Smith proceeded to put his foot on the accelerator. The car sped away for 130 yards. PC Meehan clung on to the driver's side of the vehicle on which the only hand holds were the door handle and the vertical bar of the quarter light of the driver's window, there being nowhere for his feet. The car began to zig-zag and PC Meehan was thrown into the roadway into the path of oncoming traffic. His body was struck first by an elderly Austin saloon, then by a Ford Popular, next by an earlier model of Ford Prefect and finally by a BMW Isetta 'bubble car'.[28] He was struck by this vehicle with very considerable force, severely damaging its bodywork, with the result that he died at the scene from massive injuries.

Had there been no traffic coming from the opposite direction it is possible that PC Meehan would not have been killed. While Smith was clearly endeavouring to escape arrest by driving on, dumping the stolen goods in a side street, he immediately returned to the scene of the incident and inquired after the policeman's welfare and, on being told that he was dead, gave himself up, expressing according to a police witness, great concern, saying: 'I know the man.[29] I wouldn't do it for the world. I only wanted to shake him off'. Smith later denied using the last few words.

In the police car on the way to Woolwich police station, Smith is said to have kept muttering to himself, 'It is a terrible thing. I know his family and

27. The value of the goods stolen from Birchin Lane was in excess of £2,000 at 1944 prices. The estimated value of the 271 stolen scaffolding clips in 1960 was estimated to be £60.
28. The three wheeled Isetta, though lightweight, was powered by a BMW motorcycle engine and was of comparatively robust construction.
29. Smith had previous convictions for stealing metal and had been arrested by PC Meehan for the theft of copper wire some months before.

I know he has kids'. Having been arrested and cautioned he is reported to have said: 'I didn't mean to kill him, but I didn't want him to find the gear'.

Mr de Antiquis, like Captain Binney before him, in attempting to execute what is known as a citizen's arrest, was behaving as a police officer would have done.[30] Police constable Meehan, whose death was at the centre of the case of *DPP v Smith*, like Binney and de Antiquis, had been attempting to stop a motor vehicle whose occupants had, or who were suspected of having, committed what was then termed a felony.[31] Although there are differences in the detail, the fundamental link between *Hedley and Jenkins* and *DPP v Smith* is the question of what the driver intended when he chose to drive on rather than stop as he had been enjoined to do. Did Hedley determine deliberately to drive at Captain Binney, or was it an unavoidable accident that the driver had no chance to avoid? What did Smith foresee when he drove off with PC Meehan hanging precariously onto the side of the car, notwithstanding that the 'reasonable man' would have been aware that the police officer might suffer serious injury or even death as a consequence?

While we can conclude that on all the evidence before the jury, Hedley was properly convicted of murder and that his subsequent appeal was rightly judged to be without merit, the situation in *Smith* is by no means as straightforward, since the Court of Criminal Appeal set aside the verdict of murder and substituted one of manslaughter. Yet again the conduct of the 'reasonable man' is applied to the interpretation of the evidence and in *Smith* it is challenged, initially with success. The argument is foreshadowed in *Hedley and Jenkins* when the trial judge told the jury:

> If you think that in the excitement of the moment he did not realise that he was knocking down Captain Binney and that he did not intend to knock him down, you may find that it is a case of manslaughter.

At first sight, the behaviour of Hedley and Smith appears to have been similar, though it was, in totality, very different. One sought to deny involvement while the other readily admitted what he had done. One drove at

---

30. See: *Walters v Smith (W.H.) and Son Ltd.* [1914] 1 KB 595.
31. The distinction between felonies and misdemeanours was abolished by the Criminal Justice Act 1967. The contemporary term is 'arrestable offence'.

speed for a considerable distance leaving his victim in the roadway mortally injured; given the ground clearance of the car it is scarcely conceivable that in the course of travelling more than a mile he could have been unaware of an obstruction beneath the vehicle. The other, once he had dumped the stolen property, shortly returned to the scene and inquired solicitously of the constable's condition. In one case the driver's companion appeared to have done nothing to dissuade his accomplice from driving on, while in the other the passenger (who was not prosecuted) maintained that he had tried to restrain the driver, saying: 'For Christ's sake, stop, will you!'

When, on 10 May 1960, the Court of Criminal Appeal set aside Smith's conviction for capital murder and substituted one of manslaughter, the presiding judge was Mr Justice Byrne. It was a scenario with which he was personally familiar for it had been he who had prosecuted at the trial of Hedley and Jenkins in 1945. In the course of Smith's trial before Mr Justice Donovan, the prosecution had relied upon the maxim that a man must be taken or presumed to intend the natural consequences of his acts. The jury had been given no explanation in general terms of the meaning or effect of the word 'presumption' nor told that any such presumption might be rebutted. The passage in the appeal judgment is illuminating.

Whatever may have been the position last century when the prisoner could not go into the witness box and the distinction between presumptions of law and presumptions of fact was not so well defined, it is now clear, as was naturally conceded by Mr Griffith-Jones,[32] that the presumption embodied in the above maxim is not an irrebuttable presumption of law.

The law on this point as it stands today [1960] is that this presumption of intention means this: that, as a man is usually able to foresee what are the natural consequences of his acts, so it is, as a rule, reasonable to infer that he did foresee them and intend them. But, while that is an inference that may be drawn, and on the facts in certain circumstances must inevitably be drawn, yet, if on all the facts of a particular case it is not the correct inference, then it should not be drawn.

---

32. Prosecuting counsel.

The idea that, if on a review of the totality of the evidence, there was room for a jury to take more than one view was by no means novel. Rather, there was authority in a judgment, though not in a murder case, given by Goddard LCJ, sitting with Atkinson and Cassells JJ, in 1947.[33] In *Hedley* the best response the defence could make to the prosecution evidence that the driver had, after initially knocking him down, stopped and then driven over him again, trapping him beneath the car, was that it had been pure accident and that the driver had 'no chance' to do otherwise. The jury doubtless considered that totality of the evidence supported the presumption. But the totality of the evidence in *Smith* disclosed a very different state of affairs. PC Meehan was carried on the moving car, not because it had been driven at him and he had been involuntarily trapped by its movement, but because he had hung on to the driver's door and window. Exactly how he came to fall off was a matter of dispute, but the undisputed fact was that he was struck by a succession of oncoming vehicles and finally killed. This was not something over which Smith could have had any direct control. The most damning interpretation of his behaviour was to suggest that it was the deliberate manner of his driving that cast the police officer into the roadway.

When, on 11 March 1960, the officers of the Director of Public Prosecutions received an early report from the Metropolitan Police about the unlawful killing of PC Meehan nine days before, there was little doubt from the known facts that this was a case falling within one or more of the categories of capital murder in the Homicide Act 1957, namely murder done in the course or furtherance of theft, murder of a police officer acting in the execution of his duty and murder in the course of, or for the purpose of, resisting or avoiding or preventing arrest. The ensuing indictment reflected the triple lock that might be placed on a verdict of capital murder, if indeed this was a case of murder and not manslaughter.

But at the opening of the trial on 4 April 1960 at the Central Criminal Court, the indictment was amended to delete the alternative counts of murder in the course or furtherance of theft and murder in the course of resisting arrest. The indictment bore the mark of simplicity: that Jim Smith 'murdered Leslie Edwin Vincent Meehan, a police officer, in the execution

---

33. *R v Steane* [1947] KB 997.

of his duty'. The only conceivable explanation for the amendment of the indictment was to focus the jury's attention on the murder of a policeman. In the eyes of the Crown this emphasis on the identity of the victim of the homicide elevated the intrinsic seriousness of the crime to the highest level, rather than reflecting the precise extent of the culpability of the police officer's killer. Between 1948 and 1960 five officers of the Metropolitan Police had been killed on duty.[34] In some instances the trials excited immense publicity at the time and lingered in popular consciousness long afterwards. At the time of the Homicide Act 1957, the shooting of police constable Miles by Christopher Craig would have been still fresh in the recollection of politicians when the whole question of the abolition of capital punishment was coming to the boil. The killing of a policeman at this time could not have other than considerable political resonance.

However justified were—and still are—the scathing attacks on the reasoning (and the result) of the House of Lords' decision in *DPP v Smith*, there is every reason why the decision of the Court of Criminal Appeal should be applauded. Any lawyer reading in detail, as we have done, the transcript of the two-day hearing before that court can hardly fail to be impressed by the cogency of judicial interventions during the course of oral argument. The simple point in the court's reserved judgment—the decision was given immediately at the end of the hearing on 10 May 1960 and the reserved judgment on 18 May—was that Smith had not driven the vehicle *at* PC Meehan and the latter's death was the indirect result of an indifference and lack of foresight as to the fatal consequences of the manner of his driving The judgment of Mr Justice Byrne, an experienced criminal law practitioner and criminal judge, specifically noted the contrast with the case of Ronald Hedley in 1945 (when Byrne had himself been counsel for the Crown) in which the driver of the escaping stolen vehicle drove deliberately at, and directly killed, Captain Binney who was seeking to stop the thieves. Any reader of the judgment of Court of Criminal Appeal would instantly nod in agreement with its decision. Yet the court was not oblivious to the seriousness of the crime. When Mr Edward Clarke QC (on behalf of Smith) submitted—rather imprudently, if not impudently—to the judges that

34. In February 1948 PC Edgar was shot, as was PC Miles in 1952. PC Summers was fatally stabbed in 1958 and DS Purdy was shot in July 1959. PC Meehan died in March 1960.

they should treat the substituted verdict of manslaughter as a case of 'motor manslaughter', he was later roundly reproved by Mr Justice Byrne:

> This court is unable to regard this as a case of what is called 'motor manslaughter'. It is in fact a very serious case of manslaughter. The sentence of the Court upon the Appellant will be a sentence of 10 years imprisonment.

Jim Smith's offence was indeed serious. It merited a sentence of ten years' imprisonment, a long sentence by the standards of 1960. No reasonable observer could possibly demur.

The complete acceptability and intellectual integrity of the decision of the Court of Criminal Appeal prompts the question of why the Attorney-General was so ready to grant his certificate enabling the Crown to take the case to the House of Lords. It is not impossible, indeed we think it is likely, that the politics of capital punishment, together with the widespread belief that crime generally, and criminal violence in particular, was increasing rather than diminishing were in the mind of the Attorney-General, Sir Reginald Manningham-Buller. Under the *fiat* system, which operated until its demise that year (1960), the certificate had to be on the footing that the case involved a point of law of *exceptional* public importance and that in the Attorney-General's opinion it was desirable in the public interest that a further appeal should be brought. There was little here that could be regarded as novel, let alone 'exceptional'. Was his perception of the verdict of the appeal court a disagreeably unwelcome a factor in his decision? Was this the considered choice of the lawyer or the politician?[35] One might yet have hoped for the sort of response made by Lord Sumner in 1918[36] when expressing regret that the *fiat* had been issued in an appeal. He said the case 'raises no new principle of law; it elucidates no new aspect of familiar principles. It is a mere question of the application of the rules of evidence to this particular case'.

The same could be said of the point of law in *Smith* — the case involved only an interpretation of a rule of evidence: the nature of the presumption

---

35. In mitigation it might be said that Manningham-Buller's forensic abilities were not always of the highest order.
36. *Thompson v R* [1918] AC 211, at 236.

that a person intends the natural consequences of his acts. The Court of Criminal Appeal got it right. The presumption is a 'may', not a 'must'.

The Social Background

In the period after 1945 the level of crime rose to reach a peak in 1951. Whereas before the war the prison population of England and Wales had actually fallen, by the 1950s it had risen to an historical high of around 25,000 inmates.[37] In pre-war Britain, its social classes largely insulated from each other, crime had not been seen as a major item of political concern. The delinquent conduct of the lower orders of society was essentially a matter for the police to control.

This so-called 'crime wave' in which 'Teddy boys' now roamed the streets stimulated a belief that crime was seriously eroding the social order of society. 'Juvenile delinquency' became a focus issue for the popular press. Following the shooting of PC Miles in Croydon in 1952, the *Daily Mirror* proclaimed across its front page:

VICIOUS YOUNG FOOLS STILL PARADE IN A TOWN OF TRAGEDY[38]

One reaction to this sense that social order was now subject to serious threat was that the police came to enjoy more public support. There emerged the noble stereotype of the 'British Bobby', to be immortalised by the actor Jack Warner in the film *The Blue Lamp* and later in the television series *Dixon of Dock Green*. Dixon was solid and honest, the kindly but firm embodiment of law and order, bidding his audience a warm 'Evening, all'.[39] The killing of police officers[40] became identified as a particularly heinous crime. In November 1952 PC Sydney Miles was shot dead by Christopher Craig as he and Derek Bentley were committing burglary at a commercial

---

37. This contrasts with almost four times that figure today.
38. 'I saw 100 in the Craig mould in one street—curly headed hooligans and Mama's little bullies. From decent, comfortable homes in tree-lined roads'. *Daily Mirror* (Monday 15 December 1952).
39. Corrupt police officers simply did not figure in this cosmography.
40. In *The Blue Lamp* Dixon was shot by a teen-aged delinquent.

warehouse in Croydon; in 1958 PC Raymond Summers was fatally stabbed by Ronald Marwood; in 1959 Detective Sergeant Raymond Purdy was shot dead by Gunter Fritz Podola[41] and in 1960 PC Leslie Meehan was killed having fallen from the car driven by Jim Smith. Bentley, although he had no gun and was in custody at the time,[42] was nevertheless hanged, as were Marwood and Podola. The above victims were by no means the only police officers to be killed in the execution of their duty in this period, but their deaths had a very high profile.

These events could nevertheless divide opinion. On the one hand there was great concern at the killing of police officers, not least by shooting or stabbing them when the unarmed 'Bobby' had been a feature of policing since the inception of modern policing in 1829. Unlike his 'continental' or American counterpart, he carried no gun as he patrolled the streets, his sole weapon being the wooden truncheon. Killing policemen was seen as a cowardly, and thereby an even more despicable crime. On the other hand, the opponents of capital punishment, and even some who were not, were concerned that it was Bentley, rather than Craig who had actually fired the fatal shot, who was hanged. Hundreds demonstrated outside Wandsworth Prison on the morning of his execution in 1953. There were again serious public disorders outside Pentonville Prison on the morning in 1959 that Marwood, a man who came from that area of north London, was hanged. In the case of Podola, the amnesia that was central to his defence became the subject of speculation not only that it might be genuine, but also that it had somehow come about as a result of events in the course of his arrest.

But the widespread view by the late 1950s was that the British Bobby was now seriously vulnerable to lethal violence. Many who favoured the retention of capital punishment not only maintained that it acted as a deterrent to murder generally—without it, there would, it was argued, be many more killings—but in any event it was the necessary and wholly just desert for those who killed policemen. The Homicide Act 1957 could, if need be,

---

41. Podola was represented by Mr Frederick Lawton QC in one of his last cases before his elevation to the Bench in what is still recognised as a masterly performance. Amnesia was a central issue in his defence.
42. Fifty years later, Bentley's conviction was quashed by the Court of Appeal (Criminal Division) on a reference from the Criminal Cases Review Commission, the summing-up by Lord Goddard being declared manifestly unfair: *R v Bentley* [2001] 2 Cr App R 307.

place the triple lock on the death sentence; the murder of a police officer in the execution of his duty was capital, like murder by shooting or murder in resisting arrest.

The Granting of the *fiat* and the Composition of the Court

Quite apart from the question of whether the 'Gypsy' Jim Smith's case raised an 'exceptional' point of law there is a further issue never, as far as can be discovered, raised at the time, but which would certainly be the subject of criticism today. When in 1935 the Attorney-General granted his *fiat* in *Woolmington*, he granted it to the defence. In *Smith* in 1960 the Attorney-General in granting it to the appellant was granting it to the Crown—of which he was a law officer. Not only that, in his role as Attorney-General he appeared in person for the Crown to argue its case, together with Mr Mervyn Griffith-Jones (who had represented the Crown in the court below). In *Woolmington* the Lord Chancellor, Lord Sankey, had indicated that Mr Casswell, who had earlier represented the defendant, should be led by a Silk; in this forthcoming appeal Mr Griffith-Jones was in the same position and therefore it was entirely appropriate that he should be likewise led by a Silk. But it need not have been the Attorney since it would have been perfectly acceptable for that role to have been assumed by a Silk at the criminal bar of the prosecution's choice.

One is drawn to the possibility that the Attorney-General was motivated to grant his certificate for the same reason that the original indictment was amended, but, as in so many instances of past decisions, there is no paper trail, no body of undeleted email correspondence, to provide any clue. In the absence of any available evidence or persuasive argument to the contrary, we might perhaps be entitled to conclude that the unlawful killing of a police officer—who suffered a most violent death—sufficed to make the administrators of justice seek the most robust political response to the perception that serious criminality in post-war Britain was a growing threat. Not only that, in the course of legislating the Homicide Act 1957, though capital punishment was no longer the mandatory penalty for murder, the death penalty had been retained for offences that had been marked out as particularly heinous, which included the murder of police officers.

If the judgment of the Court of Criminal Appeal had been the last word, no member of the public would have had cause to feel less protected by Jim Smith's 10-year sentence for manslaughter than by his death on the gallows. Smith, though a small-time thief, was no ruthless robber with violence. The argument that the death penalty was an effective general deterrent was always unpersuasive.

Of the five judges who sat for five days at the end of June, only two of them, Lord Tucker and Lord Denning, were full-time Law Lords. Denning was a retentionist who was to remark on the utility of capital punishment years after it had been altogether abolished. The other three supernumerary Law Lords were the Lord Chancellor, Lord Kilmuir (the former Sir David Maxwell Fyfe), Lord Goddard, the recently retired Lord Chief Justice, and Lord Parker, his successor.

Kilmuir, it should be noted, was the Home Secretary at the time of the Craig and Bentley case who, notwithstanding a petition signed by over 200 Members of Parliament and an unprecedented public clamour for Bentley's reprieve, declined to recommend exercise of the prerogative of mercy. Interviewed some 20 years later, Kilmuir's widow is recorded recalling his reasoning in the Bentley case: he believed that the police had to be protected and if a young man 'got off' because he was accompanied by an even younger man who could not hang, then this might lead to further incidents.[43]

More evidence, this time in the course of legal proceedings respecting Kilmuir's refusal to recommend that the Royal Prerogative be exercised to reprieve Bentley from the gallows, came to light in July 1993 when his decision was formally challenged in *R v Secretary of State for Home Affairs ex parte Bentley*.[44]

A memorandum from Philip Allen to the Secretary of State and endorsed by the Permanent Under-Secretary, Sir Frank Newsam, advised that effect be given to the jury's recommendation for mercy, adding that such a plea

---

43. Fenton Bresler. *Lord Goddard: A Biography of Rayner Goddard, Lord Chief Justice* (Harrap, 1977).
44. [1994] QB 349, before Watkins and Neill LJJ and Tuckey J.

rested principally on the ground, which had been held valid in previous cases, that it would not seem right to exact the supreme penalty from the accomplice when the principal offender is escaping with his life.[45]

Also before the court was a copy of Maxwell Fyfe's minute in which he wrote, *inter alia*:

> It was a very bad murder, involving the death of a police officer, committed at a time when there is much public anxiety about numbers of crimes of violence . . . .I feel it is important to protect the unarmed police.

Nevertheless, the court held that 'there is a compelling argument that even by the standards of 1953 the then Home Secretary's decision was wrong'.[46]

Such an enthusiast for capital punishment ought, in our opinion, never to have been involved judicially in what was an appeal by the Crown made possible by the grant of a *fiat* by the Government's chief law officer.

But to place this in context, Kilmuir (as he was later to become in the role of Lord Chancellor) appears no different from the conservatively-minded politicians and lawyers of his time who argued strongly that hanging was a deterrent. Not all disguised their belief that it was also a just desert. Given that they were able to express their opinions freely, not all of those who comprised the court had kept silent on the issue of the death penalty. Those who bestrode the worlds of politics and the law like Kilmuir, the Lord Chancellor, and Manningham-Buller, the Attorney-General, had been involved in the legislative process that led to the Homicide Act 1957.

How far the *Smith* case excited the concerns of the political establishment may be gauged from a brief but highly indicative minute from the Prime Minister of the day, Harold Macmillan,[47] dated 29 July 1960, addressed to the Lord Chancellor, Lord Kilmuir:

> You know I am an amateur of the Law. I read with the deepest interest your judgment in the Director of Public Prosecutions v. Smith. I was interested also to see that all

---

45. At p.355.
46. At p.365F.
47. Harold Macmillan, 1st Earl of Stockton (1894-1966): *Kilmuir Papers* (PREM 11/3034).

four Judges sitting with you agreed with your view against the Court of Criminal Appeal. This must be rather an unusual position and I would have thought that from a common-sense point of view the House of Lords was right — as so often.

Kilmuir wrote by return that day:

Thank you very much for your minute. I am glad to think that my judgment in Smith attracted your agreement. The unanimous reversal of the Court of Criminal Appeal by the Lords is unusual and has very seldom happened before.

May I send my congratulations on the Session and every good wish.

Later that year on 14 September Kilmuir, speaking in Canada at the Second Commonwealth and Empire Law Conference, referred to the influence of Oliver Wendell Holmes, both on constitutional doctrines and the spirit in which lawyers approach the law, as being 'incalculable'. He added: 'I quoted him with gratitude and admiration in the last judgment I delivered'.[48] The quotation by the House of Lords in *Smith* from Holmes' *The Common Law* (1881) is essentially extra-judicial material. Moreover, the judgment employs it out of context and in contradiction to Holmes' radical view of criminal homicide. We take the view that for Kilmuir to have so extolled Holmes' legal writing was both inapt and inept and serves only further to discredit the controversial House of Lords decision in *DPP v Smith*.

In referring to 'the last judgment I delivered', while Kilmuir was technically correct in that he did indeed deliver it, other material in the Archives[49] confirms what was widely believed at the time, namely that the author was the new Lord Chief Justice, Lord Parker.[50] There is correspondence relating to the discovery by a sharp-eyed law student (a certain 'P English') of an error in the *Smith* judgment, namely that referring to the case of *R v Faulkner* (1877) the Lord Chancellor in giving judgment had stated that the conviction (for the arson of a ship) had been upheld whereas in fact it had been quashed. Though irrelevant to the decision, a correction to the Law

---

48. This was, of course, *DPP v Smith*.
49. *Kilmuir Papers* (LC02/8517).
50. See Note 58 below.

Report was made. On 21 November 1960 Lord Parker wrote to Sir George Coldstream at the Lord Chancellor's Office:

> As I told you on Thursday night, I am horrified to find that mistake is entirely mine and I hope you will express my sincere regret to the Lord Chancellor. The mistake, as you say, in no way affects the argument but how I ever came to make it I really do not know.

The following day Coldstream wrote to Kilmuir:

> As the Judgment of the House of Lords which you delivered had been prepared by Lord Parker, I wrote to him on Thursday of last week drawing attention to P English's letter. Underneath this minute you will find his reply to me of today (sic) in which he takes the entire blame for the error.

Although never a politician in the Parliamentary sense, the recently retired Lord Chief Justice, Lord Goddard, like both the Lord Chancellor and the Attorney-General, had been involved legislatively in the Homicide Act 1957. But that fact certainly did not deter him from participating in the proceedings in *Smith*. During the Lords' debate on the Bill to abolish the death penalty in 1955, Goddard (then Lord Chief Justice) railed in no uncertain terms against the reform, and in the process declared, incorrectly, that the High Court judges were unanimously supportive of retaining the death penalty. Since Goddard was also a participant, legislatively speaking, in the 1957 Act, he should have disqualified himself from sitting judicially on a case that involved issues under the Homicide Act, specifically section 1 which purportedly had abolished the concept of constructive malice and was now under direct judicial scrutiny in *DPP v Smith*. He could scarcely have claimed impartiality on that issue. His distinct bias towards severity in the criminal law was of long standing and not limited to debates in the House of Lords. In court his remarks from the Bench at times disclosed an irascibility of temperament towards defendants and those who represented them.[51] Eyewitness accounts of his conduct as the judge in the Craig and

---

51. In this, save for his being a scholarly lawyer, as he aged he seemed increasingly to resemble Lord Hewart.

Bentley trial indicate his capacity for ill-tempered and partisan intervention. Indeed, if there is one case which damages Goddard's reputation in
this regard it is undoubtedly that of *R v Craig and Bentley*. When in 2001 the
issue was again before the courts, this time in the Court of Appeal (Criminal
Division)[52] following a reference from the Criminal Cases Review Commission with regard to the conviction of Bentley for murder, the judgment,
while generously recognising Goddard's standing as a criminal judge, did
not, in this instance, spare him judicially from the criticism that had been
heaped upon him at the time. In quashing the conviction Lord Bingham,
in his judgment found it necessary to observe:

> It is with genuine diffidence that the members of the court direct criticism towards
> a trial judge widely recognised as one of the outstanding criminal judges of this
> country. But we cannot escape the duty of decision. In our judgment, the summing
> up in this case was such as to deny the appellant that fair trial which is the birthright
> of every British citizen.[53]

The judgment went on to add:

> It must be a matter of profound and continuing regret that this mistrial occurred
> and that the defects we have found were not recognised at the time.[54]

While these comments relate directly to Bentley's trial and conviction it
is possible to speculate what was in the mind of the court when it included
the final words of this passage. We would argue that it was Maxwell-Fyfe,
as he then was, who ought, as a Home Secretary who was also a lawyer, to
have recognised these defects at the time, never mind the observation of the
memorandum from Philip Allen which advised, but implied no compulsion to grant, a reprieve.

Goddard's legislative interventions in the House of Lords debates in the
1950s disclosed a distinct bias. Indeed one might legitimately ask why was
he seen to be needed on the final court of appeal for it was his presence that

---

52. *R v Bentley* (2001) Cr App R 21, at pp.307-351.
53. At p.334.
54. At p.340.

is perhaps most noteworthy, not least since he was by now retired and had been succeeded by Lord Parker. He was still a dominant figure with a high public profile with regard to crime and for most of the post-war period his influence had been immense. He was set in ways that reflected the values of his class and generation and in this was little different from many of his brethren whose privileged lives had been spent in public schools, Oxbridge colleges and the Inns of Court. Though not aristocratic in the conventional sense, these representatives of the Establishment inclined to the mentality of an *ancien régime* and were, for the most part, deeply suspicious if indeed not openly hostile to the 'new-fangled' psychiatry.[55] At a time when average life expectancy was lower than today, many of the senior judiciary were relatively old men, some sitting into their eighties. In many instances they were living links with the values of a world that had existed before 1914[56] and it was hardly surprising that their frequently illiberal approach[57] was deeply sceptical if not openly hostile to new thinking.

More significantly, the presiding judge and ostensibly the author of the single judgment[58] given four weeks after the oral hearing was the Lord Chancellor, Lord Kilmuir. His refusal to recommend a reprieve for Bentley in 1953 marks him down as the sort of person Voltaire had in mind when in *Candide* he satirised the death sentence on Admiral Byng[59] as being *pour encourager les autres*. At that time it was not uncommon for a Lord Chancellor to choose to exercise his prerogative of sitting judicially, and presiding over the Appellate Committee, but it was nevertheless highly objectionable that such a political figure should have chosen to sit and hear the appeal in *DPP v Smith*. Like Goddard, he had been actively involved in the legislative processes of he Homicide Act 1957.

---

55. A notable instance of this was the treatment of Professor Henry Yellowlees, one of the most distinguished psychiatrists of his generation and an expert witness at the trial of John Haigh (the so-called 'acid bath' murderer) before Mr Justice Humphreys in 1949.

56. Goddard's first judicial appointment was as Recorder of Poole in Dorset in 1917. Travers Humphreys, who was ten years his senior, had appeared at the trials of Oscar Wilde and Dr Crippen and in 1949, in his 83rd year, tried John Haigh, the so-called 'acid bath' murderer.

57. Notably with regard to the reform of the law relating to homosexuality and what were termed 'obscene publications'.

58. Alan Paterson suggests (rightly as it turns out) that the judgment was in fact prepared by Lord Parker: *Law Lords* (Oxford Socio-Legal Studies/Macmillan, 1981) at p.93.

59. Court-martialled and shot for having lost the island of Menorca to the French in 1756.

The most intriguing aspect of this oddly composed court[60] was its fifth member. Lord Parker was not a Lord of Appeal in Ordinary, but became a peer on his appointment in 1958 as the successor to Lord Goddard as Lord Chief Justice. Parker, unlike the others, was generally considered within legal circles to be a welcome and overdue breath of fresh air in contrast to the stifling atmosphere of reaction in penal affairs exhibited by his predecessor. Indeed, he quickly displayed his dislike for the workings of the Homicide Act 1957 later in the course of the abolition debates in 1965 when he advocated life imprisonment as a maximum and not mandatory penalty for murder. He declared his distaste for the Act, not least for its retention of 'fine lines and theoretical distinctions'.

He had already, in September 1959, publicly attacked the Homicide Act in what was then for a Lord Chief Justice a peculiarly uninhibited way: so much so that the Home Secretary, R A Butler, wrote to the Lord Chancellor, Lord Kilmuir, taking particular exception to the allegation that he, the Home Secretary, had gone in for 'an indiscriminate commuting of death sentences'.[61] The speech and the ensuing private correspondence were redolent of more recent clashes between incumbents of the Home Office and the higher judiciary. Should this not also have precluded Lord Parker from sitting, it being the only occasion that he sat in the Lords during his tenure as Lord Chief Justice? *DPP v Smith* resonates with argument that would be entirely superfluous if there were no 'fine lines and distinctions' to be drawn between murder and manslaughter, and it is hard to reconcile his role in *DPP v Smith* with his evident enthusiasm, five years later, to rid the law of murder of 'the fine lines and technical distinctions' that permeated the law of homicide.

By several criteria the composition of the court was highly objectionable and can only have been determined by a process that owed as much to the politics of penology—whether illiberal or liberal is of no account—as the rational administration of the court's business. It is inconceivable that anything like it would be tolerated today. Moreover, the court managed to get

---

60. The composition of the House of Lords in *Woolmington* was the Lord Chancellor, the Lord Chief Justice and three Lords of Appeal in Ordinary.

61. In fact, of the 19 capital sentences, by the summer of 1959 Butler had only had to consider eight.

everything wrong, so much so that its judgment produced a howl of disapproval that not only echoed round every seat of academic learning but also resonated as far as some of the most senior judges in the British Commonwealth. It was as if their Lordships were affirming the most extreme aspects of Coke's concept of constructive malice, notwithstanding that it had been abolished by the Homicide Act 1957: the notion that a man might commit murder by accident.

When Jim Smith was tried for the murder it was a clear indication of how the matter was viewed at the highest level. That the Court of Criminal Appeal should see fit to reverse the verdict and substitute manslaughter was a distinctly unwelcome result for those who considered that Smith should end his days on the gallows. The decision of the Attorney-General to grant his *fiat* reflected an evident concern that the distinction between murder and manslaughter in this instance was a matter of such public importance that it was 'exceptional'. In the social sense this may well have been the case, but where was the exceptional point of law? Unlike in Woolmington's case the *fiat* had been sought not by the defence, but by the prosecution. If the House of Lords decided to reverse the Court of Criminal Appeal, would this mean that Smith would, after all, be hanged? It happened that this awesome dimension of the case was happily removed before their Lordships even began their deliberations. For the one figure who emerges from this event with towering integrity is none other than the Home Secretary R A Butler. As soon as it became known that the case was to go to the Lords he announced that, were their Lordships to restore the capital verdict of the jury, Smith would be reprieved from the gallows. In ensuring that the jurisprudential outcome had no penal conclusion Butler stands out as a humane and far-seeing reformer.[62]

---

62. When, during his time as Home Secretary, visiting magistrates ordered a prisoner to be flogged or birched for an offence against prison discipline, Butler invariably refused to confirm such orders, on occasion positively enraging some JPs in the process.

How Did Their Lordships Decide as They Did?

Why was Smith ultimately convicted of murder, and not manslaughter? The rule laid down by the House of Lords, in a single judgment of the Lord Chancellor (Lord Kilmuir) who presided, can be shortly stated. Putting aside the case of an intention to kill (this was not such a case) a person is guilty of murder if three conditions are satisfied. First, the accused must intend to do something unlawful to the other person, in the sense of 'aiming at' someone. Second, the act must cause death; and third, the unlawful act must be of such a kind that serious harm (or death) is the natural and probable result. The prosecution did not have to show that an ordinary person would have foreseen the likelihood of death—only that he would have foreseen the likelihood of really serious harm, and that need not be sufficiently serious to involve the foreseeable likelihood of death. On that conclusion, it was not surprising that a distinguished Australian judge, Mr Justice Fullagar, expostulated in private correspondence, to his Chief Justice Sir Owen Dixon: 'Well, Dixon, they're hanging men for manslaughter in England now'. Three years later Dixon, in an Australian case,[63] described the *Smith* judgment as 'palpably misconceived and wrong', saying that it would not be used as judicial authority in Australia.

The final judgment laid down a definition of intention that was wholly objective. Once a defendant is 'unlawfully and voluntarily doing something to someone', the law deems that the person intends any consequences of his conduct that a reasonable man would have foreseen, and that is irrespective of what he himself intended or whether he foresaw what might happen. At a practical level, the result was harsh on an individual like Jim Smith who expressed sincere remorse at the killing of a friendly policeman. At a theoretical level the result was regarded as highly objectionable. It extended the boundaries of intention so widely as to swallow up acts of recklessness or gross negligence. That conduct should be reserved for the lesser crime of manslaughter. Predictably, Parliament responded, but only to cure an absurd rule of evidence. The substantive law discussed in the judgment that had stood for 400 years was left intact, its shortcomings amplified by the

---

63. *Parker v The Queen, The Times* Law Reports (12 June 1963).

distinction between capital and non-capital murder, introduced into the law in 1957 wholly against the advice of the Royal Commission on Capital Punishment of 1949-1953.[64]

DPP v Smith was yet another contribution to the 'mess' which characterises the law of homicide in England.

---

64. We deal with this more fully in *Chapter 3* of this work when discussing the wisdom of Oliver Wendell Holmes and the unreformed English law of murder.

CHAPTER 7

A TALE OF TWO AMENDMENTS: OR ONE FIXED PENALTY FOR ANOTHER

The Problem

As anyone who has learned the art of splicing an eye in a rope knows well, if at the outset one of the three basic strands is wrongly placed, every subsequent part of the work will replicate the defect. No matter what is done to adjust the other strands, it will be impossible to eliminate the problem: the whole splice will be defective, unfit for purpose, and must be done again.

The wrongly started splice might well be a figure for the crime and penalty for homicide. Here, the three strands consist of:

(a) the substantive law of homicide;

(b) the defences and partial defences to the charge of murder, the latter reducing the offence to manslaughter; and

(c) the penalty.

What Parliament did in 1965 was in effect to alter the substantive law insofar as it would no longer distinguish between capital and non-capital murder. But, far from seeking to address the already perceived and growing problems associated with provocation and diminished responsibility that reduced a homicidal offence from murder to manslaughter, it did nothing to rectify any of the evident defects that persisted after the Homicide Act 1957.

Most important of all, Parliament failed (deliberately, as we will show) to address the potential consequences of simply substituting the sentence of life imprisonment for the penalty of death. The best that can be said is that, at the time, it was assumed that the system developed down the years for dealing with those reprieved from the gallows by the exercise of the Royal Prerogative of Mercy (administered by the Home Secretary, advised by competent and thoughtful civil servants in the Home Office) would serve just as well in respect of all murderers of whatever character or desert. When prisoners were detained for very long periods, the overriding considerations were those related to public safety.

It is the mandatory penalty of life imprisonment which is the problematic strand, in that nothing can be done to reform the law of murder, let alone the law of homicide, while that inflexible penalty remains in place. Every attempt constructively to deal with the other two strands will encounter the jurisprudential obstacles it places in the way. Unless and until the defective splice is taken apart and that strand of the law which is the penalty is repositioned in relation to the other two, every attempt to amend either the substantive law or the defences will be at best a temporary repair and at worst a complete botch. Indeed, the retention of the partial defences, which prompted the Government in 2003 to ask the Law Commission to report on the state of the defences to murder, simply exacerbates the present 'mess' identified by the Law Commission. And the changes to the two partial defences in the Coroners and Justice Act 2009 do little to remedy the defects of the law of murder.

The Executive Takes Over: the Invention of the Tariff

It can, of course, be argued that the establishment of the Parole Board by the Criminal Justice Act 1967 went a considerable way towards rationalising the process of managing all prison sentences, including life sentences, but such improvement has to be offset against the distinctly unhelpful political interventions of Government during the 1980s, notably the invention of the 'tariff'. Seeking to allay the vocal dissatisfaction of those sections of the public which had come to express increasing anxiety over what they perceived to be the paradox of an increase in crime and 'lenient' sentencing, this was an expression of 'getting tough' on 'law 'n' order', as criminal justice issues were now termed. Thus the idea that the first part of any life sentence would consist of a period to reflect 'deterrence and retribution' in respect of a particular criminal event which must expire before any consideration of release, arose not out of any ordinary Parliamentary debate, but rather, *ex cathedra* from a Secretary of State whose actions seemed to suggest, though without specifically claiming, an aura of infallibility.[1] From this there spawned a more expansive doctrine that included the 'whole life' tariff. Lesser tariffs, moreover, could be subject to such increase (in at least one instance without the prisoner even being aware) should the Secretary of State on reconsidering the circumstances of the crime deem it to be appropriate.[2] The Home Secretary, Mr Michael Howard (now Lord Howard), in a letter to the Home Affairs Committee of House of Commons dated 4 August 1995, reminded its members of what his predecessor, Mr Leon Brittan, had said in 1983 when introducing the so-called 'Brittan guidelines':

Taking account of the public concern about violent crime, in future I intend to exercise my discretion so that murders of police or prison officers, terrorist murderers, sexual or sadistic murderers of children and murderers by firearm in the course of robbery can normally expect to serve at least 20 years in custody; and there will be cases where the gravity of the offence requires a still longer period.[3]

---

1. Although immediately challenged, those who sought relief were eventually confronted with the judgment that the Home Secretary had acted neither unlawfully nor unreasonably— *Findlay v Secretary of State for the Home Department* [1985] AC 318. They were represented by Mr Stephen Sedley QC (now Lord Justice Sedley) and Mr Edward Fitzgerald (now a QC). It was, perhaps, a sign of the times that Mr Brittan had announced the new guidelines not to the House of Commons, but to the Conservative Party Conference at Blackpool on 11 October 1983.

2. While one cannot go beyond speculation as to the nature of the advice given by Home Office officials in these matters, the period of the 1980s was that in which Government ministers in many departments appear to have begun to be unusually sensitive to what they perceived to be popular opinion. Any decline in the influence exerted by civil servants which began at this time was not, however, to result in a social vacuum; in the last two decades the influence of other advisers has increased, some might say exponentially.

3. HC Home Affairs Committee, *Murder: The Mandatory Life Sentence*, First Report (13 December 1995).

What Happened in History: Events at the Time of Abolition

It was but only a matter of time before what was effectively to become a wholly improper arrogation of a judicial function by the Executive would be challenged at Strasbourg—and with a predictable outcome.

Once the setting of tariffs had, in terms of the European Convention on Human Rights, been defined as an exclusively judicialised function, the mischief of political intervention was reduced, though only to be confused by the tariff-setting introduced by Schedule 21 of the Criminal Justice Act 2003. But in 1965, during the debates on the abolition of the death penalty, although it was possible to identify differing opinions, those opinions (notably in the House of Lords) were sharply focused on the issue: party political interests played no discernible role. The present situation is entirely different in that, as between Government and Opposition, the last decade has seen a succession of Home Secretaries who have appeared to be pursuing very similar policies in respect of 'getting tough' on crime. Michael Howard's argument for retention of the mandatory penalty was fully endorsed by Jack Straw, by Charles Clarke, by John Reid and their successors in office. The remit to the Law Commission to examine the law of murder, subsequent to its review of the partial defences to murder, while precluding any consideration of the mandatory penalty has, for the time being, made it impossible to have any discussion about the reconstruction of the splice.

The many hours that have been spent in the courts by advocates, the deliberations of jurors and a ceaseless stretch of case law in appellate tribunals, even the energies of politicians eager to assuage what they perceived to be public opinion, would have been saved if, in 1965, the first amendment to the Murder (Abolition of the Death Penalty) Bill providing for complete judicial discretion in sentencing for murder, moved by the Lord Chief Justice, Lord Parker of Waddington (and carried by a small majority), had remained in place. Instead, it was withdrawn and replaced by a second amendment which was to become section 1(2) of the 1965 Act, by which the judges, having passed the mandatory sentence of life imprisonment, would be given no more than the discretion to make a recommendation (not part of the sentence) with respect to the minimum term the prisoner should serve. We subsequently refer to the alternate amendments as *Parker I* and *Parker II*.

It is one of the ironies of history that, but for the pressing issue of Parliamentary time, and the accompanying anxiety of the Bill's promoters that all could be so easily and perhaps irretrievably lost, it would have been *Parker I* that would now be enshrined in present law. Those Parliamentarians who, in 1965, reluctantly mourned the withdrawal of *Parker I* in favour of *Parker II* could scarcely have known how accurate their forebodings would prove to be.

In the Beginning: A Tale of Two Amendments

When Sydney Silverman MP launched his Private Member's Bill in 1964 to abolish capital punishment for murder, his sole intention and that of his co-abolitionists was to rid the country of the death penalty (the remaining death penalties for treason, piracy and arson in HM Dockyards were later abolished); the Bill's prescription was to replace the fixed penalty of the death sentence with the fixed penalty of life imprisonment. Apart from the significant change of statutory language from 'death' to 'life', which was definitive of the penalty and symbolic of the resolve to consign the hangman's noose to the museum of penal history, the legislation was unconcerned with the question of the duration of a life sentence. The authors of the Bill were content to let the process of releasing life-sentenced prisoners on licence from custody follow the long-established pattern of executive and administrative action for which the Home Secretary was answerable to Parliament: a system developed over many years to deal with those murderers who had been reprieved from the gallows and, later, for those convicted of non-capital murder under the Homicide Act 1957.

During the passage of the Bill through the House of Commons during the first half of 1965, a good deal of anxiety was expressed by many MPs about the dissociation of the judiciary from the actual assessment of how long a convicted murderer (who had automatically been sentenced to life imprisonment) should remain in prison before being on licence. To that issue, there were a number of proposed amendments contemplating judicial involvement in the sentencing process. All these proposed amendments, seeking to resolve these anxieties, were rejected by the sponsors of the Bill, if only on the ground that the sponsors were desirous of avoiding any legislative complexities in their determination to ensure the success of their abolition-ist enterprise. There was a strong disinclination to tamper with the existing procedure for implementing the mandatory sentence for all those convicted of murder, if only for fear of losing the cause of abolition. When, in the final stages of the Bill, there was an amendment in the House of Lords which became section 1(2) of the Act (the trial judge's power to recommend a mini-mum term to be served by the life sentence prisoner), Barbara Wootton (the sponsor of the Bill in the Lords) said that, while accepting the amendment, she still hankered for a Bill without it. She was adhering to the sponsors' desire simply and decisively to consign the hangman's noose to the status of a ghoulish curiosity.

The various amendments, proposed—and all lost—were unacceptable, and not just to the Bill's sponsors, with their fixation on the riddance of the death penalty. The Home Secretary (Sir Frank Soskice QC) proclaimed the orthodox view that it was not right to include a power whereby the judges could impose a minimum penalty, but that it was better left to the discretion of the Home Office.[4] And when the Bill came to the Lords, the Government Minister Lord Stonham (Joint Permanent Under-Secretary of State at the Home Office) observed: 'The only alternative that I know to death is life',[5] but he went on, significantly, to concede[6] that the matter did not strictly arise on the Bill. And a former Home Secretary, Henry Brooke, who became converted to abolition in the light of his experience at the Home Office and the ill-fated Homicide Act 1957, likewise observed that arrangements for reviewing life sentences should be a matter for later consideration. He had in mind that sentencing policy and practice would be reviewed by the Royal Commission on the Penal System, which he had set up in 1964 and which was still functioning.[7] (It was, uniquely, dissolved by Roy Jenkins in 1966.) Its replacement, the Advisory Council on the Penal System, published a

---

4. *Hansard* HC Vol 704 Col 930.
5. *Hansard* HL Vol 268 Col 567 (19 July 1965).
6. At Col 931.
7. *Hansard* HC Vol 704 Cols 906 and 914. *See also Hansard* HC Vol 716 Col 445. In none of his interventions in the debates is there any reference to any *quid pro quo* between abolitionists and retentionists. Brooke was the author of the amendment to the Bill which required that abolition should only become final if Parliament were to re-affirm the position at the end of five years.

report in June 1978, *Sentences of Imprisonment: A Review of Maximum Penalties*, which contained a chapter entitled 'The Penalty for Murder',[8] in which it recommended the substitution of a discretionary life sentence. The anxieties that the abolition Bill's passage should be unimpeded resurfaced during the Committee stage in the House of Lords, the Bill having come from the Commons unamended, save for one question of the timing of final abolition, namely the suspension of the Act on 31 July 1970 unless Parliament resolved to continue it indefinitely, which it did in December 1969.

The impetus for judicial involvement in determining the penalty for murder had been the Homicide Act 1957, which had sought to neutralise the abolitionist movement of the post-war period by categorising murders into those which alone should continue to attract the ultimate sanction and the remainder which would become non-capital. The Act was a scarcely mitigated and utterly friendless disaster, as the Royal Commission on Capital Punishment (the Gowers Commission) had predicted such a legislative step would be, since any search for categorising degrees of murder would be chimaerical. More than this, the Act provoked the judges to express outright hostility, none more so than the Lord Chief Justice, Lord Parker of Waddington, who had succeeded Lord Goddard (a devout retentionist) in 1958. Lord Parker had expressed his dislike for the Act in public speeches in the early 1960s, most particularly at a conference of probation officers in Margate in 1961. His intervention in the Parliamentary process in 1965 assisted in producing a vote both for abolition and for the debate on the sentencing process.[9]

During the committee stage of the Bill in the House of Lords on 27 July 1965, Lord Parker moved two amendments. The first was to provide that the penalty of life imprisonment would no longer be mandatory; the trial judge would, in future, have complete discretion in sentencing, as he had for any other criminal offence, including, significantly, manslaughter.

His alternative amendment provided for the retention of the mandatory life sentence, but gave discretion to the trial judge to recommend a minimum term of imprisonment, which would *not*, however, be part of the sentencing process, but merely an indication to the Executive of how long the prisoner should serve in prison. Lord Parker's first amendment was carried by 80

---

8. Chapter 12, pp.106–15.
9. *Hansard* HL Vol 268 Col 1211 (27 July 1965) and Vol 269 Col 423 (5 August 1965).

votes to 78; every Law Lord voted for it, including Viscount Dilhorne, a leading protagonist for the retention of the death penalty. Among the Law Lords, only the Lord Chancellor, Lord Gardiner, voted against, doing so in his capacity as a Government Minister in a Cabinet singularly committed to abolition, while retaining the exclusive Home Office power to determine how long each life sentence prisoner should serve in custody. Lord Gardiner's explicit support for the *status quo* was directed to the need for official control over those murderers who exhibited a risk of future dangerousness and for whom trial courts at the time of sentencing could not properly prescribe a timetable for release. By implication, Lord Gardiner found acceptable the principle of determinate sentencing by the trial judge for purposes of deterrence and punishment for the homicidal event.

Following the recollection in 1995[10] of the events of 1965 by the late Lord Shepherd (Government Chief Whip in the Lords at the time) a myth was accorded increasing credibility that somehow the mandatory sentence of life imprisonment was the price of a bargain or pact between abolitionists and retentionists that secured the end of the death penalty. The myth was accepted without question by the Home Affairs Committee of the House of Commons in 1995 and has been assiduously rehearsed by Government ministers and others since, besides being repeated in the media. Evidence from the time is strongly persuasive that there was, and is no basis for this account.[11]

It is important at this point to recall the fact that *Parker I* was warmly supported by both abolitionists and retentionists alike. Moreover, all the Law Lords, with the exception of the Lord Chancellor, Lord Gardiner, voted for it. Not least among its supporters was Lord Dilhorne (the Lord Chancellor immediately preceding), who was among the strongest advocates of the death penalty and found *Parker I* infinitely preferable to *Parker II*.[12]

---

10. During a debate on an amendment, tabled by Lord Ackner, to the Criminal Appeal Bill then before the House. *Hansard* HL Vol 565 Col 535.

11. Our extensive search of the evidence, including, *inter alia*, the volumes of *Hansard*, the Cabinet papers of the time and the private papers of the Lord Chancellor, Lord Gardiner, revealed not a scintilla of collateral evidence in support of Lord Shepherd's account. See Blom-Cooper and Morris, *With Malice Aforethought: A Study of the Crime and Punishment of Homicide* (Hart Publishing, 2004) pp.93-125.

12. *Hansard* HL Vol 268 Col 240 and Vol 269 Cols 405, 406,

The evidence is that the mandatory life sentence, far from being the outcome of any 'pact', was by no means set in stone. In March 1970, only three months after Parliament had affirmed abolition, the Home Secretary, James Callaghan, charged the Criminal Law Revision Committee in the following terms:

> To review the law relating to, *and the penalties for*, offences against the person, including homicide, *in the light of, and subject to, the recent decision of Parliament to make permanent the statutory provision abolishing the death penalty for murder.*[13] (our italics)

It would seem inconceivable that, if so recent a Parliamentary bargain had been struck whereby opposition to abolition had been bought off at the price of the mandatory life sentence, a Minister of the stature and experience of Callaghan would have simply either ignored it or brushed it aside.

A Lost Opportunity

Had *Parker I* found its way on to the Statute Book, tariff-fixing by administrative process, formally introduced by Leon Brittan as Home Secretary in 1983, would never have been necessary, if indeed desirable. Hours of debate would have been saved. Lord Parker's slender victory was, however, to be short-lived. By the time of the report stage on 5 August, he had been prevailed upon, almost certainly by the Home Secretary (Sir Frank Soskice QC) or his Minister of State, Lord Stonham, to withdraw his amendment and move, successfully, to his alternative.

Parker II became section 1(2) of the Murder (Abolition of Death Penalty) Act 1965, the only concession in the Act to particularity in the life sentence. In practice, the recommendation was to be little used — initially in fewer than 5% of cases — and the Court of Appeal (Criminal Division) pronounced in 1972 that the minimum recommendation should be not less than 12 years,[14]

---

13. See: CLRC Twelfth Report, *Penalty for Murder* Cmnd 5184 (HMSO 1973).
14. *R v Flemming* (1973) 57 Cr App R 524. This was an incidental pronouncement since the issue in *Flemming* was whether a recommendation could be made in respect of a sentence under section 53 Children and Young Persons Act 1933. The court ruled that section 1(2) of the 1965

thereby clearly indicating that the judges thought that the minimum recommendation was designed solely to cater for the dangerous prisoner, and did not permit short *minima* for cases of extreme mitigation such as mercy killings. That had not been the general intention behind the provision for a minimum recommendation, since the Home Secretary (Sir Frank Soskice QC) had assured Parliament that the minimum period could be lengthy, or short if there were mitigating circumstances.[15]

The story surrounding the two Parker amendments is more than an account of a mere historical event; it is highly instructive. During the report stage in the House of Lords, Lord Parker explained that he was content to accept the second compromise amendment as being 'right in principle and indeed logical', although doubtless he, like other peers, expected that the minimum recommendation would be used as an alternative to judicial discretion to determine any sentence, even a non-custodial penalty. In the course of the debate, Lord Parker referred to correspondence he had had in February 1962 with Mr Gerald Gardiner QC (as he then was)[16] in which the latter had suggested a solution to the sentencing problem by imposing by statute:

(a) a sentence of life imprisonment;

(b) subject to the Home Secretary possessing the power of release whenever he thought fit;

(c) such release not to be effected 'before such terms of years as the trial judge may fix'.

Two observations can be made. First, *Parker II* gave far less power to the trial judge. As a 'recommended minimum' it possessed no legal effect. The 'fixed' term of years would not provide a binding limitation on the prison administration. Second, the Gardiner formula (which indicated at least some

---

Act did not apply.

15. *Hansard* HC Vol 718 Col 376, 28 October 1965. This had been stated by Lord Stonham (Minister of State at the Home Office) on 5 August 1965, when he observed that a judge could recommend anything from a very short sentence to a very long one: *Hansard* HL Vol 269 Col 420, 421.

16. *Hansard* HL Vol 269 Col 414.

judicial input to the question of 'how long is life') is now reflected in the tariff system spelled out in Schedule 21 of the Criminal Justice Act 2003.[17]

Parker II was acceptable to both the sponsors of the Bill and the Government (which had orchestrated the legislative process) but was, however, only reluctantly accepted by some peers. As we have earlier indicated, Viscount Dilhorne, a former Conservative Lord Chancellor and Attorney-General, who throughout the passage of the Bill had remained in favour of retaining the death penalty for murder (and voted accordingly at the final stage of the Bill in the Lords), expressed a distinct preference for *Parker I*. And, significantly, that view was echoed by MPs on all sides of the House of Commons when the Bill was reconsidered on 28 October 1965.

Coda: Further Words on Parker I and Parker II

Following Sydney Silverman's acceptance of the Lords' amendment, providing for the trial judge's minimum recommendation, the Conservative spokesman on home affairs, Mr Mark Carlisle (later a Home Office Minister in 1970, Secretary of State for Education in 1979, and eventually Lord Carlisle of Runcorn QC), described the amendment as 'a dismal compromise'.[18] He strongly supported Lord Parker's initial approach, favouring the courts giving all murderers a determinate sentence. He would clearly have supported *Parker I*, but in view of the late stage of the session was disposed not to vote against *Parker II*. Mark Carlisle's preference for *Parker I* was shared by Sir John Hobson QC (a former Attorney-General), Mr Reginald Paget (a Labour MP of highly independent views) and Sir Richard Glyn (a prominent Conservative MP). Mr Henry Brooke (a former Home Secretary 1962-64) declared himself against *Parker II*, without declaring a preference for judicial discretion in sentencing.

Most notable among those who spoke in the debate was Mr Peter Thorneycroft, a former Conservative Chancellor of the Exchequer. He declared that the amendment 'had not a friend in the House; except for the Home

---

17. See the judicial interpretation of the tariff system by the Court of Appeal (Criminal Division) in a guidance decision in *R v Peter, Palmer & Campbell*, 1 March 2003.
18. *Hansard* HC Vol 718 Col 370.

Secretary'. That was clearly the majority view.[19] He added that it would not be proper to lose the Bill now over 'some muddle concerning a Lords' amendment'.[20] Given the lateness in the parliamentary process and the manifest desire of Lord Gardiner and his abolitionist colleagues in and out of Cabinet, it is reasonable to assume that, particularly had time permitted, judicial discretion in sentencing those convicted of murder would have been accepted by Government and MPs. The overwhelming desire, however, to ensure the end of capital punishment undoubtedly prevailed, as against the *dirigisme* of the Home Office to retain administrative control of the 'lifer system'. Had the battle over the exclusivity of judicial sentencing, which was ultimately won in the 1990s (via the jurisprudence of Strasbourg), taken place three decades earlier, forty years of fruitless efforts by penal reformers would have been avoided.

The unfinished business of the 1965 Act should now be completed. Those who persist in maintaining loyalty to the spirit of abolition might respect the overwhelming view, expressed in *Parker I,* to ensure that an independent judiciary should decide the appropriate penalty for murder, as it does for every other criminal offence (including manslaughter).

The mandatory life sentence for murder has no place in the penal system of a civilised country.

---

19. *Hansard* HC Vol 718 Col 381.
20. *Ibid,* Col 380.

Hubert Lister Parker, Baron Parker of Waddington and Lord Chief Justice 1958-1971. In the debates on the Bill abolishing the death penalty Lord Parker expressed the view that 'there is one offence of homicide' and, identifying the mandatory life sentence for murder as an anomaly, he attempted — unsuccessfully — to establish judicial discretion in the sentencing process. © National Portrait Gallery, London.

Rayner Goddard, Lord Chief Justice 1946–1958. Perhaps the most publicly prominent judge of the post-Second World War period he had a reputation for severity in sentencing. An enthusiast for capital punishment, he is now irreversibly associated with the controversial conviction and hanging of Derek Bentley in 1953. Although the decision not to reprieve Bentley from the gallows was that of the Home Secretary, Sir David Maxwell Fyfe, Goddard was heavily criticised when the conviction was quashed by the Court of Appeal in 2001. 'In our judgment, the summing up …was such as to deny the appellant that fair trial which is the birthright of every British citizen'.

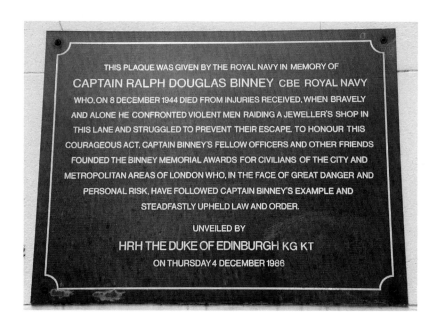

THIS PLAQUE WAS GIVEN BY THE ROYAL NAVY IN MEMORY OF

CAPTAIN RALPH DOUGLAS BINNEY CBE ROYAL NAVY

WHO, ON 8 DECEMBER 1944 DIED FROM INJURIES RECEIVED, WHEN BRAVELY AND ALONE HE CONFRONTED VIOLENT MEN RAIDING A JEWELLER'S SHOP IN THIS LANE AND STRUGGLED TO PREVENT THEIR ESCAPE. TO HONOUR THIS COURAGEOUS ACT, CAPTAIN BINNEY'S FELLOW OFFICERS AND OTHER FRIENDS FOUNDED THE BINNEY MEMORIAL AWARDS FOR CIVILIANS OF THE CITY AND METROPOLITAN AREAS OF LONDON WHO, IN THE FACE OF GREAT DANGER AND PERSONAL RISK, HAVE FOLLOWED CAPTAIN BINNEY'S EXAMPLE AND STEADFASTLY UPHELD LAW AND ORDER.

UNVEILED BY

HRH THE DUKE OF EDINBURGH KG KT

ON THURSDAY 4 DECEMBER 1986

Close-up of the plaque erected in memory of Captain Binney in Birchin Lane in the City of London. On 8 December 1944, attempting to frustrate the escape of robbers, Binney was run down and carried beneath their getaway car for over a mile, dying later of his injuries. © Terence Morris

Birchin Lane today. Save for the yellow no-parking lines it remains virtually unchanged since 1944. The Binney Memorial plaque can be seen on the wall in the right distance, close to where Captain Binney was run down, on the side of what in 1944 was Wordley and Co's jewellers shop. © Terence Morris.

The 1956 Ford Prefect 100E driven by Jim Smith on 2 March 1960. Various models of the Prefect were in production between 1938 and 1959. Unlike earlier versions, the 100E had no running-boards. The paintwork of the front of the vehicle and the visible distortion of the front bumper are suggestive of earlier collision damage. © Metropolitan Police Service.

The oncoming vehicles by which Police Constable Meehan was struck. The first was a pre-war Austin 10 Cambridge saloon (in production July 1936–April 1939), the second a Ford Popular 103E (in production 1953–59), the third an earlier Ford Prefect E493A (in production 1949–53) and the fourth a BMW Isetta motor tricycle popularly known as a 'bubble car' (produced 1957–62). © Metropolitan Police Service.

Plumstead Road adjacent to Beresford Square, Woolwich as it is today. Unlike Birchin Lane, it has changed considerably, though some of the original shops are still visible. The main road is now a dual carriageway to the left of the trees and the original road is pedestrianised. The oncoming stream of vehicles into whose path Police Constable Meehan fell would have been coming towards the camera. What happened here in 1960 led to a turning point in English legal history. © Terence Morris.

Beresford Square today. Where Smith was stopped is now paved over and a busy street market but the older shops to either side remain much as they were at the time.
© Terence Morris.

Reginald Woolmington. On trial twice in 1935 for the murder of his teen-aged wife he was, perhaps against all the odds, successful in his appeal to the House of Lords which affirmed that it was not for him to prove that the gun had gone off by accident, but for the prosecutor to prove the contrary. The judgment in *Woolmington v DPP* was to set aside some three centuries of precedent in English homicide law. From an old newspaper clipping.

Viscount Sankey Lord Chancellor 1931-1935 Sankey, in delivering the judgment that set Woolmington free, used a phrase that has entered the legal lexicon: 'Throughout the web of the English criminal law one golden thread is always to be seen - that it is the duty of the prosecution to prove the prisoner's guilt ...' Among other things, the authors argue that the law concerning defences to murder (as opposed to a new definition of that offence) leads to unnecessary use of court time and avoidable expense.

Terence Morris and Louis Blom-Cooper © Waterside Press

CHAPTER 8

HUNTING THE CHIMÆRA[1]

The jurists of the Middle Ages and their successors in the 17th century were concerned with the law of murder largely in terms of the issues of malice and its constructive extensions. Apart from the sanctions applicable in the 'clergyable'[2] exceptions, homicide, like many other offences, was punishable by death. In the 19th and 20th centuries the focus had shifted away from definitions of the law of homicide and towards its limitation in the context of capital punishment. By the second half of the 19th century, limitation of the death penalty had become so extensive that it effectively applied only to what the law now defines as murder.[3] The pressure for the total abolition of capital punishment, however, continued to grow, predicated for the most part upon the argument that it was a barbarous relic of past times which ought to have no place in a modern society which saw itself located at the pinnacle of contemporary civilisation. In the event, progress towards abolition was to prove very protracted.

Perhaps as with no other criminal offence, discussion about the definition of murder became increasingly inextricable from consideration of its penalties. Indeed, this has been the besetting problem for reforming the law of homicide as distinct from the penalties attaching to it. By presuming the jurisprudential legitimacy of fragmenting homicide into distinct offences, each with its specific penal consequences, murder became, quite literally, 'a crime apart'. The wider issues of legal liability and moral culpability were

---

1. This phrase was used by the late Sir Ernest Gowers, Chairman of the Royal Commission on Capital Punishment 1949-53 in conversation with the present authors some 40 years ago. He was suggesting that the search for a way of categorising murders (such as had been employed in the Homicide Act 1957) was an impossible task. The *chimæra*, a fabulous monster of Greek mythology, was described by Homer as having a goat's body, a lion's head and a dragon's tail. Born in Lycia, it was slain by Bellerophon.

2. See *Chapter 1*.

3. Exceptions remained, largely those related to national security in times of war.

eclipsed by attempts to identify malicious intent, express, implied or constructive. In May 1864 after a debate in the House of Commons on capital punishment a Royal Commission was appointed:

> To inquire into the provision and operation of the laws under which the punishment of death is now inflicted in the United Kingdom, and the manner in which it is inflicted, and to report whether it is desirable to make any alteration therein.

The Commission reported in January 1866[4] in a mere six pages.[5] The Commissioners could not agree on the subject of abolition, but they were of one accord in finding the current law of murder unsatisfactory. While they accepted the accepted definition of the crime as killing unlawfully with malice aforethought, they were exercised by the way in which the courts had variously interpreted these terms. Interpretations of malice aside, the defence of provocation was by no means uniform in character. Provocation, by means of words, looks, gestures, or trespass to land or goods, was held to be insufficient to reduce the crime to manslaughter. The Commission did, however, make an attempt at distinguishing between two degrees of murder, only the first being capital. The first degree was to consist of those murders deliberately committed with express malice aforethought, such malice to be found as a fact by the jury. Additionally punishable by death were to be those committed in the context of other acts such as escape after, or in the perpetration of, the felonies of murder, arson, rape, burglary, robbery or piracy. For the rest, the penalty was to be penal servitude for life, or for any period of not less than seven years, at the discretion of the court. Prior to the Consolidation Acts of 1861, the judges had enjoyed the power to record the death sentence but not pronounce it; if this were to have been restored, it would have had the effect of giving the judges the discretion to decide whether a defendant convicted of first degree murder would suffer the death penalty rather than this remaining within the Royal Prerogative of Mercy.[6] Fitzjames Stephen, Recorder of Newark at the time, was not only strongly

---

4. *Report of the Capital Punishment Committee.* Cmnd 3590 (1866).
5. In contrast to the 700 pages or so of Minutes of Evidence and other material.
6. No longer exercised by the sovereign after the accession of the 17-year-old Victoria in 1837, but originally by the Home Secretary and now by the Justice Secretary.

in favour of retaining the death penalty but believed public hangings were a powerful deterrent.[7] While he would have reduced the scope of the crime of murder he considered that the proposed bifurcation of murder into two degrees would be productive of nothing but further complication in the definition of murder bringing numerous injustices in its train.[8]

Four months after the publication of the Royal Commission's report, the Lord Chancellor, Lord Cranworth, introduced a Bill in the Lords with this precise intention, based upon the recommendations of the Commission. The voting for and against was equal and Cranworth substituted a new clause limiting the definition of murder to instances in which the accused intended to kill or do grievous bodily harm to the person killed or any other person. Although this managed to survive a Third Reading, a change of Government frustrated its successful passage through the Commons. But for this quirk of political events, reform of the law of murder, as distinct from the penalty, might have made a quantum leap in the direction of constructive reform. Throughout the next two decades there were a number of attempts to tackle the issue, none successful. The Bill introduced in 1867 is of particular interest in that it anticipates the approach embodied in the Homicide Act 1957 by identifying five conditions having the effect of defining the crime as capital, namely:

(i) a deliberate intention to kill or do grievous bodily harm to the deceased or another;

(ii) that the crime was committed with a view to, and in or immediately before or immediately after the commission of the felonies of rape, bur-

---

7. James Fitzjames Stephen, *A History of the Criminal Law of England*, London (1883), vol 2 at p.89. He argued that such a shameful death was 'much harder to go through in public than in private'. Stephen had a tendency towards the hyperbolic in expressing some of his most punitive views. He favoured making more felonies capital on grounds of deterrence and thought that such an extension would result, in a short time, in 'really bad offenders' becoming 'as rare as wolves'.

8. Stephen, writing in *Fraser's Magazine* of February 1866. In 1872 Stephen, who enjoyed a substantial reputation as a jurist, was invited to draft a Bill that would define and amend the law relating to homicide. It was presented in 1874.

glary, robbery, piracy, or arson to a dwelling house any person being therein;

(iii) that the crime was committed for the purpose of thereby enabling himself or any other person to commit murder or any of the above mentioned felonies;

(iv) that the crime was committed in the act of escaping from, or for the purpose of enabling himself or any other person to escape from or avoid lawful arrest or detainer, immediately after he or such other person had committed or attempted to commit murder or any of the above mentioned felonies;

(v) that the accused murdered a constable or other peace officer, acting in the discharge of his duty.

Neither this Bill, nor any of its successors,[9] was to reach the statute book.[10] Stephen's draft Bill of 1874 was referred to a Select Committee of the House of Commons; it is notable in respect of a clause (Clause 24) which, had it become law, might have avoided what was to prove to be almost a century of ensuing debate about the so-called 'insanity defence'.

Some seven decades were to elapse before major reform of the law of murder once more became the concern of Government as distinct from individual Members of Parliament seeking to promote the abolition of capital punishment. The Criminal Justice Bill of 1948, promoted by the Labour Government elected in 1945, was, not unlike British motor cars in the immediate post-war period, a pre-war design in almost every respect. In this instance it was based very broadly upon the Bill of the same name proposed in 1938 by a Conservative administration but overtaken by events that were to bring about

---

9. Murder Law Amendment and Appeal Bill 1871; Homicide Law Amendment Bill 1874; ditto 1876; Homicide Law Amendment Bills 1877 and 1878; Law of Murder Amendment Bill 1908; Criminal Justice Bill 1948 (Clause 1 and Schedule of Government Amendments to Lords Amendments, also clauses proposed by Basil Neild KC MP and Hector Hughes KC MP).

10. The passage of these various Bills in the later Victorian period is considered in detail by Leon Radzinowicz and Roger Hood in vol. 5 of their seminal *History of English Criminal Law*, London (Stevens and Sons, 1986), pp.661-676.

World War II. The abolition of capital punishment was, however, a 'bolt-on' modification that has to be understood in the context of the enormous pressure for abolition that had been building on the Government back benches, led by the indefatigable Sydney Silverman MP. In the event a combination of hostility in the Lords and the doubts entertained by the Prime Minister, Clement Attlee, that abolition consequent on a constitutional battle with the Upper House would be a politically hazardous enterprise,[11] proved fatal. It was not for a further decade that Parliament was again to be exercised on the issue, once more in the context not of reform of the law of homicide *per se*, but of its modification in order to reduce the scope of capital punishment. Although abolition was clearly not going to be recorded in history along with the foundation of the NHS as one of its great achievements, the Attlee administration was responsible for the establishment of the Royal Commission on Capital Punishment in 1949 under the chairmanship of Sir Ernest Gowers.[12] The combination of a powerful and intellectually incisive chairman with some notable specialists among the Commissioners, it had the advantage of having as its secretary Francis Graham-Harrison, who was to emerge as one of the ablest figures in the post-war Home Office. The report, which appeared in September 1953, was, however, to a Conservative Government headed by the elderly Churchill.[13] Its essential findings were that, short of abolition, there was no way in which it was practically possible to reform the law, and that the idea of 'degrees' of murder was a non-starter. Attempts to get a Commons debate on the report in February 1954 were stonewalled by the Home Secretary, Sir David Maxwell-Fyfe.[14] The Lords had debated the report in the preceding November. Further attempts were made, but to no avail, to persuade the Government to change its mind; nor would it even indicate what steps, if any, it proposed to take with respect to the Commission's recommendations. Not until a further year had elapsed

---

11. There is reason to believe that Herbert Morrison, Attlee's deputy and effectively his political manager, urged this counsel. Morrison (a policeman's son) was opposed to abolition.

12. Hitherto, Gowers, himself a distinguished civil servant, had been better known for his work in attempting to persuade others in the civil service to employ plain English.

13. How far he was, in his eightieth year, concerned with such issues is a matter for speculative doubt. The onset of old age was beginning to take its toll of this gargantuan figure.

14. Maxwell-Fyfe is elsewhere remembered as the Home Secretary whom Goddard LCJ had expected to reprieve Derek Bentley, but chose to let the law take its lethal course.

did the opportunity for debate finally arise on 10 February 1955. Silverman, his Parliamentary energy seemingly inexhaustible, attempted to amend the Government motion to 'take note' of the Gowers Report by moving that the death penalty be suspended for five years. Maxwell-Fyfe had meanwhile been succeeded as Home Secretary by Major Gwilym Lloyd George and Sir Reginald Manningham-Buller[15] was now Attorney-General. The combination of an Attorney-General and a Home Secretary, neither of whom favoured change, together with a divided House, ensured not merely the defeat of Silverman's amendment but sterilised the debate about capital punishment in the immediate future — or so it seemed in the early months of 1955.

But, once more, it was to be public disquiet with individual cases involving the death penalty that guaranteed that the issue simply would not go away. The hanging of Timothy Evans in 1950 (subsequently pardoned) and the subsequent conviction of his landlord John Christie (for serial murders in the same house) in 1953 had projected into popular consciousness the spectre of an innocent man going to the gallows; the hanging of Derek Bentley, aged 19, while his accomplice, Christopher Craig (accused of firing the fatal shot), had been too young to receive the death sentence, aroused a sense that the law was capable of monstrous unfairness which offended the common man's sense of justice. The carrying out of the death sentence on Ruth Ellis in the summer of 1955[16] served to re-ignite the debate which the Government thought had been quenched some five months earlier. These three can be identified as being the cases which changed the law. But the politics of abolition at this period were complex[17] and the outcome scarcely surprising in view of the resistance to abolition which was still marked, certainly in Parliament. What was to emerge could most charitably be described as little more than a legislative botch. It failed to placate the diehards among

---

15. In his forensic style, Manningham–Buller had not a little in common with Sir Edward Coke.

16. Although much 'played down' by both the Metropolitan Police and the Home Office, accounts of the scenes outside Holloway on the morning of 13 July suggested outrage, with the crowd chanting 'Evans! Bentley! Ellis!' Official 'denials' of the circumstances surrounding the execution of the death penalty remained until almost the very end of capital punishment. As it happened, Ruth Ellis was to be the last woman to be hanged in the United Kingdom.

17. See Brian P Block and John Hostettler, *Hanging in the Balance* (Waterside Press, 1997); also Terence Morris, *Crime and Criminal Justice in England Since 1945* (Basil Blackwell, 1989) pp.77-85.

the retentionists, but succeeded, simultaneously, in providing ammunition to be used in the cause of abolition.

The Homicide Act 1957[18] must rank as one of the most unsatisfactory examples of legislation affecting criminal justice in the 20th century. Instrumentally reactive rather than constructively proactive, it began its working life with few friends and the number of its critics grew with the passage of time.

To be fair, it began bravely. It served to abolish the doctrine of constructive malice. That, at least, was the intention, though how far 'constructive malice' lingered on in other guises suggesting that the snake had been scotched rather than killed, is a matter for some debate. It plunged with not a little courage into the deep and dimly illuminated waters of what had become known since the days of M'Naghten[19] as the 'insanity defence' by introducing the concept of diminished responsibility (the burden of proof to be on the defence) and upon a jury thus finding, providing for a substitute conviction for manslaughter. The grounds for provocation were extended to cover 'things said' as well as 'things done' or a combination of the two, and, to deal with the tragic predicament of the surviving party to a suicide pact (the burden of proof of fact again being upon the defence) a further provision for a manslaughter verdict. Thus far, the new Act was to liberalise the law of homicide by making concessions to a long line of critics that stretched back for years, if not centuries.

However worthy these intentions, they were largely set at nought by the fact that, contrary to the advice of the Gowers Commission — and indeed, to many of the critics who had taken part in the Parliamentary debates in later Victorian times — the Act forged ahead with categorising murders into capital and non-capital. We cannot be certain what was the source of this initiative; certainly, there was at the time a current view that public opinion, by no means enthusiastically abolitionist, would only tolerate so much by way of change and would look ill upon the hangman becoming redundant.[20] It is not impossible that the political managers considered the Act as

---

18. Elizabeth II. Ch. 11. It was not long before it became known among lawyers as the 'Reggie-cide' Act since the Attorney-General, Sir Reginald Manningham-Buller (later to become Lord Chancellor as Lord Dilhorne) was one of its principal architects.

19. See *Chapter 4* of this work for a more detailed discussion of the 'insanity' defence.

20. Part of the problem was that public sentiment was volatile: those convicted of horrific murders would enjoy little sympathy and many would wish them speeded on their way to the

FINE LINES AND DISTINCTIONS

a way of getting the issue of total abolition put to sleep for many years to come. On the other hand, there was among the younger generation of Conservative politicians, especially those who were lawyers, a recognition that, complete removal of the death penalty apart, changes were needed. Each of these is likely to have weighed advantageously in the balance against taking the advice of the Royal Commission and, as for the lessons of history, they could be readily set aside as having little relevance to the mid-20th century,[21] yet it requires little imagination to presume the reaction of Stephen to the proposal.

The five categories of capital murder were those done:

(a) in the course or furtherance of theft;

(b) by shooting or causing an explosion;

(c) in the course or for the purpose of resisting or avoiding or preventing a lawful arrest, or of effecting or assisting an escape or rescue from legal custody;

(d) any murder of a police officer acting in the execution of his duty or of a person assisting a police officer so acting; or

(e) in the case of a person who was a prisoner at the time when he did or was a party to the murder, any murder of a prison officer acting in the execution of his duty or of a person assisting a prison officer so acting.

Provision was also made for the death penalty for those convicted of murder who had been so convicted in Great Britain of another murder done on a different occasion.

---

gallows, while others would engender a sense that to inflict the death penalty was unjust or unfair. *Vox populi* might chant the names of Evans, Bentley and Ellis, but not those of Heath, Haigh or Christie.

21. There is a view, attributed to George Santayana, that those who know no history are destined to re-live it.

In these categories echoes of the past resonate with a familiar clarity. We see homicides done in the course of other crimes singled out for the capital penalty. Theft, which included robbery, being one of the old felonies, remained capital. Similarly, homicides done whilst resisting arrest or escaping from custody. Officers of the peace are, however, limited to police officers, and prison officers emerge as a new category of those said to require the special protection of the death penalty.

In the case of those murders for which a court was to be precluded from passing sentence of death, the Act provided that the sentence should be one of life imprisonment. The comparatively brief life span of the Act was one factor that ensured that the meaning of life imprisonment was unlikely to become a contentious matter, but, in any event, the assumption appeared to be that such life sentences would be no different from those life sentences served by those who had been reprieved from the gallows. Reprieve was traditionally granted in compassionate cases and non-capital murders were now statutorily differentiated as less heinous than those for which the penalty of death was reserved. Only since total abolition has the meaning of the life sentence become a matter for what is almost exclusively political debate. As we shall consider later,[22] the concept of imprisonment for life currently arouses feelings in politics and the media that equal, if not surpass, those generated by the debates about capital punishment. Indeed, the situation is multi-dimensional since it involves the legal definition of 'life' as well as the implications of the cumulative increase in the 'lifer' population for the administration of prisons.

While it can be argued that imperfections could be discerned everywhere in the 1957 Act, it was in the distinctions between capital and non-capital offences that its flaws were most transparent. Every attempt to categorise the various manifestations of homicide is predicated upon the presumed existence of a hierarchy of heinousness. In plain language, the law is employed to say that *this* kind of killing is worse than *that* and therefore deserves a greater penalty to be inflicted on the offender. The assumption is that there is a readily discernible consensus on the matter. But neither in 1957, nor, for that matter, today, is such uniformity of view other than an illusion.

---

22. In *Chapter 16*.

The inclusion of police officers was no surprise, not least since at the time of Coke various agents of justice had been identified as requiring special protection[23] and it was widely believed that the deterrent quality of the death penalty provided this. The inclusion of prison officers occasioned some surprise, not least since the phenomenon of prison staff being killed by their captives was (and indeed, remains) exceptionally rare. The inclusion of killings in the course or furtherance of theft was, again, historically consistent with the view that it was deemed appropriate for certain felonies to be marked by some penal premium.

Since the death penalty was to remain the centrepiece of the legislation, the Home Secretary, Major Gwilym Lloyd George (later Lord Tenby), elaborated on the reasoning behind the new role of capital punishment. The Government had a prime duty to maintain order in society and it recognised a real fear in the public mind that to remove the ultimate penal sanction would lead to increased violence. Those murders involving such violence as to be inimical to public order and those most likely to arouse fear in the minds of members of the public at risk were deemed to be prime instances of capital crimes. The progenitors of the Act failed to consider either the incidence of such crimes or the way in which the circumstances of particular offences or the characteristics of many of the offenders involved might result in anomalies, let alone apparent injustices.

The present authors examined each of the 764 cases of persons indicted for murder in England and Wales between the coming into force of the Act on 24 March 1957 until 31 December 1962.[24] In practice, not all popular conceptions of heinousness were recognised in the Act by the identification of certain offences as capital. Killings that involved poisoning (long regarded as one of the most despicable homicides), those occurring in the course of sexual offences and the killing of children after abduction were omitted from the capital category.[25] The use of firearms, thought to be the

---

23. Whether this was significantly afforded by the law relating to constructive malice is a matter for argument.

24. Terence Morris and Louis Blom-Cooper, *A Calendar of Murder* (Michael Joseph Ltd, 1964).

25. In 1961 *Jones* was convicted of non-capital murder of a 12-year-old girl whom forensic evidence indicated had been raped. The defendant had previously been convicted of raping an 11-year-old. Consequent upon the failure of his appeal to the Lords his sentence of life imprisonment, consecutive upon the existing sentence of 14 years' imprisonment for rape, was

preserve of professional criminals, was by no means absent from what are more accurately termed domestic homicides. *Walden* (1959) shot and killed the young woman with whom he was infatuated and her boyfriend[26] while *Neimasz* (1961) shot his male victim but killed his female companion with the butt of the shotgun immediately afterwards.[27] *King* (1959) was acquitted of capital murder but convicted of section 2 manslaughter and sentenced to life imprisonment. In the course of a domestic dispute during which King appears to have been under the influence of alcohol, he terrorised his estranged wife and her parents. When a constable attempted to get the gun away, King shot him in the groin; he then shot his wife in the back. A police inspector who tried to pacify him was then shot in the chest and died later. The trial of Gunter *Podola* (1959) who shot and killed Detective Sergeant Purdy was beset with the issue of fitness to plead since it was claimed he was suffering from hysterical amnesia following events at the time of his arrest. The truth of the matter will never be known since he was hanged[28] having been refused the Attorney-General's *fiat* for an appeal to the House of Lords. At most it can be said that Podola seemed far removed from the average passenger on the Clapham omnibus.

But perhaps an instance of how the law remained in an unsatisfactory state during the currency of the 1957 Act was the case of *Vickers*. The Act had been in force barely a month when Vickers (aged 22) killed a woman of 72 who had attacked him as he attempted to burgle her shop. Knocking her down with a blow from his fist he searched for money and finding none fled the scene. His only previous conviction was for theft at the age of eleven. The killing was done in the course of theft, but was it murder when a pathologist's report suggested that the blows inflicted on the victim were moderately severe to slight? Far from being a straightforward instance of the kind of violence which would normally result in serious harm to the victim, the blows were such as to put the implication of malice in some considerable doubt. In the Court of Criminal Appeal[29] it became clear that while the Act

upheld. *R v Jones* [1962] AC 635.

26. Walden was hanged at Leeds Prison (Armley Gaol) on 14 August 1959.

27. Neimasz was hanged at Wandsworth Prison on 8 September 1961.

28. At Wandsworth Prison on 5 November 1959.

29. [1957] 2 QB 664.

had, as it were, struck a mortal blow against the doctrine of 'constructive' malice, the notion of implied malice was alive and flourishing: a full court of five judges dismissed his appeal. The Attorney-General subsequently refused his *fiat* for an appeal to the Lords, provoking a motion of censure on the part of some 68 Labour MPs who argued that the case raised a point of law of exceptional public importance.

Four months from the date of his original conviction, Vickers became the first person to suffer death under the new Act and was hanged at Durham.[30] It is not without irony that the first trial for capital murder under its provisions should have demonstrated, and so clearly, that the notion of 'malice', the relic of three centuries of criminal justice, should continue to present problems of interpretation. The issue of what constitutes 'serious harm', though the case of *Vickers* is now almost half a century distant, remains unresolved. The Supreme Court may one day have to consider two questions which arose from a case in the Court of Appeal in Northern Ireland in 2003:[31]

1. whether implied malice (an intention to commit grievous bodily harm) constitutes sufficient *mens rea* for the crime of murder, or whether the prosecution must prove express malice (an intention to kill);

2. if implied malice constitutes sufficient *mens rea*, whether it must be proved that the defendant knew or foresaw that his act might endanger the victim's life.

During its brief lifetime, the Homicide Act 1957 could be accounted a success in at least one regard: it succeeded in pleasing no-one. If concern about the conviction and hanging of Vickers was limited to articulate abolitionists, a reverse concern undoubtedly existed in the public mind about the fact that the majority of the most serious instances of homicide in the context of some form of sexual activity were not only excluded by statute from the capital category but also appeared to provide some form of penal discount through the medium of the verdict of manslaughter by reason of diminished responsibility.

---

30. On 23 July 1957.
31. *The Queen v Samuel Anderson* [2003] NICA 12 (7 April 2003).

In 1958 *Matheson* (aged 52), a casual labourer, had met his victim, a 15-year-old boy and had gone with him to premises in Newcastle for the purpose of homosexual relations. He killed the boy with blows from a bottle and a hammer and then took £35 in cash from his person. Hiding the body until the following day, he crudely dismembered it and put the body parts into a drainage sump in the building. He finally surrendered to police in Glasgow. Two issues, central to the new Act, emerged at his trial at Durham Assizes, the first relating to the definition of murder 'in the course or furtherance of theft' and the second with regard to his plea of diminished responsibility. The trial judge,[32] observing that the term was entirely new, raised the question of its interpretation: was theft the motive or intention that led to the murder, or was the intention of the accused to murder, perhaps during the course of the sexual offence, and the theft just followed?

On the question of diminished responsibility, three doctors, including the medical officer of the prison in which he had been remanded to await trial, gave evidence of Matheson's mental history. Most of his life had been spent in various penal institutions and he had been a voluntary patient in a mental hospital. He had sought treatment for his sexual condition but suffered from the handicap of an IQ of only 73, having a developmental age of ten. He was also described as having a psychopathic personality. His appeal to the Court of Criminal Appeal was heard before a full court of five judges, with Goddard LCJ presiding. The appeal was grounded primarily in the argument that the jury had come to an unreasonable verdict, against the weight of the evidence of diminished responsibility. Three doctors had testified on the matter and there was no evidence the other way. On this argument the appeal was allowed, and a verdict of manslaughter (under section 2 of the 1957 Act) and a sentence of 20 years' imprisonment substituted.[33] In giving judgment the court affirmed that while it was for the jury to decide the question of diminished responsibility it must be founded on the evidence offered.[34]

---

32. Mr Justice Finnemore. For more extensive discussion of *Matheson*, see *Chapter 14* of this work.

33. [1958] 1 WLR 74. Matheson's eventual discharge from prison was not back into the community but into a secure mental hospital.

34. A similar issue had arisen in *Spriggs* [1958] 1 QB 270, where the accused was convicted of capital murder a month or so before Matheson (by shooting a barman who had earlier ejected him from licensed premises over a relatively trivial issue). Mr Justice Austin Jones, having

In 1960 there were two instances of murders with powerful sexual over-tones that arrested public consciousness by their horrific details but which were, again, defined as non-capital under the Act.

Patrick *Byrne*, a 27-year-old labourer, was a voyeur who prowled about a women's hostel. Entering the room of a resident he strangled her and having done so embarked upon the savage mutilation of her body. Byrne entered a plea of diminished responsibility and medical witnesses gave evidence of his being an aggressive psychopath with a long history of sexual pathology. This evidence was not rebutted, nevertheless the jury convicted him of non-capital murder. It was argued on appeal that the trial judge[35] had misdirected the jury by so interpreting section 2 that the jury were effectively precluded from finding a verdict under the section. The Court of Criminal Appeal allowed the appeal arguing that, properly directed, the jury could not have come to any other conclusion than that the defence of diminished respon-sibility was made out. A verdict of manslaughter pursuant to section 2 was substituted and a sentence of life imprisonment affirmed.[36]

A third homicide involving substantial mutilation in an overtly sexual context was prosecuted in the case of Michael Dowdall some three months before. A 19-year-old guardsman, he went with a prostitute to her home where, after intercourse, a quarrel degenerated into physical violence between them. The defendant took a large ornament and battered her to death, subsequently subjecting the body to mutilation and other indignities. The defendant was not in fact arrested until eleven months later, following a similar attack on another woman who fortunately survived and was able to give a description. Forensic evidence was sufficient to link him positively with both crimes. In support of a plea of diminished responsibility substan-

---

meticulously rehearsed the medical evidence to assist the jury, then confined himself to hand-ing them a copy of the terms of section 2. Dismissing the appeal in the Court of Criminal Appeal, Goddard LCJ had observed: 'It was not for a judge, where Parliament had defined a particular state of things, as they had here, to redefine or attempt to define the definition'. The Attorney-General refused his *fiat* for appeal to the Lords but Spriggs was reprieved by the Home Secretary (R A Butler) three days before execution of the death warrant and the sentence commuted to one of life imprisonment.

35. Mr Justice Stable.

36. The court's interpretations of 'abnormality of mind' and 'mental responsibility' in section 2 were subsequently approved by the Judicial Committee of the Privy Council in *Rose v The Queen* [1961] AC 496.

tial evidence was offered, the senior medical officer at the remand prison describing him as a psychopathic personality liable to act aggressively and to become physically violent without evident provocation. He had apparently attempted to hang himself at the age of 17. He was not the material of a good soldier, thought to be difficult, and given to the heavy consumption of spirituous liquor. A senior officer thought he exhibited delusions of grandeur, occasioned by the fact that he was in fact 'weak and insignificant'. So compelling did this evidence appear that the Crown offered nothing by way of rebuttal and following a conviction for section 2 manslaughter a sentence of imprisonment for life was imposed.

It so happened that on the day that Dowdall was sentenced at the Old Bailey[37] James Barclay was on trial at Newcastle Assizes. The defendant had gone with a prostitute to a hotel where her naked body was later discovered, indicating signs of battering and other assault. A plea of diminished responsibility having been entered, substantial evidence of the defendant's long history of mental disorder combined with a propensity to violence towards women was given. The verdict was manslaughter under section 2 and a life sentence was imposed.

It can be argued that the Homicide Act 1957 at least ensured that when presented with compelling evidence of mental illness or abnormality in the context of a section 2 plea, juries had an opportunity to make a finding other than of murder. In the years of mandatory capital punishment juries had not infrequently felt constrained to make recommendations for the exercise of the prerogative of mercy in distressing and compassionate cases—which included instances of apparent mental disorder of various kinds as well as provocation, so-called 'mercy killings' and unwanted survival in suicide pacts. In practice this had meant that while substantially mitigating factors were identified by juries—of whom it could be said that they were as close to the evidence as anyone—there was no guarantee that the Home Secretary would necessarily act upon their recommendations, however forcefully urged at the conclusion of their verdict. The existence of the provisions whereby verdicts of manslaughter could be returned in cases involving mental disorder, a wider definition of provocation and suicide pact survival meant that

---

37. 21 January 1960.

their conclusions could be both intellectually assured and legally secured. That there were categories of murder specifically identified as capital could, however, frequently vitiate this process. In capital cases, these considerations, though they might go to the heart of the matter, whether concerning the circumstances of the offence or the character of the offender, were largely subordinated to determining the issues which identified the killing as capital murder.

While there were capital cases which undoubtedly involved the kinds of professional criminal activity that did not eschew the commission of homicide, by no means all those charged with the commonest form of capital murder—a killing committed in course or furtherance of theft—were aware of the kinds of killings that were capital and those that were not. The desire to be hanged was expressed in a disturbing minority of instances of non-capital murder, suggesting that the Act, when poorly understood, by no means offered the universally appreciated deterrents that it authors had believed would be clear to all intending killers.[38]

Experience of the 1957 Act strongly indicated that the deterrent effect of the death penalty remained as variable as it had always been and the situation was complicated in some instances by offenders being unaware of the differences between capital and non-capital crimes. But this could be numbered among the least of the weaknesses of the Act. The attempt to distinguish certain offences as particularly heinous failed, and miserably, to persuade the public that it had been done with any sense of logic, still less any reference to how the public at large viewed the nature of particular crimes. That the killers of children, especially those who had sexually assaulted them beforehand, should merely go to prison for life,[39] while the killers of policemen went to the gallows, was perceived as inequitable in terms of desert. Quite apart from the uncertainties of interpretation that were never entirely absent from the minds of either judges or juries, the public increasingly perceived its workings as frequently capricious. In the so-called 'towpath' murder there was but a single criminal event: the brutal killing in the course of an attempted

---

38. In our original research based on those indicted for murder under the 1957 Act we were able to identify at least eight such instances.

39. 'Whole life' sentences at this time were not only extremely rare, but in effect only resulted from the continuing perceived dangerousness of the offender.

robbery of a young man by a group of four youths aged between 17 and 23. One, aged 20, was convicted of non-capital murder and sentenced to life imprisonment. The 17-year-old, who had injured the victim, was sentenced to be detained at Her Majesty's pleasure; the remaining two were sentenced to death and hanged though only one had caused injury, the other having merely gone through the victim's pockets. The prosecution established a common purpose or design involving all four in the crime: yet, though on this point the conclusion of the criminal law mirrored that of common sense, the imposition of three kinds of sentence on four defendants, including the death penalty on two who were clearly not equally responsible (in the physical sense) for the death of the victim, appeared to many people if not as capricious then as powerfully indicative of the law's capacity for absurdity.

The Homicide Act 1957, by any test, was a legislative failure. But it was more than that. It was a demonstration of a belief that an argument that had been around for almost a century — that it was impossible to identify distinctive categories of homicide based upon their heinousness and embody them with clarity and no ambiguity with the substantive law — could somehow be overcome. The pressure for reform in the face of the public disquiet generated by particularly troubling cases provided the stimulus for what rapidly proved to be an unsatisfactory law enveloped in a political fix. In the event, the fix turned out to be a botch creating new problems rather than radical solutions to old ones. If it did anything, it was to serve the interests of those who were pressing for total abolition of the death penalty.

The Act, insofar as it sought to establish a hierarchy of heinousness that mirrored the gradient of public opprobrium, is now long gone, though its provision of the defences relating to diminished responsibility and certain forms of provocation, in their essence, remain. Politically, however, it would seem to have come back to haunt us, albeit in a somewhat disembodied guise, its *geist* an echo in the penal philosophy of New Labour. In place of the arguments that once raged over the provision of the death penalty there is now a new division of opinion over the interpretation of the meaning of 'life' imprisonment. And as alarming as it is inexplicable, save in the context of appeasing a perceived populist desire simply to punish (to the exclusion of all other objectives within the framework of criminal justice) the Bill currently in Parliament proposes, yet again, a hierarchy of heinousness in criminal homicide. No matter that to do so has been proclaimed impossible, not least by Parliamentarians for almost a century and a half; no matter that the 1957 Act lies in the sands of the political desert, like the fallen image of Ozymandias for all to see and reflect upon; the Government is preparing, once more, to hunt down that elusive and mythical creature, the Chimæra.

CHAPTER 9

CLEARING UP THE MESS: OR THE LAW COMMISSION ATTEMPTS TO MAKE BRICKS WITHOUT STRAW

What Went Before

At the time of the establishment of the Law Commission in 1965 to review the law, and systematically develop its reform, there existed, outside of Government, an independent agency advising on referred topics of criminal law and criminal justice. It was, therefore, entirely sensible that, within three months of the Parliamentary confirmation in December 1969 of the 1965 statute abolishing the death penalty for murder, the Home Secretary (then Mr James Callaghan) should have requested the Criminal Law Revision Committee to 'review the law relating to, and the penalties for, offences against the person, including homicide, in the light of the recent decision of Parliament to make permanent the statutory provisions abolishing the death penalty for murder'.[1] The committee was a highly respected advisory body composed of senior judges (the chairman was always a Lord Justice of Appeal), legal practitioners, administrators in criminal justice and academic lawyers. Until 1986, when the committee ceased to function (it appears never to have been formally dissolved), the Law Commission was a bystander on criminal law reform. Before 1980 it engaged in reviewing the criminal law on only five occasions.[2] Nevertheless, in answer to a limited circulation questionnaire

---

1. When the reference was made on 4 March 1970 the Criminal Law Revision Committee was preparing its Eleventh Report which was a general survey of criminal evidence including a recommendation that restricted the right of an accused to remain silent both at the police station and in court: Cmnd 4991 (1972). At that time (June 1972) there were three Lords Justices on the Committee — Edmund-Davies, Sellers and Lawton.
2. *Conspiracy and Criminal Law Reform* (1976), *Defences of General Application* (1977), a draft Criminal Liability (mental element) Bill (1978), *Imparted Criminal Intent* (*DPP v Smith*)

compiled by the Criminal Law Revision Committee, the Law Commission, in an unpublished memorandum of February 1978, commented specifically on the substantive law of murder and the appropriate penalty.

The Criminal Law Revision Committee had earlier, in 1972, published in its Twelfth Report[3] its provisional conclusions exclusively on the penalty for murder in advance of its consideration of the law of homicide and other crimes of personal violence. Its provisional report of 1973 examined at some length the arguments for and against the mandatory penalty of life imprisonment. It also considered them in its final report (the Fourteenth) in 1980. After 'long and anxious discussions' the members were 'deeply and almost evenly divided';[4] as a result the committee was not in a position to recommend that there should be any change, although the members clearly envisaged that the rival arguments would assist the Government and Parliament in coming to a conclusion. The committee did not claim that its members' experience of criminal justice accorded their views 'any special weight', but it emphasised that the working lives of its members did at least bring them 'closer to the administration of justice than most'. By that time (1980) two other official committees composed not only of lawyers — the Butler Committee on Mentally Abnormal Offenders in 1975[5] and the Home Secretary's Advisory Council on the Penal System in 1978[6] — had unanimously recommended the abolition of the mandatory penalty. Alongside these reports there was judicial activity. The House of Lords in its judicial capacity had handed down in 1974 its divided judgment in *DPP v Hyam*,[7] in which one of the two dissenters, Lord Kilbrandon, concluded his judgment with the opinion that, once the death penalty was removed as the exclusive penalty for murder, it was unnecessary any more to maintain the law's distinction between murder and manslaughter, the conclusion being that one simple offence of criminal homicide would thereafter carry a discretionary life sentence as the maximum penalty.[8] According to the biographer of

---

(1967) and a working paper on malicious damage (1969).

3. Cmnd 5184.

4. Cmnd 5184, para 4.2.

5. Cmnd 5244, paras 19.14-19.16.

6. *Sentences of Imprisonment: a review of maximum penalties*, para 256.

7. [1975] AC 55.

8. *Ibid*, at para 90.

Lord Hailsham, who presided over the Appellate Committee in *Hyam* and delivered one of the majority judgments, he privately held the view that there should be a single homicide offence.[9] In its questionnaire the Criminal Law Revision Committee had specifically, and not unnaturally, asked its consultees whether they supported the remarks of Lord Kilbrandon. The Law Commission responded positively, that it both endorsed the remarks of Lord Kilbrandon and favoured the abolition of the mandatory life sentence, although it did enter a cautionary note to the effect that the public might not readily favour the removal of the mandatory penalty. That acknowledgment of populism was prophetic. For the next two decades, politicians of whatever hue have stubbornly refused to cede any ground to the growing support among legal professionals (judges and practising lawyers) and other interested parties to get rid of the mandatory penalty. Were the Criminal Law Revision Committee (or its counterpart, the Law Commission) to revisit the penalty for murder, it would undoubtedly come off the fence in favour of the plea made by Lord Parker in July 1965.

A Parliamentary Diversion

In the mid-1980s, under the impressive drive of its chairman, Sir Ralph Gibson, the Law Commission turned its attention to codification of the general principles of criminal law, with the ambition, still sadly unfulfilled, to move towards a Code of Criminal Law. It commissioned an academic report, under the chairmanship of the late Sir John Smith QC, on the general principles of law applicable to codification of the criminal law.[10] The Law Commission, no doubt aware by then of the apparent demise of the Criminal Law Revision Committee, nevertheless appeared content to leave reform of the law of homicide to others who were pressing for legislative change, both of an incrementally messy case law emanating from frequent judicial excursions

---

9.   Geoffrey Lewis, *Lord Hailsham: A Life* (Jonathan Cape, 1997) at p.315.
10. The Law Commission has been a consistent advocate of codification since its Second Programme in 1968, but since 1985 the prospect of a Code of Criminal Law has not been advanced. The Law Commission Act 2009 has provided a Parliamentary impetus to the work of the Law Commission: see a comment in *Public Law* (July 2010) at pp 441-2, *Reform? Reform? Aren't things bad enough already?*

in appellate courts and the absurd inflexibility of the mandatory penalty of life imprisonment. That process found its manifestation at the hands of the House of Lords in its deliberative capacity. A Select Committee had been set up in 1988 by the House of Lords, under the chairmanship of Lord Nathan, to examine the problems both of murder and life imprisonment. A series of all party amendments to the Criminal Justice Bill of 1991 stemmed from the proposals of the Select Committee. They were as follows:

1. that in future no court should be required to sentence a person convicted of murder to imprisonment for life; and

2. that judicial procedures should govern both the setting of the length of the penal term contained within an indeterminate sentence of life imprisonment, and the decisions on release or continued detention of life prisoners on expiry of the penal term.

The new provisions would apply whenever a court passed a life sentence, whether for murder or any other serious offence for which life imprisonment was the maximum sentence. The judge would be required to give reasons in open court for imposing a life sentence in preference to a determinate sentence, and for the quantum of punishment. This would be expressed in the form of a penal term based upon the requirements of retribution and deterrence. It would not be open to revision by Ministers, but would be subject to appeal by either side. At the expiration of the penal term, the decision whether the prisoner should be released or further detained would be considered by judicial tribunals constituted to conform to the case-law of the European Court of Human Rights. Any life sentence prisoner convicted of murder would be released only on life licence, with the Home Secretary retaining the power to revoke the licence. Recall to custody would be subject to the consent of the tribunal. If the tribunal determined not to direct the release of a life prisoner, usually because of the risk to the public of further serious offences being committed, his case would be referred back for fresh consideration within a maximum period of three years. The tribunal would be subject to procedural rules enabling the prisoner to make his or her representations in person or to be legally represented; to know what was said about him or her; and to have the opportunity to challenge reports and other information before the tribunal.

On 18 April 1991, amendments along these lines, supported by the two surviving former Lord Chancellors (Lords Hailsham and Havers), the Lord Chief Justice, the Master of the Rolls and five Law Lords, were carried against the Government by a large majority. When the Bill went back to the Commons, regardless of a plea in a letter to *The Times* from the chairman of JUSTICE that the issue be treated as one of conscience and not one appropriate for recourse to party whips, the House voted strictly on party lines to reject the amendments. The Home Secretary, Kenneth Baker, like other speakers on the Government benches, made no attempt to meet the arguments that had been put forward, simply repeating the assertion that retaining the mandatory sentence was essential to mark the uniquely heinous nature of the crime of murder. The public, whose views on capital punishment were (it was assumed) clearly known, 'would feel very let down if there were a weakening in the mandatory sentence for murder'.[11] The same plaintive cry was made from Government by Lady Scotland (then Minister of State for the Home Office) in a debate on the Criminal Justice Bill in October 2003 that 'the death penalty for murder was abolished *on faith* that the criminal justice system would continue to treat the offence with the utmost gravity'.[12]

As a positive response to the concerns expressed in the Lords, the Government was prepared in 1991 to amend the procedures, but only relating to discretionary life sentences. It was unwilling to go any further, on the argument that mandatory life prisoners, who were not applicants before the court, were not entitled to have their cases reviewed by an independent judicial body after the expiry of the penal term, because the lawfulness of their detention for life had been determined once and for all at the moment of conviction and sentence. Any subsequent release was regarded as a matter of mercy and privilege; not of right.

These concepts were most clearly expressed by the Minister of State, Angela Rumbold, on 16 July 1991 in the following terms:[13]

---

11. *Hansard* HC Vol 193 Col 868 (25 June 1991).
12. *Hansard* HL Vol 653 Col 837 (italics supplied). This myth has been exploded: see *Chapter 7*.
13. *Hansard* HC Vol 193 Cols 311-312.

Mandatory life sentence cases, however, raise quite different issues and the Government do not agree that it is appropriate to extend a similar procedure to these cases. In a discretionary case, the decision on release is based purely on whether the offender continues to be a risk to the public. The presumption is that once the period that is appropriate to punishment has passed the prisoner should be released if it is safe to do so. The nature of the mandatory sentence is different. The element of risk is not the decisive factor in handing down a life sentence. According to the judicial process, the offender has committed a crime of such gravity that he forfeits his liberty for life without the necessity for judicial intervention. The presumption is, therefore, that the offender should remain in custody until and unless the Home Secretary concludes that the public interest would be better served by the prisoner's release than by his continued detention. In exercising his continued discretion in that respect the Home Secretary must take account, not just of the question of risk, but of how society as a whole viewed the prisoner's release at that juncture. The Home Secretary takes account of the judicial recommendation, but the final decision is his.

The result of these various arguments during the passage of the Bill was a new procedure adopted in the Criminal Justice Act 1991 in the case of discretionary life prisoners. This is to be found in section 34 of that Act. The effect is to give the judge power to state the term of years which he deems it appropriate for the prisoner to serve by way of punishment for the crime and to order the sanctions that apply at the conclusion of that period. The Home Secretary can be required by the prisoner to refer his case to the Parole Board. The Board then decides whether it is any longer necessary for safety reasons to keep the prisoner in custody. As a result of a growing distaste among the higher judiciary for the Government persistently brushing aside widespread professional and other public opinion on the mandatory penalty for murder, the Prison Reform Trust set up in 1993 a committee, under the chairmanship of Lord Lane, who had recently retired from being a distinguished and professionally respected Lord Chief Justice.

The Conflicting Philosophies

At the outset of its investigation, the Lane Committee observed that practice had been shown to have departed from theory. The theory propounded by Angela Rumbold in 1991 was founded on the concept that murder is such a grave offence that it invariably demands imprisonment for life — a penalty which may sometimes in mercy be softened by release on licence. In practice, as Leon Brittan made clear in 1983, and his successors have obstinately maintained, there is, inside the indeterminate life sentence, a fixed term of years which represents the proper penalty by way of retribution for the crime's nature or moral obliquy and also by way of deterrence. It did not require a lengthy study of the two theories — that of Angela Rumbold and that of Leon Brittan — to observe their mutual inconsistency. As Lord Mustill said in *Doody*, in a speech with which the rest of their Lordships agreed, 'These two philosophies of sentencing are inconsistent. Either may be defensible, but they cannot both be applied at the same time'. Of the two, their Lordships had no hesitation in deciding that the regime installed by Leon Brittan is that which had been in operation, with modifications, ever since 1983 under the aegis both of Leon Brittan and his various successors.

The Howard Statement: Rumbold Revived

The Home Secretary, Michael Howard, made a statement in the House of Commons on 27 July 1993 making clear, however, that Angela Rumbold's explanation of the new approach to the detention of mandatory lifers was to be adopted, so as to defeat any argument based on parallels between discretionary and mandatory lifers. The Home Secretary asserted that the two-phase system of detention under the mandatory life sentence introduced by Leon Brittan was to be altered in two ways:

(i) first, the Secretary of State maintained his right to revise upwards the tariff period fixed and communicated to the prisoner at the start of his imprisonment if, at some later stage, he considered it to be insufficient to satisfy the requirements of retribution and deterrence;

(ii) second, the Secretary of State made it clear that he claimed the right to continue to detain a prisoner who had completed his tariff period and was no longer a danger to the public, on the basis that his 'early release' (that is, release before the prisoner's death) would not be 'acceptable to the public'.

This statement was quite inconsistent with a number of earlier statements by successive Secretaries of State since 1983 which:

(i) defined the tariff as 'the period' necessary to satisfy the requirements of retribution and deterrence, and *not* some provisional assessment of the period subject, years later, to revision upwards; and

(ii) did indeed confirm that there were only two phases of detention—namely the punitive and the preventive period—and that, after the completion of the punitive period, a prisoner could legitimately expect release unless he constituted a danger to the public.

It was hardly surprising that the Lane Committee concluded that the mandatory penalty for murder should be abolished. If (as anticipated) it received a sharp rebuff from the Conservative Home Secretary (repeated in 1998 by Jack Straw as Home Secretary in the incoming New Labour administration) the Lane Committee's report was embraced — to borrow the words of the CLRC in 1980—by those 'closest to the administration of justice'. The battle for supremacy in sentencing convicted murderers and fixing the tariff was fiercely joined, and ultimately won by the judges in 1999, only partially qualified by Parliament in Schedule 21 of the Criminal Justice Act 2003.

On 1 March 2007, in a debate in the House of Lords ostensibly on the Law Commission's report of November 2006, every speaker (with the exception of Lady Scotland and, to some extent, the late Lord Kingsland as Shadow Lord Chancellor) spoke powerfully against the mandatory penalty. The Law Commission's proposals on the substantive law of murder were only marginally touched upon in the debate. The Parliamentary diversion during the debates on the Criminal Justice Act 1991 had left the law and penalty for murder in the anomalous state, so authoritatively described by Lord Mustill in 1998. It was time enough for Government to turn to the Law Commission for a way out of a messy law and a penal dilemma.

Enter the Law Commission, Belatedly

Whether as a direct result of the judicial disagreement and professional criticism over the case of *R v Smith (Morgan)* or growing dissatisfaction among politicians for the way in which the law accommodates the phenomenon of provocation in cases involving domestic violence, the Government decided in 2003 to refer the question of the two partial defences—provocation and diminished responsibility—to the Law Commission (the Law Commission had already entered the fray with its report on familial homicides which was enacted in the Domestic Violence, Crime and Victims Act 2004[14]). While recommending, in two consultation documents,[15] changes to both section 2 (on diminished responsibility) and section 3 (provocation) of the Homicide Act 1957, the Law Commission indicated that the partial defences could properly be reviewed only in the context of the substantive law of murder. And so it naturally recommended that the Government should refer the review of the law of murder to itself—who else?

After some political hesitancy to comply with the Law Commission's request, the Home Secretary (by then Mr Charles Clarke) did make a limited reference, restricting the review, however, to the established distinction between murder and manslaughter and putting the mandatory penalty of life imprisonment out of bounds. Whatever new structure might emerge, it would of necessity be built from bricks made without straw. At the same time, the Home Secretary indicated that the Law Commission's review would be part of a two-stage process. The Law Commission did not demur. Any self-respecting law reform agency should not have bowed to the constraints of politicians heavily engaged at the time in penological rhetoric. The Law

---

14. *Children: their non-accidental deaths or serious injuries (criminal trials)*, Law Com No 282 (September 2003) and the earlier *Consultative Report*, Law Com No 279 of April that year. See *Chapter 12* of this work.

15. *Partial Defences to Murder*, Law Com CP No 173 (2003) and *Provisional Conclusions on Law Commission Consultation Paper 173* (2004).

Commission went ahead and issued a consultation paper in November 2005[16] and reported finally in November 2006 recommending the three-tier system of Murder 1, Murder 2 and Manslaughter, with an updated version of its suggested amendments to the partial defences to murder.[17] It was expected that the Law Commission's report, based as it had to be on restricted terms of reference, would not preclude the follow-up, comprehensive review by officials in the Ministry of Justice. But the Government changed tack in July 2008[18] and engaged in planning to legislate only in relation to the two partial defences, together with a change in the law on infanticide. A fourth topic, joint enterprise in homicide cases, was left to be considered separately. Provocation was to be transformed into a partial defence of loss of self-control, and diminished responsibility would be updated to take account of advancement in knowledge of forensic psychiatry. The changes appeared in the Coroners and Justice Act 2009.

Given the politically imposed restriction on its terms of reference, the Law Commission has contrived to shore up the 'rickety structure set upon shaky foundations'[19] by carving out from the present two tier system yet a third: to create a system that would embody Murder 1, Murder 2 and Manslaughter. Apart from the downgrading of those homicides of perceived lesser seriousness and some adjustments to the partial defences of diminished responsibility and provocation, each of which should provide some clarity to the present law, the retention of the basic ingredients of the crime — the act of killing and the mental element reflected in the accused's specific intent — can hardly be regarded as reformist. Juries will be, marginally, assisted in grappling with the patchwork of rules that will continue to make coherent directions to juries unnecessarily difficult.[20] At no point in the Law Commission's scholarly report (which some readers might consider somewhat excessively legalistic) is there any serious consideration given to the possible impact that the proposed new structure might have on the task of juries. The Law Commission, in considering the question of determining

---

16. *A New Homicide Act for England and Wales?* Law Com CP No 177.
17. *Murder, Manslaughter and Infanticide* (Law Com No 304).
18. *Murder, manslaughter and infanticide: proposals for reform of the law.*
19. Law Com No 304 (28 November 2006) p.3 at para 1.8.
20. *See* the comments of Lord Carswell in *Attorney-General for Jersey v Holley* [2005] 2 AC 580 at para 77.

the requisite element of fault in the homicide offence, came to the surprising conclusion that juries are not confused, because

> there is no evidence that the existing law gives rise to any confusion in the jury room. If the law confused juries we would expect juries to be consistently sending notes to judges asking for explanation. We have not received reports that this has occurred.[21]

Unfortunately, there is little by way of evidence — other than anecdotal — of what actually transpires in the jury room. That juries do not necessarily bombard judges with notes seeking explanations of the law or some forensic technicality might equally be taken to indicate something quite else. While they may have misunderstood the law, or been in error in applying the law to the facts, the jury may have been confident in the belief that they had indeed understood it, and had applied it correctly. Alternatively, bemused juries may well give up the task to which they find themselves unequal and render what is, effectively, an 'instinctive' verdict.

Without research within the the jury room itself (which is constitutionally impossible), it would, in our view, be safer to proceed on the basis that if, as the Law Commission freely admits, 'the law is in a mess' there is the corresponding possibility that some juries may well be confused by it; unless, that is, they are at critical times possessed of the forensic equivalent of second sight. Even if confusion is not an ignoble condition of the human mind, a disordered plethora of road signs at a roundabout is inherently likely to confuse even the most attentive driver. The same might well be said of the jury.

The Law Commission specifically recognises that the differences between intention, knowledge, and belief in the context of fault are not substantial, but prefers, for their proposed offences of Murder 1 and Murder 2, the concept of intention. If, however, knowledge were to be the criterion of the required mental element the task of the jury would, we think, be immeasurably eased. Yet the Law Commission does not explain why that elusive element of the accused's innermost thought at the moment of killing is so vital to establishing the criminal liability of unjustified homicide.

---

21. p.58, at para 3.3.

Much of any improvement in the functioning of murder trials will depend upon the policy adopted by those responsible within the Crown Prosecution Service. Yet, given the widespread view that killings involving deliberation of one kind or another need to be marked by severe penalty, the variation in penalty between Murder 1, carrying mandatory life imprisonment, and Murder 2, for which (like manslaughter) life imprisonment constitutes the maximum, we cannot see how Murder 2 will not be seen as a kind of 'downgrading' of the offence in the public mind. This, given that it is proposed that Murder 2 encompasses intention to cause *injury* (as distinct from *serious* injury[22]) fear, or risk of injury, when the accused was aware that his conduct involved a serious risk of causing death.

Criticism of Our Proposals

In its consultation paper of November 2005, the Law Commission paid us the compliment of describing our plea for a single offence of criminal homicide 'as a powerful force in the argument for reform of the law of murder' (para 2.33, p.32). But in the next breath (para 2.34) the compliment was undermined; the Law Commission took away the credibility of our argument. The Commission said that 'even if it were within our terms of reference to consider it [the argument for a single offence of homicide], we do not agree that it is the right course to recommend the creation of a single offence of unlawful killing'.

Granted that the Commission was debarred by its terms of reference (about which it might justifiably have complained that the restricted reference was handcuffing its scholarly review of a crucial part of the criminal law) we found it strange that it should have been so singularly dismissive of a reform that had considerable backing from authoritative quarters. No less a person than the Lord Chief Justice, Lord Parker, in the abolition debate in the House of Lords on 27 July 1965, pronounced his dislike of the 'fine lines and technical distinctions' between murder and manslaughter. Were those remarks unworthy of consideration 40 years later? Ten years later Lord

---

22. Our italics.

Kilbrandon, a Scottish Law Lord of distinction, and aware of the different approach in Scots law, made the same point in a judicial forum. Moreover, the Law Commission itself had gone on record in its memorandum of February 1978 (to which we drew attention in our submission) as specifically approving of the Kilbrandon formula. Yet the Law Commission made no acknowledgement of its own previous conclusion that was the very opposite of its considered view a quarter of a century later. It was perfectly entitled to disagree with its predecessor. But it should have indicated that it had undergone a change of opinion, and why.

The Law Commission's rejection of our thesis was grounded on the absence of any fault element in the formulation of a single offence of unlawful killing. If our explanation led to that conclusion, we must confess that we may not have made it clear that we positively postulate a necessary fault element in the offence of unlawful killing. Knowledge by the accused that his act involved killing the deceased with foresight of the consequences of his act clearly involves blameworthiness and excludes the possibility of an accident.

The Consultation Paper of November 2005[23] concluded its section under the heading 'The argument of Sir Louis Blom-Cooper and Professor Terence Morris' by saying that its provisional proposal is that to maintain a firm and clear connection between the sanctity of life and the structure of the law of homicide, intentional killing should be made into a unique offence: 'first degree of murder'.[24] It is unsurprising to us that this argument was not advanced in the Law Commission's final report.[25]

Given that in that report no reference was made to any of the argument by way of response to the criticisms of our case for a single offence of homicide and other matters that had been made earlier in the consultation paper, we consider it important to set them out again in the same terms.

We are grateful to the Law Commission at least for its comments on the proposal in our book, *With Malice Aforethought: A Study of the Crime and Punishment for Homicide*[26] for a single criminal homicide offence to replace the crimes of murder and manslaughter, even though our proposal does not

---

23. *A New Homicide Act for England and Wales?* Law Com CP No 177.
24. p.33, at para 2.38.
25. *Murder, Manslaughter and Infanticide.* Law Com No 304.
26. Hart Publishing, 2004.

fall within the restricted terms of reference given to the Law Commission by the Home Secretary. Accordingly, we have taken it upon ourselves in the following submission to answer the Law Commission's rejection of our proposal. We trust that the Law Commission will feel able to include in its final report to the Home Secretary a further comment on our proposal, in the light of this response.

The remainder of this chapter, therefore, deals with three topics only:

(a) the reliance of the Law Commission on the notion of the sanctity of life to sustain a contemporary law of murder and manslaughter;

(b) a rejoinder to the Law Commission's rejection of a single criminal homicide in the manner of the Kilbrandon formula; and

(c) the persistence of the Government to retain the mandatory penalty for murder.

The Concept of the 'Sanctity of Life' in the Context of Law

Consultation Paper No 177 refers at paragraph 2.20 to the concept of the 'sanctity of life', a term used so emphatically in the context of the law of murder by the Criminal Law Revision Committee (CLRC) in its report of 1980.[27] The word 'sanctity' derives from the Latin *sanctus*, generally translated as 'holy', and the term 'sanctity of life' has therefore strong religious connotations. Thirty years ago, when the CLRC was deliberating, there was probably less awareness of the fact that society was changing significantly in its ethnic and confessional characteristics, and it would have been accepted that ideas drawn from the Judaeo-Christian tradition were dominant; this notwithstanding that it had been long established that Christianity formed no part of the law of England.[28] This is not the case today, when other religious faiths are now recognised as a major feature of the social landscape. While

27. Criminal Law Revision Committee Fourteenth Report, *Offences Against the Person* Cmnd 7844 (1980), para 15.
28. *Bowman v The National Secular Society Ltd* [1917] AC 406.

it is certainly the case that there is still a widespread religious belief in the unique quality of human life, it may be expressed in different ways. No less important, however, is the fact that our society is nevertheless predominantly secular, a fact which is reflected in the character of its institutions, including law. Their function is to provide a *lingua franca*, in which those ethical principles that are consonant with wide cultural diversity can be both expressed and approved without dissent or ambiguity.

We would argue strongly, therefore, that terminology which employs concepts such as 'sanctity' is unhelpful and ought to form no part of the jurisprudence of homicide, not least since the matter of the inviolability of life is better accommodated by reference to Article 2(1) of the European Convention of Human Rights which is now incorporated within domestic law. Article 2 initially provided that the right of everyone to life shall be protected by law and that none shall be deprived of it intentionally save in the execution of a sentence of a court following conviction for a crime for which death is the penalty prescribed by law. Effectively this is no longer applicable since capital punishment has been abolished within the various jurisdictions of the Convention signatories as a consequence of the Sixth and Thirteenth Protocols. Article 2, however, sets out the conditions in which deprivation of life constitutes a contravention of the Article with the proviso that this was, *ab initio*, a limited as distinct from an absolute right. Nevertheless, it has been judicially identified as one of the most fundamental provisions in the Convention from which there can be no derogation under Article 15. Consequent upon the Protocols excluding capital punishment, it has to all intents and purposes acquired a character that is difficult to distinguish from an absolute right.

The obligation of the State under Article 2(1) extends beyond its primary duty to secure the individual's right to life, by requiring the State to put in place effective provision in criminal law to deter the commission of offences against the person.[29] It further includes the establishment of a criminal justice system which provides for the trial and punishment of those who take life. The nature and extent of the provisions of the criminal law are left to be determined by the individual state.[30]

---

29. *Osman v UK* (1988) 29 EHRR 245.
30. See: R Clayton and H Tomlinson, *The Law of Human Rights*, Oxford (OUP, 2000) 7.08 at

We would strongly argue that the term 'sanctity of life' be no longer employed in discussion of reform of the law of homicide, and the term 'right to life' be substituted: it has a pragmatic (as distinct from theological) character that can be accepted and readily understood by any reasonable participant in the debate.[31] For this purpose it can be regarded as an absolute right identified in proactive terms that contrast with 'sanctity of life' which at best is no more than ambiguously descriptive.

There are further arguments against the use of the term 'sanctity of life' in the context of the law of homicide. In paragraph 2.23 the Consultation Paper makes reference to the distinction to be drawn between intentional and accidental or careless killing. In our view, while it is entirely logical to recognise that homicidal events encompass a very wide range of culpability and intention, the outcome of such events is that a life has been lost, whether by intent, accident or failure of duty to care. It is a simple and incontrovertible matter of fact that the dead are dead, however death may have come about.

It is this which is central in the minds of those who have been bereaved, and upon which the culpability or intention of the person responsible can have only a bearing, usually to accentuate it in proportion to the degree of recklessness, irresponsibility or evidently malicious intent. It would be difficult to maintain that the grief of a parent whose child has died under the wheels of a drunken driver is generically distinct from that of a parent whose child has been killed by a paedophile. Whatever the circumstances, the inalienable right to life has been violated, or, to employ the term that the authors of the document would evidently prefer, the sanctity of that life has been profaned. The quality of the life that has been lost is entirely *sui generis*, and is no way contingent upon the nature of the killing by which

---

p.341 and 7.35 at p.354; J Rowe and D Hoffman, *Human Rights in the UK* (Pearson Longman, 2009) p.105; N Jayawickrama, *The Judicial Application of Human Rights Law* (Cambridge University Press, 2002); *R v Weir* [2001] 1 WLR 421, para 18 at p.427.

31.   In this context we would consider the term 'inalienable' to be the corollary of 'right'. It is, however, important to note that the right defined in Article 2 is not entirely consonant with the idea of 'sanctity of life': indeed, recalling that for centuries religious believers have been content to put to death not only offenders against the criminal law but those who have been defined as heretics or unbelievers, it can be said to go well beyond it by way of positive guarantee.

it has been prematurely terminated, although doubtless the circumstance attending the event may aggravate or mitigate the sense of grief.

In this context we note that paragraph 2.26 of the Law Commission's Consultation Paper cites Exodus 20:2-17 as 'Do no murder'. The Authorised ('King James') Version of the Bible published in 1611 does not use the word 'murder', but the broader term 'kill', as does the Douai Version of 1609 which is a direct translation of the Latin Vulgate. In Latin there is no word corresponding 'to murder' that is distinct from the word 'to kill'.[32] 'Kill' is also used by the Revised Standard Version in all its three editions of 1881-5, 1901 and 1952. The Ecumenical Edition of the RSV, published in 1973 and accepted by Roman Catholic scholars, similarly uses the word 'kill'. The New International Version published in Chicago in 1973 appears alone in employing the term 'murder' in this text from Exodus.

In that by the end of the 16th century the term 'murder' as distinct from manslaughter had emerged within the common law,[33] it is not unimportant to note that Biblical scholarship, both Anglican[34] and Roman Catholic, remained consistent with the approach of the mediaeval jurists for whom the distinction was much less apparent.

Although in paragraph 2.28 there is a quotation from Finnis, Boyle and Grisez[35] in which the Law Commission cites Exodus 20:13 as 'Do no murder', they go on with their analysis of its meaning by reference not to the word 'murder', but 'kill' or 'killing', no fewer than four times in a single paragraph. One must conclude either that this is simply a case of termino-

---

32. All forms of killing are understood by the general term *interficere*, to 'do away with' or 'put an end to' and by *caedere*, literally to 'cut down' or 'beat' from which the word *homicida* derives: literally 'cutting a man down'. What is not without interest is that Latin, while not attempting to distinguish killings in terms specific to categories of culpability, is nevertheless the source of words that identify the victims of homicidal events in concepts such as 'patricide', 'matricide', 'fratricide', 'infanticide' and 'regicide'.

33. The term 'murder' first appears in Statute in 1532 (23 Hen. VIII. Ch. 1). Although it might be seen as a term to describe what is essentially deliberate killing, our view that Coke's subsequently highly idiosyncratic interpretation of the law of homicide has been a legacy of dubious value (set out in *With Malice Aforethought: A Study of the Crime and Punishment for Homicide*, at pp.15-32) remains unaltered.

34. The *Book of Common Prayer* of 1662 in using the term 'murder' in its text is, no doubt, representing the usage that had developed in the 130 years since the term appeared in the Tudor statute and the 30 years following the publication of Coke's Institutes.

35. *Nuclear Deterrence, Morality and Realism* (1986) at p.78.

logical inexactitude, or that they acknowledge murder to be no more than a synonym for unlawful killing. It is significant that they also, within this same passage, refer to 'reckless homicide'. The essence of their argument, however, would seem to be to draw a distinction between recklessness, however blameworthy, and the deliberate killing of the innocent.

Again, this raises problems, for if we are to pursue the argument that the worst kind of homicide consists of deliberate killing, that must extend beyond situations involving innocent victims to those where that label cannot possibly be attached. Let us suppose that an armed police officer, called to a house, finds a man who has just killed his wife and is standing over her body holding a golf club. The officer shoots the suspect through the head, killing him instantly.[36] The circumstantial evidence points to the shooting having been deliberate, and in circumstances in which the disparity in weaponry was self-evidently extreme.[37] While it could not be said that the suspect so killed was innocent, since he had evidently just killed his wife, the police officer would have had no licence to take the suspect's life and could, as the law presently stands, be properly charged with murder. The life thus taken could certainly not be described as that of an innocent man, since he had shortly before clubbed his wife to death and one would need to stretch the concept of 'sanctity of life' to reason that, notwithstanding the evidence of deliberate homicide, that 'sanctity' was in no way compromised.

The central issue here is not the 'sanctity', or otherwise, of the life of the uxoricide, but the violation of his inalienable right to life that his conduct, unlawful and morally reprehensible though it may have been, has in no way affected. Not only is this association of the concept of deliberation with that of innocence a *non sequitur*, it is also highly misleading. 'Innocence', or indeed any specific characteristic of the victim, is not a necessary element in establishing the criminal guilt of the offender, although such factors are likely to be highly relevant in establishing culpability for the purposes of sentencing.

---

36. If this example seems bizarre, we would pray in aid a practice of forensic exaggeration for academic purposes of which Professor Kenny was a noted exponent.

37. Apart, perhaps, from a highly contrived argument in support of a plea of diminished responsibility, it is difficult to think of a plausible defence against the charge. At the same time, there is no certainty how a jury might find, no matter how clearly and impeccably the judge may have summed up the facts and the law!

Our example is a clear case in which the right to life, underwritten by Article 2, must be the paramount consideration, notwithstanding that in the circumstances the moral desert of the husband might be regarded as negligible. A right is either violated, or it is not. In the 19th century trial of Dudley and Stephens the defendants, who, cast adrift for days after shipwreck and without food or water, had chosen to eat and kill the cabin boy, unsuccessfully ran the defence of 'necessity'.[38] It is instructive in its demonstration that even in a situation as grave as theirs, the right to life enjoyed by the cabin boy was inalienable.[39] (Under the Law Commission's proposal Dudley and Stephens would be guilty of first degree murder.)

In 2.30 it is stated that the provisional view of the Law Commission is that the connection between the law of murder and the view that life is sacrosanct is best expressed through the creation of the crime of 'first degree murder'. The proposition that 'life is sacrosanct' needs to be more closely examined in the ways in which the law has considered the taking of human life. The mediaeval notion of what were termed the 'petty treasons' is instructive in demonstrating that the lives of some members of society were regarded as more important than those of others. The essence of such treasons consisted of a failure of duty owed to one deemed a social superior, primarily within the framework of feudal obligation.[40] This graduated hierarchy of superiority among homicide victims is reflected in Coke's analysis of what he terms 'malice implied'. Thus: 'As if a magistrate or known officer, or any other that hath lawful warrant, and doing or offering to do his office, or to execute his warrant, is slain, this is murder, by malice implied by law'.[41] The notion of there being special categories of homicide victims, largely concentrated among those responsible for law enforcement, was much in evidence in the various proposals for amending the law of homicide in the latter part of

---

38. Here 'necessity' can be distinguished from the defence of 'self-defence'. The cabin boy Richard Parker in Dudley and Stephens was not a threat to the lives of his killers. Aquinas, who in the *Summa* argues a case for necessity by which it is licit for a starving man to steal food to preserve his life, does not extend this to a situation in which the 'food' supply arises directly from a homicide.

39. [1884] 14 QBD 273. See: A W B Simpson, *Cannibalism and the Common Law*, London and Chicago (University of Chicago Press, 1984).

40. See: Theodore Plucknett, *A Concise History of the Common Law* (4th ed.) (Butterworth & Co, 1948) at p.418.

41. Coke, *Institutes* vol 3, 51-52.

the 19th century and was very much in evidence in the Homicide Act 1957 in which the killing of a police or prison officer was a specific instance of a capital murder.[42] Why fire service and ambulance personnel were considered unworthy of such putative protection has never been satisfactorily explained.

Nor is it the case that in the workplace human life has always been regarded as sacrosanct. Throughout the 19th century the mortality of those employed in the construction industry — mining, quarrying, fishing and shipping — was extremely high. In the merchant shipping industry it was not unknown before 1874[43] for unscrupulous owners to send vessels to sea that were known to be unseaworthy, risking the lives of their crews which were regarded as expendable, while in the knowledge that their cargoes were insured. 19th century Blue Books are replete with evidence that the lives of workers were frequently regarded as of little account, not least when the supply of labour was plentiful. The practice subsequently initiated after fatal industrial incidents, of bringing criminal prosecutions under the Factory Acts rather than for manslaughter, continued throughout the 20th century and remains essentially unchanged. The reason for this is undoubtedly the extreme difficulty in prosecuting corporate manslaughter, but the penalties are manifestly less onerous, both in quantum and social stigma, than those possible on conviction for a homicidal offence. The effect is to send a signal that no matter what the magnitude of failure in respect of a duty of care, the loss of life is not so great a matter as it would have been had the penalty been one imposed upon a conviction for murder or manslaughter.

By the same token, the hiving-off of the offence of causing death by dangerous driving by the Road Traffic Act 1956, providing substantially lesser penalties than those available following conviction for manslaughter, sent a signal that to kill a person with a mechanically propelled vehicle upon a public road was not as serious as killing a passenger by driving a train through a signal set at danger, or, indeed, in the course of any other system of public carriage.

---

42. One might note that the slaying of judges and magistrates in the execution of their office was no longer a capital matter such as Coke would have most certainly regarded as an instance of 'malice implied by law'.

43. The Act piloted by Samuel Plimsoll MP.

Our point, therefore, is a very simple one. If human life is regarded as 'sacrosanct', the evidence both of history and the patterns of prosecution suggest that, to adapt Orwell's phrase, the law regards the lives of some people as more sacrosanct than those of others. That, in our view, is a consequential defect of the disarray in the present law, which we maintain is remediable by returning to a single crime of criminal homicide.[44]

The Argument for a Return to a Single Offence of Criminal Homicide: Our Rejoinder to its Rejection

Admitting that murder, though co-extensive with deliberate killing, has not hitherto been confined to it is a recognition of what we have elsewhere defined as the 'penal premium', deriving from Coke's notion of constructive malice.[45] The anxiety of the Criminal Law Revision Committee three decades ago that to abolish the separate crime of murder and with it the mandatory sentence of life imprisonment would be to give a public signal that murder was no longer a 'specially or uniquely grave crime' was understandable, given the circumstances of the time when capital punishment had only recently been abolished.

Yet, although the criticism of the Kilbrandon formula in the Consultation Paper is directed towards our advocacy of it, we cannot fail to note that in its Fourteenth Report, rejecting it (as the present Commissioners approve), the Criminal Law Revision Committee notes that in response to their Working Paper of 1976 in which they invited attention to Kilbrandon, *the Law Commission in February 1978 alone shared his opinion* (present authors' italics). It is, of course, accepted that the present Law Commissioners cannot be bound by the conclusions of their predecessors. Nevertheless, having now had the opportunity of reading the comments of the Law Commission in 1978[46]

---

44. Unless it is suggested that some violations of Article 2 be treated as matters intrinsically for the civil jurisdiction we see no reason why they should not be dealt with by the criminal law since, as we have argued in terms of right, one instance of homicide cannot be treated differently from any other.

45. See: Blom-Cooper and Morris, *With Malice Aforethought: A Study of the Crime and Punishment of Homicide* (Hart Publishing, 2004) at pp.25-27.

46. We are grateful to the Law Commission for having furnished us with material upon our request.

upon the Criminal Law Revision Committee's Working Paper on Offences Against the Person (which run to some 24 pages) we are somewhat puzzled as to why the Consultation Paper, in rejecting the Kilbrandon formula, made no reference to earlier support for it.

The Law Commission's response of February 1978 was almost certainly drafted by Mr Derek Hodgson QC (later Mr Justice Hodgson). Mr Justice Cooke was the chairman of the Law Commission at the time.

That the disappearance of 'murder' as a discrete category of homicide might be interpreted as a 'signal' that the deliberate killing of another is no longer to be considered the gravest of crimes is a point that cannot be ignored. But, as an argument against what we term the Kilbrandon formula, we consider it defective. By what reasoning can deliberation be demonstrated to be the source of its uniqueness? Deliberation is undoubtedly indicative of a high degree of moral culpability and such killings can give rise to feelings of the greatest revulsion. But what of instances of reckless disregard for the welfare of others such as the terrorist who plants a bomb in a public building, whether a specific duty of care is owed to them or not? What of the conduct of the aggressive drunken driver who forces an oncoming vehicle off the road after having deliberately overtaken other traffic, with the result that its occupants are killed? While it cannot be said that he deliberately killed them, not least since he had no foreknowledge of their presence, their right to life has been violated by his unlawful conduct. To drive whilst intoxicated is to invite moral opprobrium and, when combined with reckless irresponsibility and aggression behind the wheel, must surely invite substantial amplification of that opprobrium. If, on conviction, the offender demonstrates remorse, a wish that he had never become the author of his own penal misfortune, rather than genuine contrition manifested in a desire to express a sincere regret at the enormity of the consequences of his conduct, then surely the crime merits the description of substantially grave, if it is not uniquely so.

No less important is the general perception that it is the severity of the penalty that is the benchmark against which the gravity of the offence is measured, not the label by which the offence is identified. This is demonstrated across the whole spectrum of statute law and exemplified in the varying level of maximum penalties attaching to particular offences. If, in our lexicon, a criminal homicide is proved and the circumstances of the criminal event disclose not only deliberation but also other aggravating circumstances of the gravest kind, then there would be absolutely no reason why a sentence reflecting those facts would not be available to the court, up to and including imprisonment for life or any other order the court considered necessary in the public interest. The assumption of what is now termed murder into the generic offence of criminal homicide would have no bearing upon the penalty, save to provide the court with the flexibility — and thereby the ability better to serve the public interest — that it is presently denied by the existence of the mandatory penalty of life imprisonment on conviction of murder. Moreover, a strict liability offence, which we are proposing, emits as strong if not a stronger message than liability that requires a specific intent.

We would underscore this point by saying that it was the statutory separation of killing by the drivers of mechanically propelled vehicles from that part of the general *corpus* of homicide known as manslaughter by the Road Traffic Act 1956 and its (initial) maximum penalty of five years' imprisonment that led to this category of crime being reduced in its perceived social importance. By no means all road deaths result in this being charged at all. Indeed, in some instances it is now largely a matter for determining damages in tort, with the element of criminality being marginalised to what the relatives of the dead frequently perceive to be derisory penalties.

We turn now to paragraphs 2.32–2.38 in which the document considers our argument for what we term the Kilbrandon formula. We suggest that:

a. in important respects our argument has been misunderstood; and that

b. the fact that what we would consider a return to the single offence of criminal homicide is a proposal that has discernible support within the constituency of judicial opinion places an obligation upon the Commission to expand its contrary argument beyond the seven paragraphs in which it is rejected.

We consider that the approval of Victim Support for what is in effect the Kilbrandon formula in their response to Consultation Paper 173,[47] *Partial*

---

47. Law Com CP No 173 (October 2003).

Defences, is important, in that it would reduce the adversarial dimension of the criminal trial generated by attempts by the defence to achieve a reduction in the outcome from murder to manslaughter. In our view the defences which seek to reallocate the homicidal event from the category of murder to that of manslaughter are the source of much of the 'mess' which presently characterises the law of murder. Not least are they a source of difficulty in that such technical reallocation inevitably redefines the character of the conduct in ways which may be an additional source of distress to those who have been bereaved. To be convicted of manslaughter is to suffer less moral opprobrium than to be convicted of murder. To be convicted of causing death by dangerous or drunken driving, with its lower statutory maximum penalty, serves to diminish the mark of opprobrium still further. Indeed, to employ the argument of the CLRC, the effect of the Road Traffic Act 1956, in hiving-off road killing from the general body of manslaughter, notwithstanding a subsequent increase in the maximum penalty, has been to send out a signal that he or she who kills with a mechanically propelled vehicle on a public road commits a crime less serious than a train driver who goes through a signal set at danger or one who kills with a broken glass in a public house brawl. Such offenders remain at risk of receiving a discretionary life sentence. Not only is the law of homicide in a 'mess'; its apparently capricious interpretation can only serve to diminish public confidence in the objectivity of criminal justice.

Thus, *pace* the argument of the CLRC, which the Law Commission clearly approved in 2.30, if it is indeed the available penalty which signals the degree of opprobrium attaching to the offence, it must by the same token give an indication of the degree of 'sanctity' attaching to the life that has been lost. Yet it is difficult to accept that the life of one who dies as the outcome of a road crime is somehow less sacred than that of one whose throat is severed with a broken beer glass or one who is shot to death in a gangland killing, simply as a result of the circumstances of the criminal event. 'Innocence', whether demonstrable or merely putative, is not even an issue. We return, therefore, to underscore our earlier argument, namely, that by defining unlawful homicide as a violation of the right to life enshrined in Article 2, in this respect every life taken in the course of unlawful conduct is, by definition, of equal value.

It is stated by the Law Commission in 2.34 that:

> If, for Blom-Cooper and Morris, fault is merely a factor to reflect in sentence then
> that could logically be said to be true of the outcome (the victim's death) as well.
> Why single out unlawful killing for separate treatment, when it may purely have
> been chance that the victim died and the result could have been more or less serious
> bodily harm done?

We confess to some difficulty in following this line of reasoning. In this context we understand 'fault' as a neutral term to describe no more than liability. The right to life enshrined in Article 2 places an obligation upon state and citizen alike, analogous to a general duty of care, in that the duty to preserve life involves both a range of positive conduct as well as inaction. What happens in criminal homicide is that D has taken the life of V. The nature and circumstances of the criminal event will inevitably vary, but what will remain invariable is the fact that V's right to life has been violated by the conduct of D. By the same token, the circumstances of that conduct will vary in respect of the blameworthiness of the action.

Having considered Professor Robinson's material in detail,[48] we must now state that we approve of his point that the rule that is violated in homicide can be said to be the rule prohibiting unjustifiably harming someone *simpliciter*. We have no difficulty with this, since it is a statement of the inclusive nature of the prohibition of unjustifiable harm. It would be unjustifiable for a householder to use excessive force against an intruder; likewise, it would be unjustifiable for the householder to kill him. Once the boundary between the force necessary to restrain or expel the intruder has been exceeded, the harm becomes unjustifiable. It would be as 'unjustifiable' to break a burglar's leg as to break his neck.

We re-affirm our argument that in criminal homicide it is the right to life that is violated; a right which is the corollary of membership of civil society and which cannot be modified or qualified, since it is enjoyed by every citizen irrespective of the circumstances in which it has been violated.

---

48. In paragraph 2.35 the Commissioners quote Professor Robinson as arguing that causing death, can, like the more culpable of the mental elements (intention/recklessness), be regarded as simply a matter of grading.

Footnote 20 to paragraph 2.34 refers to our definition of criminal homicide in which it is suggested that we distinguish between 'simply causing serious physical harm to another person in which the various fault elements … are relevant and the crucial fatal result, to which they are not'. Again, we believe this to misunderstand our position.

In employing a definition that encompasses an act or omission—an intention to cause serious harm, or the manifestation of recklessness, gross negligence, or failure of corporate management—we seek to identify the necessary circumstances which must be proved to have existed before a death can result in a conviction for criminal homicide. The essence of Professor Robinson's argument, as we understand it, is that as the law presently stands *mens rea* and *actus reus*, far from being conceptually distinct as necessary elements that must be established before criminal guilt is determined, are unhelpfully confused. And that is where we and Professor Robinson are in agreement (see our *Chapter 2*, final paragraph).

Attempting to assess the intention of the offender, whether by subjective or objective criteria, in order to determine criminal guilt (for example whether murder or manslaughter, or in the application of partial defences, such as provocation or diminished responsibility), has given rise to not inconsiderable difficulty. Our argument is that, given the problems of balancing *mens rea* and *actus reus* at the trial stage, it is better to ask the prosecution to establish its case on an altogether simpler basis. Was the death the result of an act or omission by the defendant? Can it be demonstrated that the defendant intended to cause harm? Was this conduct manifesting recklessness or gross negligence? Did the defendant possess foresight of the consequences of the harmful act? Was there evidence of failure of corporate management? Did such conduct cause harm, even though not intended? Was the death the result of such harm?

In short, we would approve proof of guilt in criminal homicide to approach more closely to the norm of strict liability. While it might be immediately suggested that we are doing that which the late Professor Glanville Williams criticised in the House of Lords judgment in *Smith*,[49] namely, that it is possible to commit murder (or criminal homicide) by accident,

---

49. *DPP v Smith* [1961] AC 290.

that criticism is valid only if the consequence of conviction is the imposition of what Lord Reid in *Sweet v Parsley*[50] described as a 'disgraceful penalty'. Since it is our argument that some of the evidence presently adduced for the purpose of establishing a partial defence, together with other evidence neither relevant nor necessarily admissible in the course of trial, should be presented after a finding of guilt but before sentence, it follows that a court can perfectly well take such matters into account. The circumstances of the criminal event might be at the very margins of blameworthiness, as in a so-called 'mercy killing' or assisted suicide. Alternatively, they might be such as to attract a condign penalty, as in a so-called 'contract' killing.

Degrees of Murder and the Mandatory Penalty

At the heart of all the difficulty in reforming the law of homicide in England, whether the concern is specifically with murder or with the entire *corpus* of homicide law, is the mandatory penalty of life imprisonment. It is an impediment to any attempt at applying reason in the process of reform. The introduction of categories of murder that is proposed differs from earlier proposals in that the basis of distinction consists not in the identity of the victim but possibly in the deliberation or otherwise of the offender. In one sense, that is an undoubted improvement upon all the suggestions for degrees of murder that have been proposed and deservedly foundered in the past 150 years.

As the distinction is presently proposed, we see it is having an effect no different from the distinction in the Homicide Act 1957 between capital and non-capital murder. It would provide the court with the opportunity of passing the sentence of its own choice as distinct from the mandatory sentence which would still apply to first degree murder, irrespective of any mitigating circumstances. Just as the 1957 Act produced some quite absurd anomalies,[51] the present proposal would undoubtedly be vulnerable to the sometimes capricious decision-making of juries.

---

50. [1969] 2 WLR 470.
51. A man who shot his wife with a gun committed capital murder, but if, having run out of ammunition, he had still failed to kill her and finished the task by battering her with the butt

237

The Three-Tier Structure: Overview

Presented with the restricted remit of 2005, the Law Commission might have appropriately declined to embark upon the task of reforming the law on this important crime. Given, however, its willingness to conduct a review so severely handicapped by the terms of reference, its product in 2006 was a brave, but unavailing, attempt at clearing up the 'mess'. Now that the partial defence of provocation has been displaced[52] by the more restrictive term 'loss of self-control' (with all the implications of new, complex directions to juries)[53] the Law Commission might have sought to complete the task of reviewing the law and penalty for murder.

---

end he could only be indicted for non-capital murder.

52. A notable exclusion from the partial defence is any reference to sexual infidelity.
53. The widening of the other partial defence of diminished responsibility in section 56 Coroners and Justice Act 2009 should not call for any great adjustment in the direction of juries. Both partial defences came into force in October 2010.

CHAPTER 10

HOMICIDE ON THE ROAD

Introduction

> Public opinion as a rule accuses [criminology] of trying to whitewash and to pamper the criminal. In two cases however, the charge is different: whenever criminologists turn their attention to the white collar criminal or the traffic offender, public opinion makes a *volte-face* and accuses them of being unduly harsh and punishment-minded. It is in fact the prevailing popular theory that these unfortunate victims of the motor age have been brought into the sphere of the criminal law and the criminal courts only by a deplorable combination of legal tricks and social and moral misjudgements which should be put right without delay.[1]

In England and Wales each year fewer than a thousand people are 'murdered'—to use that imprecise term of art—while around three thousand die as a consequence of a variety of incidents involving road traffic. The comparison is imprecise in that just as the data for 'murders' do not include every kind of unlawful killing, so not all deaths on the road come about as a result of unlawful acts. But, that given, we know that a substantial number of those who die on the road do so as a result either of their own behaviour or,

---

1.   Hermann Mannheim. Foreword to T C Willett, *Criminal on the Road: A Study of Serious Motoring Offences and Those Who Commit Them*. London, Tavistock Publications, 1964. Mannheim (a former distinguished German judge who fled the Nazis to become the founding father of modern British criminology) had an approach to criminological issues not unlike that of Edwin Sutherland. (See: Roger Hood in Jack Beatson and Reinhart Zimmermann (eds.), *Jurists Uprooted: German-Speaking Émigré Lawyers in 20th Century Britain*, OUP, 2004)). Willett's work was the first seriously to focus on the issue of road traffic offenders and remains a classic.

more commonly, the conduct of other road users potentially falling within the general ambit of the criminal law.

Killings on the road, which almost exclusively arise from the use of mechanically propelled vehicles, may well illustrate one of the most acutely problematic issues in homicide law. Yet both the general pattern of their prosecution, the severity of the penalties provided by statute, and the pattern of sentencing, normally result in relatively lenient penalties which are in marked contrast to those which are the norm in cases of murder and manslaughter. Indeed, it is a contrast that is, in certain instances, positively stark. That this is often a source of bewilderment to — and no little resentment by — the relatives and friends of those who die in what are commonly referred to as 'road accidents' is well known.[2]

The starting point of any analysis of this situation must embrace an historical perspective.

Road traffic law is, in the context of the general *corpus* of the criminal law, of comparatively modern provenance: its origins are identifiable in the Stage Carriage Act 1832, the Highways Act 1835, some of the provisions of the Metropolitan Police Act 1839, and the Town Police Clauses Act 1847. While almost all the vehicles on public roads at that time were horse drawn and individual horse riders were common,[3] mechanically propelled road transport in the form of steam driven road locomotives were appearing in larger numbers by the middle of the century.[4] Section 35 Offences Against the Person Act 1861 provided for a maximum penalty of two years' imprisonment with or without hard labour for those in charge of carriages or vehicles whose conduct resulted in bodily harm 'to any person whatsoever'. But that provision notwithstanding, the regulation of mechanically propelled vehicles developed, as did much other regulatory legislation in the 19th century, in

---

2. In contrast to the subject of so-called 'mercy killings' about which a whole range of interest groups from lawyers to theologians are greatly exercised, killing on the road, and the law relating to it, has never been subject to the same degree of moral or jurisprudential scrutiny.

3. For many years bicyclists were defined as 'riders', and, not being distinguished from horse riders, were also prosecuted under these statutes for such offences as 'riding furiously'.

4. The Locomotive Act 1861, amended in 1865, restricted their speeds initially to a maximum of ten and later to four miles per hour and required an attendant with a red flag to go ahead of them. The 'locomotives' were essentially traction engines used for pulling loaded wagons, but the category also included other vehicles such as mobile threshing machines and road rollers, known until recent times as 'steamrollers'.

what might be termed a parallel jurisprudential universe from the common law generally and the criminal law in particular. It was predicated upon the notion that these offences, as practical means of ensuring public welfare, were to be regarded as *mala prohibita* rather than *mala in se*.[5] The exceptions were those in which deaths resulted from negligent or reckless behaviour, a situation in which individual railway signalmen and engine drivers were prosecuted for manslaughter.[6] In contrast, the corporate liabilities of the railway companies following death or injury in train crashes were matters for the civil law.

Gentlemen in Leather Coats and Goggles

In 1884 Gottlieb Daimler produced the first vehicle to be propelled by an internal combustion engine using petroleum, and other inventors and manufacturers followed. Within a decade there were substantial numbers of rich and often socially influential owners of these new 'motor cars', as they became known. Motoring organizations began to be formed and pressure was applied in political circles for new legislation. This resulted in reform in the shape of the Locomotives on Highways Act 1896[7] which raised the speed limit and removed the red flag requirement for unladen vehicles of under three tons. There followed a period of great public hostility towards motor cars and those who drove them, especially in the countryside.[8] The Motor Car Act 1903 addressed the question of speed limits but went further to deal with dangerous driving and failure to stop or report accidents, while providing power to endorse and suspend licences to drive. Its provisions were extended to motorcycles.

---

5. Many police forces until almost the end of the century recorded offences against the Factory and Education Acts as 'quasi'-crimes.
6. It can be argued that it was their status as 'railway servants' that suggested that the application of the criminal law was appropriate. The view that the offences of 'servants' could be distinguished from those of other individuals was related to their imputed 'trustworthiness'. For most of the 20th century the Larceny Act 1916 identified 'larceny by a servant' as a distinct category of theft until replaced by the Theft Act 1968.
7. Commemorated annually in the veteran car run from London to Brighton.
8. Quintessentially encapsulated in the pages of Kenneth Grahame's *Wind in the Willows* (1908).

Although the numbers of draught horses reached a peak in the decade before 1914 and were extensively used by the armed services in World War I, motor transport became increasingly important and by the early 1920s commercial motor vehicles in the form of motor lorries, omnibuses[9] and what were known as *charabancs*[10] had become a common sight on both country roads and city streets. More important was the emergence of the new mass-produced motor car in this period. Legislation, however, moved only slowly; although a Royal Commission had been set up in 1906 to examine the working of the Act of 1903 and to make recommendations, these were effectively shelved for two decades. Notably, section 40 Criminal Justice Act 1925 made it an offence for a person to be drunk in charge of a mechanically propelled vehicle on the highway[11] and provided for mandatory disqualification from driving, but broader issues of regulating the use of motor vehicles remained in urgent need of consideration. The increasing number of small cars, the so-called 'family saloons' whose occupants no longer needed the protection of stout coats and goggles, was an element in the inexorable social change that was taking place in British society.

Enter the Respectable Middle Classes

Whereas in the 1890s and early 1900s motor cars had been the large and expensive accessories of the wealthy, their bodywork the opulent manifestation of the bespoke coachbuilder's art, the mass production of small family cars by William Morris (later Lord Nuffield) and Sir Herbert Austin, following the example of Henry Ford in the United States, had brought motoring within the reach of the moderately affluent middle classes. The Austin Seven

---

9. The first of these were developed in France under the name *voiture omnibus* (literally 'carriage for all'). George Shillibeer began a horse-drawn omnibus service between Paddington Green and the City of London in 1829. In 1934 the London Passenger Transport Board officially adopted the abbreviation of 'bus'. In the countryside, the motor bus came to replace the carrier's cart as a mode of transport for poorer people.

10. An increasingly popular form of transport for groups of the otherwise relatively impecunious and a competitor with the railway excursion (from the French *char à banc* or 'cart with seat'). By the 1960s the demotic term for this vehicle, commonly known as a 'sharrabang' or 'sharra', had become 'coach'.

11. Such people would previously have been prosecuted under the Licensing Act 1872.

(1923) and the Morris Minor (1928) became the British equivalents of the Ford Model T. Those less affluent bought motorcycles and motor tricycles, which attracted a significantly lower rate of excise duty than motor cars.[12] The organs of Government stirred. The first Report of the Royal Commission on Transport in 1929 was shortly followed by the Road Traffic Act 1930 which removed the 20mph speed limit, introduced compulsory third party insurance and increased the penalties for dangerous and drunken driving.

As road casualties rose steeply in the early 1930s[13] pressure mounted for further and more restrictive legislation that came in the form of the Road Traffic Act 1934.[14] Urban speed limits were re-imposed, all new drivers were required to pass a test[15] and marked pedestrian crossings were introduced.[16] The most significant provision of the Act, as far as homicide law is concerned, was that which provided for juries to convict for dangerous driving where the charge had been manslaughter.

It is perhaps one of the great ironies of the history of road traffic legislation that a Parliamentary advocate of improvements in road safety should himself have been prosecuted for the manslaughter of the driver of a car with which

---

12. The three-wheeled Morgan fitted with a motorcycle engine was among the most popular, but not so common as the 'motorcycle combination': a motorcycle which carried a pillion passenger and other (often child) passengers in a sidecar bolted to its frame. The Morgan survives as a highly sought-after conventional modern-day sports car, while one of the most successful of sidecar manufacturers, Swallow Sidecars, later built motor cars under the name of the 'SS Jaguar'. The 'SS' was dropped following World War II after which the original company continued as Jaguar Cars.

13. One must assume as a result of the combination of increased vehicle numbers and those being driven at higher speeds with poor roadholding and often abysmally poor brakes. In 1934 there were approximately 1.4 million motor vehicles on the roads with road deaths amounting to some 7,300. In 2008, by which time vehicle numbers had increased to some 34 million, road deaths had fallen to approximately 2,500.

14. The Motor Vehicles (Construction and Use) Regulations 1934 (as frequently updated since) established minimum standards, especially for brakes and lighting.

15. The driving test was suspended during World War II and new drivers were issued with provisional driving licences. Those who renewed these without any break in the post-war period were allowed to convert them into full licences although they had not passed any test. Those who had become approved drivers in the armed forces during the war were similarly advantaged.

16. The distinctive illuminated orange globes on striped poles marking these crossings were for many years known as 'Belisha Beacons' (commonly — but erroneously — pronounced as 'Belissher') after Mr Leslie Hore-Belisha, the Minister of Transport who had overseen their introduction.

his vehicle had been in collision. In his maiden speech in the House of Lords in 1928[17] Edward Russell, 26th Baron de Clifford, argued that applicants for driving licences should be subject to a mandatory test. He was also in favour of speed limits. In August 1935 he was involved in a head-on collision as a result of which the driver of the other car died. A coroner's jury held him to be responsible and he was subsequently charged with what was then the felony of manslaughter. The case was, however, a landmark in legal history, though for an entirely different reason. Having initially been committed for trial at the Central Criminal Court it emerged that he was entitled to be tried not there, but in the House of Lords by a jury of his peers who had jurisdiction to try the case, a right enjoyed by peers since the early Middle Ages but rarely used in modern times. Russell's defence that the fault lay with the other driver was accepted and he was acquitted of manslaughter.[18] However, his troubles were not yet over, for he faced a further trial at the Central Criminal Court on an indictment for dangerous driving. Proceedings were, nevertheless, subsequently discontinued. There is no record of his having spoken again in Parliament on the subject of road safety.

The 1956 Act: Sand is Thrown from the Descending Balloon

Until 1956, although the concept of causing death by dangerous driving was employed in legal proceedings, individuals responsible for deaths on the road arising from the negligent or reckless driving of a mechanically propelled vehicle on a public road that was susceptible to criminal prosecution (as distinct from civil suit) were prosecuted for manslaughter at Common Law. The Road Traffic Act 1934, following the case of *Stringer*,[19] allowed juries to find a defendant guilty of dangerous driving rather than the specific homicide offence of manslaughter. Though juries did sometimes exercise this option

---

17. He was aged 21 at the time.
18. This proved to be the last time that a trial of a peer charged with felony would take place there, the right being abolished in 1948. In that the Lords, in the shape of the Judicial Committee, gave their judgment in *Woolmington* that year, it might be said that 1935 was a landmark in the judicial history of the Upper House.
19. *R v Stringer* [1933] 24 Cr App R 30.

it scarcely simplified the law. By 1937 it had become clear from *Andrews*[20] that there were a number of degrees of negligence which the jury needed to consider even though the victim's unlawful death was no in doubt.

It was the Road Traffic Act 1956 that was to establish the modern offence of causing death by dangerous driving, in contrast to the Road Safety Act 1967 that established an objective measure of alcoholic intoxication, following years in which juries had not infrequently declined to accept prosecution evidence of drunken driving. The Road Traffic Act 1956, while it gave the prosecution a clear objective in proving the cause of death, could still offer no warranty against juries simply declining to convict.[21] Speaking in support of the clause in the Bill relating to causing death in the course of Parliamentary debate, the Lord Chief Justice, Lord Goddard, said that he had urged the necessity of such an offence to the Minister of Transport in 1933, having been continually astounded at the perverse verdicts in cases where manslaughter had been charged.[22]

What, in effect, the 1956 Act did was to recognise the not infrequent defeat of the prosecution case at the hands of what in some instances were perverse juries. If they would not convict for manslaughter, notwithstanding the strength of the case, then there was no alternative but to lower the bar by providing for a new offence with a comparatively modest penalty of a maximum of five years' imprisonment. But unlike the alcohol limit set at 80mg per 100ml of blood, which, if exceeded, could result in nothing other than conviction, the concept of dangerous driving attracted an element of subjective *assessment*, something that cannot be similarly measured. Indeed, the concept of 'dangerousness' has a quality that defies reliable objective gradation and can only be estimated by reference to the circumstances present in the context of the particular event. A well-maintained vehicle, in the hands of a competent and responsible driver, that is travelling at 70 mph on a motorway with only light traffic, can scarcely be said to constitute an immediately

---

20. *Andrews v DPP* [1937] 26 Cr App R 34, at p.39.

21. In road traffic offences involving death, like those involving intoxication, the findings of juries have often suggested a flaw in the jury system. Where the interpretation of the culpability of the defendant is subjected to the criteria of jury *choice* rather than any objective test, it may be tempted to consider first the consequences of conviction, declining to convict where those consequences are considered unacceptable.

22. *Hansard* HL, 15 February 1955.

evident risk of danger. Not so one in poor condition and driven at high speed, on a busy urban street on which the speed is restricted to 30 mph, by an inexperienced youth seeking by the manner of his driving to impress his passengers. The combination of an inexperienced driver, the state of the vehicle, the manner in which it is being driven and the ambient conditions on the road itself, represent a high degree of potential danger; the possibility that, nevertheless, nothing disastrous *might actually* happen is an entirely irrelevant issue. If it were otherwise all efforts to improve safety, whether on the roads or anywhere else, could be held to be largely unnecessary.[23]

The new statutory offence, created in 1956 as an alternative to a charge of manslaughter, was, in effect, a device designed to encourage juries to behave differently. But as far as deterring potentially homicidal drivers was concerned, there were those on the Bench who doubted the deterrent effect of heavy sentences in serious motoring cases, including those of drinking drivers. In 1959 *The Times*[24] reported Mr Justice Stable as saying in court:

> If I thought that by sending people to prison I should save thousands of people killed on the roads every year, then I would do it. Personally I don't believe that sending bad drivers to prison is going to achieve that result.

His view echoed that of the Hon. Ewen Montagu QC, who sat as a Recorder in Hampshire and Middlesex, who, also speaking from the Bench but specifically about the drinking driver, maintained that in many cases (he)

> has not been drinking a lot, and is an eminently responsible man to whom a small fine means a lot.[25] (Sic!)

Such sympathetic attitudes towards bad and irresponsible drivers were probably mirrored among juries trying cases in which dangerous, careless or drunken driving had resulted in death. Few such drivers, if indeed any,

---

23. Arguments about the compulsory wearing of seat belts, like current arguments about helmets for pedal cyclists, often seek to rely on evidence that not *all* crashes or collisions result in injuries that either a seat belt or a helmet would otherwise have prevented.
24. *The Times*, 27 October 1959.
25. *The Times*, 12 December 1959.

could be said to have *intended* the fatal consequences of their actions: indeed, it can be reasonably assumed that the overwhelming majority would have regretted them for a variety of reasons. But, being unintended, it was only a small step to regarding them as 'accidental' in the sense of not being primarily perceived as blameworthy. This, of course, neglects consideration of the moral responsibility of the driver to exercise a general duty of care when behind the wheel.

The presumption that the motoring offender was a species to be distinguished from the traditional criminal classes was widely held and there is little to suggest that the creation of an offence of causing death by dangerous driving, even if it made juries less reluctant to convict than they might otherwise have been, had the charge been manslaughter, did little to change matters. Where death on the road was concerned, the concept of the 'road accident', with its imputation of tragic but unintended consequences as distinct from a morally culpable act, was deeply entrenched.

'It was a dreadful accident': the Offender as Co-Victim

There is some evidence which suggests that there remains a popular view that those whose driving conduct results in the death of others and who are also killed are not to be seen as offenders. Rather they are viewed as victims along with those whom have they have killed by their driving. The lack of intention to *kill* is seen as neutralising the offender's culpability. Even those who have deliberately *chosen* to drive unlawfully — the intoxicated, the uninsured, the disqualified, the so-called 'joy rider' or car thief — should they themselves die are often curiously absolved from moral obloquy; a process made easier by the fact that they have not lived to be successfully prosecuted for their conduct.

The primary identification of a deceased drunken, dangerous, uninsured or otherwise potentially offending driver as a victim is an essential part of a process whereby guilt and responsibility are neutralised. Indeed, one might note the stark contrast with how the murder of children by a parent, followed by parental suicide, is viewed.

A road death, if it can be shown to have come about as a direct result of unlawful conduct, can only be properly described as a homicidal offence. It is of no avail for the careless driver to say that he never intended to kill the cyclist whom he did not see, nor for the dangerous driver to argue that at that time of the day he never expected oncoming traffic on a blind corner. We need to consider matters in terms of what the prudent and reasonably competent driver would foresee as being potentially hazardous. The erroneous notion that an intention to achieve particular outcome can be the *only* test of criminal guilt is deeply embedded in what might be termed popular ethics, yet the question that is frequently not asked is: 'To what end is the intention directed?'. If it was to make or receive a mobile telephone call, notwithstanding the legal prohibition on the use of handheld equipment, the intention was obviously not to injure another, still less to kill. But what if the outcome is the death of another?

It can be argued that the driver who knowingly and with conscious deliberation breaks the law, with the albeit unintended consequence of killing another person, is in a position that is impossible to distinguish from that of the man who, having lost his temper, inflicts an injury which unexpectedly proves to be fatal. Neither he, nor the driver using his hand held mobile device, can be considered, *prima facie,* as having any intention to achieve the death of another. The driver using his telephone may simply have wanted to speak with someone and it is often difficult precisely to know what might have been in the mind of an angry person who has, albeit temporarily, lost all control of himself. What is critical is the combination of their knowledge of the potential risks involved (including the extent to which awareness of such risk is clear and unambiguous) and the individual's decision to pursue his intention without being deterred, notwithstanding his understanding that his actions may well be against the law.

Recognition of this is frequently obscured by what might be termed linguistic neutralisation in which the term 'accident' is frequently employed. If a tree, battered by a high wind, suddenly crashes down on to a passing vehicle killing its driver, it might reasonably be termed an 'accident'.[26] No human hand has brought about his death and a tree can bear neither moral

---

26. To be compared with the (possibly unfortunate) term 'act of God' that can feature among the exclusory clauses of some insurance policies.

responsibility nor criminal guilt. Not so in the case of the death following a collision between two vehicles, one of which is being driven dangerously: the death, however unintended, has been a direct consequence of the conduct of the dangerous driver and no 'accident' to be compared to that of the falling tree. That road traffic offences were, in the early days of motor transport, largely committed by the relatively affluent members of society who could be readily distinguished form the so-called 'criminal classes' has resulted in road traffic offences becoming regarded as largely *sui generis* and effectively devoid, if not of complete moral obloquy then certainly of a *criminal* character in the accepted sense of the term. Matters would be helped if the police were to refer to road traffic *incidents* rather than road traffic *accidents*.

Fortunately, road traffic incidents mostly involve damage to vehicles and non-fatal injuries to the person. Most of these are dealt with by resort to negotiated settlements between the parties (or more commonly, their insurers) by way of financial compensation. Certain cases, however, may go to litigation in the courts.

The idea that individuals owe a responsibility to compensate the losses or injuries of others, even if unintended, is well established and forms part of that moral catechism that is located within a culture of reparation in which insurance and the availability of civil suit are essential elements. In contrast, it is held that *crime* can only come about when the individual deliberately *intends* to do that which he succeeds in doing. This belief provides the essential device for the purpose of neutralising both guilt and responsibility in their moral dimension. Should the offender have suffered any hurt he is thus readily translated into co-victim.

This is, of course, founded upon an egregious nonsense, since the individual has a general duty of care, certainly when behind the wheel of a motor vehicle, to avoid injury to others at large. That logically precedes any action that may result in the necessity of compensating another for injury. Moreover, a successful candidate in the driving test is able to acquire a *licence* to drive, not an inalienable right to do so, and certainly not to drive as he pleases. The guidelines respecting his driving behaviour are enshrined in the Highway Code and also in road traffic law and while candidates for the test are not required to be proficient in their familiarity with the latter, knowledge of the Highway Code is an integral part of the test procedure. A

249

driver who observes the provisions of the Code at all times is most unlikely to fall foul of the law.

Thus it can be presumed that those with licences to drive have not only reached a standard of competence but are aware, through their study of the Highway Code, of the manner of driving which is expected of them. It is therefore logical that the law, in cases of alleged infringement, should apply as a general criterion the objective standard of a competent driver. This, however, is to portray a perfect world. How, it may be asked, could it be otherwise?

Until the early 1980s, a number of those in possession of a driving licence had never taken a normal Department of Transport driving test, either because they had held a licence prior to 1934 or, more commonly, because they had converted a wartime provisional or military licence into a full civilian licence by the simple expedient of renewing it at annual intervals. They had never been required to take a test. Given the uncertain nature both of the quality of their initial instruction and in the case of the service licence the often rudimentary original test of 'competence', their standard of driving would scarcely be susceptible to objective criteria of evaluation. These drivers are now a small and rapidly diminishing minority.

Not so those whose licences date from between 1950 and 1970. While older drivers are less likely to be involved in road traffic incidents than those younger and less experienced, the statistical data are almost certainly skewed by the fact that those over 70 tend to drive lower mileages and often avoid doing so in conditions requiring extra skill, such as at night or in adverse weather. It may also be true that behaviourally, they may be generally more cautious.

The problem here is twofold. First, both the quality of professional driving instruction and the rigorousness of testing has changed substantially in the last half-century. Second, much of what older drivers learned is no longer relevant and much of what is currently relevant they were never taught. No longer is the test candidate required to know the signals given by the rotating whip of the horse-drawn cart ahead, but, equally, the older driver will initially have had less long-term experience of driving on dual carriageways or negotiating large gyratory systems. But there will be nothing to prevent him or her, decades after having passed the test, from driving on a motorway.[27] The exponential increase in the volume of road traffic in the last two decades alone has meant that the driving skills demanded, not only on motorways but also on urban roads, are now significantly greater than in the 1950s and 1960s. Very large articulated commercial vehicles are nowadays a significant proportion of high-speed traffic on motorways and constitute a significant proportion of delivery traffic in urban areas. In addition, the modern policy of concentrating children in fewer and larger schools has meant that there is now a new dimension to traffic in the form of the so-called 'school run'. Provided the older driver is medically fit to drive and is not ordered to do so by a court, he need never take a test again.

The issue of regular driver testing is one which, however frequently raised, seems never to attract the interests of the legislature. Yet those elderly drivers who are concerned about their skills and who decide voluntarily to undertake professional assessment, often discover not only the existence of new and improved driving techniques, but that over the years they have lapsed imperceptibly into what are undoubtedly bad driving habits. However, younger drivers, even though they will have been instructed in modern roadcraft, may equally fall into more relaxed patterns of driving once the test is out of the way and they have became more confident and experienced. There are strong arguments for re-testing all drivers, however experienced, at regular intervals and particularly young and relatively inexperienced drivers who are involved in a high proportion of road traffic incidents. Drivers who have been involved in a higher than average number of collisions, whether or not the subject of prosecution, would also appear to be proper candidates for re-testing. Only drivers who have been convicted of a road traffic offence and are ordered to do so by order of a court can be required to re-take the driving test.

There is a case for re-examining not only the procedures for the driving test but also the nature of driving instruction. While the number of professional driving schools has grown employing officially approved instructors, their services are a matter of choice for the novice driver. There may well be

---

27. The first section of motorway did not open until 1959.

merit in requiring test candidates to have undergone a minimum period of training by a qualified and approved instructor.

But however far it may be possible to improve driver training and promote a culture of safe and considerate behaviour on the road, the law will always be required to control the conduct of those who choose deliberately to drive as they please, however inconsiderately. Perhaps in no other area of homicide is it possible so clearly to distinguish between incompetence and ineptitude and deliberate lawbreaking as on the public road.

Modernising the Law — Again

Currently conduct on the road is governed primarily by two comparatively recent pieces of legislation: the Road Traffic Act 1988 and the Road Safety Act 2006. While it remains possible for a driver who causes death on the road still to be charged with what is essentially a generic form of homicide, namely manslaughter,[28] the law now identifies a number of specific offences regarding death by driving.

(a) causing death by dangerous driving;

(b) causing death by careless driving;

(c) causing death by careless driving while under the influence of drink or drugs;

(d) causing death by driving when driving unlicensed, disqualified, or uninsured; and

(e) causing death by aggravated vehicle taking.

Forensically, the advantage of this legislation is that it provides an objective test, both of what is dangerous and what is careless. In the former the manner

---

28. Where the defendant is grossly negligent regarding the risk of *death* as distinct from the risk of injury or damage. See *Ademako* [1995] 1 AC 171.

of driving must fall *far* below that expected of a careful and competent driver and in the latter the standard must simply fall *below* that standard.[29]

In cases of causing death by dangerous or careless driving we are looking at a relationship between a standard of driving which must be demonstrated to fall below or far below the objective standard, and its consequence. When we come to the other categories, the notion of a penal premium can be discerned, since in each of these the offender commits the offence of causing death without there being any need to establish his standard of driving. His standard of driving is not at issue; what matters is that he has killed someone whilst driving when the law, in one context or another, has made it unlawful for him to do so. Not that this is any guarantee that if his driving has in one way or another indeed fallen below the objective standard, he does not remain in hazard of prosecution for a more serious offence.

In real life it is often the case that the standard of driving of a driver impaired by drink or drugs is likely in any event to fall below or well below that of the competent and careful driver, which is why the end result may so readily be the death of another. Lawbreakers though they undoubtedly are, such drivers may also be foolish risk-takers, or possibly people whose original decision to drive has itself been seriously impaired by alcohol or drugs.

Unlicensed, disqualified, and uninsured drivers[30] and those who are driving stolen vehicles are in a different category. None of these characteristics could be regarded as in any sense an impairment. With perhaps the exception of the driver who honestly believed that he was insured to drive when in fact he was not, every offender in this group will:

(a) have had foreknowledge of the prohibition on his driving; and

---

29. It can of course be argued that even this process is one of estimation rather than precise measurement. A traveller to the polar regions would not require a thermometer to discover that it was very cold indeed, any more than one to the tropics would need one to realise that it was extremely hot. Assessment of driving is not so very different since contextually it is largely self-evident.

30. It is estimated that uninsured and untraced drivers are responsible for around 160 deaths and 23,000 injuries every year (Press Release, Department for Transport, 11 January 2011). What we do not know is what proportion of 'untraced' drivers are uninsured, disqualified, driving with excess alcohol in their blood or under the influence of drugs.

(b) have nevertheless made a deliberate decision to do so.

It is hard to understand how a disqualified driver, one who has never held a licence, or one who has never paid an insurance premium, can be unaware of any of those acts, any more than a car thief can be unaware that it is an offence to drive a vehicle that has been taken unlawfully from another. These may be towards the extreme end of the scale of serious offences, but there is other behaviour, no less hazardous. Drivers who simply disregard the law relating to speed limits or the use of mobile telephones are a daily sight on every public road. Here the law, however sensibly its provisions may have been constructed, is handicapped by the consequences of low levels of enforcement. But short of serious mental impairment it can be presumed that every driver who deliberately drives in a manner or circumstances prohibited by law will have had foreknowledge of that prohibition.

Matching the Penalty to the Fault

Following the Criminal Justice Act 2003 the maximum penalty for causing death by dangerous driving increased from five to fourteen years' imprisonment. Causing death by careless driving while under the influence of drink or drugs carries the same maximum of fourteen years. Otherwise causing death by careless driving carries a maximum of only five years; causing death while driving unlicensed, disqualified or uninsured carry maxima of only two years. In the instance of aggravated vehicle taking, if death results, the maximum rises from two to fourteen years. But if such vehicle taking constitutes an aggravating (in the sense of being the opposite of mitigating) dimension to the offence of homicide, by what logic is driving whilst unlicensed, uninsured or disqualified any less an aggravating factor? The preliminary circumstances in all these instances will have been characterised not by any pharmacological impairment of behaviour (by alcohol or drugs), nor inattention, nor incompetence, but by conscious deliberation.

By inference we may assume that in distinguishing between deaths resulting from dangerous as distinct from careless driving, Parliament had in mind the need to reflect the magnitude of the fault element in the offence.

Clearly, an utterly reckless disregard of the risks involved in driving in a self-evidently dangerous manner can be distinguished from an instance of momentary inattention. To that extent the dangerously reckless or aggressive driver who is contemptuous of the law's constraints is considerably more blameworthy than the carelessly inattentive one, and if the 'fault' element is to be determined by the character of their respective driving, it is logical that there should be a difference in the maximum penalty.

But what if we do *not* limit the fault element to the nature of their driving, but extend it to cover its consequences? Which is of greater moral and social consequence, that one individual had driven dangerously while the other has only done so carelessly, or that the outcome in both cases has been the unlawful death of another person? Is there, perhaps, room for a new concept of 'constructive harm'[31] — as distinct from constructive malice? It is, after all, the law that an intention to do a person serious harm is sufficient to prove murder should death result. The fact that a person drove in a particular fashion at a particular time is, intrinsically, no more than that. But the consequent death, apart from its sheer magnitude and irreversibility, may well have a series of future consequences for the relatives and friends of the victim that will be felt throughout their lifetimes.

When we come to the penalties for causing death by driving when disqualified, unlicensed or uninsured, or in the context of aggravated vehicle taking, the *manner* of the defendant's driving is irrelevant save as an aggravating feature of the offence. Were such a driver simply to decide to take to the road in defiance of the law then the 'fault' would reside in that decision. But where death occurs, the higher penalty indicates that in the mind of Parliament the 'fault' resides not only in the manner of driving but also in the homicidal outcome. But again, one must ask, what is the logic that distinguishes in terms of the maximum penalty between drivers who are banned from the road by a prior legal prohibition and those who, in the course of what is essentially a serious property offence — the unlawful taking of a vehicle without the owner's consent — happen to kill whilst driving it?

---

31. Constructive malice aside, other spheres of the law seem not to experience difficulty in accommodating the concept of 'constructive' in such guises as 'constructive dismissal' or 'constructive desertion'.

Indeed, the question that needs to be asked is whether the penalty for causing death in any of these circumstances should depend primarily upon some prior 'fault' or upon the outcome of the offender's driving. By 'driving' we would include both the manner of driving and the decision to drive when to do so is already prohibited. If, however, the focus is upon the more serious issue, namely the consequential death, then it is necessary to establish to what extent the defendant should be regarded as having had foresight of that possibility.

While causing death by dangerous driving may come about as a result of serious negligence it may also arise from aggressive behaviour, sometimes referred to as 'road rage'. An angry driver who may be in control of a large and powerful vehicle has a potentially deadly weapon at his disposal.[32] What reason is there for not regarding him in the same way as any other man in a rage with a deadly weapon such as a gun or a knife to hand? The case for sentencing such drivers with comparative severity would appear to be on all fours with the proper approach in instances of aggressive behaviour in other situations which result in death.[33] Where careless driving is concerned the case for greater leniency ought logically to be based upon the premise that there is a difference between overt aggression on the road and relative incompetence or misjudgment.

Wrong Concept: Wrong Place

Given its great diversity, there are good reasons for identifying areas of human behaviour that require to be regulated by the criminal law but in different ways and by appropriately distinct sanctions. Offences of dishonesty contrasted with those of violence to the person might be cited as an example. But where homicide is concerned, the situation is entirely unique: it stands alone as the one event whose consequences can be neither reversed nor significantly ameliorated by any act of reparation or compensation. Whether

---

32. The common practice known as 'tailgating', particularly if the offending driver is at the wheel of a heavy commercial vehicle, is both seriously intimidating and highly dangerous.

33. Having a bad temper, while conceivably of marginal value as mitigation, is scarcely any defence to a charge of homicide.

the instrument of death is the human hand, a weapon, or mechanical device can makes no difference to the terminal outcome: they are no more than means to that end and there is no basis for generic distinction.

We return, therefore, to what is a fundamental theme in our approach, namely the need for a unitary offence of criminal homicide. As we have said elsewhere, we regard the distinctions drawn between murder and manslaughter to be essentially artificial, shot through with illogicality and arbitrariness. The same is most certainly the case with the law when it attempts to draw a distinction between deaths involving one means of transport from those involving any other.

Moreover, in distinguishing between death arising from 'careless' and that from 'dangerous' driving, it defines the offence—albeit with some serious attempt at objectivity—in terms of the defendant's putative culpability. This is in complete contrast with, say, the law of theft. A theft is a theft, whether it involves a child stealing a bar of chocolate from the counter of a sweet shop or a gang of professional adult thieves stealing goods going from store to store in a shopping centre. Likewise robbery, an offence that can technically involve child offenders and child victims no less than bank staff and masked and armed men. Again, as we argue elsewhere, the place for examining issues of relative culpability is not in the course of the trial of a particularly defined offence but in the process of determining sentence. Where deaths arising in the context of road traffic offences are concerned, this would mean in practical terms that the prior elements of the present offences of homicide on the road would remain, but as aggravating features of the offence of criminal homicide.

As we argue throughout this book, the sentence for the offence of criminal homicide should be at large, with a maximum of imprisonment for life, and this should be equally applicable to death on the road no less than in any other situation. But it does not follow that in this context properly constructed sentencing guidelines would not be able to ensure that sentences were appropriate to the circumstances of the individual offence any less than the instance of homicides committed in other circumstances. Moreover, given that juries would be effectively relieved of making what are essentially subjective judgments about driving behaviour, their verdicts would be more sharply focussed upon facts.

A Final Consideration

Are road traffic offences 'crimes' in the sense that the word is generally used? Those who perceive the driving of motor vehicles to be a 'right' as distinct from a licensed and thereby privileged activity, tend to regard road traffic legislation as a curtailment of that freedom rather than as a rational system of regulation having the general object of road safety. Given that, there is no reason to consider such offences as falling squarely within the generic category of crime, bearing in mind that different crimes constitute different threats to the general well being of society, ranging from the relatively trivial to the most serious. Offences committed by drivers include both the relatively trivial and the most serious of all, namely homicide. And just as the law regards the killing of a householder in the course of a burglary as a grave instance of homicide, notwithstanding that the offender never specifically intended it and claims it to have been an 'accident', so too a death caused by an aggressively dangerous driver can properly be regarded as an instance of criminal homicide, no matter that the emollient use of the word 'accident' may be employed in an attempt to sanitise the description of a violent and unlawful killing.

If, then, road traffic offences are, as we would forcefully argue, to be regarded as criminal offences in the accepted sense of the term, it is legitimate to consider the matter of their prevention, no less than with respect to other forms of crime. Here the three 'E's of engineering, enforcement and education may be compared with crime prevention in other spheres. Just as locks and alarms may prevent or seriously restrict theft, so modifications to road layouts may serve both physically to restrict the dangerous driver[34] and minimise the consequences of careless or incompetent driving. Enforcement is more problematic, not least since many such measures are often resented as instances of a 'war on the motorist' — often by those who have no difficulty with the concept of a 'war' on other kinds of crime. A segment of popular culture promotes the idea that speed cameras are installed primarily for the purpose of raising revenue and that they are somehow objectionable as an invasion of freedom and privacy.

---

34. Such devices can include humps on the carriageway, chicanes and traffic 'pinches'.

Given that traffic policing is vulnerable to retrenchment in times of financial stringency, the probability of detecting road crime is proportionately lower and offenders are likely to be emboldened; ignoring speed limits and using handheld telephones whilst driving, to cite but two examples, both of which are done with relatively impunity by what would appear to be a significant number of drivers.

While the sanctions of fines and disqualification from driving have an important part to play, more imaginative consequences are worthy of consideration, such as the confiscation and possible destruction of vehicles in appropriate cases. The education of drivers both initially and subsequent to their being licensed to drive has and can still be improved. There would seem to be little doubt that the quality of driver instruction and the increasing sophistication of the driving test, both written and practical, can only contribute towards ensuring that those who are licensed to drive are not only competent, but aware of the risks to life and property that are ever present on the public roads.

But in contemporary society the motor car is far more than a means of transport. It has, in many respects, become inseparable from the individual's sense of freedom and proprietorial autonomy. For some drivers, their vehicles are an expression of the self or conspicuous consumption and a virtual extension of personality. Radio and recorded music are at the driver's fingertips, along with mobile telephones and satellite navigation equipment. Advances in design have also created a sense of security amounting at times to feelings of virtual invulnerability. Braking and lighting are superb compared with vehicles of only a generation ago, and onboard computers can compensate for driver errors. As a consequence, collisions between vehicles are less likely than in former years to result in major or fatal injuries to those inside. Vehicle bodies with modern soundproofing and airbags designed to protect the occupants also have the potential to isolate the driver not only from a sense of risk but also from positive awareness of other road users, not least the more vulnerable, such as motorcyclists, pedal cyclists and pedestrians. Moreover, aspects of what might be termed the 'car culture' may well encourage an emphasis on perceived rights rather than responsibilities and compared with previous generations there will be many young drivers who will have had no experience of riding a bicycle or motor-cycle. Protective

259

parents frequently discourage their children from such pursuits and the more affluent may buy them cars as soon as they are legally able to drive. In short, there may be a degree of cultural and behavioural 'unawareness' on the part of many drivers of the vulnerability of other road users.

But more than this, although few people can be unaware that certain conduct behind the wheel is illegal, not all are aware of the penalties attached. Given the comparatively low level of traffic policing in this country, many drivers will act on the basis that, even if they do break the law, their chances of being prosecuted are slim. Nor do all those who come before the courts for the first time appear to learn their lesson but go on, much to their chagrin, to acquire points on their licences and eventually be disqualified as recidivists. That repeated driving convictions are likely to attract increasingly prohibitive insurance premiums is by no means a guarantee of restricting the activities of bad drivers. Some will pay up, but others will simply fail to insure at all.

There will always, with respect to any offence, be a number of individuals on whose behaviour the existence of sanctions has little, if indeed any, deterrent effect. They may be prepared both to calculate the risks of detection and to treat any sanction imposed with contempt. Where disregard for road traffic law on the part of such individuals has resulted in their acquiring a multiplicity of convictions, disqualification from holding a licence may be completely ineffectual. A significant number of such drivers simply ignore the sanctions imposed by the courts and continue to drive, disqualified and uninsured. It might be that just as one certain, if expensive, way of ensuring a recidivist burglar is restrained from committing more offences for at least a while is by holding him in prison, so a driver who commits repeated road traffic offences might be restrained by the confiscation of his vehicle, should he own one. Given that many road traffic offenders are comparatively affluent members of a property-owning class, this might also act as a powerful deterrent.

Homicide on the road is perhaps the one area in which unlawful killing has the greatest potential for reduction. In the long term, it must depend upon improved programmes of driver education at the tuition stage and by better testing. There is no doubt but there have been quantum improvements in recent years[35] but there is room for more. No driver ought to go untested for a near lifetime. More importantly, there is an argument for suspending the licences until re-test of those who, while not having been prosecuted, have been involved in a disproportionate number of insurance claims involving collisions.

Road traffic legislation in Britain over the last 100 years, whatever its shortcomings, has nevertheless been a guarantee against the lethal anarchy that characterises driving in some other parts of the world. Though the criminal law is an imperfect instrument when it comes to controlling human behaviour, it will nevertheless continue to be needed to deal with those who make deliberate choices to behave as badly behind the wheel of a motor vehicle on a public road as some others do elsewhere. Those who commit road traffic offences, whatever the magnitude of their seriousness, are offenders no less than those who offend in more traditional ways. In this they are not entitled to consider themselves as distinct or less deserving of penalty.

---

35. The introduction of the theory test being one.

CHAPTER 11

CORPORATIONS IN THE DOCK

Introduction

The Corporate Manslaughter and Corporate Homicide Act 2007,[1] which came into effect on 6 April 2008, is the result of a 20-year battle to change the law on corporate homicide and enhance the legal responsibility of large companies as distinct from resorting to the less serious offences under health and safety legislation.

In a sense, the foundation-stone for reform was laid on 6 March 1987, when the P&O ferry *Herald of Free Enterprise* sank in the outer harbour of Zeebrugge, Belgium, with the loss of 187 lives. The ferry had set sail from Zeebrugge with its bow doors open, the crew member responsible for ensuring they were properly closed and secured being asleep in his bunk, having failed to hear the signal for 'harbour stations'. Yet there were no safeguards in place to prevent the vessel from sailing with the doors open.[2] 'By the autumn of 1986, the shore staff of the company were well aware of the possibility that one of their ships would sail with her stern or bow doors open. They were also aware of a very sensible and simple device in the form of indicator lights which had been suggested by responsible masters'.[3] The Board of Directors, according to the report, 'did not have any proper comprehension of what their duties were ...From top to bottom the body corporate was infected with the disease of sloppiness'. Indeed, when discussing liability for

---

1.   Hereafter referred to as the CMCHA.
2.   For a more detailed analysis of the events leading up to this sinking, see Blom-Cooper and Morris, *With Malice Aforethought* (Hart Publishing, 2004) at pages 135-137.
3.   *MV Herald of Free Enterprise Report of Court No 8074*, Department of Transport, 1987, para 18.8. Such warning lights (to indicate on the bridge whether the doors were open before sailing) were fitted by the company within days of the tragedy.

the disaster, the report stated: 'A full investigation into the circumstances of the disaster leads inexorably to the conclusion that the underlying or cardinal faults lay higher up in the company [than the crew member whose duty it was to ensure the doors were closed]'. Yet, despite all of this, neither the company nor any of the senior directors was convicted of manslaughter.

Over the following years, a succession of tragic events fuelled the calls for reform. On 18 November 1987, 31 people died in a fire at King's Cross Underground Station — the report of the public inquiry[4] drew attention to serious lapses by the most senior company officers of London Underground Ltd, with safety recommendations from the fire brigade, the police and the Railway Fire Prevention and Fire Standards Committee (which might have prevented the disaster) having not been adequately considered by senior managers. Again, no criminal proceedings (either for manslaughter or under health and safety regulations) were brought.

In July 1988, an explosion and fire on the Piper Alpha oil and gas platform in the North Sea killed 167 workers; a train crash near Clapham Junction railway station on 12 December of the same year killed 35 passengers. Neither of these disasters resulted in a successful conviction for manslaughter (although, following the Clapham Junction crash, British Rail was prosecuted for health and safety offences and fined a derisory £250,000[5]). Similarly, three more high-profile train crashes, with a combined loss of 18 lives (Southall in 1997, Hatfield in 2000 and Potters Bar in 2002) failed to bring a single conviction for gross negligence manslaughter, despite there having been clear evidence of inadequate safety systems. As Mr Justice Mackay, the trial judge in the Hatfield case, commented: 'This case continues to underline a long and pressing need for the long-delayed reform of the law in this area of unlawful killing'. For reasons which we shall state, large companies escape the clutches of prosecution for any homicide offence and are dealt with (if at all) under health and safety legislation, while the small company and its limited directorship are visibly caught by the prime criminal offence of manslaughter.

---

4. *Investigation into the King's Cross Underground Fire*, November 1988, known as the Fennell Report after Sir Desmond Fennell who chaired the inquiry.

5. The trial judge commented that 'a swingeing fine could only be met by British Rail by either increasing the burden on fare-paying passengers or by reducing the finance available for improvements to the railway system' — as reported in *The Guardian*, 5 June 1991.

Health and Safety: an Alternative to Prosecution for Homicide

The first piece of enforceable corporate health and safety legislation was the Factory Act 1833. Although it applied only to textile factories, it was a groundbreaking piece of legislation inasmuch as it allowed for Government-appointed inspectors to ensure its provisions were met. The 1867 Factory Act extended health and safety provisions beyond the textile industry, and a series of Acts introduced more and more comprehensive health and safety codes for public workplaces, until the provisions were consolidated by the Factories Act 1961.

Following the report of the Government's Committee on Safety and Health at Work, chaired by Lord Robens (as chairman of the Coal Board in the Aberfan school disaster), in 1972, the Health and Safety at Work Act 1974 was passed, setting up a new administrative system, with the Health and Safety Executive created, amalgamating the powers of previous Government inspectors. The Act also, in theory, widened the scope for criminal prosecution of those found to have breached health and safety legislation.

The 1974 Act did not take effect until 1 April 1975, and thus was not applicable when, on 1 June 1974, 28 people were killed and 36 injured following an explosion at the Nypro (UK) site in Flixborough, North Lincolnshire. A bypass pipe ruptured, and 40 tonnes of cyclohexane escaped in the form of a cloud. On contact with an ignition source, the cloud exploded, causing what was, at the time, the largest peacetime explosion ever seen in the UK. The official report into the disaster drew attention to the fact that the key post of works engineer was vacant at the crucial time and that apparently none of the senior personnel of the company was capable of recognising the existence of what was in essence a simple engineering problem, let alone of solving it. The Under-Secretary of State for Employment, Mr Harold Walker, told the House of Commons:

> As for prosecution, I understand that under the law as it was at the time of the disaster there were inadequate grounds on which to base a criminal prosecution. However ... the new Act, particularly in section 2, enormously widens the scope. I am advised by the director of the Health and Safety Executive that had this disaster

occurred at a time when the provisions of the new Act were operative and effective, he would not have hesitated to go for a prosecution on indictment.[6]

The Flixborough disaster no longer has the dubious distinction of being the largest peacetime explosion in British history. In the early hours of Sunday 11 December 2005, a series of explosions and fires took place at the Buncefield Oil Storage Depot at Hemel Hempstead, Hertfordshire. Nobody died, but 40 people were injured. Five companies, including Total UK,[7] are at the time of writing being prosecuted for breaches of health and safety legislation.

But health and safety legislation has, in practice, proved inadequate at bringing individual company directors (particularly in large corporations) to justice for fatal breaches. The Southall rail crash led to a £1.5 million fine for Great Western Trains; the Hatfield crash cost Balfour Beatty £7.5 million and Railtrack £5m for breaches of health and safety legislation. In neither case was an individual company director held to be at fault. The Health and Safety Offences Act 2008, while increasing the courts' sentencing powers for breaches, is unlikely to influence this trend.

The Difficulty of Prosecuting for Gross Negligence Manslaughter — the 'Identification Principle'

At common law, before a successful prosecution for manslaughter could be brought against a company, it was necessary to show that an individual at the very top of the company, someone who represented 'the directing mind and will of the company', was personally guilty of manslaughter.

A living person has a mind which can have knowledge or intention or be negligent and he has hands to carry out his intentions. A corporation has none of these: it must act through living persons though not always one or the same person. Then the person who acts is not speaking or acting for the company. He is acting as the

---

6. *Hansard* HC 12 May 1975 vol 892 col 42.
7. Total UK were found to have been negligent in a preliminary hearing on 23 May 2008, but deny that the destruction and damage was a foreseeable consequence of their negligence. See *The Times*, 24 May 2008.

company and his mind which directs his acts is the mind of the company. There is no question of the company being vicariously liable. He is not acting as a servant, representative, agent or delegate. He is an embodiment of the company or, one could say, he hears and speaks through the persona of the company, within his appropriate sphere, and his mind is the mind of the company. If it is a guilty mind then that guilt is the guilt of the company.[8]

The essential problem with the identification principle was clarified in a Government Consultation Document in May 2000:

The governing principle in English law on the criminal liability of companies is that those who control or manage the affairs of the company are regarded as embodying the company itself. Before a company can be convicted of manslaughter, an individual who can be 'identified as the embodiment of the company itself' must first be shown himself to have been guilty of manslaughter. Only if the individual who is the embodiment of the company is found guilty can the company be convicted. Where there is insufficient evidence to convict the individual, any prosecution of the company must fail. This principle is often referred to as the 'identification' doctrine.

There can often be great difficulty in identifying an individual who is the embodiment of the company *and who is culpable*. The problem becomes greater with larger companies which may have a more diffuse structure, where overall responsibilities for safety matters in a company can be unclear and no one individual may have that responsibility. In such circumstances it may be impossible to identify specific individuals who may be properly regarded as representing the directing mind of the company and who also possess the requisite *mens rea* (mental state) to be guilty of manslaughter: in such circumstances, no criminal liability can be attributed to the company itself.[9]

---

8. *Tesco Supermarkets Ltd v Nattrass* [1972] AC 153 at 170E. Perhaps the earliest iteration of the theory that a corporation is not itself subject to the criminal law can be found in Sir Edward Coke's judgment in the *Sutton's Hospital case* (1612) 77 Eng Rep 960, 973.

9. *Reforming the Law on Involuntary Manslaughter: The Government's Proposals* (Consultation Paper, May 2000).

This principle meant that, in the *Herald of Free Enterprise* case, when the cases against two directors and a senior manager failed through lack of evidence of their individual culpability, P&O was automatically acquitted, a decision which, according to David Bergman, Director of the Centre for Corporate Accountability, 'highlighted a serious defect in the legal principle of corporate liability'.[10] It was a defect that was not to be remedied until the CMCHA. Between 1992 and 2005, only six companies were successfully prosecuted for manslaughter, and all six were either sole traders or small companies. At common law, large companies seemed immune from prosecution for manslaughter, a situation which led to public outrage and calls for reform.

Reforming the Law: an Act is Raised

The first steps towards change in the law on corporate manslaughter can be seen in the 1994 consultation paper by the Law Commission reviewing the law of involuntary manslaughter.[11] Two years later, the Commission recommended the creation of an offence of 'corporate killing', whereby a death 'should be regarded as having been caused by the conduct of a corporation if it is caused by a failure, in the way in which the corporation's activities are managed or organized, to ensure the health and safety of persons employed in or affected by those activities',[12] and that the offence would 'be committed only where the defendant's conduct in causing the death falls far below what could reasonably be expected'.[13] These were followed in 2000 by a Government consultation paper on *Reforming the Law on Involuntary Manslaughter*,[14] which accepted the majority of the Law Commission's proposals, but went further, suggesting that directors and officers of corporations could be held

---

10. See Bergman, *The Case for Corporate Responsibility: Corporate Violence and the Criminal Justice System* (Disaster Action, 2000) at p 27.
11. Law Commission, Consultation Paper No 135, *Criminal Law: Involuntary Manslaughter*.
12. *Legislating the Criminal Code: Involuntary Manslaughter* (Law Com No 237, 1996), recommendation 11(4).
13. *Ibid*, recommendation 11(2).
14. Home Office, *Reforming the Law on Involuntary Manslaughter: The Government's Proposals* (2000).

individually responsible for contributing to the offence of corporate killing.[15] By the time of the draft Corporate Manslaughter Bill (this did not appear until 2005), however, the proposals for individual liability had been excised, and the final Corporate Manslaughter and Corporate Homicide Act specifically states that 'an individual cannot be guilty of aiding, abetting, counselling or procuring the commission of an offence of corporate manslaughter'.[16]

The End of the 'Identification Principle': Moving Forwards or Treading Water?

As we have already seen, the greatest obstacle at common law to the successful prosecution of an organization for manslaughter was the 'identification principle', and the calls for reform were heeded by those who drafted the CMCHA. The offence of corporate manslaughter relies on five elements. (1) An organization which is subject to the Act[17] (2) which owed a relevant duty of care to the deceased (3) caused a person's death; (4) the death was attributable to a 'gross breach' of the duty of care;[18] and (5) that the way in which the organization's activities were managed or organized by its senior management was a substantial element in the breach.[19]

At first sight, then, the CMCHA offers a new direction, and a move away from the much-criticised 'identification principle'. But, under the new law, will successful prosecutions against large or medium corporations be any easier to achieve than they were under the previous common law? One critic of the new Act, Professor James Gobert, thinks not.

> The Southall train crash illustrates the point. The primary cause of the crash and ensuing fatalities… was the failure of the driver to pay sufficient attention to signals

---

15. *Ibid*, paras 3.4.7 to 3.4.12.
16. CMCHA, section 18(1). Section 18(2) provides the same bar on individual liability for the Scottish offence of corporate homicide.
17. This includes corporations, departments or other bodies listed in Schedule 1 to the Act, police forces and partnerships, trade unions or employers' associations that are employers.
18. Defined as conduct falling 'far below what could reasonably have been expected of the organization in the circumstances'.
19. CMCHA, section 1.

that would have warned him of the looming danger. But arguably of equal or greater importance was the failure of management to provide a functioning Automatic Warning System that would have alerted the driver to the potential danger, or, better yet, an Automatic Train Protection System that would have brought the train to a halt without the need for driver intervention when a red signal had been passed. Both systems were installed on the train in question but neither was operative. The Southall case is not atypical in that the person whose negligent acts were most directly connected in time and space to the resulting deaths was an ordinary employee and not a senior officer of the company. In contrast, the senior managers who approved the policy of allowing company trains to operate without adequate technological safeguards (or even a back-up driver) may have been too far removed in time and space from the resulting harm to satisfy traditional tests of causation. As was the case under the identification doctrine, such an approach to causation will work to the disadvantage of small companies and organizations, where the causal link between a death and a responsible official will be easier to establish than it will be for a large corporation or multinational with a diffused command structure.[20]

This and other criticisms will be tested as the Act is applied in practice. Yet there is one aspect of the Act that cannot be described as ambiguous. Somewhere between 2000 and 2005 (when the draft Bill was presented) the Government shrank back from its plan to fix liability on individuals for corporate killing. Whether because of heavy pressure from members of the business community, worried about their reputations or possible prison terms on conviction, worried that junior staff might feel unwilling to accept more senior posts with responsibility for health and safety, or for whatever other reason, the legislature missed its opportunity to expand the liability for corporate manslaughter from the corporation to those who might earlier have been described as 'directing minds'. Needless to say, this met with disappointment and disapproval from the unions, whose members would find themselves most at risk in the event of negligence or breaches of health and safety legislation. 'The Bill was a severe disappointment for [construction union] UCATT as it failed to include clauses which would have allowed

---

20. James Gobert, 'The Corporate Manslaughter and Corporate Homicide Act 2007—Thirteen years in the making but was it worth the wait?' (2008), 71 MLR 413 at pp.418-9.

the imprisonment of company directors, if their negligence had led to the death of a worker'.[21] The Transport and General Workers' Union noted that

> ...the Bill's greatest weakness is its complete failure to tackle individual liability. Organizations do not kill people — those who own and run them do. The Bill's failure to legislate for individual as well as corporate liability means that it will not be effective in stimulating the safety culture required, nor will it deliver justice for those lives lost and damaged through negligence.

The CMCHA was born out of the ferry and rail disasters of the 1980s and 1990s, and the desire to see justice done for the victims of those disasters by removing the evidentiary obstacles posed by the identification principle, and making it easier to hold large companies and corporations to account for negligence leading to people's deaths. Yet it appears that, in practice, the new Act has done little to facilitate the prosecution of large and medium-sized companies, and has missed a golden opportunity to expand the law to allow the prosecution of the individual directors or officers actually responsible for breaches in health and safety policy. Legislation requiring large companies, above a certain size, to nominate a director of health and safety, who would be responsible for overseeing the policy and who, in the event of negligence by the company leading to death, would be an identifiable person who could be prosecuted, would not inevitably lead to an increase in malicious prosecutions: rather, it would give rise to a situation where that director, knowing he or she was personally liable for the company's health and safety policy, would be certain to take more of a personal interest in the implementation of that policy, would be more likely to notice areas where problems might occur, and deal with those problems effectively. If, in 1987, the senior managers of London Underground Ltd had known that they could be held individually liable for corporate manslaughter, might they not have given the safety recommendations of the fire brigade a little more thought? Might a director of health and safety at P&O not have been more keen to heed the request to equip the company's ferries with warning lights had his own liberty or job security been on the line?

---

21. Alan Richie, the General Secretary of UCATT, described the legislation as 'a hollow victory'.

The Parliamentary Select Committee which scrutinised the draft Bill in 2005 called for an individual offence; these calls have been echoed by the press, MPs, safety campaigners and the trade unions. An extension of the Corporate Manslaughter and Corporate Homicide Act 2007 to incorporate individual liability for the offence should be a priority. Every public company (the size to be determined statutorily) would be required by law to designate an executive director as responsible for the health and safety of the company and under a duty of care to its employees and others to whom it supplied goods and services.

Corporations and Their Controlling Minds

In 1612, in the case of *Sutton's Hospital*, Sir Edward Coke identified what is perhaps the heart of the problem:

> They [corporations] cannot commit treason, nor be outlawed, nor excommunicated, for they have no souls, neither can they appear in person.

The very notion of a body corporate implies that, if it has a being, it is that of a legal, not a human being. The universe in which it exists is a reality that is essentially an intellectual construct, bearing no resemblance to the universe of existence in which human beings find themselves. The process of reification from which corporations emerge serves to give them a legal identity and with it both rights and duties. But such rights and duties are different from those applicable to human individuals. In that they are essentially constructions they may have more than a little in common with robots, but even a robot is not without direction. The modern motor car, when the driver uses 'cruise control', becomes a robot, a central computer receiving signals from various sensors and translating them into instructions to different mechanical parts. The on-board computer is its 'controlling mind'. Thus when various forms of corporate activity have serious and sometimes devastating consequences for human beings the search begins for this 'controlling mind'. As we have noted, in small organizations the individuals who have made decisions and are effectively the authors of various acts or omissions are relatively easily identified, unlike the processes in large corporations that may have a national or even global management structure within which there is a complex division of responsibilities. The significance is this: while individuals make decisions, they may not necessarily be, in themselves, the decisions that directly bring about the unlawful event. It is sometimes the case that when things go seriously wrong it is as a result of an amalgam of a series of independent individual decisions. Experience tends to show that what are colloquially known as 'cock-ups' can come about in this way.

More than 60 years ago, the great American criminologist Edwin Sutherland in a lecture entitled 'The Crime of Corporations' made the important point that businessmen (the 'controlling minds') do not normally regard themselves as criminals, even when they have broken the law, because they do not perceive themselves as conforming to the stereotype of the lawbreaker. And as Coke observed that corporations 'have no souls', so Sutherland was colourfully to argue they had no psyche:

> We have no reason to think that US Steel has an Oedipus complex, or that the Armour Company has a death wish or that Du Ponts desire to return to the womb. [22]

Self-perception apart, there is something fundamentally inequitable about the differential vulnerability to prosecution of particular decision-makers that arises not from any variation in their alleged responsibility for the harm done, but solely from the ease or difficulty whereby they may be identified. More than that, the idea of a 'controlling mind' is suggestive of an individual with sole responsibility, while in complex organizations that is seldom the case. Collective decision-making with respect to particular policies (which may subsequently have deleterious effects, perhaps years later) serves only to complicate matters.

There is an important place for health and safety legislation in ensuring the workplace is as safe an environment as is reasonably possible (some tasks will always be inherently hazardous) and that the public will be protected

---

22. Edwin Sutherland, 'The Crime of Corporations'. A lecture given to the Toynbee Club at de Pauw University, Indiana in 1948. Reprinted in A Cohen, A Lindesmith and K Schuessler (eds.). The *Sutherland Papers*. Indiana University Press, 1956.

from any potential harm arising from industrial activity (within which public transport may be subsumed). But what if death or deaths should result?

Health and safety legislation is, by definition, pro-active in this context; the criminal law of homicide is precisely the opposite. In some of the cases we have cited earlier in this chapter where death has resulted it is clear that by and large prosecutors have attempted to find a way through what is indeed a grey area — a fog perhaps — in making a choice of which route to take. In many instances, given the pragmatic test of likelihood of success, the choice will naturally fall upon enacting health and safety law, given the initial difficulties in identifying individuals who might be deemed to be responsible.

The prosecution of the Metropolitan Police Service for a breach of health and safety legislation following the death of Jean Charles de Menenzes who was tragically mistaken for a terrorist bomber may well represent the extreme of the spectrum in deciding what course a prosecution should take. Some might consider the decision to be something of a parody of the concept of health and safety — there is, after all, more than a difference of degree between a death resulting from, say, poorly maintained equipment and being deliberately (if erroneously) shot at close range. Yet even if the tragic shooting of de Menenzes had occurred after 6 April 2008 would a prosecution for corporate manslaughter have been possible under the CMCHA? The answer would seem to be that it would not. For while police forces are specifically included as corporations subject to the Act, section 5 states that no relevant duty of care exits in cases where the police are 'dealing with terrorism, unrest or civil disorder' and 'officers or employees of the public authority in question come under attack or violent resistance, or face the threat of attack or violent resistance, in the course of the operations'.

The law in this area remains deeply unsatisfactory and the solution to the problems posed is by no means simple. What is required is a firmer resolve constructively to address them rather than allow matters to continue to drift.

CHAPTER 12

FAMILIAL HOMICIDE

Few victims of homicide are strangers to their killers; the most common example of victims unknown to their killers arises from terrorist activities. The preponderance of homicides (at present, approximately 700 a year in England and Wales) derives from a pre-existing relationship of killer to victim that is sometimes fleeting or of short duration, occasionally episodic or, often, long-standing. Of the latter most occur within the domestic scene: husbands and wives, sexual partners, and parents or carers of young children who figure prominently in the annual homicide statistics. Rarely are young people (under the age of 16) themselves killers, although they are often the victims.

Familial homicides, because they occur not in public but in the privacy of the household, frequently with no witnesses to the killing, present evidential problems in the criminal process. There is often a paucity of evidence beyond the forensic evidence of the deceased's body, the one constant factor that not infrequently gives rise to conflicting expert testimony. The problems of prosecuting familial homicides impact awkwardly upon the law and practice of homicide; they contribute to the messy state of the law.

A common occurrence in the deaths of young children has long posed a specific problem for the criminal law. It was highlighted by the series of public inquiries in the 1980s into child abuse. When the dead child is cared for by two people within the household of the carers, the death occurring as a result of ill-treatment, it is frequently unclear which of the carers is directly responsible for the ill-treatment causing the death. When faced with the accusation of unlawful killing the two carers may present a wall of silence, a kind of conspiracy against criminal justice, which is thus stymied: the two are able literally to get away with murder, so long as their silence in the criminal process is maintained. As the law stood until 2004[1] the criminal trial could not proceed beyond the stage of a defence submission of 'no case to answer'. It even became difficult to establish that, though one parent may not have struck the fatal blow, he or she was an accessory to the criminal offence, either through having participated in the killing or by failing to protect the child from the risk of death or serious injury. How then to remedy this stultification of the criminal process? It took over a decade for a suitable proposal to come from the Law Commission. In its report in September 2003[2] it recommended a new offence of 'cruelty contributing to death' — an aggravated form of the existing offence of child cruelty under the Children and Young Persons Act 1933. (It also recommended a new offence of 'failure to protect a child'.) This new offence, which would carry a maximum penalty of 14 years' imprisonment, would arise where three conditions were met. First, the carer of the child is aware, or ought to have been aware, that there is a real risk that one of a list of specified offences against the child might be committed. Second, that the carer failed to take reasonable steps to prevent the commission of the offence. And, third, the commission of a listed offence was anticipated, or ought to have been anticipated.

The proposal considered a two-track approach. The first was to maintain the current focus of the law in seeking to establish who caused the physical harm to the child. The alternative (or possibly additional) approach would be to craft changes to the substantive law in order to convict of some different type of offence all those adult carers who had responsibility for the welfare of the child at the time of the death. The basis of this approach was that the defendant was guilty of a 'wrong' underpinning the offence — namely, of failing adequately to ensure the safety of the child. The fundamental difference would be that the courts would not be convicting a greater proportion of those who caused harm, but of a greater proportion of those whose child suffered non-accidental injury. In the event, the Law Commission opted for engrafting the aggravated child cruelty offence onto the existing legal basis. But it proposed to alter the rules of evidence in the adversarial system, by postponing submissions of 'no case to answer' until after the close of the defence case, the idea being to encourage the defendant to give evidence,

1. *R v Lane and Lane* (1986) 82 Cr App R 5.
2. Law Com No 282, para 6.77.

failure of which would lead to an adverse inference from their silence. Parliament duly obliged.

In its comprehensive report, the Law Commission specifically rejected proposals to amend the law of manslaughter. By implication, it also did not seek to disturb the existing law of murder. In the Law Commission's later review of the law of murder, in November 2006,[3] no allusion was made to the problem of child killing, and no reference was made to the intervening legislative solution adopted in the Domestic Violence, Crime and Victims Act 2004. That Act broadly followed the recommendations of the Law Commission in its proposed Offences Against Children Bill, while positioning the reforms in the context of domestic violence. Yet, despite the change in nomenclature, the legislation overlooked (or at least made no provision for) placing the problem in the context of the child protection system and, more particularly, in the civil justice system operating in the Family Court. The experience of the new offence of familial homicide has thrown up an apparently unforeseen consequence.

Many, if not most, child killings in the home occur coincidentally with other young children demonstrably also at risk. The urgency to protect the surviving children leads inexorably to prompt care proceedings in the Family Court which, while investigating the intervention by the children's department of local authorities, may be asked to determine which of the carers inflicted the fatal injury— precisely the issue facing the prosecuting authorities in any criminal trial. If the criminal proceedings are limited to charging the two carers only with a section 5 offence of failure to protect the child, the criminal trial will be evidentially uncomplicated: the criminal court will possess the valuable material adduced before the Family Court. Unfortunately, the legislation contemplated that the carers can at the same time be charged with murder and manslaughter. But what if, in the care proceedings (which are bound to precede any criminal proceedings), the court is unable to point the finger of homicidal responsibility at one or other of the carers? And, even if the killer is identified, there is no guarantee that a murder/manslaughter verdict will be easily obtained, given the higher standard of proof required in the criminal trial.

---

3. *Murder, Manslaughter and Infanticide*, Law Com No 304.

It might be thought that the new offence of familial homicide of a child by a carer under section 5 of the 2004 Act provided exclusively the homicidal offence. Yet Parliament clearly indicated that the section did not preclude additionally a prosecution for murder or manslaughter. A charge of familial homicide could be supplemented by counts in the indictment of murder or manslaughter. But what if initially the parents are charged only with familial homicide, but in the care proceedings, before the criminal trial, evidence emerges that would warrant charges for murder or manslaughter? Would the prosecution be able accordingly to amend the indictment? Defendants in the criminal trial could contend that they faced charges only of familial homicide and the prosecution should not be allowed to change tack in the midst of the legal proceedings, with the motive of heightening the criminality of domestic violence. A circuit judge at Cambridge Crown Court (in a case related below) held[4] that if, before the criminal trial, there was evidence to show that whoever caused the death of the child committed murder, then 'not only would it be permissible for the Crown to add a count(s) for murder, it would be highly desirable' so long as the contents of the defendant's statement of intended evidence meant that at the close of all the evidence there would be admissible evidence to show which carer had inflicted the fatal injury. In effect, the introduction of the familial homicide of a child into the law of homicide under the 2004 Act did not in any way modify the normal rules governing the inclusion in an indictment of the more serious homicidal offence, if in the circumstances there was evidence to suggest murder. Other trials of parents for the offence of unlawful killing have started out on the basis of the two offences, but, in the course of the trial, the charge of murder against either one or both parents has been withdrawn. Where the twin offences are pursued, there are inevitably evidential problems in pursuing the parallel accusations. All this adds to the protracted and much duplicated nature of proceedings,[5] over and above the

---

4. *R v Inman and Akinrele*, 6 November 2008; the case was adjourned and was tried at Ipswich Crown Court in 2009.

5. The case of *R v Inman and Akinrele*, *ibid*, involved a six-week old child's death in December 2006, almost three years before the final trial at Ipswich Crown Court. The female defendant pleaded guilty to failure to protect the child, and was sentenced to three years' imprisonment, thereby effecting her immediate release. The male defendant was convicted of murder, and sentenced mandatorily to life imprisonment, with a tariff of 16 years.

primary adjudication of the circumstances of the death by the Family Court in the care proceedings.

The Case of Inman and Akinrele[6]

Kelly Inman and her partner Olusola Akinrele had two very young children, born respectively on 7 July 2005 and 7 November 2008, the latter dying on 30 December 2008 primarily as a result of a serious injury (among other marks of child abuse) inflicted at their home in Peterborough earlier that month. The survival of their first-born child instantly prompted care proceedings in the Family Division of the High Court to protect the older child.

The two carers were ultimately charged with murder as well as causing or allowing the death of a child contrary to section 5 Domestic Violence, Crime and Victims Act 2004. Before their criminal trial in 2009, in which Akinrele was convicted and Inman acquitted of murder (she having pleaded guilty at the start of the criminal trial to the section 5 offence of allowing the child's death) care proceedings were conducted by Mrs Justice Parker who found that, although the two of them were actively aware of exactly what had happened to the abused child, she was quite unable to conclude 'which of them caused which injury'.[7] Following the convictions on 5 November 2009 when Akinrele received a sentence of life imprisonment with a minimum period of detention of 16 years and Inman was sentenced to three years' imprisonment for the pleaded offence of allowing the child's death, the latter restored the care proceedings for adjudication in the light of the criminal trial result. On 9 March 2010 Mrs Justice Parker said that while she was bound by the jury's verdict, it was not in conflict with her findings in the care proceedings two

---

6.   [2010] EWCA Crim 2972.
7.   Between a midwifery visit of 24 November 2006 and her admission to hospital after her collapse on 18 December 2006 the child suffered multiple injuries. She had 22 fractures to the ribs. These were bilateral and close to the spine. There were a total of five metaphyseal fractures to upper and lower limbs. Her nose and fingers had been bitten; the bites to the fingers had caused underlying fractures to the fingers. She had a fracture to her right femur which produced swelling. She had a fracture to her skull. This was initially thought to have been part of a fatal injury but, on the Crown's medical evidence at trial, it occurred prior to 18 December 2006.

years previously, although that might seem puzzling. While she was bound to repeat her earlier finding, that either of the two could have inflicted the fatal assault, there was no other reason to undermine her instanr finding of her inability judicially to say 'who was the perpetrator or to exonerate the other of perpetration', other than the unarticulated verdict of the jury.

Faced with the appeal of Akinrele against his conviction for murder, sandwiched between the two judgments of Mrs Justice Parker, how significant were her findings in the civil court to be considered by the Court of Appeal (Criminal Division) in Akinrele's appeal in October 2010? The answer given was none. The evidence given in the care proceedings was different, that given in the second hearing subsequent to the criminal trial 'added little that was new; there was no fresh evidence [sic], only a re-affirmed conclusion of the same judge'. It mattered not that another division of the High Court was unable to unravel the question in a familial homicide of which carer of the child had inflicted which injury. Lord Justice Thomas, giving the judgment of the court, rounded off his rejection of the fact-finding in the two care proceedings with the remark: 'There is, in our system of justice, no reason to prefer the [reasoned] decision of a judge to that [unreasoned verdict] of a jury on a matter such as this'. The issue, however, is not that stark and uncomplicated.

There is no question of any rivalry or competition between two modes of trial, civil and criminal. But there is always a question of evaluating the findings of fact made in parallel proceedings that are relevant to the identical issue before the two courts on the individual responsibility for the criminal homicide of a child. It is insufficient for the appellate court, reviewing the totality of relevant evidence, to say that the findings were based on different evidence. Evidence about the abuse of a child is bound to be different (if only due to the lapse of time) when adduced separately with different procedures of admissibility in care proceedings and in a criminal trial at different periods in the process of administering justice. Different or not, the evidence must all be relevant to the issue posed for adjudication, namely, which person inflicted the fatal injury. Moreover, the reasoned verdict of the civil court might sensibly assist an appellate tribunal over the unarticulated reasoning of the criminal trial jury.

Whatever the right approach in such cases as *Inman and Akinrele*, the result indubitably demonstrates the need to resolve the inherent conflict between two systems for dealing with the protection of children. Since the familial homicide offence appeared for the first time in legislation directed to domestic violence and the plight of victims, one might assume a general object of child protection.

Resolving Conflict Between the Criminal and Family Courts

Where the Family Court in the course of its fact-finding exercise has made findings of fact, then the Crown should not be allowed to indict either carer for any offence, proof of which would involve the jury in making findings of fact which went beyond those found by the Family Court, unless of course subsequent to the family proceedings fresh evidence comes to light. Such evidence must be such as, in the opinion of the criminal trial judge, would justify a jury making such findings (as they did in the *Inman and Akinrele* trial). Such further evidence might come from a source quite independent of either defendant, in which case there would be no problem. Where, however, the proposed new evidence comes from one of the defendants, that should not preclude the judge from giving leave to add counts which would not be justified on the findings of the Family Court. It should be for the jury to evaluate the new evidence in light of the old. If the new evidence is to come from a defendant, it is likely that, in the absence of some convincing explanation to the contrary, the jury will reject it, or regard it as too dangerous to act upon, on the basis that it has been made up since the family proceedings, and, consequently, has more to do with that defendant saving his or her own skin than any desire to assist the jury to find the truth. If, however, the explanation for not revealing the new evidence in the earlier family proceedings is compelling, the jury may well act on it. The essential point is that it will not be for the judge hearing the application for leave to add counts to evaluate the evidence. His task must be limited to deciding whether such evidence, if believed, would be sufficient to justify a jury convicting a defendant of an offence which would not have been justified on the findings of the Family Court.

281

There may be a sound social purpose in the law ensuring that no escape route is available to a child killer from a conviction for murder or manslaughter. The new law appeared effectively to remove the tactical advantage which operated, adventitiously and illogically, to parents keeping silent about their criminality. But if, since 2004, the complexities of the legal process can be avoided by exclusive use of the familial homicide provision, would that not suffice to assuage any public feeling that unlawful killers are able unjustifiably 'to get away with murder'? And if not, is there any feasible solution to the overlapping jurisdictions of the Family Court and the Crown Court envisaged by the 2004 Act? The prospect of such overlapping appears not to have been contemplated by the Law Commission in an otherwise comprehensive review of the law, with its emphasis on ensuring, in the suggested reform of the substantive offence, a fair trial. One practical step would be to arrange for the judge in the Family Court proceedings to be nominated to try the criminal case. Some Family Court judges might be unwilling to perform the dual task. But the practice could be employed.

Conclusion

Where the child is killed within the familial setting, the new section 5 offence of failure to protect the child ought generally (or perhaps invariably) to involve charging without resort to murder or manslaughter. The offence of familial homicide in section 5 can sit easily with our suggested merger of murder and manslaughter as criminal homicide. An avoidance of any conviction of murder and manslaughter might give rise to a problem of sentencing. Following the Court of Appeal's judgment in *R v Ikram and Purveen*[8] the judge must pass sentence on the basis that both carers failed to protect the child. But where it is not possible to identify the killer to the criminal standard of proof, it might be considered unjust to the non-harming carer, where identification could nevertheless be made. The answer may be that the severe requirements of the criminal process may sometimes call for an adjustment of the outcome in the jury verdict. Even if identification

---

8.   [2008] EWCA 586.

can be shown in the sentencing process, justice might be achieved by parity of sentence on the lower end of the scale of moral culpability for the two carers who together failed to protect the child from unlawful killing. If child protection is the law's aim, no greater deterrent is provided by upgrading the homicidal offence. The penalty structure amply supplies a just outcome.

The Children Act 1989, apart from establishing the concept of parental responsibility for their children, provided a social framework for the child protection system: it was supplemented by the Children Act 1989 (Amendment) (Children's Services) Planning Order 1996 which inserted a new provision requiring local authorities to prepare and publish plans for the provision of children's services in their area, and to keep those plans under review. But systems are constructed to facilitate and promote good practice, as well as underpin social justice. Under the 1996 Order local authorities are required to consult health and education authorities, certain voluntary organizations, the police, the probation service and other relevant bodies—a statutory recognition of an inter-disciplinary approach to the needs of child welfare. As part of the spectrum of protective devices for vulnerable children, the Family Court provides the judicial means for intervention by local authorities into family life. What is needed is some method of interweaving the powers of the courts into that spectrum of the child protection system. Judicial activity, be it civil or criminal, needs to be more closely related to social policy, particularly where the State is justified in intervening in family life.

CHAPTER 13

EXPERT EVIDENCE ON TRIAL

Fictional representations of the criminal trial may nourish in the popular mind the idea that, among those who stand in the dock, the innocent may be as numerous as the guilty; the experience of practitioners is that the guilty will probably be in the majority. When scientific evidence enters upon the forensic scene, it can often be compellingly persuasive to a jury of the defendant's guilt. But in trials for murder, things do not always go as smoothly, not least in cases of infant deaths that are in some way unascertained or even unascertainable. Violent and brutal parents are generally not difficult to identify, but what of evidently loving and caring parents whose infants — sometimes more than one — suffer deaths that remain unexplained? Among those parents standing trial in recent cases for the murder of their children in such circumstances have been Sally Clark, Angela Cannings and Trupti Patel. Sally Clark and Angela Cannings were both convicted of murder and sentenced to the mandatory penalty of life imprisonment; Trupti Patel was acquitted by the jury. This trilogy of cases in the first decade of the 21st century will undoubtedly be noted by future historians of the criminal law as cases which were to change it, not least in consequence of the judgments given in the appeals of Sally Clark and Angela Cannings quashing their convictions. In each of these cases the jury was confronted with a mass of highly complex expert medical evidence. If there is a lesson to be learned here, it is that there is an urgent need for the court itself to take early possession of expert evidence, not least within the context of court management, if juries are not to become confused and, more importantly, if those parents to whom no blame should be attached are to be spared the humiliation and public obloquy that follow a conviction for murder, not to mention their loss of liberty.

Every trial of a defendant charged with an offence of homicide is likely to involve the calling of expert medical (and sometimes other scientific) evidence, if only to ascertain the cause of the victim's death. Usually, the evidence of the forensic pathologist who conducted the post-mortem will suffice. The pathologist conducting the autopsy is both a witness of fact — of what he finds respecting the condition of the corpse — and an expert witness as to the import of those facts. It will normally be uncontroversial and uncontradicted, simply because the cause of death will be manifest. It will establish readily whether the death was from natural or unnatural causes, but even if a violent or unnatural death, the precise instrument that killed may be in doubt.

The problems associated with the reception and assessment of forensic evidence in a system of trial by judge and jury are anything but new; they have become accentuated over the passage of time and advances in medical knowledge. Writing in 1859 James Fitzjames Stephen (later to become Mr Justice Stephen) said:

> Few spectacles, it may be said, can be more absurd and incongruous than that of a jury composed of twelve persons who, without any previous scientific knowledge or training, are suddenly called upon to adjudicate in controversies in which the most eminent scientific men flatly contradict each other's assertions. How, it might be asked, can ordinary tradesmen and farmers, who have never been accustomed to give sustained attention to any subject whatever for an hour together, be expected to weigh evidence, the delivery of which occupies many days and which bears upon subjects which can only be described in language altogether new and foreign to their understanding?[1]

And he concluded:

> We ought to take seriously that when scientific questions are involved in a criminal trial, the verdicts upon which courts of justice pronounce judgment should represent the settled opinions of men who have made a special study, and not the loose impressions of unscientific jurors.[2]

---

1. James Fitzjames Stephen, *Trial by Jury and the Evidence of Experts* (London Papers of the Juridical Society, 1858–1863), volume 1, Paper XIV, at 236.
2. *Ibid.*

How to handle scientific or technical knowledge in the context of a criminal trial before a jury as the exclusive fact-finder is an issue of increasing complexity and importance. Is the jury the right instrument to adjudicate upon conflicting medical evidence? If so, how can it be assisted by the manner in which that evidence is elicited, set out and placed before the court, either before or at the trial? Failure to heed the words of Fitzjames Stephen and to accommodate opinion evidence on scientific or technical matters constituted a reproach to successive administrators of criminal justice over nearly a century and a half.

No criminal trial, heavily dependent upon expert (medical) evidence has exposed so demonstrably the deficiencies in our system of criminal procedure than the recent case of Sally Clark. The quashing of Mrs Clark's conviction (at the second attempt, in April 2003) was fully justified, but it was achieved in circumstances that give cause for disquiet about the procedure for adducing expert evidence in criminal justice. Nor does it stand alone. Similar concern was expressed at the trial of Trupti Patel (acquitted by the jury at Reading Crown Court later that year) and in the appeal by Angela Cannings in January 2004 where there was no extraneous non-medical evidence. The earlier case of the young schoolboy Damilola Taylor attacked on his way home from school threw up the problem of a delayed medical report challenging the Crown's version of the cause of the victim's death. Sally Clark's case, however, is an exemplar.

At Chester Crown Court on 9 November 1999, before Mr Justice Harrison and a jury, Mrs Clark, a solicitor, was convicted of the murder of her sons, Christopher and Harry, when they were aged eleven weeks and eight weeks respectively. At her trial no fewer than nine experts were called — belatedly: five by the prosecution and four by the defence. There was some other non-forensic evidence, which in the eyes of the jury may have tilted the scales against the accused, but clearly the prosecution relied primarily and heavily on the medical evidence supporting the opinion that each child had either been suffocated or subjected to severe shaking at the hands of their mother. They were not, the Crown argued, deaths from natural causes.

Sally Clark's appeal to the Court of Appeal (Criminal Division) on 2 October 2000 was unsuccessful. The Court, composed of Lord Justice Henry, Mrs Justice Bracewell and Mr Justice Richards, delivered a judgment of 274 paragraphs (approximately 40,000 words). Under the heading *The strength of the case at trial* it concluded:

> We have considered with care the extensive evidence placed before the jury at trial, and we have concluded that there was overwhelming evidence of the guilt of the appellant on each count.[3]

At paragraph 272/3 the Court had stated:

> We consider that there was an overwhelming case against the appellant at trial. If there had been no error in relation to the statistics at the trial — a reference to a piece of evidence from [Professor] Sir Roy Meadow, a consultant paediatrician and an expert on cot deaths[4] — we are satisfied that the jury would still have convicted on each count. In the context of the trial as a whole, the point on statistics was of minimal significance and there is no possibility of the jury having been misled so as to reach verdicts they might not otherwise have reached. Had the trial been free from legal error, the only reasonable and proper verdict would have been one of guilty…The error of approach towards the statistical evidence at trial…did not render the convictions unsafe.

In July 2002 the Criminal Cases Review Commission referred the case back to the Court of Appeal, on the basis that there was a real possibility that the court would find that 'the new evidence renders Mrs Clark's convictions for the murders of Christopher and Harry unsafe'.

The 'new evidence', which the second Court of Appeal admitted as 'fresh evidence', related to hospital records of the results of microbiological tests performed on samples of Harry's blood, body tissue and cerebrospinal fluid, gathered at the post-mortem on the child. The results were not disclosed at trial, but when submitted to medical experts it was suggested that Harry might not, after all, have been killed, but may have died from natural causes.

At the Court of Appeal hearing on 28/29 January 2003 Mrs Clark's counsel made what were identified as 'two essential points'. First, and principally, the

---

3. There were two separate counts, one for each murder.
4. The term 'cot death' is a popular term employed to describe otherwise inexplicable deaths in infants. The term 'sudden infant death syndrome' or 'SIDS' has greater scientific currency.

failure of the Crown to disclose the information contained in the microbiological reports meant that important reports relating to the cause of death
were never considered at trial. Second, it was contended that statistical information given to the jury about the likelihood of two sudden and unexpected
deaths of infants from natural causes misled the jury and painted a picture
that was now considered as overstating, very considerably, the rarity of two
such events happening within the same family.

Counsel for the appellant did not seek to argue any other point — in
particular, she did not review the effect of the expert evidence given at trial,
which the first Court of Appeal comprehensively covered in concluding
that it presented an overwhelming case of unnatural death at the hands of
the children's mother.

The second Court of Appeal, comprised of Lord Justice Kay, Mr Justice
Holland and Mrs Justice Hallett,[5] delivered its judgment on 11 April 2003.
The judgment ran to 182 paragraphs (approximately 20,000 words). Nearly
two-thirds of the judgment was devoted to a rehearsal of the expert evidence
at trial, and concluded as follows:

> The medical evidence at trial, which we have set out in detail, made clear that on
> any view this was a difficult case. There was a wide difference of views in respect of
> each death as to the conclusions that could properly be drawn from the available
> evidence. However, a number of factors seem to us to emerge, which are of relevance
> to this appeal:
>
> 1. In each case, before a conclusion adverse to the applicant could be drawn, the jury
> would have had to be sure that they could rely upon the evidence of Dr Williams
> [the forensic pathologist who conducted both post-mortems]. There were important
> features said to have been found at each post-mortem examination which depended
> both upon the competence of Dr Williams in carrying out the post-mortems and
> upon the extent to which he could be considered as a reliable and objective witness
> as to his findings. There were features at that time that must have caused the jury to
> hesitate. His change from a conclusion that Christopher died of a lower respiratory
> tract infection, to an opinion that there was no evidence that he had such an infection

---

5.   Mrs Justice (now Lady Justice) Hallett had been the trial judge in the case of Angela
     Cannings.

that could have led to his death, and the acceptance by the Crown that Professor Luthert (a consultant ophthalmologist) was right about the intra-retinal haemorrhaging of the eyes being the result of an error in slide preparation, were the most obvious examples of the need for caution. Anything further that cast doubt upon the approach of Dr Williams must, therefore, have been of potential significance to the jury's conclusions.

2. It was of potentially crucial importance that there was no evidence of any illness or infection suffered by Harry that might have explained his death. If this was not a true SIDS case, as the doctors were largely agreed, and since there was no apparent natural explanation for the death, the evidence pointed towards unnatural death. The only disagreement between the doctors was whether it did so to sufficient degree to permit a firm conclusion that the cause of death was unnatural, or whether the case had still to be classified as an unascertainable cause of death. Thus any evidence which positively suggested that Harry died from natural causes was of potentially crucial relevance to the jury's considerations and might very well have resulted in different verdicts.

3. The evidence in respect of Christopher's death, if it had stood in isolation, would not have justified a finding of murder and if, therefore, there had been evidence that suggested that Harry died from natural causes so that the jury accepted this was a possibility, it seems inevitably to follow that they could not have been sure that Christopher was murdered.

The Court of Appeal dealt peremptorily with the statistical evidence given by Sir Roy Meadow:

Finally, we should say a little about the statistical evidence before the jury. The matter was the subject of only brief argument before us and we certainly heard none of the evidence.[6]

and observed:

---

6. At para 172.

The Court of Appeal on the last occasion would, it seems clear to us, have felt obliged to allow the appeal but for their assessment of the rest of the evidence as overwhelming. In reaching that conclusion, the Court was as misled by the absence of the evidence of the microbiological results, as were the jury before it. We are quite satisfied that if the evidence in its entirety, as it is now known, had been known to the Court it would never have concluded that the evidence pointed overwhelmingly to guilt.[7]

Thus, in effect, the sole argument before the second Court of Appeal was the non-disclosure to the trial court of the hospital records of the microbiological tests on Harry. That non-disclosure in itself either constituted an unfair trial, or was insufficiently serious to justify the sobriquet of unfairness.

Since the sole issue was the failure of the prosecution to disclose the microbiological tests (which had a significant impact on the question whether the deaths of the two infants were the result of natural or unnatural causes) it mattered not one whit, for the purpose of concluding the verdict to be unsafe, how and why the reports were undisclosed, or indeed who was to blame for the failure to disclose.

For the purpose of determining the appeal, on the legal consequences of non-disclosure of important evidence, the court had no need to review the case, since it had been contested without the undisclosed material. The statistical evidence provided a basis for adjudication distinct from the undisclosed evidence, and did not affect the ultimate result. Why then did the Court engage in a lengthy, even prolix, rehearsal of the medical evidence given at trial and fully reviewed by the Court of Appeal in October 2000, minus the fresh evidence of the microbiological tests? Unfortunately, one can only speculate.

Reviewing (and re-reading) paragraph 93 of the judgment, we conclude one of two possibilities.

1. By implication, the second Court of Appeal had come to the conclusion that their judicial brethren in October 2000 had wrongly concluded that the case was overwhelmingly proved against Mrs Clark. A review of the experts' evidence disclosed that there was no consensus about the cause

---

7. At para 179.

of death, but a clear conflict between those who were in favour of death from natural causes and those who were doubtful whether the cause was simply 'accidental', 'unascertained' or even 'unascertainable'. On that analysis, the jury should have entertained a reasonable doubt (even if the issue should not have been left to the jury by the trial judge). Surprisingly, it did not. It may be that the jury, utterly confused by the welter of conflicting medical evidence, relied on the non-forensic evidence of the accused and her husband to guide them to their verdict. If that was so, what an appalling way to treat forensic evidence in a criminal trial!

2. If that is the true interpretation, either the second Court of Appeal should have declined to say anything about its predecessor's decision (and dealt only with the question of non-disclosure), or it ought to have stated that it positively disagreed with the earlier decision: it should have said that the jury's verdict was unsafe, whether or not the microbiological tests had been disclosed.

If neither of the two possibilities is correct, the only other explanation is that the second Court of Appeal, for the purposes of public relations, was desirous of quelling public disquiet about other cases in the pipeline for review on appeal. One gleans that much from a somewhat unusual final paragraph in the judgment, in which the Court wrote:

> We are aware that there is public speculation as to whether other convictions of mothers for killing their babies where the babies have died sudden deaths, are similarly unsafe. The matters to which we have referred are directly referable only to this case. If any other case is brought before this court, it will receive the same anxious scrutiny by the court that we would like to think we have given to this case.

That 'any other case' must surely be a reference to that of Angela Cannings, hearing of whose appeal came before the court in December 2003 with the judgment at the end of January 2004. If, in Sally Clark's case, the court had felt obliged to engage in the exercise of publicly demonstrating its familiarity and full understanding of the medical evidence, it might more profitably have turned its attention to the practice and procedure in our criminal courts of adducing evidence which produced such a flawed procedure. But it singularly failed to address the problem of how courts in a modern world should handle scientific evidence.

In its judgment of 2 October 2000, the first Court of Appeal in the Sally Clark case had observed that it was not until the medical witnesses for the defence were called to give oral evidence on the ninth day of a 13-day trial that it became clear that those medical experts called by the defence accepted that neither the death of Christopher Clark nor the death of Harry Clark 'was a true SIDS death'. It is a grave reflection on the English criminal process that an issue so crucial to the outcome of the trial should be exposed only at such a late stage in the proceedings. It stems from the fact that the expert evidence (as with the testimony of eye-witnesses) is fitted procedurally into an adversarial system that requires the Crown to prove its case. Only if there is a *prima facie* case will the defence then call its evidence, which, at best, will reveal fully the nature of the case against conviction.

In the case of expert testimony, the totality of such evidence (whether emanating from Crown or defence) might sensibly be heard in a discrete fashion as a preliminary body of evidence, to be evaluated by the trial judge alone, or by the judge leaving the jury to assess its weight in the light of other, non-expert evidence adduced by the parties. This evaluation, after judicial examination, could be incorporated within the process of court management.

Our recommendations hereafter are designed to promote a procedure which gives effect to that overriding need for a separate function for expert evidence in the criminal jurisdiction, especially in homicide cases. The recommendations are made in the light of the provisions of section 30 Criminal Justice Act 2003, which inserts into the existing procedure in section 6 Criminal Procedure and Investigations Act 1996 a requirement on the part of the defence to notify the Crown of experts instructed by the accused. Section 6D(1) follows the wording of Part 35 of the Civil Procedure Rules in that 'if the accused instructs a person with a view to his providing any expert opinion for possible use as evidence at the trial of the accused', the expert's name and address must be supplied to the court and the Crown. Thus, experts' reports, which are sought for the purpose of advice and not for potential use at trial, are not subject to notification and possible disclosure. It is not clear whether the Crown can seek disclosure of any notified expert's report. We suggest that, in accordance with the recommendations of Sir Robin Auld in his *Review of the Criminal Courts in England and Wales,*[8] such reports should be disclosed, but not any other reports outwith the provisions of section 30 Criminal Justice Act 2003. We think that expert evidence, which is opinion evidence based on given data (such as a post-mortem report in a homicide case), ought to be treated as available to the court, whether its provenance is the Crown or the defence. While we would not support any replica derived from Part 35 of the Civil Procedure Rules of 'a single joint expert', we do think that there should not be any proprietorial interest in any experts' reports. They belong to the criminal court of trial, irrespective of their origins.

Additional to the provision of the expert evidence emanating from the parties, we suggest that, exceptionally, the trial court might call for expert evidence in a particular area of expertise relevant to the issues at trial, the Sally Clark case providing just such an example. The court might in the instant case have required the Macclesfield Hospital to send the results of the microbiological tests performed on the one child. These were tests that the jury had requested to see, but were told were not available. Under our proposals, the court could have required them to be produced at an early stage. At the pre-trial stage, a report might also have been sought from an obstetrician and gynaecologist to explain whether the fracture to Harry's rib could have been caused by a breech birth[9] even if, as it appears, the birth was a normal vaginal delivery.

An initiative from the court to call additional expert evidence might conventionally be subject to the concurrence of the parties. But should the parties not agree, the court should be empowered to order such evidence. Likewise, the court should have the power to limit the number of experts from a particular specialty. Mr Justice Harrison at trial observed that the jury 'might be forgiven perhaps for thinking that you had heard almost too much medical evidence'. The judge's explanation, 'that a murder trial involves very serious issues and therefore these matters must be investigated thoroughly', we think, is misguided. On the contrary, the sheer volume of evidence from the pathologists (five from the prosecution and four from the defence) and

---

8.   Published 8 October 2001.
9.   See para 271(c) of the judgment of the Court of Appeal.

from neurological pathologists, paediatricians, anaesthetists and ophthalmologists may well have served only to confuse rather than to elucidate the cause of death of the two babies. Indeed, the parties seem to have indulged in a protracted expedition to find medical experts to support their respective cases. The Crown Prosecution Service has explained its actions publicly:

> The experts were instructed and as the case unfolded it became clear that the prosecution required specific expert evidence. For example, the pathologist Dr Alan Williams suggested that the Crown contact Professor Green. In a similar way, the other prosecution experts were selected. Naturally, every report and statement from prosecution experts has been served on the defence and made available to the court.

> We have been asked to explain why a microbiologist was not instructed at the outset. The answer is that there was nothing to indicate that the microbiology was of any significance, and expert evidence in this regard was therefore not required.

The judgment in *Cannings* delivered by Lord Justice (now Lord Chief Justice) Judge offers an important point of reference, when considering the problems arising from a plethora of expert witness evidence:

> We have some sympathy for the jury. We have to reflect an anxiety which has struck us throughout our own deliberations, whether notwithstanding these clear directions [by Hallett J, which were found to be faultless], the whole course of the trial, the sheer numbers of experts called by the defence, and the complex specialist fields in which these distinguished men and women worked, the jury may not, inadvertently, unconsciously, have thought to itself that if between them all, none could offer a definitive or specific explanation for these deaths, the Crown's case must be right.

We shall need to return to the judgment in *Cannings* later, since it must now be regarded as a landmark, not merely for the present but for the future conduct of trials of parents arising from infant deaths in suspicious circumstances where direct evidence of violence, deliberate neglect, or the involvement of third parties, such as carers, is absent. But why should decisions about the calling of expert evidence be so perilously left to the parties, effectively unregulated in the way they conduct their case, and delayed in their presentation until trial, often many months after the event?

This is a very particular species of evidence. Frequently its significance may be demonstrated only after the specialist language of experts has been translated into a vernacular that can be readily understood by a jury. Moreover, lawyers, however keenly their professional skills in the techniques of presentation and cross-examination may have been honed by years of experience, are rarely independently possessed of qualifications in medicine and forensic science. In criminal trials in which the issue of proof can be so finely balanced upon the evidence of expert witnesses, not least those in which the charge is murder, the volume and availability of expert evidence cannot be subject to *laissez-faire* arrangements. Even if there are to be a great number of witnesses giving a prodigious volume of evidence, it should be a predictably ordered process.

Our considered view, based on examination of cases in which reliance has been placed upon such evidence, and especially those that have been the subject of successful appeal, is that the court, at a pre-trial stage, should have the power to restrict the number and nature of expert witnesses to be called to give oral evidence. Experts' reports should, wherever possible, be advanced by way of opinions written for the purpose of the all the parties.[10] In the Sally Clark case the parties appear to have sought sequentially to identify medical experts who would put a favourable gloss on what was up until then very ambiguous opinion evidence.

We think, nevertheless, that such a power should be conditional on some distillation of the evidence contained in the written reports. The condition would be that the parties should identify those areas in which there is agreement and those in which there is disagreement. The matters thus identified would need then to be further explored by formal discussion among the experts.

In the civil courts, and particularly in the Family Division, there is a long tradition of a not dissimilar practice whereby experts enter into discussions before trial, often held face-to-face. With the introduction of the Civil Procedure Rules 1998, such discussions have become widely used in

---

10. There is a well-established model for this in the pre-sentence reports prepared *for the court* but made available to the defendant.

civil litigation of all kinds. The discussions assist the court in defining the matters of agreement and disagreement between opposing experts. Sometimes, the discussion obviates the calling of expert evidence at trial, for there is no substantive point of difference; an agreed statement is submitted. More commonly, where agreement is not complete, the experts are able to tell the court which points of difference remain.

Applying this principle to the criminal jurisdiction would have considerable advantage in the case of complex medical evidence. It would, in the trial of Sally Clark, have revealed at a stage long before trial the extent of agreement between the pathologists that the cause of death of both Christopher and Harry was unascertainable, but that they were certainly not cot deaths (SIDS), something that was to emerge only nine days into the trial.

But there are also important questions of interpretation of expert evidence in which it is key that juries are properly directed. Angela Cannings had originally been charged with the murder of her daughter Gemma — a charge not proceeded with — as well as those of her sons Jason and Matthew of whose murder she was convicted. The jury was to hear evidence, not only about the deaths of Jason and Matthew, but also about a number of so-called 'ALTEs' (Acute or Apparent Life-Threatening Events) relating to Jason, Matthew and a surviving daughter, Jade. In her directions to the jury Mrs Justice Hallett reminded them that both sides were inviting them to look at all the evidence:

> Be careful how you approach Gemma's death. It was a long time ago … It is part of
> the background and it is relevant. It may, for example, be relevant as to whether or
> not there is a genetic defect. But be very wary how you approach Gemma's death.
> You know the pathologists carried out a very careful post-mortem and decided that
> the death effectively was SIDS, or cot death, and no suggestion of maltreatment.
> You have not heard about Gemma's death to justify the kind of approach referred to
> by Mr Mansfield [Michael Mansfield QC, counsel for Angela Cannings]; the Lady
> Bracknell approach. [11]'This is not a case whereby you could say 'to lose one baby is
> misfortune, two carelessness, three murder'. As you will appreciate as members of
> the jury, that is just inappropriate — totally.[12]

11. From Oscar Wilde's play, 'The Importance of Being Earnest'.
12. *R v Cannings* [2004] EWCA Crim 1, paras 167, 168.

The jury at Winchester Crown Court went on to convict Angela Cannings, though their reasons for doing so are likely to remain as inscrutable as the present law permits. The jury at Reading Crown Court hearing the case against Trupti Patel was directed in not dissimilar terms by Mr Justice Jack:

> You have heard from some of the prosecution witnesses the idea that the fact of three deaths makes it more likely that the cause was unnatural. Certainly with three deaths one must be suspicious and look the more carefully, for potentially it is a very serious situation. But I am going to ask you to put out of your minds the idea that because there are three that makes it more unlikely that the causes are unnatural:...I think that would be a dangerous approach in this case ...[13]

We interject only to say that we think that the Lady Bracknell test might well be reversed. To lose one baby who appeared healthy enough is suspicious, two losses arouse concern as to the possibility of a killing, and three point in the direction of a plausible genetic explanation.

The jury in the Patel case, eschewing that 'dangerous approach', took the different view and acquitted the defendant. It would, of course, be quite wrong simply to contrast the finding of one jury with that of another, notwithstanding that in both instances the directions of the trial judge were clear and unambiguous. Indeed, one might be forgiven for thinking that there are times when, whatever social and mental processes there may be at work, ratiocination may be for some jurors the very last tool they employ to assist them in their task. What is almost certainly more relevant to the task of understanding the verdict in *Patel* is the chronology of final outcomes in each of the three cases to which we have referred. In the case of Sally Clark it required more than one attempt in the Court of Appeal before the jury's verdict was quashed, following a reference back by the Criminal Cases Review Commission, on the basis of new evidence supplied by those advising Sally Clark. The outcome was known by the time of the Patel trial.

Clark can be portrayed as the initial movement of a critical stone in the existing forensic structure which did not, however, dislodge it. *Patel* was responsible for knocking it away; while the successful appeal in *Cannings*

---

13. Quote in *ibid*, para 165.

can be thought of as the forensic JCB that cleared away the debris, leaving the intellectual ground ready for a new and more efficient and effective construction.

In January 2004, shortly after the Court of Appeal had delivered its reasons for quashing the convictions of Angela Cannings, the Attorney-General, Lord Goldsmith QC, ordered a review of the 258 cases in which a parent or carer has been convicted of killing a child under the age of two since 1994. The Director of Public Prosecutions, Sir Ken MacDonald (now Lord MacDonald) QC, undertook at the same time to review personally the 15 prosecutions pending in order to determine whether they should proceed. The announcement occasioned criticism that in Family Court proceedings children had been removed from the care of their parents on the basis of not dissimilar expert evidence; this prompted a further announcement that a similar review of old cases would take place, but with the *caveat* that the process in these civil cases might well take substantially longer.[14] The reported comments of the DPP on the broader issues are not without interest. Commenting that

> One can hardly imagine a worse miscarriage of justice than a woman who has lost her baby [being] convicted of murder, and then sentenced to life imprisonment.

He also observed that there was an 'attraction' in the procedures employed in some other European countries:

> ... in other jurisdictions, these cases don't come into the criminal justice system. They go before a family law panel.[15]

The application of the practices employed in the civil jurisdiction with respect to expert evidence can scarcely present any significant difficulty. Guidelines on the conduct of such discussions have been published in the

---

14. Whereas in criminal cases involving the death of a child or children the quashing of convictions and the release of prisoners goes some way towards righting an injustice, the situation in civil proceedings is altogether more complicated. It may not be in the best interests of a child for it to be restored to its parents if the child is now well settled in foster care; in instances where adoption has taken place the presenting problems appear intractable.

15. Reported in *The Guardian* of 11 February 2004.

Code of Guidance on Expert Evidence, produced by the Working Party established by the Head of Civil Justice in December 2001 and published in the Spring 2002 edition of the White Book. Central to their success is the production of closed questions, on a tight agenda, usually to be agreed by the parties, with the court retaining the ultimate power to set the agenda. A similar procedure should apply to the criminal jurisdiction. Nowhere would it be better to make a start than in all homicide cases.

It is worth questioning, however, whether the current procedure for handling expert evidence in the criminal jurisdiction complies with Article 6 of the European Convention on Human Rights; and whether the reforms we suggest would be Convention-compliant. Our view is that the present English law, which procedurally favours the accused in relation to pre-trial disclosure of expert evidence, is entirely compatible with Article 6(1). Nor, however, would any change in English law which might hereafter equiparate, as between prosecution and defence, the treatment of expert reports, violate Article 6(1), in that, by itself, such treatment would fail to maintain the principle of the equality of arms. Only if the trial were subsequently, on consideration of the entirety of the proceedings, held to be unfair would the court, so finding, be bound to take account of the manner in which the expert evidence functioned.

The European Court of Human Rights would not regard the multiplicity of experts, even if numerically favouring the prosecution, as unfair. Nor would the Court also regard any restrictions on the number of experts, given parity in quantity and quality, as a violation of Article 6(1). Likewise, a court-appointed expert, where the existing experts disagreed, would not be an unfair practice. A procedure whereby experts meet to decide the areas of agreement and disagreement would also not constitute any violation of a fair trial.

That the situation needs urgently to be addressed is underlined by the fact that some medical experts have expressed a growing sense of unease about becoming involved as expert witnesses. In March 2004 the Royal College of Paediatrics and Child Health published the results of a survey questionnaire sent to all paediatricians in the United Kingdom of whom a very substantial proportion (78 per cent) responded. The survey results indicated that the number of complaints against paediatricians involved in child protection work had increased from fewer than 20 in 1995 to over 100 in 2003. Of these, some 11 per cent were sufficiently serious to be referred to the General Medical Council. Of the cases so referred 41 per cent were dropped and 59 per cent were found not proven.[16] At the same time, the BBC's *Today* programme reported that just under a third of members of the Royal College had expressed fears of being made scapegoats or the subject of malicious complaint if they became involved in child protection work; some have been the recipients of 'hate mail' and one the subject of a death threat.[17]

There can be little doubt that the high profile of a number of recent cases has attracted a great deal of attention in the media, which in turn has had a bearing upon public perception of the phenomenon commonly known as Munchausen's Syndrome by Proxy (MSBP), in which the children of those affected with the condition will either have a fabricated illness or an induced illness. Both the Royal College and the Department of Health now use the term Fabricated or Induced Illness (FII) rather than MSBP. What has happened in these cases, in which expert evidence has effectively come to grief in the appellate process, is that the prominent conjunction of what is an unsafe conviction (with its attendant consequences for the parent concerned) and the importance of such evidence in securing the original conviction has placed some expert witnesses in a highly unfavourable light. It is a short step to generalised criticism on a 'profession-wide' basis.

Expert witnesses are there to give an expert opinion upon the evidence that is before the court, based on their knowledge and experience; witnesses of fact are there to be just that. But whereas a witness of fact, assuming he or she is not lying in the witness box, can be *mistaken*, the situation with an expert witness is quite different. Opinion evidence given by one expert is not more than that, and may well be at variance with the import given to the same facts by another expert; the dichotomy of truth and falsehood has no relevance as is frequently the case with those who are no more than witnesses of fact. But for the jury comprised of ordinary men and women, frequently quite unfamiliar with the sophisticated nuances of the forensic process, the task can often be far from easy. Experts, of necessity, need to employ technical language, but even if this can be translated into the demotic,

---

16. Royal College of Paediatrics and Child Health, Press Release of 8 March 2004.
17. *Press Association News*, 8 March 2004.

an array of expert evidence (the meaning of which may be the subject of the differing expert opinion) can be bewildering, not least when it is presented for many hours, day after day.

In our view, however, the substantially greater source of difficulty resides in the unsatisfactory way in which the management of the court process in the criminal trial presently permits the presentation of expert evidence in a manner that precisely reflects the adversarial character of the trial process itself. The feature with which the public is probably most familiar from fiction and television drama is the cross-examination of a witness. It is the entirely proper task of the cross-examiner to test the witness's evidence in such a way as to cast doubt upon its reliability, whether by challenging the witness about its factual basis or — and by no means uncommonly — by challenging the probity of the witness. This, of course, must apply to witnesses of fact; with the expert witness, who offers an opinion, the challenge must of necessity be on a different basis. The view of one distinguished lawyer[18] was that the forensic offensive should be mounted against the expert's methodology rather than be directed at his probity.

But because in the popular mind the distinction between the two types of witness is imperfectly understood or not even appreciated to exist. When expert evidence is successfully challenged it is perceived as having been *untrue* rather than unreliable as a consequence of some flaw in analysis or methodology. It follows that when a conviction in a high profile case, in which expert evidence has played a substantial part, is quashed, it can be readily (if quite wrongly) assumed that the expert evidence was in some way mistaken or inaccurate or, at worst, derived from some malice or hostility towards the defendant.

The remedy, in our view, is for the courts to take ownership and responsibility for expert evidence, particularly at the pre-trial stage. In homicide trials the Crown will always need the evidence of a forensic pathologist, stating the facts found on a post-mortem examination; the witness who conducts the post-mortem will bestride the roles of witness of fact and expert witness. If specialists who are willing to serve the administration of justice are deterred from participating in criminal trials, an imbalance between

---

18. The late Sir Frederick Lawton (a retired Lord Justice of Appeal) who had long experience at the criminal Bar.

prosecution and defence may well develop, to the detriment of the equality of opinion evidence before the court upon which homicide trials are so frequently dependent.

Our proposals for change can be summed up as follows:

1. In any prosecution, where the case involves difficult, controversial expert evidence, a judge in a pre-trial direction should decide whether trial of such issue should be by jury, or by judge alone. In the event that the matter goes before a jury, opinion evidence from expert witnesses should be treated as forensically residing within the province of the judge.

2. In any event, where the trial by jury primarily involves complicated expert evidence, arrangements should be made for all the expert witnesses to be called in succession in a trial-within-a-trial. There should not be a division between experts called by Crown and defence. While experts are called by the parties, they are all the court's witnesses.

3. Whenever possible, experts should be advised pre-trial to attend a meeting among themselves, with a view to defining the areas of agreement and disagreement, thereby reducing the areas of conflicting evidence.

4. The trial judge should draw a distinction between those experts giving eyewitness testimony (for example, a pathologist conducting a post-mortem) and those giving opinion evidence only on established data.

The matters that we have examined in this chapter, at times technically complicated in both the scientific and legal sense, and baffling as they might appear to a jury, go to the very heart of that justice which is itself at the epicentre of the criminal prosecution. For Sally Clark, Angela Cannings and Trupti Patel, the possibility of a mandatory sentence of life imprisonment, imposed for crimes of which they protested their innocence, could have been nothing if not awesome, even mind-numbing. Perhaps the best we can say is that those who sit captive in the dock, charged with the murder of their own children, yet fervently clinging to the hope, if not expectation, that their innocence will appear transparent, no longer risk perceiving the outline of the hangman's noose in some chance shadow upon the courtroom wall. But there remains for such defendants the prospect of a sentence which some would wish to be transformed from being a constructive punishment for those convicted of homicide, with the prospect of rehabilitation and eventual release, into a symbolic entombment characterised by punitive retribution alone. If guilt in cases so reliant upon expert evidence cannot be ascertained with certitude, then that 'dreadful possibility' to which Lord Justice (now Lord Chief Justice) Judge so poignantly and pointedly referred becomes a reality:

> If murder cannot be proved, the conviction cannot be safe. In a criminal case, it is simply not enough to be able to establish even a high probability of guilt. Unless we can be sure of guilt the dreadful possibility always remains that a mother, already brutally scarred by the unexplained death or deaths of her babies, may find herself in prison for life for killing them when she should not be there at all. In our community, and in any civilised community, that is abhorrent.[19]

---

19. *R v Cannings* [2004] EWCA Crim 1, at para 179.

CHAPTER 14

A MATTER FOR THE JURY

The most usual triall of matters of fact is by 12 such (jury)men; for *ad quaestionem facti non respondent judices;* and matters in law the judges ought to decide and discusse; for *ad quaestionem juris non respondent juratores.*[1]

Whether the jurors deliberately threw the law into the discard, and rendered a verdict out of their own heads, or whether they applied the law correctly as instructed by the court, or whether they tried to apply it properly but failed for lack of under-standing—these are questions respecting which the verdict discloses nothing ...the general verdict serves as the great procedural opiate ...draws the curtain upon human errors, and soothes us with the assurance that we have attained the unattainable.[2]

A Fundamental Institution

Whatever its imperfections, defects, or shortcomings (both theoretical and practical), trial by jury in England (strictly speaking, trial by judge and jury) is deeply rooted in the culture that has produced Anglo-Saxon legal systems. By all accounts, mostly anecdotal and impressionistic, it steadfastly retains the confidence of the public; any attempt by the legislature to dilute its application arouses stout opposition.

Many an alleged shoplifter has preferred to take his or her chances before a jury rather than elect summary trial.[3] Indeed, although only a small per-

---

1. Sir Edward Coke, *Coke upon Littleton, Institutes* vol 1, 1628 ('Questions of fact are not for the judges and questions of law are not for jurors').
2. Jerome Frank, *Courts on Trial: Myth and Reality in American Justice*, Princeton (Princeton University Press, 1949) at p.114.
3. Both fearful and resentful at the prospect of a criminal conviction, believing, no doubt, that such would be the likely outcome in a magistrates' court, and in the notion that 'Who steals

centage of criminal cases in England and Wales are decided by juries, the language employed by some of its most vocal champions would seem to regard it as something almost sacred, as if the right to trial by jury[4] were fundamental to the idea of freedom under law and the warranty given by the State to its citizens that none, no matter how serious or trivial the crime of which they stand accused, shall be condemned save by the judgment of a dozen of their peers who will have listened to the evidence and brought to bear upon it that highly prized intellectual commodity, otherwise known as common-sense. More recently, Government has failed to introduce trial by judge alone in cases of serious fraud.

Given its near-permanence in the upper reaches of criminal justice, it is nevertheless apposite to ask how the task of such a non-professional and amateurish body in determining the guilt or innocence of the accused can be improved. How can the burden of decision-making by the jury be lightened by the directions it receives from the trial judge, and how may the attendant judicial process be made more even-handed? More particularly, can the summing up to the jury be so phrased as to enhance the judicial approach to decision making? It certainly can be, if the law is simple and clear.

The report by Lord Justice Auld in 2001[5] brought a hail of criticism. Some of it was (erroneously) founded on the belief that any restriction of the right to jury trial would represent the abrogation of a constitutional right; notwithstanding that those accused of a vast number of minor offences had never enjoyed any such right. Some of his eminently sensible proposals, such as that requiring juries to give answers to judges' questions and thereby making their reasoning more transparent, would have made the jury a more effi-

---

my purse steals trash ... but he that filches from me my good name robs me ... and makes me poor indeed'. (*Othello* Act 3, Scene 3, line 155).

4. Lord Justice Auld in his *Review of the Criminal Courts in England and Wales* observed that 'there is no constitutional, nor indeed any form of general right to judge and jury, only a general obligation to submit to it in indictable cases,' London (The Stationery Office, 2001) at p.137, paras 5 and 7. The argument that any such right exists deriving from Article 6 of the ECHR, that requires a 'fair trial' before an 'independent and impartial tribunal', would, we suggest, be unlikely to succeed at Strasbourg. Moreover, the division of criminal offences into those triable only upon indictment (and thereby by a jury), those for which only summary trial is available, and those triable either way, derives from pragmatic rather than constitutional concerns. But see also our comments on *Taxquet* below.

5. *A Review of the Criminal Courts of England and Wales* (September 2001).

cient mechanism of justice, rendering it less susceptible to perverse verdicts. Another was a suggestion that offences such as burglary, theft and assault could properly be tried by a district judge sitting with two justices, and yet another that where there were grounds for believing that a jury had reached a perverse verdict, an appeal should be possible.

But the general drift of his critics was that to modify the jury system in any way would be fundamentally unacceptable. The Bar Council, the Law Society, and the Criminal Bar Association each affirmed their faith in the jury system and considered that for the Government to change it would be a grave mistake. The chairman of the Bar Council was quoted[6] as saying that in a survey of some 900 people, 81% considered a jury trial to be fairer than that conducted by a judge, and 80% considered a jury system was capable of producing better justice, while 73% thought a jury more likely to reflect their views and values. It was thought to be the view of Government ministers that change appearing to weaken justice in the public mind would not only be profoundly unpopular but also a serious electoral miscalculation.

Leaving aside the fact that, when jury service was based upon property qualifications, there were individuals who sought to *avoid* jury service, and others who were statutorily exempted or excluded from it,[7] the history of the jury prompts two initial observations. First, it was the case that prior to the introduction of adult suffrage as its basis by the Criminal Justice Act 1972, jury membership had been severely restricted by property qualifications.[8] The notion that offenders, drawn as they very largely are from the ranks of those of limited means and little property, have always been subject

---

6. *BBC News online*, 30 January 2002 at 1220 GMT.

7. For example, members of such corporate bodies as the Metropolitan Water Board, the Port of London Authority and the Mersey Docks and Harbour Board, justices of the peace, active and retired members of the professional judiciary, solicitors, barristers and serving and retired police officers were all exempt. Persons with criminal convictions and those subject to orders under the Mental Deficiency and Mental Treatment Acts were disqualified.

8. In 1951 a person was qualified for jury service if he or she was: aged between 21 and 60; and a registered local government elector; either (a) a resident beneficially possessed of £10 p.a. in real estate or rent charge, or £20 p.a. in leaseholds held for not less than 21 years or determinable on any life or lives, or (b) a householder residing in premises of rateable value of not less than £30 p.a. in the counties of London and Middlesex or £20 p.a. elsewhere in England and Wales. In 1951 most manual workers would have needed to work 60 or more hours each week to take home more than £10 in wages, suggesting that manual workers were under-represented on juries.

to the judgment of their peers is therefore hardly defensible; rather, their experience was, and often remains, one of being tried by those richer and more powerful than themselves—certainly those regarded as more 'respectable'—be it in the guise of justices of the peace, a district judge or jurors. Second, if knowing of and participating in the process of jury trial 'maintains public trust and confidence in the law',[9] then one must ask whether, by comparison, the ordinary citizen perceives the processes of summary justice as fundamentally flawed?

If the survey results at the time of the Auld Report are evidence of that perception, then, it can be argued, its corollary must surely be a substantial public distrust, not only of summary justice before lay magistrates and district judges but, by the same token, of the adjudications of the Criminal Division of the Court of Appeal, the House of Lords (now the Supreme Court) and the Privy Council. What might be inferred from this is that the populist caricature of the judiciary as socially remote from the world in which most people live and ignorant if not insensitive to their values has taken disturbingly deep root. Perhaps it is indicative of a belief that juries are likely to be sympathetic to those whom they identify as being like themselves. Yet, if jurors do indeed make such identification of those whose causes they are sworn faithfully to try according to the evidence, then there must be an ever-present risk that such partiality may lead, however unwittingly, to perversity of judgment. But perversity or not, 'the jury', though the name has been there for centuries, has undergone many changes both in its composition and its functions. The question that must be asked is whether such changes have been synchronous with changes in criminal law and procedure. Given the major advances in forensic science in the last fifty years, and the consequent increase in the complexities of technical evidence, it is undeniable that a great deal more is demanded of juries, certainly those in homicide trials, than was previously the case.

Although it was probably his radical views about the range of offences for which jury trial would be appropriate which attracted the greater volume of critical comment, Auld also addressed the question of disclosure of the processes within the jury room. Section 8 Contempt of Court Act 1981 creates

---

9. Baroness Kennedy of the Shaws speaking in the House of Lords during the debate on the Criminal Justice (Mode of Trial) No 2 Bill on 28 September 2000.

an offence of 'obtaining', 'disclosing' or 'soliciting' any arguments, opinions or statements made by jurors in the course of their deliberations. Given that anecdotal evidence (despite its illegal provenance) suggests that there are jury rooms in which events occur which might well undermine rather than reinforce pubic confidence, besides those instances in which appeals result in jury verdicts being set aside, it is not unreasonable to infer that its deliberations, wholly unscrutinised, the jury may well fall short of perfection.

Auld went so far as to argue that the ban on disclosure was both indefensible and capable of causing serious injustice.[10] Nevertheless, there have been cases of jurors so concerned about events in which they have been participants that they have voiced their concerns[11], only to fall foul of section 8 of the 1981 Act. In *Mirzah*, although the majority on the court upheld the position in section 8, Lord Steyn (who had dissented) strongly argued that there was a contravention of Article 6 of the ECHR, guaranteeing a right to a fair trial before an independent and impartial tribunal, and that presently the situation was 'morally indefensible' — a term remarkably similar to that earlier used by Auld. The ECHR figured again in *Scotcher*, again in the House of Lords, this time in the shape of Article 10 relating to the right to freedom of expression. Article 10, however, being a qualified right, afforded the juror in question no protection against a charge of contempt under section 8. The judgment did, nevertheless, indicate that a concerned juror might take his concerns about a possible miscarriage of justice to an officer of the trial court. In this instance the juror had written of them in a letter to the defendant's mother.

The arguments in support of the present law include the need to protect the jury from external pressures, not least subsequent intimidation or reprisals by disgruntled parties, besides ensuring that accounts of what had transpired in the jury room are not being sold to the press. Lord Steyn (judicially) and Sir Robin Auld (extra-judicially) have taken a contrary view to that expressed by the House of Lords in *Mirzah*, while Professor John Spencer[12] in arguing that the current system is 'almost certainly incompatible

---

10. Auld, *op.cit.* Chapter 5, *Juries*, at p.173, para 98.

11. *R v Mirzah* [2004] UKHL 2; [2004] 1 AC 1118 and *R v Scotcher* [2005] UKHL 36, on appeal from [2003] EWHC 1380 (Admin).

12. Professor of Law in the University of Cambridge.

with Article 6'[13] would appear to take a different view from the judgment in *Scotcher* making the important point that '*Scotcher* does not address the basic risk that a defendant has been convicted not because the jury thought him guilty but because it did not like him'.

Clearly, jurors must be protected from external pressures of any kind, no less than should be their freedom to exercise their own judgment, but the problem of ensuring that the conduct of their private deliberations is above reproach, whether in respect of bias, prejudice, or irrational assessment of the evidence before them, is both real and as yet unresolved. Our view, which we elaborate later in this chapter, is that the problem needs to be addressed not by devising what are in effect invasive techniques of surveillance, but by those which concentrate on making transparent the stages by which the jury has arrived at a reasoned verdict.

What Happened in History?

Since those who tend towards a trenchant defence of the jury trial against any significant change or limitation frequently pray in aid its ancient and venerable origins, we cannot ignore that fact. But when history is cited to authenticate popular belief, fable is seldom entirely absent. Never mind the lack of evidential proof, every schoolchild knows that Aelfred, who was a good king, was sadly no reliable custodian of cakes. John, however, we know to have been a bad king who, not content with carelessly losing the crown jewels in The Wash and being greedy (to the point of dying from over-eating of lampreys) oppressed the people generally and especially upset the barons, who brought him to heel at Runnymede and forced him to sign the *Magna Carta*. From this Great Charter, it is not infrequently asserted, all our liberties essentially derive.

In reality the *Magna Carta* of 1215, far from being a specifically seminal instance of criminal justice legislation, was essentially concerned with the politics of a changing feudal system. Where liberties were under-written, they were the liberties of *freemen*. The liberties of those below them in the

---

13. Quoted in 'Media Law: Non-Disclosure', *The Guardian* (17 September 2007).

feudal hierarchy were not at issue. Trial by peers (equals) was, in fact, an importation from mainland Europe consisting of the solemn trial of a vassal by his fellow vassals in the court of their lord. Indeed, John himself was tried by his peers in the court of King Philip II of France who was his local overlord, the matter arising from John's tenure of lands in Aquitaine.

The jury, no less than Parliament and the institution of monarchy, has a history that is long and complicated, the true narrative often bearing little resemblance to the substance of popular belief. But the jury, and its close relative, the coroner's inquest, have undergone substantial change in the course of that history. In the Middle Ages, various devices were employed to determine the truth or otherwise of complaints of crime: trial by battle, by ordeal, and by jury. Trial by ordeal, such as being precipitated into water or made to carry a red-hot iron during the Mass, was officially abolished by a decree of Pope Innocent III, also, as it happens, in the year 1215. By the 12th century the jury had come to consist of twelve, or some other number of jurors fixed by the court according to circumstances, who were called upon to swear, not to the facts of the case, but that from their knowledge of the accused, his word was to be believed. These jurors, termed 'compurgators',[14] would attest to the oath of innocence taken by the accused being 'clean' or founded in truth, thus purging him of guilt. Over time, the judges ceased to play an inquisitorial role, assessing the weight of the evidence themselves, leaving this task to a new kind of jury that developed in the 13th century, whose verdicts came to be accepted as unquestioningly as the outcome of the ordeal.

In his *Concise History of the Common Law* Theodore Plucknett, Professor of Legal History in the University of London and among the most respected scholars in this field in the 20th century, writing of what he terms the 'supposed Anglo-Saxon origins of the jury' observes:

> Ever since the seventeenth century when juries began to express sentiments against the government, there has been a tendency for the jury to become, at least in popular thought, a safeguard of political liberty. It is only natural, therefore, that its history

---

14. From the Latin *purgare*, 'to cleanse'.

should have been idealised and traced back for patriotic reasons to the supposed golden age of Anglo-Saxon institutions.[15]

When Sir Patrick (later Lord) Devlin delivered his Hamlyn Lectures on trial by jury,[16] he seemed scarcely, if indeed at all, concerned with the vagaries of its history. There seems little doubt but that he subscribed to what might be termed the 'golden view' in which the origins and functions of the jury were perceived to belong in a world in which, although Great Britain possessed it in no written form, the 'British Constitution', like the roast beef of Old England, was to be understood as intrinsically superior to anything that might have emerged from any foreign source. The truth of the matter is that while the modern jury bears remarkably little resemblance to its medieval predecessors, it has an ancestry suggestive of Scandinavian as well as Frankish roots. Moreover, it has had, down the centuries, a variety of functions including being an instrument of royal inquiry in both administrative and criminal matters, a mode of trial in property cases, besides that which most nearly approaches its contemporary function in criminal prosecution, namely as a replacement of earlier modes of trial such as that by ordeal.

The thesis that, since the 17th century, the jury has been the custodian of popular liberty is questionable. It could be argued that much depended upon the degree to which the jurors identified or sympathised with the defendant and his cause. James II with his Romish religion was heartily disliked and it

---

15. (4th ed.) London (Butterworth, 1948) at p.105. One is immediately prompted to recall the trial of the Seven Bishops, and the account of the consequent worsting of the Roman Catholic James II that, in the 19th and early 20th centuries and by way of many a school textbook, had become part of the folklore of triumphant Protestantism. There is a much later instance of a jury taking a robust — some would say an assertively political — stand in a criminal trial: that, not of Seven Bishops, but of seven dockers at the Old Bailey under the wartime Order 1305 which prohibited strikes at a time of national emergency and which was invoked at the time of a dock strike in 1951. While it was widely seen in union circles as a triumph for the freedom to strike, it was also a source of humiliation for the Labour Government whose Attorney-General, Sir Hartley Shawcross, had conducted the prosecution. For a discussion of the conduct of 18th century juries in cases involving the infamous Waltham Black Act between 1723 and 1827 see E P Thompson, *Whigs and Hunters,* New York (Pantheon Books, 1978). Thompson cites their reaction to it as a classic instance of the 'rule of law', in contrast to those among his Marxist peers who argued that the concept was, by definition, a sham.

16. Sir Patrick Devlin, *Trial by Jury,* London (Stevens and Sons, 1956) (the published version of his Hamlyn Lectures).

is scarcely surprising that the Seven Bishops went free. Not so the Tolpuddle Martyrs in early 19th century Dorset, whose attempt at the unionisation of agricultural workers resulted in convictions for criminal conspiracy and sentences of transportation to Australia.

The resolution of some of the great issues of constitutional liberty has arisen, not from the robust and challenging verdicts of juries, but from judicial pronouncement. Though Parliament did not see fit to outlaw the slave trade until 1807, or slavery itself until 1833, it was Lord Mansfield who, in *Summersett's Case* in 1771, decided that if a slave had been brought to England he must be treated in all respects as a free man. And it was not a jury (which had convicted him of murder) but a bench of judges who were to set free another Dorset farm labourer, Reginald Woolmington, by disapproving a feature of the common law that had gone unchallenged for centuries.[17]

When Devlin wrote so passionately about the jury the penalty for murder was death. The passage of time has rendered remote its awful finality and intrinsic generation of horror, perhaps even to those who, from personal experience, remember all too clearly not only the atmosphere of the courtroom but also of the prison as the hour of execution approached. Yet although after the abolition of the death penalty some forty years ago it appeared as if a doorway into modern times had been opened, the penalty of life imprisonment has, in the ensuing period, taken on a shape in which it would not have been recognised in the 1960s.

The substitution of imprisonment for life, though no longer an irreversible sentence, retains an awesome quality: it remains as something to be feared by all condemned to it, saving perhaps those few mentally aberrant offenders for whom anything beyond the present, or its immediate temporal vicinity, has no reality. The 'life' sentence, though it may not come to mean lifelong incarceration, nevertheless proffers a potential prospect of seemingly endless time in which days follow each other into weeks, weeks into months, and months into years, such that time itself acquires a new dimension. Schedule 21 to the Criminal Justice Act 2003 ensures that any time served will be never less than substantial. Added to the corrosive *ennui* that is the common characteristic of long-term imprisonment may be a gnawing sense of

---

17. *Woolmington v DPP* [1935] AC 462. See *Chapter 6, supra.*

guilt amplified by the knowledge that the life taken can never be brought back. It is small wonder that those convicted of murder and sentenced to life imprisonment are often considered to be at risk of suicide in the early months of their time in prison.

It is not least for these reasons that those who stand trial for murder and who firmly maintain their innocence of the crime, while they may hope for much within the trial process, place their final trust in the jury to deliver a true verdict. Herein lies perhaps the greatest strength as well as the greatest weakness of the system.

Objective Judgment — Guaranteed

The task with which jurors today are charged is to determine whether or not the prosecution has made out its case and, in so doing, to entertain no reasonable doubt as to their own concluding judgment. Terms like 'on balance' can have no place in their thinking. They have to be 'sure'. They will have heard an outline of the prosecution case and the testimony of its witnesses. They will have heard those witnesses cross-examined by the defence and the testimony of defence witnesses, to be cross-examined in their turn by the prosecution. They will have had the benefit of a summing up of the evidence by the judge and, in a trial for murder, a careful statement of the law, enabling them to test what they decide are the established facts against it. All this will have occupied many hours and demanded considerable and continuous concentration on the part of the jury.

It is presumed that, being ordinary citizens randomly drawn from the local community, their approach will be determined by a realism deriving from their experience of ordinary life. The remainder of the cast of the courtroom drama who have the speaking parts — professional lawyers all — are, in contrast, generally believed to be more distant from the world inhabited by ordinary people. To some extent this is true, given their generally privileged social background, but they are not as socially unaware as their critics often portray them.[18] Their professional careers can make them fully alive to the way in which their fellow citizens conduct their lives.

The contemporary requirement of a civilised system of criminal justice is now expressed in Article 6 of the European Convention on Human Rights as a fair trial before an independent and impartial tribunal conducted in public: that is to say, nothing more nor less than that provided by the common law of England. These are the primary criteria against which the jury system must itself be judged. Each of these is wholly and self-evidently met, save, perhaps, for the issue of impartiality. For it is not that we have reason to believe that juries *are* partial: rather, that because they conduct their deliberations in private, there is simply no way of knowing how objectively and impartially each member of the jury approaches the task. Because the jury room is literally closed to outside scrutiny, even to the most professionally conducted research, we have, where real cases are concerned, nothing upon which to rely save for anecdotal accounts of what may have transpired. If the jury does experience difficulty, part of the problem arises from the circumstances in which juries have to deliberate when perhaps none except the foreman has had any experience either of jury service, or indeed of the criminal justice system.

Before 1965, when both rational selection and training were introduced into the system of lay magistrates,[19] the larger part of the business of the criminal courts was conducted by people who had never been trained to view matters judicially. To 'think' a defendant was guilty, or to be 'pretty sure', never mind to speculate on the nature of events beyond what was disclosed by the evidence, would, nowadays, be recognised by every newly-fledged magistrate as no basis upon which to establish a criminal conviction. Lay justices came to recognise that while the details of the law were not their direct problem, assurance for the standards laid down in *Woolmington* was very much their responsibility. Jurors, in contrast, and who, by definition,

---

18. While it is doubtful whether any contemporary judge would seriously need to inquire as the nature of a bikini, any more than would counsel, in addressing a jury, make reference to the moral welfare of their servants, judges who ask questions relating to demotic language or popular culture are still not exempt from criticism. They may well be seeking to elucidate matters for the jury.

19. One of the reforms actively propelled by the enthusiasm of Gerald Gardiner during his time as Lord Chancellor.

are called upon to deliberate in substantially more serious cases than lay magistrates, receive no such extensive training; only some introductory information and an implied encouragement to do their best.

Assuming an effort on the part of each juror to set aside his or her own feelings about the evidence in a homicide case and their natural reactions as human beings, to what further pressures may they be subjected? The essential virtue of the jury is that it is encapsulated in a reliance on the collective view of twelve ordinary citizens, having the ability, by using their commonplace experience of human behaviour, jointly to determine whether the prosecution has succeeded in making them sure of its case. Trials of homicide, which instinctively arouse the deepest concern of the community because of the violence employed and the resultant grief of the victim's family, are particularly susceptible to adjudication by an admittedly amateur body but one whose members nevertheless have knowledge of the ways in which most people live their lives. Selection on the basis of a universal adult suffrage, though it may not always produce the kind of random sample that might be regarded as ideal for socio-legal research, is nevertheless likely to provide a deep reservoir of social experience relevant for the purpose. When the criminal trial is primarily concerned with assessing and evaluating eyewitness evidence the jury is a very suitable body to undertake the task.

Since most homicides are committed within the compass of domestic relations—killing by strangers is comparatively rare—jurors can readily identify the patterns of social behaviour that lie behind the homicidal event. The shortcomings of the modern jury system relate much less to the identity of the jurors and their varying abilities, but rather to the nature of the tasks with which they are sometimes presented. The jury must make an assessment of technical evidence when need be, whatever their own background knowledge or training.[20] But perhaps the most daunting task consists of assessing that part of the evidence of the prosecution that seeks to establish

---

20. Medical and scientific witnesses are generally possessed of knowledge altogether beyond that of even the most intelligent and well-educated lay person. Though certainly less likely today, in the past, juries could be in awe of pathologists like Sir Bernard Spilsbury (1877-1947) of whom a defence counsel (Mr J D Cassels KC) was once driven to complain: 'It will be a sorry day for the administration of justice in this land if we are to be thrust into such a position that, because Sir Bernard Spilsbury expressed an opinion, it is impossible to question it'. Keith Simpson, *Forty Years of Murder*, London (Granada Publishing Ltd, 1980) at p.30.

the necessary *mens rea* essential to the verdict of guilty. There are times when the jury must make the attempt to see into the defendant's mind.

The modern criminal trial of homicide before a jury, in contrast to its historical counterpart, is likely to be both more protracted and more complicated. In the 18th and early 19th centuries, trials in capital cases were often completed within a matter of hours; a trial that forty years ago might have occupied a matter of days is now likely to require weeks. Given the sheer volume of evidential material, the average juror is at risk of suffering what is nowadays known as 'information overload'. At the end of the trial so much will have been said that it would be hardly surprising if a person unused to receiving information in this way did not experience some degree of confusion, not to say mental exhaustion.

Yet, given constructive improvements to the way in which juries go about their work, there is no reason to abandon the system. We conclude that our proposals for a single homicide offence and for the issue of *mens rea* to be removed from the trial to the sentencing stage of the criminal justice process will reduce some of these pressures and remove many of the complexities in the modern trial of homicide.

The Problem of Bias

As justice depends upon, and indeed, may be considered to consist of the exclusion of arbitrariness, so too it can have no accommodation with bias. In common parlance 'justice' is synonymous with 'fairness', a concept that is at the heart of the fair trial enshrined in Article 6 of the European Convention. Though in ordinary speech a variety of words may be used to identify 'unfairness', in the context of the criminal trial the problem is rather more than one of semantics. 'Bias', 'prejudice', 'partiality' and 'preconception' are often used interchangeably but, as we seek to demonstrate with regard to the qualities of jurors, they are by no means the same.

When in 2007 the House of Lords was faced with a challenge to the position of serving police officers and a member of the Crown Prosecution

Service acting as jurors in three separate criminal trials,[21] on the ground that each of them, by virtue of their general involvement in the administration of criminal justice, was biased (and hence not impartial), the court relied instinctively on that overworked aphorism of Lord Hewart CJ in *R v Sussex Justices, ex parte McCarthy*:[22]

> It is not merely of some importance but is of fundamental importance that justice should not only be done, but should manifestly and undoubtedly be seen to be done.

While these words have been considered generally as an essential ingredient of English procedural law, they were clearly relevant to the subject matter of bias. Yet their citation in these House of Lords judgments was unaccompanied by any recitation of the facts in *Sussex Justices*.

What constituted partiality (personal bias) in that case was the undeniable fact that the substitute clerk to the justices, who had retired with his magistrates to advise them on any legal issues, turned out to be a partner in the firm of solicitors acting for the injured party in the civil proceedings, and therefore had a specific interest in the outcome of the criminal proceedings. As Lord Hewart stated:

> The question therefore is not whether in this case the deputy clerk made any observation or offered any criticism which he might not properly have made or offered; the question is whether he was so related to the case in its civil aspect as to be unfit to act as clerk to the justices in the criminal matter... Nothing is to be done which creates even a suspicion that there has been an improper interference with the course of justice.[23]

Seventy seven years later, in the leading case of *Porter v Magill*,[24] Lord Hope of Craighead, in holding that the question of bias is one of whether the fair-minded and informed observer, having considered the facts, would

---

21. *R v Abdroikof, Green, Williamson* [2007] UKHL 37.
22. [1924] 1 KB 256, at 259.
23. *Ibid*. On the matter of the conduct of justices' clerks in summary criminal trials see *R v Consett Justices ex parte Postal Bingo Ltd* [1967] 2 QB 9.
24. [2001] 2 AC 357.

conclude that there was a real possibility of bias, rejected the challenge of bias on the grounds of specific evidence failing to establish that perceived partiality on the part of the auditor in the auditing of the accounts of Westminster City Council for the years 1987/8 to 1994/5. The alleged partiality was based on there having been a televised press conference arranged by the auditor at a provisional stage of his inquiry, at which he expressed himself 'in florid language' and supported his views by reference to the thoroughness of the investigation which he claimed to have carried out. The Divisional Court concluded that

> unless it was being implied that the persons under investigation might wish to steal the documents (which were displayed in a stack of ring binders at the press conference under the protection of a security guard, bearing the name of the auditor's firm for the benefit of the cameras) it is not clear what was the purpose of the posturing.[25]

This evidence about the state of progress in the audit was only inappropriate because it was made at an ostentatious press conference and created a risk of unfair reporting. Yet it appeared to the court that there was nothing in the words used by the auditor that indicated a risk of there being a real possibility that he was biased. Objectively speaking, there was not a real possibility of bias.

In the conjoined appeals of *Abdroikov and others* there was no direct evidence to support the undoubted suspicion (in other words, a source of potential bias) that those normally engaged in the prosecution of criminal cases in their various professional capacities who had been called as jurors possessed any specific interest in the result for the specific defendant.

In two cases, those of *Abdroikov* and *Green*, both juries had included a police officer whose presence was considered by the appellants to be a source of potential bias, although the precise details differed in each case. In a third, that of *Williamson*, the juror whose presence was considered objectionable was a solicitor employed by the Crown Prosecution Service who was a higher court advocate and had previously been a prosecuting solicitor for a large metropolitan local authority. In the event, the court divided three to two;

---

25. (1997) 96 LGR 157, at 173 G-H, cited approvingly by the House of Lords.

Lords Bingham, Mance and Lady Hale dismissing the appeal of *Abdroikov* and allowing those of *Green* and *Williamson*, but with the proviso that the case of *Williamson* should be remitted to the Court of Appeal to quash the convictions and rule on any application for a retrial. The minority, Lords Rodger of Earlsferry and Carswell, were for dismissal of all three appeals.

What is of considerable interest here is to observe how opinion has changed in the last forty years regarding the principles governing the qualification and disqualification of jurors.

A number of aspects of jury service were considered by a Departmental Committee under the chairmanship of Lord Morris of Borth-y-Gest that reported in 1965.[26] When that committee set about its task, membership of the jury was still governed by the Juries Act 1870 and later statutory modifications, such as the inclusion of women by the Sex Disqualification (Removal) Act 1919.[27] While the Morris Committee had sensibly insisted on dealing with exemption from jury service on a basis more fitting to the 1970s than the 1870s, it argued strongly that two groups ought to remain exempt — namely, those comprising members of professions concerned with the administration of justice and the police. It was concerned with the risk that such jurors, given the specialist knowledge and standing attaching to their occupations, might emerge as 'built-in leaders' in the jury room.[28] Given the need fully to satisfy the requirement of justice being seen to be done, it was thought important to exclude this form of potential bias from the privacy of the jury room, no less than to ensure that objectivity in the assessment of the evidence was not imperilled by any prejudice, conscious or otherwise, on the part of such 'professional' jurors.

Opinion about the recruitment of jurors has undoubtedly undergone what might be described as a seismic shift and, prompted by Sir Robin Auld's review of the criminal courts, Parliament, in the Criminal Justice Act 2003,[29]

---

26. *Report of the Departmental Committee on Jury Service*, Cmnd 2627 (HMSO, 1965).

27. Women continued to be effectively excluded from jury service after 1919, since many either remained below the threshold of the property qualifications or were without title to property at all.

28. Morris Report, para 104. The committee listed all those ineligible 'by reason of their close connection with the administration of law and justice'; that included members of the prison and probation services.

29. Section 321 and Schedule 33.

rejected the Morris Committee's view.[30] Newer arguments cannot, however, be set aside since understandably in this period notions of 'fairness' at common law have come into sharper focus, not least as a consequence of the Human Rights Act 1998 and the development of Strasbourg jurisprudence. It can be argued that just as it does not follow that every lawyer or police officer must, by reason of his or her calling, be automatically prejudiced against a defendant—not least a defendant who is clearly no stranger to the halls of justice—so too, it does not follow that an ordinary citizen must be assumed to be devoid of prejudice and free of all subjectivity of approach. What of the juror, trying a case of causing death by dangerous driving, who has had a loved one killed or maimed in a road traffic crime, or a juror who has been the victim of a street robbery or a burglary hearing evidence against defendants charged with such an offence? There are many other ingredients that might be added to this brew, such as class, ethnic or religious prejudice against defendants unlike themselves. Nor can one dismiss the alternative possibility that the ordinary juror might be favourably disposed *towards* a defendant for these, or indeed other reasons having no bearing whatever upon the evidence in the case. Improper preference can constitute bias no less than dislike or prejudice.

The Court of Appeal, in a judgment of Lord Woolf CJ, had earlier taken the view that

> The fact that there were 12 members of the jury of which at least ten must be agreed is a real protection against the prejudices of an individual juror resulting in unfairness to a defendant. In addition, it is to be hoped and expected that those who are employed in the administration of justice will be particularly careful not to act in a manner which is inconsistent with their duty as members of the jury and, in particular, to exercise the independence of mind which is required of all jurors and to be on their guard to reach their verdict only on the evidence in accordance with the directions of the trial judge.[31]

One can perhaps conclude from the House of Lords' judgments in these appeals that, given the current basis of universal suffrage for the selection of

---

30. Ch 5.14.
31. [2005] 1 WLR 3538 at para 29.

jurors, the way to deal with alleged bias is in part for any serious allegation to become known to the court at the earliest opportunity, and in part to recognise that human beings, by their social characteristics, will inevitably entertain preferences, no less than prejudices of which they may themselves be conscious in varying degrees. The argument encapsulated in the dissenting judgment of Lord Rodger of Earlsferry[32] is, we would suggest, compelling:

> In my view, while recognising that there was a possibility of bias on the part of the juror concerned, the informed observer would also realise the risk was actually no greater than in many of the other situations that occur every day. Like all other jurors, be they clergymen, defence lawyers, butchers, estate agents, prostitutes, petty crooks or judges, police officers and CPS lawyers [they] sit as private individuals. Each brings his or her own particular experience to bear on the case they have to try. They are repeatedly reminded by counsel and the judge both of their solemn undertaking to faithfully try the defendant and to give a true verdict according to the evidence and of the need for them to put aside their prejudices. Unless the contrary is shown, the law presumes that the jury will comply with those directions and that their verdict will be impartial.

What is striking about all the five judgments handed down by their Lordships is the interchangeability of language to determine the circumstances in which a decision-maker (be he or she a judge sitting alone or with colleagues in an appellate court, or as a juror in a trial by judge and jury) is disqualified from sitting in judgment. Bias (alternatively, the absence of impartiality) is not the same as prejudice.[33] Bias requires some evidence to sustain the perception of the real possibility that the decision-maker has a distinct interest in the outcome of the trial of the matter before the court. We are all innately, if not also interstitially, filled with preconceptions and prejudices; the process of justice requires such human foibles to be acknowledged and for their effects in decision-making to be countered, in jurors no less than in judges.

---

32. Regarding the appeal of Williamson: [2007] UKHL 37 at para 37.

33. In *Matheson* (*q.v.* below) Lord Goddard's use of the archaic and pejorative term 'sodomite' as a description of the appellant suggested his personal distaste for his sexual conduct and he concluded (without any suggestion of dissent on his part) that the jury might well have been so revolted by the crime that it considered the death penalty appropriate. But in allowing the appeal, the judgment was transparently free of bias.

But factors extraneous to that of human psychology which interpose so as to excite a specific interest in the audience are appropriately different in effect. The matter has perhaps been never better, nor more eloquently, enunciated judicially, than by that great American judge and jurist, Jerome Frank in the case of *J P Linahan Inc.* in 1943. The judgment bears powerful contrast with the majority opinions in the conjoined appeals of *Abdroikov and others*.

Frank's argument in the US Second Circuit Court of Appeal might be summarised, almost epigrammatically, in the following extract:

> If ...'bias' and 'partiality' be defined to mean the total absence of preconditions (in the mind of the judge), then no-one has ever had a fair trial and no-one ever will.[34]

We would suggest that to establish a real possibility of bias (usually *perceived* bias) in a juror, there must be some material evidence of it before the court, which is qualitatively distinct from any *prejudice* in the individual juror. We are quite content to countenance the persistent feature of prejudice, even strong prejudice, in the juror, if only because the juror's prejudice will be paraded potentially before eleven other prejudices. We would add that the clue to the avoidance of bias would seem to lie in transparency, not merely with respect to bias, whether substantive or perceived, but with respect to the process whereby the jury has arrived at its conclusions.[35] Both the public and any subsequent appellate body ought to be able, like the examiner in a mathematics examination, to see the rough working in the margin.

The Jury in Trials of Homicide

Whatever may have been demanded of it in former centuries, what is asked of the contemporary jury in such a trial is, on the face of it, very straightforward.

---

34. *In Re J P Linahan Inc.*138 F.2d 650. We would maintain that in this context 'judge' can be taken as synonymous with any judicial decision-taker, including juror or member of any tribunal.

35. In our view, the subjection of individual jurors to a lengthy *voire dire* at the outset, though a frequent occurrence in the American courts, would have little to commend it. In England a *voire dire* (a corruption of the Norman French *vrai dire*, to speak truly), used to consist of the examination of a witness suspected of having an interest in the cause.

Yet that demand can be deceptive, for the apparent simplicity of the task serves to conceal its intellectual complexities.

What is fundamentally required of the jury in any criminal trial is that, collectively, it must find a true verdict; that is, having heard the evidence, and an explanation of the law as it bears upon that evidence, it must assess all this information for the purpose of determining whether the defendant is guilty as charged or, on occasion, whether he or she is guilty of another offence. It is something upon which they must be in agreement, either unanimously or by a legally determined majority. If they should determine the defendant to be guilty of an offence it must be based upon their being *sure* in the sense that none of them entertains any lingering doubt or uncertainty about the nature of the verdict. And that sure verdict must be founded, not upon any supposition or conjecture, but upon the evidence alone, subject to any judicial commentary or summary for their assistance with which they may have been provided. No less importantly, it must be founded upon the jury being persuaded of the case presented by the prosecution; nothing else will do. No conjecture on the part of jurors can enter their deliberations, nor can any failure on the part of the defence to establish innocence of the crime.[36] In modern parlance, their decision cannot be other than 'evidence-based'. When evidence-based decisions are made in other spheres of social and economic activity, it is generally presumed that those who are charged with the task have training and experience in the interpretation of evidence. Apart from some technical familiarity with the data—or at least a minimal capacity to appreciate the information—decision-making is normally predicated upon the employment of scientific method. That is to say, the process must accord with the canons of rationality.

The assessment of evidence by a jury therefore demands both intellectual rigour and objectivity of approach, something that in the training of lay magistrates is often referred to as 'thinking judicially'. But unlike lay magistrates whose powers are strictly limited to the trial of comparatively minor offences, jurors undergo no comparably long hours of training, even

---

36. The 'golden thread' identified by Lord Sankey in *Woolmington v DPP* [1935] AC 342 overturned what had previously been held to be a cardinal principle in the common law of murder. See also: Louis Blom-Cooper and Terence Morris, *With Malice Aforethought: A Study of the Crime and Punishment for Homicide*, Oxford (Hart Publishing. 2004) at pp.17-18.

though in the past they might, by their verdict, have condemned a convict to death and even now may make a life sentence inevitable. Indeed, a juror may never have been inside a court before until called for jury service, and while fictional criminal trials are frequently a feature of television entertainment they may be no sure guide to a reality which is of a very different order. Whereas in the world outside the courtroom decision-making may be determined by all manner of processes, the irrational and capricious not excepted, the process of determining criminal guilt can admit of nothing but an independent and objective rationality. This is the mental dress which the juror must put on, leaving his or her everyday habit outside.

The juror, frequently entirely unfamiliar with the criminal law, may have quite erroneous misconceptions about the law of homicide. There is, for example, a widespread (and very understandable) belief that to prove murder, the prosecution must prove an intent to kill, and the juror may be astonished not only to learn that the Crown need establish no more than an intention to do serious harm but also that a majority of murder convictions come about in this way. Manslaughter is something the meaning of which many laymen are at a loss properly even to understand: it is often thought that manslaughter is just a crime of murder that someone has somehow—and inexplicably—'got away with'.

Then there are the defences, about which the juror may be no less untutored. Self-defence does not license the use of unlimited force, no more than a householder is at liberty to do what he will with a trespasser who is intent on nothing beyond the crime of burglary. It would be a rare verdict that on such a basis held the act of shooting a burglar dead to fall within the compass of 'reasonable force'. At such points the layman might well muse that if the law offers some protection to the criminal, it perhaps is overgenerous. Ought the wounded burglar to have any 'human rights'? The populist response might be a resounding negative.[37]

So the juror, empanelled for the first time, has much to learn and much to discard. But the process must be a speedy one. In the vernacular, it is known as 'learning on the job'. The majority of criminal trials are, for the most part,

---

37. Indeed, much of the poorly informed hostility to the Human Rights Act 1998 appears to incorporate the idea that once a person has embarked upon a crime, that ought to result in the automatic extinction of any rights to which he might otherwise be entitled.

humdrum affairs, most of those in the sparsely occupied public gallery generally being the friends and relatives of the accused. Trials for homicide, on the other hand, though not attracting public and press attention as in the days of capital punishment,[38] are still, in a sense, *sui generis* since criminal homicide remains both sociologically and psychologically a crime apart from all others. Many formal public occasions that focus upon matters of great and symbolic importance, including trials for homicide, take the form of solemn theatre: within a formal structure of interaction individuals perform particular roles and are identified by distinctive costume and language. Wig and gown in the courtroom are functional no less than cassock, surplice, or mitre in the church. But whereas the ecclesiastical theatre is governed by a predictable liturgical text that determines both structure and content, its forensic counterpart provides no more than structure and the dramatic content unfolds as the actors speak *extempore*.

It is in these circumstances that we entrust the jury with playing a major, perhaps in one sense the *leading* role, in that thespian phenomenon which is the trial of criminal homicide. Silent throughout, only at the end is it for the jury to devise and speak the penultimate lines pronouncing guilt or acquittal. When the final act is concluded the curtain falls with the pronouncement of sentence or order of discharge. In the event of a guilty verdict, although a grisly epilogue is no longer enacted upon a gallows, there remains the certainty of the long sunless years of a life sentence with the possibility that the words 'imprisonment for life', solemnly uttered by way of penalty, may have what one judge once identified as their 'awful, terrible meaning'.[39] It is hardly surprising that the jury occupies so important a place in the public mind.

---

38. Before 1965, long queues of the curious, awaiting the opening hour of a murder trial, were a common sight outside the Old Bailey.

39. A phrase understood to have been employed by Mr Justice Stephen Chapman at Reading Crown Court when sentencing the particularly brutal killer of a police officer (in an unreported case).

The Jury With a Mind of its Own: the 'Downside' of Independence

But what of the jury that may contain those who dissent, not from an interpretation of the evidence upon which guilt must be founded, but from what they perceive to be the possibility of an unacceptable outcome in the form of a sentence which they would consider inappropriate? Here, we are confronted with the spectre of the perverse verdict, about which the law itself can do comparatively little when a properly instructed jury has, nevertheless chosen to follow its own inclinations and declined to convict.

Before the Road Traffic Act 1956, juries were frequently reluctant to convict drivers who had been charged with manslaughter at common law following deaths resulting from road traffic incidents. It is widely accepted that it was this reluctance on the part of juries that encouraged Parliament to create the statutory offence of causing death by dangerous driving punishable with a maximum of five years imprisonment.[40] In so doing it had the effect — notwithstanding it might have been an unintended consequence — of defining this variety of criminal homicide as being altogether less serious than manslaughters dealt with by the common law. We have, of course, no way of knowing that this reluctance on the part of juries to convict was because they knew that a conviction for manslaughter might result in a substantial determinate sentence of imprisonment — never mind the possibility of a life sentence — both of which outcomes they might have disapproved, and that this was a factor in their reluctance. The possibility is by no means far-fetched. Nor is it impossible that jurors who, while they might find the greatest difficulty in identifying with common criminals, could be tempted to apply the 'there but for the grace of God' formula in cases involving homicidal drivers. It could well be that they saw themselves as sitting in judgment on the conduct of those with whom they readily identified as otherwise essentially law-abiding citizens who had suffered the misfortune of unintentionally causing a death on the road. There is a parallel here in prosecutions for drunken driving before the Road Safety Act 1967.

---

40. Such clearly instrumental legislation might be compared to casting deck cargo overboard to ensure the safety of a ship in a storm: in principle undesirable but likely to improve the situation in the short run.

In the absence of an objective standard of intoxication it was frequently difficult, if not nigh impossible, for a prosecutor to secure a conviction. The introduction of the legal limit of 80mg per 100ml in blood samples rendered obsolete the more primitive tests of counting coins and walking in a straight line that were often previously presented as evidence by the prosecution.

The problematic dimension of jury trial of which this is an example is that of the quasi-political quality of the process. History, and particularly ancient history, is replete with examples of systems of justice in which both the determination of the cause and the nature of the subsequent resolution came from the ruler whose power was to all intents absolute.[41] Both the *Magna Carta* and the Bill of Rights coming almost four centuries later are illustrative of a long-standing contest between forms of representative Government (however limited) and absolute monarchy.[42] It is hardly surprising that so many of its most enthusiastic advocates emphasise the symbolism of the jury as a bastion of liberty. But if the jury that acquitted the Seven Bishops sought to defy the King in what was essentially a religiously focused dispute, then other juries have been no less ready to arrive at what might be termed 'politically tinted' verdicts, sometimes affirming and at other times challenging what Parliament had in mind at a particular time.[43] The difficulty here is that what Parliament has 'had in mind' at various times has not necessarily always been coincident with either popular sentiment or a sense of fairness or moral rectitude. Given that a Dorchester jury in the 1830s would have been representative of a constituency likely to be hostile rather than sympathetic towards incipient trade unionism, it is scarcely surprising that they affirmed what had been in the mind of Parliament when it passed the Combination Acts. Similarly, as we shall see in a moment, the Lord Chief Justice, Lord Goddard, observed that in 1958 a Durham jury might well have concluded that Matheson was a proper candidate for the gallows.

To say that in trials involving crimes of such gravity as homicide — and, for that matter, in all trials of indictable offences — the jury must deliberate

---

41. The judgment of Solomon in the famous case of disputed maternity neatly combined both. The essence of such *kadi* justice might be said to be 'the only rule is that there are no rules'.

42. As late as 1672 Charles II was able without warning, by means of simple *fiat*, to prevent anyone who had made a loan to the Exchequer from being able to call it in. In their conflicts with the legislature the later Stuarts tended to behave as if the Civil War had not yet ended.

43. See note 15 above.

upon the evidence and set aside any personal opinions as to the acceptability or otherwise of the relevant law is to state the obvious. For while it can be argued that in their interpretation of the law in the appellate context judges can, in a sense, 'make' law, that is not something any jury is entitled to do. In the last analysis, it is for Parliament alone to amend, no less than to enact it. What approximates to universal suffrage as far as jury service is concerned is not the same as democratic election. The proper forum for challenge is not the jury room, but either the courtroom[44] or Parliament itself. For all that, it does not mean that what Parliament has enacted is always above criticism. Authority and wisdom, unlike wool and mutton, are not invariably in joint supply.

Here we need to return to the issue of contempt. It is one thing to celebrate and indeed to protect the independence of the jury, but quite another to deal with the independence of individual jurors. It has always been open to an individual juror or jurors to take a stand against the opinion of a majority of their fellow jurors. If they were not eventually persuaded to go along with the majority, the outcome would usually result in the re-trial of the case before another jury.[45] But what of the juror who has been unable to have any effect upon his or her fellows and, conscientiously persuaded of the need to speak out against what he or she believes to be a miscarriage of justice, deliberately commits contempt under section 8(1) of the 1981 Act. Though their numbers have been relatively few, the issues have been far from insignificant.

The question here is focused not on the substantive matter of alleged impropriety within the jury room, but the manner in which such concerns may properly be brought to judicial notice.[46] Mr Scotcher had been before the Divisional Court[47] in May 2003 that held that motivation on the part of a juror in order to expose a miscarriage of justice was not an available defence to a charge of contempt under the 1981 Act. Accepting that he had, therefore, committed contempt in terms of section 8(1), he was sentenced

---

44. Whether by appeal or judicial review.
45. A situation now moderated by the provision for majority verdicts.
46. The judgment in *Scotcher*, given by Lord Rodger of Earlsferry, contains, *inter alia*, useful background material on the problem.
47. Scott Baker LJ and Pitchford J.

to two months imprisonment suspended for one year and ordered to pay costs of £2500.[48]

However, in 2004 Lord Woolf CJ issued a *Practice Direction*[49] in the following terms:

IV.42.6. Trial judges should ensure that the jury is alerted to the need to bring any concerns about fellow jurors to the attention of the judge at the time, and not wait until the case is concluded. At the same time, it is undesirable to encourage inappropriate criticism of fellow jurors, or to threaten jurors with contempt of court.

IV.42.7. Judges should therefore take the opportunity, when warning the jury of the importance of not discussing the case with anyone outside the jury, to add a further warning. It is for the trial judge to tailor the further warning to the case, and to the phraseology used in the usual warning. The effect of the further warning should be that it is the duty of jurors to bring to the judge's attention, promptly, any behaviour among the jurors or by others affecting the jurors, that causes concern. The point should be made that, unless that is done while the case is continuing, it may be impossible to put matters right.

The reference contained in the penultimate sentence of this *Practice Direction* to 'any behaviour among the jurors' could be construed as inclusive of, for example, a refusal on the part of any juror or jurors to give proper consideration to the evidence of a medical witness for the defence, or a clear disregard for any part of the directions that had been given by the trial judge in respect of particular evidence — in short, behaviour that was in clear violation of the juror's oath faithfully to try the case.

The concerned juror might therefore be seen as having a duty to bring such things to the attention of the trial judge and to do so promptly. But given the importance of the unfettered independence of the jury, it must nevertheless be protected from irresponsible cries of 'foul!' from individual jurors disgruntled by the experience of a majority view prevailing over their

---

48. His subsequent appeal to the Lords included an argument about the Convention right of freedom of expression provided by Article 10, to ensure a defendant's right to a fair trial as enshrined in Article 6.

49. *Crown Court: Guidance to Jurors* [2004] 1 WLR 665.

own. At the same time, the task of the conscientious whistleblower ought not to be made more difficult than it already is. It must be recognised that taking part in a criminal trial in the Crown Court is scarcely a marginal experience, certainly not for a juror new to the scene who finds himself now additionally ill at ease with the conduct of a fellow juror or jurors, some of whom may have served on a jury before and who might consider themselves 'old hands'. He or she needs to know whom initially to approach among what may appear an intimidating array of experienced professionals among the *dramatis personæ* in this forensic theatre, and, no less importantly, how to do it.

The arrogant or opinionated juror who dismisses rational argument or who is not prepared to consider the whole of the evidence; the idle juror whose mind is elsewhere or has been inattentive; the juror who is anxious to be away attending to his own business and insists that fellow jurors 'get on with it': each is a potential source of injustice no less than one who has been corrupted by an external source. Whoever exposes any serious deficiency in the jury does a public service, not least since it may obviate the need for lengthy inquiries and appeals in the future. It should be for the court to determine the merit of any complaint and only the juror who goes about raising concerns in an improper way should be at risk of being in contempt.

Perverse Convictions

So far we have dealt with situations in which the jury has declined to convict, notwithstanding the evidence, and those in which individual jurors have been at troubled variance with their fellows with regard to conviction. But there remain those situations in which the jury, having a collective mind of its own, gets it wrong by convicting for the wrong reason, deciding to do so when it might nevertheless have undoubtedly felt 'sure' of its verdict on the basis of the evidence it had heard. The trial of Albert Edward Matheson,[50] convicted of capital murder in 1958, was just such a case.

The then Lord Chief Justice, Lord Goddard, presiding over the Court of Criminal Appeal, was to describe the crime as being 'of the most horrible

---

50. *R v Matheson* [1958] 1 WLR 474.

description, so revolting as to be almost beyond belief'. The defendant, a 52-year-old casual labourer, had met and subsequently killed a young teenaged boy in the context of a homosexual encounter.[51] In addition to mutilating the body in a most horrific fashion, he had taken an envelope from the boy's possessions containing some £35 in cash — a considerable sum in those days. He subsequently sent a series of anonymous postcards to the boy's mother, the last telling her that her son was dead. He was indicted at Durham Assizes for capital murder, being murder in the course or furtherance of theft, and on 30 January 1958 was convicted and sentenced to death.[52]

Matheson was one of the earliest cases to come before the courts with the newly-enacted Homicide Act 1957 in place, and on the question of the meaning of the words 'furtherance of theft', the trial Judge, Mr Justice Finnemore, who was clearly in some difficulty himself, raised the question as to whether this had to be the motive or intention, or merely that in fact there had been a theft. Almost rhetorically, he asked the jury:

> This is entirely new. I don't know whether you have considered the point — if the theft was the motive or intention that led to the murder, or that the intention of the man was to murder, during the course, perhaps, of the sexual offence and that the theft just followed.

Perhaps he was hoping that a Durham jury, endowed with robust common-sense, would find its way through this particularly dense legal thicket. Since the criminal event had included sexual intercourse, violence and theft, it is difficult to see how the jury could ever have determined at which point the defendant had formed an intention to steal. All that was clear was that the defendant had taken the money after having killed the boy. The perplexity of the trial judge, conveyed to the jury, was entirely understandable and he thought it was a matter for them to decide. In the event they came to the conclusion that the killing *had* taken place in the course or furtherance of theft and convicted Matheson of capital murder.

---

51. For a further account of *Matheson*, see Terence Morris and Louis Blom-Cooper, *A Calendar of Murder*, London (Michael Joseph, 1964).
52. Defined as capital by section 5(1)(a) Homicide Act 1957.

We have absolutely no idea of what actually went on in the jury room. Did they spend all their time attempting to unravel the meaning of 'in the course or furtherance of theft', paying little or no attention to what they had heard of the powerful and unrebutted medical evidence of Matheson's mental state? In finding him guilty of capital murder, they had, by definition, rejected that defence to murder provided by section 2(1) of the 1957 Act by which the defence sought to prove[53] that Matheson was suffering from diminished responsibility and that the killing thereby amounted to an offence of manslaughter. The defence had called no fewer than three very eminent medical witnesses, including the senior medical officer at Durham Prison[54] where Matheson had been held on remand. Each attested to the facts that not only had he spent a great period of his life in penal institutions, but he had also been a patient in a mental hospital. In addition to having a psychopathic personality and sexual difficulties, he had an IQ of only 73 and was severely retarded in his mental and social development.

It would appear that the trial judge failed to give the jury any clear direction on this evidence. In conversation about the trial some thirty years later, Matheson's counsel (the late Sir George Waller) recalled the jury as appearing horrified by the revolting details of the crime and that they might well have considered him to be some kind of monster. In any event, they reached a verdict whereby they had concluded that he was guilty of a capital crime.

The initial hearing in the Court of Criminal Appeal was before three judges (Streatfeild, Slade and Havers JJ) but the argument never progressed beyond the issue of diminished responsibility. It went nowhere on the matter of the criteria of capital murder which had so clearly perplexed the trial judge. The court was divided: Streatfeild and Havers to dismiss and Slade to allow the appeal. Accordingly, the case was adjourned to 24 March before a five-judge court to which another puisne[55] judge had been added in the person of Donovan J, with the Lord Chief Justice, Lord Goddard, presiding.[56]

---

53. As section 2(2) required.

54. In the days of capital punishment it was common for prison medical officers to appear as witnesses for the Crown where the mental state of the accused was at issue. To appear for the defence was very rare.

55. Literally meaning 'younger' in the Norman French but in this context a judge without a distinctive title.

56. Gossip reached the defence that Streatfeild went to see Goddard, saying that it was a clear

Goddard, now 81, his cadaverous appearance consistent with his Rhad-amanthine reputation as a sentencer,[57] was firm of purpose in upholding what he emphasised to be the law. The forthright wording of the judgment is worthy of close scrutiny.

> We can well understand that a jury, faced with such an appalling crime committed by a sodomite,[58] whether from jealousy or because his victim would no longer pander to his vice, would think, as would many, that such a creature ought not to live, and that consequently a verdict involving the capital sentence was the only one appropriate.[59]

He observed that, nevertheless, the court had to bear in mind the present law and referred to the fact that there had been no evidence brought by the Crown to rebut that of the three medical witnesses for the defence, and while it was for the jury and not the doctors to decide upon the issue of diminished responsibility, its verdict must be founded upon the evidence offered.[60] The language is unambiguous:

> If…no facts or circumstances appear that can displace or throw doubt on that evidence, it seems to the court that we are bound to say that a verdict of murder is unsupported by the evidence. We prefer to rely on those words of the Criminal Appeal Act 1907, rather than on the word 'unreasonable'.[61]

He went on to say:

---

case. Goddard had agreed that it was a clear case, but a clear case of diminished responsibility!

57. In 1988 Sir George Waller suggested to one of the present authors (Terence Morris), who was in the court when Goddard delivered the oral judgment in *Matheson*, that 'his bark was worse than his bite'. He had appeared before Goddard quite a number of times on the North Eastern circuit.

58. Homosexual relations between consenting adults still constituted a criminal offence at this time, being contrary to the Criminal Law Amendment Act 1885.

59. [1958] 1 WLR 474 at p.478.

60. Goddard had made the same point in the appeal of *Spriggs* [1958] 1 QB 270. In *Spriggs*, how-ever, a prison medical officer had testified for the Crown that he had found no evidence of insanity or mental abnormality in the prisoner. The appeal was dismissed and application for the Attorney-General's *fiat* to appeal to the House of Lords refused. Spriggs was reprieved three days before he was due to be hanged on 26 January 1958, four days before Matheson's conviction.

61. [1958] 1 WLR 474 at p.479.

Having regard to what we think must have affected the jury, or any body of ordinary citizens, we should not care to say that their verdict was *unreasonable* (our italics) though we feel bound to say it was not supported by the evidence.[62]

The appeal was allowed and Matheson sentenced to 20 years' imprisonment.[63] Whatever might be said of Goddard's frequent resort to what would nowadays be termed 'robust' sentencing, he was a lawyer of great stature. One might conjecture that he was not entirely unsympathetic to the view that, given what must have affected the jury as ordinary citizens confronted with the details of the crime, this 'sodomite' was a creature who ought not to be suffered to live, and that in the circumstances they had not acted 'unreasonably'. His emphasis was on the fact that the verdict was contrary to the unrebutted evidence of the defence.[64]

There was contradictory medical evidence in the not dissimilar and contemporaneous case of *Spriggs*. The trial judge in that case, Mr Justice Austin Jones, had not, the defence was to argue on appeal, given sufficient direction to the jury on the meaning of the words 'abnormality of mind' or 'mental responsibility' in section 2(1). In contrast to Mr Justice Finnemore, who had been far more forthcoming if not necessarily helpful to the jury, Mr Justice Austin Jones simply gave the jury the text of the section to interpret themselves, unaided by any judicial assistance on the subject!

The case of *Byrne* in 1959 had some similarities with that of *Matheson*. A voyeur, he had forced his way into a room in a YWCA hostel occupied by a young woman whom he then strangled, subsequently mutilating her body in a manner suggestive of the most sadistic sexual perversion. There was unrebutted evidence in support of a plea of diminished responsibility

---

62. *Ibid.*

63. It is our understanding that he was at some later stage made the subject of an order under the Mental Health Act 1959. Part V of the Act came into force on 1 November 1960 enabling both trial judges and the Court of Criminal Appeal to make hospital orders, with or without restriction, in cases of manslaughter by reason of diminished responsibility under section 2 Homicide Act 1957. In the following two years such orders were made no fewer than 81 times. See Terence Morris and Louis Blom-Cooper, *A Calendar of Murder*, London (Michael Joseph, 1964) at pp.381-384.

64. Sir George Waller recalled a vigorous cross-examination of each of the medical witnesses in an attempt to persuade the jury to discount their testimony. What, if any, effect this had on the jury we shall never know.

that he was an aggressive psychopath with a long history of gross sexual abnormality. The jury convicted him of non-capital murder and he was sentenced to life imprisonment. The ground for appeal was that the trial judge, Mr Justice Stable, had, in his interpretation of section 2 Homicide Act 1957, effectively misdirected the jury by removing from it the possibility of returning a (manslaughter) verdict under the section. The appeal court ruled that 'properly directed [the court] did not think the jury could have come to any other conclusion than that the defence of diminished responsibility was made out'.[65]

Both *Matheson* and *Byrne* illustrate that while it was for the jury to assess the medical evidence, such assessment *must be on the basis of the whole of the evidence offered.* That is also to say, where none was offered in rebuttal, the jury could only proceed on what they had. Put another way, if the scales of justice were held up and one pan was completely empty, the outcome could not be at issue. Leaving aside the question of proper judicial direction, juries needed to be reminded that it was the law alone that must be followed, uninfluenced by any moral imperative they might perceive that suggested what 'ought' to be the verdict.

The problem for the jury in *Matheson,* and again in *Byrne,* may have been at the extremities of the spectrum, but the Court of Criminal Appeal was able to put matters right. The task of finding a true verdict in a case that required an interpretation of part of a new statute, murder in the course or furtherance of theft, besides taking into account the unchallenged evidence of the defendant's mental state in relation to an equally new statutory defence, that of diminished responsibility, was challenging, to say the least. Although not capital crimes, in prosecutions for offences of an unambiguous sexual character, the partial defence of diminished responsibility was also available. In *Byrne,* no less than in *Matheson,* we have no idea of the intellectual course of the jury's deliberations, but it would appear likely that if the jurors found the details of the crimes of the defendants morally repellent, this could only have exacerbated matters.

Though it was half a century ago, there are still lessons to be learned from it, not least about the proper direction of the jury. If an example of

---

65. [1960] 2 QB 396.

complexity is needed, there are, perhaps no better examples than those of *Holley* and *Smith (Morgan)*[66] in which the Privy Council and the House of Lords arrived at opposite conclusions with the consequence of changes in the directions to be given by judges to juries[67].

Another Problem for the Jury

In January 2011, some half a century after Lord Goddard's judgment in *Matheson*, the Court of Appeal (Criminal Division) gave judgment in the case of Peter William Coonan,[68] better known as Peter Sutcliffe, the so-called 'Yorkshire Ripper' who had in 1981 been convicted of the murder of 13 women and the attempted murders of a further seven. His offences stretched over a period of five years between July 1975 and November 1980. He was arrested on 2 January 1981, carrying a hammer and a knife, in the company of a woman whom he later admitted would have been his next victim. For the 20 offences with which he was charged he was given 13 mandatory life sentences and a further seven discretionary life sentences, with a recommendation by the trial judge, Mr Justice Boreham, that he serve 30 years before he could be considered for parole.

The substance of his case in this instance was not, however, as it had been in *Matheson*, against the jury's verdict of murder,[69] but against the imposition, some 29 years later, of a 'whole life' tariff under the provisions of the Criminal Justice Act 2003 by Mr Justice Mitting, when in July 2010 the Home Secretary had made an application to the High Court for a minimum term to be set. This was subsequent to an earlier decision in October 1997 by the then Lord Chief Justice, Lord Bingham, following an application by the Home Secretary (prior to the Act) to make a recommendation as to tariff.[70]

---

66. *Smith (Morgan)* [2001] 1 AC 46 and *Holley* [2005] UKPC 23.
67. The Court of Appeal (Criminal Division) revisited the issue in *R v James* [2006] EWCA Crim 14.
68. *R v Coonan (formerly Sutcliffe)* [2011] EWCA Crim 5 (before Judge LCJ, Calvert-Smith and Griffith Williams JJ). Sutcliffe chose to adopt his mother's maiden name after his conviction.
69. That in *Matheson* had been *capital* murder with the mandatory sentence of death.
70. Should this appear confusing to the general reader it should be borne in mind that the original arrangement established at the time of abolition in 1965 was for the trial judge to make a

But with regards to a decision by the jury, *Sutcliffe* and *Matheson* have a considerable amount in common. An Old Bailey jury in 1981 was faced with evidence of crimes so appalling as almost to put even the horrific nature of Matheson's offence into the shadows; the number of Sutcliffe's offences alone would have been shocking but they were amplified in their enormity by the magnitude of the violence to which his female victims were subjected.

As in *Matheson*, the jury, notwithstanding psychiatric evidence in its support, declined to accept the defendant's plea of diminished responsibility and convicted him on 13 counts of murder. The jury may well have concluded, as perhaps had a jury at Durham Assizes some 23 years before, when confronted with crime 'of the most horrible description, so revolting as to be almost beyond belief',[71] that the defendant deserved nothing less than the most severe penalty that the criminal law could provide.

At this point, however, on the issue of diminished responsibility, the narratives of these cases diverge. In *Matheson*, it will be recalled, Lord Goddard's judgment had underscored the fact that a jury must make its decision upon all the evidence and could not ignore the uncontradicted evidence before it of the defendant's mental state. That evidence had been based upon the observations of three medical witnesses, including the medical officer of Durham Prison, called by the defence. In *Sutcliffe* the defendant maintained that in 1967 he had heard a divine voice, whilst working in a local cemetery, telling him to kill prostitutes.[72] If the defendant had indeed heard such a voice then the psychiatric inference was that he was suffering from encapsulated paranoid schizophrenia. However, as the judgment of Lord Judge CJ in *R v Coonan* states:

---

recommendation, should he see fit to do so. The concept of the 'tariff' to satisfy the needs of retribution and deterrence was later developed such that the Home Secretary took it upon himself to set the minimum term. Subsequent challenge in the ECHR resulted initially in the 'judicialisation' of the arrangement. The Criminal Justice Act 2003, Schedule 21 put the whole matter on to a statutory basis.

71. The words used by Lord Goddard in the Court of Criminal Appeal in describing Matheson's offence. See also note 58 above.

72. Though it is important to note that not all of Sutcliffe's victims were prostitutes.

But, and it is a crucial 'but', it was accepted by all the psychiatrists that the diagnosis depended on the truthfulness of the appellant's account of the divine visitation and its continuing influence over him throughout the period of these crimes.[73]

The trial judge put three key questions to the jury. Did the defendant honestly believe that 15 years before he had indeed had that experience in the cemetery? Was he deluded in his belief that he had a divine mission to exterminate prostitutes? Did he believe that when he killed, or attempted to kill, each of his victims that each of them was a prostitute? But crucially the judge reminded the jury that

The doctors all say that their diagnosis, and opinions are based, certainly in the main—I think it is fair to say almost exclusively—upon what (he) has told them...they all agree that if the defendant does not establish the truth in what he has told them, their diagnosis cannot stand.[74]

The correctness of this approach was underscored in the judgment given by Lord Lane CJ in the Court of Appeal (Criminal Division) in May 1982 in Sutcliffe's substantive appeal against conviction, who went on to add:

The matter was thrashed out at great length before the jury and the jury came to the conclusion that...this man was probably not telling the truth to the doctors and accordingly their diagnosis was falsified, though no fault of theirs.

There is no doubt that the jury were entitled to reject Sutcliffe's plea of diminished responsibility if they thought that he was not telling the truth when he spoke of a divine injunction for his offences. Yet even if they considered him to be a liar in this regard, the objective evidence of his crimes would suggest to most reasonable people that this was a seriously strange person who apparently could so readily and with such frequency cross the threshold from normal behaviour into a world of pitiless and horrific violence.

When the Lord Chief Justice, Lord Bingham, was faced with the task of making a recommendation in 1997 he consulted Mr Justice Boreham who

---

73. At para 12.
74. *Ibid*, at para 14.

replied that he now thought it would have been better to have made no minimum recommendation. Nevertheless he added:

> However that may be, I have no doubt that this is one of the rare cases where the offences were so heinous and the perpetrator so dangerous that life should mean life.[75]

While it is not clear how much written material was available to Lord Bingham (a point forcefully made by Lord Judge when declining to endorse Lord Bingham's rejection of a whole life tariff) what is clear is that Bingham took a different view. In increasing the recommended minimum to 35 years (expiring in 2016) he made an important point:

> It seems clear that when committing these crimes, Sutcliffe's mental state was disturbed, even if his responsibility for the crime was not diminished. This leads me to the conclusion that the requirements of retribution and general deterrence should be met by a term of years rather than a ruling that life should mean life. But plainly, given the number and brutality of these crimes, and their public consequences, the term should be one of exceptional length.[76]

What, of course, was not known to the jury at Sutcliffe's trial was the fact that the Crown, represented by Sir Michael Havers QC (then Attorney-General and later Lord Chancellor), had initially been prepared to accept Sutcliffe's pleas of diminished responsibility but that Mr Justice Boreham was not at all happy with that course, insisting that the Crown give a detailed explanation of its reasoning. After a lengthy submission, from which of course the jury had been absent, the judge made the point that was eventually put to the jury, that it would be for the defendant to establish the truth upon which his partial defence of diminished responsibility was founded and that this was entirely a matter for the jury.

In contrast to *Matheson*, the Court of Appeal was not in a position to rectify any error of judgment on the part of the jury. There had been no comparable error: they had heard the evidence, they had had the benefit of

---

75. Quoted in *R v Coonan* [2011] EWCA Crim 5 at para 3.
76. *Ibid*, at para 4. In the event no tariff was set and the question remained in abeyance until the application under the Criminal Justice Act 2003 in 2010.

the judge's direction and they had come to their conclusion. The convictions and the life sentences stood and continue to stand. All that has changed has been the *quantum* of the tariff attaching to them following the new legislation of 2003 for which a jury is not responsible. But none of this addresses the question of the problem faced by the Sutcliffe jury when, while there is a clear indication of some mental disturbance, such as that commented upon by Lord Bingham in 1997, the evidence suggested that it fell short of being probative of diminished responsibility.[77] The statutory definition of diminished responsibility represents a narrow conceptual defile rather than a broad opportunity to reflect upon the abnormalities of human behaviour, however gross. Yet it raises the question of how far such abnormalities are, almost *sui generis*, indicative of some necessary course of social intervention other than that of the punishment for crime, no matter its enormity. Returning to Lord Bingham's observation that if responsibility is not shown to be diminished, then the idea of the requirements of retribution and deterrence being met by a term of years prompts one to ask whether a legal concept of diminished responsibility nevertheless implies that there is room, after all, for the criminal punishment of those offenders who, while their behaviour is self-evidently abnormal fail, for whatever reason, to satisfy the legal test.[78] It is, perhaps, small wonder that juries who bring not only their prejudices but also their common-sense interpretations of human behaviour to their task are sometimes left bemused or bewildered.[79]

---

77. Which is statutorily defined as 'suffering from such abnormality of mind (whether arising from a condition of arrested or retarded development of mind or any inherent causes or induced by disease or injury) as substantially impaired his mental responsibility for his acts or omissions': Homicide Act 1957, section 2(1).

78. If Sutcliffe's original plea of diminished responsibility had been accepted he could have been admitted to secure psychiatric accommodation forthwith. That did not happen until some three years after his conviction and he has remained so confined.

79. As we explain elsewhere, the partial defence of diminished responsibility is essentially mitigation, and should be a factor in sentencing under the general rubric of mental disorder.

Assisting the Jury to a Rational Outcome

The draftsmen of the Homicide Act 1957 must surely have believed that in their choice of words they had set out the conditions governing the defence of diminished responsibility, and indeed those of the various categories of capital murder, with sufficient clarity to dispel ambiguity. Yet early in its life, the 1957 Act was to become a source of difficulty for judges and juries alike that the appeal courts were required to resolve. As with those juries who declined to convict for manslaughter in road traffic deaths before 1956, we shall never know for certain what precisely was in the minds of those juries that had to wrestle with the then new defence of diminished responsibility, or the then newly enlarged defence of provocation. But it must be recognised that the temptation to go beyond that task with which it is charged, namely returning a true verdict, cannot, even in the instance of a well-directed contemporary jury, be warranted as having been long eradicated.

Since the disappearance of the death penalty there is little danger of the problems thrown up in homicide trials like those of *Matheson* impeding the work of the jury. But trials have become no simpler. The impression of many practitioners is that they have become longer and that expert witnesses appear with greater frequency. Sudden infant deaths, and cases in which spouses or partners kill their domestic abusers, result in an increasing volume of medical evidence ranging from pædiatrics to psychiatry.

Of the defences introduced by the Homicide Act 1957, those of diminished responsibility and provocation, not least provocation by words, can continue to present difficulty, and it is certainly the case that where defence counsel might once have striven to use diminished responsibility as a means of saving a client from the gallows, it can nowadays provide a defence to protect the defendant from its alternative, imprisonment for life. Some half a century after the 1957 Act enlarged the scope of the defence of provocation, the appeal courts have remained engaged with the issue, as we discuss in *Chapter 5*.[80] As for the defence of 'self-defence', though different in character from diminished responsibility and provocation, it is equally vulnerable to

---

80. See: *Smith (Morgan)* [2001] 1 AC 46 and *Holley* [2005] UKPC 23.

being misunderstood in the process of interpretation by reason of its definition being couched in words and phrases that have a vernacular meaning.

Simplifying the Task

The work of the jury in murder trials is no longer encompassed in a matter of hours since today the jury may be required to absorb massive volumes of evidence, hear numerous witnesses — including experts giving highly technical testimony — and at the end, take on board addresses from prosecution and defence, only to be followed by judicial summing up. The contemporary trial for murder might suggest it is more relevant, perhaps, for all those concerned to rely less upon the clock than on the calendar.

Given that the present law requires a necessary conjunction of *mens rea* and *actus reus* for there to be a conviction of crime, the jury is still required to determine the defendant's intention. The jury is asked, in so many words, to be the definitive arbiter of what was in his head at the time. But nature, even in the course of her most astonishing evolutionary designs, has as yet failed to provide for any convenient inspection hatch whereby it is possible to see at a given moment what is inside a man's head, still less to get a picture of what was there at an earlier time. The best that can ever be done is to draw *inferences* from the evidence of what has been observed of the defendant's behaviour, bearing in mind that the statement of any witness, including the defendant, can be vulnerable to selective perception and recollection, never mind the pursuit of 'economy', duplicity or plain untruth.

The task of the contemporary jury embodies the need to be satisfied both as to the facts and the defendant's intention. How can juries be better assisted, thus improving the overall efficiency of criminal justice procedures?

An Instruction Manual for Juries

The average jury is highly unlikely to be comprised of individuals who, in addition to a fair knowledge of the criminal law, will, in their everyday experience settle uncertain questions in their minds by the rigorous application of scientific method from which all hint of subjective preconceptions will have been expelled. A question might then properly be asked: how far can it be ensured that the jury will be able, without any prior instruction, to think judicially? Among the more important conclusions of the Auld Report was that jurors should be presented with questions to be answered. In our view, while that is a *sine qua non*, there is a need to go further.

It is not enough simply to argue that the jury is some profoundly deep well of common-sense that can never run dry; nor that its representativeness is any warranty that it is as free from subjective prejudice as it certain to go about its task with a rigorous logic. If, as some of its enthusiasts would no doubt maintain, the jury is indeed a mirror of society at large, then the distortions to be found there are as likely to be reflected within it.

It is, however, more probable that most of the shortcomings of the jury system arise not from any negative characteristics in the men and women who have been empanelled, but from their unfamiliarity with the arcane phenomena that characterise much of the criminal justice system as a whole. Given that the possibility of training jurors along the lines similar to that of new lay magistrates is unrealistic, the alternative is to provide them with a manual. Manuals have, in ordinary life, become increasingly commonplace, some simple, others more complex. They come with washing machines, new cars, cameras, computers, telephones and television sets. Many involve instructions for setting up equipment that are based upon the algorithm, a series of steps that must be taken in a given order.

We discovered an exemplary prototype of such a manual to assist the jury in a trial[81] of a husband indicted for the murder of his wife. It was alleged that domestic altercation had taken place that had become physically violent, in the course of which the victim had died. The defendant was said to have initially put the body outside the house, subsequently taking it covertly to a local wood where he left it hidden. It was said that some days later he returned to the wood and concealed the body more effectively, though not so well as to prevent its discovery by a dog after a further elapse of time. Meanwhile, the defendant had appeared on local television maintaining that his wife had gone missing.

---

81. At Winchester Crown Court.

In the course of the trial, several defences and partial defences were raised, including accident, self-defence, lack of intent to kill or cause really serious harm, and provocation. The trial judge,[82] mindful of the complexities of the situation furnished the jury with a brief *vade mecum* of the law of murder and a step-by-step manual of procedure. But how much simpler would be the task if the judge did not have to tell the jury that they had to identify an intention on the part of the defendant when establishment of his *knowledge* in the circumstances, of what he was doing and the probable consequences, would suffice; if he did not have to explain the distinction between murder and manslaughter at common law (Lord Parker's 'fine lines and distinctions') and did not have to deal at all with the partial defences of provocation and diminished responsibility leading to yet other species of manslaughter created by the Homicide Act 1957?

Transparency in Jury Verdicts

There is a strong, essentially Utilitarian, case for maintaining the jury in trials for criminal homicide that needs no support from any constitutional or historical embellishment. So long as there are no reliable research findings as to how juries actually function, and suggesting the contrary, we must assume that, as a mode of trial, the jury system delivers as good a quality of criminal justice as any possible alternative to trial by a professional tribunal. On the surface, at least, juries seem to work well; the legal profession on the whole supports the jury system, as indeed does the public by continuing to exhibit its confidence. But like almost all established institutions, it is capable of improvement, more particularly in the way in which the jury is asked to perform its task.

Juries need to have a brief but reliable statement of the law to which they can refer after retiring to consider their verdict, something that could well reduce the need to return to put questions to the trial judge. In practice though, while juries are normally well served in this regard, they may not necessarily be *equally* well served.[83] By working through the algorithmic series

---

82. His Honour Judge Guy Boney QC.
83. In the past, juries were not infrequently subject to what might be termed a 'circuit' (as distinct

of questions asked, and for the relevant answers to be given by the foreman in open court, the jury's reasoning would acquire complete transparency. Concluding with its verdict, it would set out for all to see not merely the verdict, but the process by which that verdict has been reached. If it became evident that a stage has been omitted, a direction clearly misunderstood, or the algorithm wrongly followed, then the error would be immediately apparent and could be appropriately addressed. The benefit of such transparency would be a reduction in the need for some verdicts to be subsequently (and expensively) examined by the appellate process.

Transparency has important implications for defendants' rights under Article 6 of the European Convention on Human Rights. More than 40 years ago, in a case at Strasbourg, the Commission stated:

> Where the convicted person has the possibility of an appeal, the lower Court must state in detail the reasons for its decision, so that in an appeal from that decision the accused's right may be properly safeguarded.[84]

If, half a century ago, the juries in *Matheson* and *Spriggs* had enjoyed the benefit of both a *vade mecum* and an algorithmic model of decision-making they would not have been left to their own devices with regard to how they should understand what was meant by 'murder in the course or furtherance of theft' or 'diminished responsibility', and, no less importantly, they would have been in no doubt that they were not only bound when considering the issue of diminished responsibility, recognising it to be central to the defence, but also to consider the issue solely on the basis of the evidence they had heard.[85] Before the jury retired it would have been made abundantly clear that while it was for them to decide whether the defendant was or was not suffering from diminished responsibility, their decision had to be founded

---

from 'postcode') lottery in this respect.

84. *X v Federal Republic of Germany*, case 1035/61 of 17 June 1963 (1963) 6 Yearbook 180-192. See also Jacobs and White, *The European Convention on Human Rights* (4th ed.) Oxford (OUP, 2006) at p.179.

85. To be fair to the individual judges in these cases, the Homicide Act 1957 was far from clear in certain aspects and a novel departure from what had gone before. Moreover, it could be said that the past was very much 'Another Country' in which judges were expected to find their own way.

upon the evidence given by the doctors. Unrebutted, their verdict would have needed to be based upon that evidence alone, however unappealing they personally might have found its consequences to be. It would not have fallen to the Lord Chief Justice to make the point after the Court of Appeal had been obliged to consider the matter, not once but twice.

Transparency and Human Rights

The question of transparency is an important dimension of the Human Rights Act 1998 insofar as it relates to the notion of a 'fair' trial. But the reasoning that lies behind a jury verdict, unlike other judicial decisions, has in the past been not only *terra incognita* but also *terra prohibita*. However, trial by judge and jury, in which the trial judge directs the jury on issues of law and sums up the facts in the case, is apparently compliant with a fair trial under Article 6. That would appear to be the result of the decision in *Taxquet v Belgium*, decided unanimously by the Grand Chamber of 17 judges of the European Court of Human Rights on 16 November 2010. Although a fair trial requires a reasoned verdict from the jury, a properly structured direction and summing-up provides adequate safeguards for the totality of the trial. The absence of a summing-up of the facts in *Taxquet* rendered the unarticulated verdict of guilty non-compliant with the Convention.

The only doubt about compliance with Article 6 by an English jury trial is whether or not the required safeguards of judicial directions and summing-up must be in writing. The Lord Chief Justice in an address to the Judicial Studies Board (Northern Ireland) has expressed the view that jury decisions as to written directions and written steps are matters for the judgment of the trial judge. Oral instructions may suffice. The resolution of any uncertainty about compliance will now presumably depend on what transpires in particular cases, with the possibility of further excursions to Strasbourg not excluded. While it would nevertheless appear to be the case that the absence of an articulated verdict from the jury, by itself, is not crucial, the question for the rational lawyer may be that ratiocination (the process of reasoning) can come only from the mouth of the decision-maker. No matter how explicit may be the process of supplying the material for the reasoned decision; that alone cannot suffice. Moreover, since Article 6 does not specifically call for the handing-down or pronouncement by the jury of a reasoned judgment, *Taxquet* leaves trial by an English jury to all intents untouched for the time being save for minor modification by way of the discourse between judge and jury.[86]

Researching the Jury System

The private deliberations of the jury, in contrast to the criminal trial itself, are conducted in total secrecy, an inviolability that is properly protected by law no less than are individual jurors from any improper approach during the trial that might affect its impartiality. But this impenetrable shroud extends beyond both trial, sentence and any appeal, such that it remains unlawful for anyone to attempt to 'get behind' the jury's verdict by asking questions of those who comprised it. Still less, as we have seen from *Scotcher*, the desire to set right a perceived wrong to the defendant provides no defence.

As a consequence, all attempts to discover how juries might work are largely limited to research by simulation.[87] As a research method, simulation has value, but also limitations. Sophisticated electronics can allow driving behaviour to be tested in the laboratory rather than the road, but even the most sophisticated equipment cannot be a perfect substitute for the reality. Similarly, it may be possible to simulate to a considerable degree the environment of the jury room at a particular time, but scarcely that of an entire trial that in homicide cases may go on for weeks.

Perhaps the only certain way of observing the jury at work would be for a jury room — chosen at random — to be equipped with hidden cameras and

---

86. This will, no doubt, come as some comfort to those disposed to conclude that *any* modification to the laws of England must inevitably be deleterious.

87. At the time of writing the latest research, usefully demolishing some of the more popular myths about the jury, has been carried out by the University of Birmingham School of Law for the Ministry of Justice. Cheryl Thomas with Nigel Balmer, *Diversity and Fairness in the Jury System*, Ministry of Justice Research Series 2/07 (June 2007). There is a considerable body of earlier research to which reference may be found in the published volume of papers presented to a Cropwood Conference in December 1974: Nigel Walker and Annette Pearson (ed.), *The British Jury System*, Cambridge (University of Cambridge Institute of Criminology, 1975).

microphones[88] that would record what went on; not that such research would be other than ethically dubious even if it were legally possible. Research on some aspects of the jury, such as selection, and conviction rates with respect to particular crimes, is undoubtedly useful, but our concern is with another question, namely that of establishing transparency and ensuring rationality in respect of the decision-making function of the jury. To satisfy Article 6 of the European Convention a defendant must have the fair trial before an independent and impartial tribunal that the Article established as his right. The final test of impartiality of a jury verdict is not in some way to monitor or reconstruct the behaviour of its members that is hidden from public view, but rather, for the jury, in presenting its verdict, to give structured reasons for it, including an account of the steps by which the process was completed. None of this would violate the privacy of the jury's deliberations, but would go far to satisfy the spirit of Article 6.

If the transparency of jury verdicts can be assured, attempts to discover how juries work go about their task become superfluous. Provided juries are presented with a clear set of instructions about how to proceed and the results are presented in detail in open court along with the verdict, the difficulty presently arising from Article 6(2) of the Convention is resolved.

Article 6(2) provides a general obligation on courts to give reasons for their judgments, a clear amplification of the quality of fairness that both informs and is embodied in the Convention. It applies to magistrates (who are responsible for both verdict and sentence) but not to juries in the Crown Court.[89] Where a jury verdict sheds no light upon why a partial defence has been rejected, or why it has opted for, say, manslaughter rather than murder, a potential appellant is disadvantaged by being forced to rely on nothing but conjecture in this regard, notwithstanding that it is their decision that he seeks to challenge. We find it difficult to identify the logic whereby both magistrates' and appellate courts are under a duty to give reasons, the critical deliberations of both tribunals being, like those of the jury, conducted

---

88. A sound recording alone, while it would record the nuances of speech, would provide no indication of the body language of the participants, often a not insignificant dimension in the analysis of human behaviour.

89. This remains the case notwithstanding the incorporation of Convention principles into domestic law by the Human Rights Act 1998. To the present writers this appears not merely anomalous but irrational.

in private, while juries are held to be *sui generis* in this respect. Quite simply, we cannot see why, if the jury has conducted itself according to its oath, to lay out its reasoning in public could in any way prejudice its integrity or independence. It surely could not do other than reinforce compliance with Article 6(2) if a jury were to indicate in open court the steps by which it had reached its verdict by answering an algorithmic questionnaire.

The principal difference from the present arrangements would be that instead of the jury needing to affirm a unanimous (or permitted majority) verdict only once, its members would need to be at one in respect of *all* the questions that needed to be answered in order to arrive at the verdict, notwithstanding that they had come to agreement by different routes.

The machinery of criminal justice has undergone many positive developments since Sir James Fitzjames Stephen could write disparagingly of jurymen as being typified as ordinary tradesmen and yeomen farmers, of short attention span, more at home discussing fatstock prices than dealing with the evidence in criminal trials,[90] and when a Court of Criminal Appeal had yet to be invented. Although Stephen was referring to juries confronted by expert evidence, his description of the jury is scarcely a flattering testimonial to its competence in criminal matters generally. Yet how far the 19th century jury normally inhabited the fictional world of *Jarndyce v Jarndyce* is, of course, arguable, and Stephen was, admittedly, at times given to a hyperbolic style of expression. But even if it bore some resemblance to what might have been a reality in the Victorian period, it bears none to the present. Indeed, it can be argued that things have moved on considerably in our own time. A jury in 2011 is different in many respects from its counterpart in 1961.[91] The replacement of the membership qualifications of the 1870 Act by universal suffrage has resulted in a much more representative social mix, including not only women but those who in the past might have been suspected as coming from the 'lower', and therefore more potentially disaffected, orders of society.

---

90. *Trial by Jury and the Evidence of Experts*, XIV. Proceedings of the Juridical Society 1858-1863 vol. 1, at p.23.

91. Not only is this true of juries. As recently as the late 1960s, members of the Magistrates' Association continued to be exercised as to whether women justices should wear hats in court.

Perhaps more importantly, the ordinary juror is better educated and better informed and perhaps less uncritically deferential towards the professionals in the courtroom. This may well be an explanation of why views about the exclusion of certain categories of professionals from jury service that were held at the time of the Morris review have little, if any, currency today. And whatever view might be held of the utility of trial by jury as a means of determining criminal guilt, the reality is that the jury is here to stay. The challenge is to ensure its fitness for purpose.

CHAPTER 15

THE APPELLATE PROCESS: EQUALITY OF ARMS

Although our argument is for a fundamental change in the existing law relating to all homicides, and the abolition of the mandatory life sentence for murder, we would expect no legislative change in the present arrangements relating to questions of conviction, save for that of the consequence of a conviction being quashed on appeal and no fresh trial being ordered. The question of sentence, however, raises issues of a very different order.

Presently, since a conviction for murder carries the fixed sentence of life imprisonment, it follows that there is no appeal against sentence. But if, as we would argue, the courts were to have the power to pass a range of sentences, appropriate to the culpability of the offender, taken together with other considerations of public policy that must form part of any rational approach to sentencing, neither the type, nor the duration of any particular sentence may be deemed satisfactory by either party to the matter. The defendant may consider that the penalty is too harsh; the prosecutor that it is too lenient. It may be that a particular sentence arouses strong public feeling which cannot sensibly be ignored. The present arrangements for appeals by the Crown against a sentence are limited by way of a reference by the Attorney-General to the Court of Appeal (Criminal Division); they relate solely to the ground that the sentence has been unduly lenient. Our view is that the powers of the Court of Appeal in this respect are deserving of more ample application. While the court should continue to address the issue of undue leniency as it is understood at present, it could be usefully extended to the appropriateness of a particular sentence. The term 'leniency', however, is capable of a variety of interpretations. It is essentially subjective. The answer you get will depend upon whom you ask — be it the prosecutor, the convicted person, the family of the victim(s) of the homicide, the ordinary member of the local community, or the public generally. The answers will rarely accord with one another.

We would not consider that sentencing at large for the proposed offence of criminal homicide should be confined within the sorts of 'starting points' that are enshrined in Schedule 21 to the Criminal Justice Act 2003, for the judiciary would, in due course, under the influence of the Sentencing Guidance Council, develop and establish patterns of sentencing that were appropriate. The review process, with its opportunities for the consideration of extensive argument, provides the appropriate forum of opportunity. While the trial judge would, no doubt, pass an appropriate sentence in the majority of cases, there would always be those in which closer scrutiny of the matter would be necessary. Given that the penalty for the new offence of criminal homicide would be at large, it follows that in many, indeed most cases, the Court of Appeal would deem the proper sentence to be one of a substantial term of imprisonment. In those cases where the future behaviour of the offender was difficult, if not, impossible, to predict, it would be likely that the court would consider the indeterminate sentence of life imprisonment to be the most appropriate penalty. We considered the proposition that defendant and prosecutor should both be equally entitled to an automatic right of appeal, but conclude that the present arrangement whereby a reference by the Attorney-General to the Court of Appeal is available on the ground of undue leniency, remains a simpler course. But because homicide is a matter of such gravity, it might well be necessary for special consideration to be given to sentencing in this instance, since the term 'leniency' will need to be examined in the light of all the circumstances of a criminal event which, while its seriousness is in no way diminished, may vary in its details very widely indeed.

But we think that something more needs to be done in order to underpin public confidence in the sentencing of homicide offenders. There is little or no virtue in maintaining the strict position that the Crown is not permitted to engage in advocacy for a particular penal sanction. The principle enshrined in Article 6 of the European Convention on Human Rights is that in matters of sentence, as well as in the trial of the substantive offence, there must be equality of arms. This entails the prosecution having an equal right of appeal against the sentence passed by the trial judge. Sentencing of all homicide cases would then be under the consistent control of the Lord Chief Justice and his colleagues in the appellate court.

Acquittal, Quashed Convictions and Innocence

An outcrop from the spate of miscarriages of justice in murder prosecutions in the latter part of the 20th century has been the voluble clamour by successful appellants (and accused persons acquitted by the jury) that they are innocent of the crime charged. The clamour stems from the undoubted principle that everyone accused of a crime is presumed innocent until proved guilty. But that principle is strictly evidential — that is to say, within the criminal process the burden of establishing the defendant's guilt rests throughout on the prosecution, and is displaced only if and when the jury brings in a guilty verdict. Outwith the criminal justice system, it has no application. But if the accused is acquitted, or his conviction is quashed on appeal, should there nevertheless follow, at least in certain circumstances, the conclusive proof of innocence?

Social policy can be ascertained from the state of the English criminal procedure today. Section 2(3) Criminal Appeal Act 1968 provides:

> An order of the Court of Appeal quashing a conviction shall, except when under section 7 below the appellant is ordered to be retried, operate as a direction to the court of trial to enter, instead of the record of conviction, a judgment and verdict of acquittal.

The successful appellant is thus in the same position as if he had been acquitted by a jury. He cannot be tried again for the offence of which a jury could have convicted him on that indictment, subject to the very limited exception under the Criminal Justice Act 2003, that a person acquitted may be tried again only if there comes to light fresh and compelling evidence indicating criminal responsibility. The double jeopardy rule has been marginally modified.

According to a controversial passage in *Sambasivam v Public Prosecutor, Malaya*[1] Lord Macdermott, giving the judgment of the Privy Council, stated:

> The effect of a verdict of acquittal…is not completely stated by saying that the

---

1.   [1950] AC 458, at 479.

person cannot be tried again for the same offence. To that it must be added that the verdict is binding and conclusive in all subsequent proceedings between the parties to the adjudication. The maxim *res judicata pro veritae accipitur* is no less applicable to criminal than to civil proceedings.

Assuming that to be a correct statement of the law, it marks the limit of the effect of an acquittal: the acquittal is binding and conclusive *between the parties to the adjudication,* that is, between the prosecution and the acquitted person. It is not binding and conclusive between the acquitted person and anyone else, or between the prosecution and anyone else. If A has been acquitted of an offence, the prosecution may subsequently indict B for aiding, abetting, counselling or procuring to commit that offence and, at the trial of B, adduce evidence and prove that A was in fact guilty of the offence of which he has been acquitted. A's acquittal is not admissible in evidence at the trial of B.[2] Where A and B are alleged to have conspired together to commit an offence, and there is evidence admissible against B (for example a confession) which is inadmissible against A, the jury may properly convict B of conspiring with A while acquitting A of conspiring with B.[3] This is so whether A and B are tried together, or B is tried after A's acquittal.

Since a jury is invariably directed that it must not convict unless the jurors are sure of the accused's guilt, the only safe deduction from a verdict of acquittal is that the jury was not 'sure'. A jury which is satisfied only that it is more probable than not that the accused is guilty, or even that it is highly probable that he is guilty, will acquit so long as it loyally follows the direction of the judge, as it is strictly bound to do. So, in 1967, the Lord Chancellor's Law Reform Committee, having considered whether acquittals should be admitted in evidence, rightly concluded:

So the acquittal, if admitted for 'what it is worth', would be worth nothing: not only would it have no effect on the onus of proof but it would be without any probative value.[4]

---

2. *Hui Chi-ming v R* [1992] 1 AC 34, a decision of the Privy Council.
3. *DPP v Shannon* [1975] AC 717, a decision of the House of Lords.
4. Fifteenth Report, Cmnd 3391 (1967), para 15.

The committee recommended that, on grounds of public policy, *defamation proceedings* should be treated differently, and that proof of an acquittal should be conclusive proof of innocence. Parliament did not accept that recommendation; the law has remained as it was in *R v Loughrans Press*.[5] In that case the defendants stated that the plaintiff was guilty of a murder of which he had been acquitted 20 years earlier. The defendants successfully pleaded the defence of justification, proving on the balance of probabilities that he had committed the offence. Since the law of libel now permits a public interest defence to an author who comments that an acquitted person is not instinctively innocent of criminal responsibility[6] there is no need for Parliamentary intervention.

It is the same when the Court of Appeal quashes a conviction as when a jury acquits. Until 1996 the Court was required to quash a conviction if it thought it was 'unsafe or unsatisfactory', and in any other case to dismiss the appeal. The fact that the court quashed a conviction did not mean, however, that it necessarily thought the appellant was innocent of the crime. Quite the reverse, the court may have been quite sure that he was guilty, but have held that the conviction was nevertheless 'unsafe or unsatisfactory' because of some defect in the trial or pre-trial proceedings. This was most strikingly illustrated in the case of *Algar*[7] where the court quashed the conviction because inadmissible (but relevant and reliable) evidence had been admitted at the trial. The Lord Chief Justice, Lord Goddard, was reported to have said to the appellant who was present in court:

> Do not think we are doing this because we think that you are an innocent man. We do not. We think you are a scoundrel.[8]

To like effect was the judgment of the Court of Appeal (Criminal Division) in *R v Davis, Rose and Another*. Lord Justice Mantell ended the Court's judgment by saying that the quashing of the conviction did not mean that the appellants were innocent, 'far from it'.

---

5.   [1965] CLY 2007.
6.   *Reynolds v Times Newspapers Ltd* [2001] 2 AC 127.
7.   [1954] 1 QB 279.
8.   *The Times* Law Reports, 16 November 1953.

The conclusion is that an acquittal, whether by jury or by the quashing of a conviction by the Court of Appeal, is of no value whatever in English law, except as between the Crown and the acquitted person.[9]

In the Criminal Appeal Act 1995 Parliament accepted the view of the Lord Chief Justice, Lord Taylor of Gosforth, that 'unsafe' and 'unsatisfactory' could conveniently be expressed under the single rubric 'unsafe'. By coalescing the two concepts — 'unsatisfactory' relating to procedural irregularities in the trial process, and 'unsafe' relating to the impropriety of the verdict of guilt — the law obscures the case of the truly innocent from the case of the person acquitted on technical or procedural grounds.

In April 2004, in the case of *Mullen*,[10] the House of Lords comprehensively dispelled the notion that a miscarriage of justice (or an acquittal) inevitably involves an assertion of innocence of the crime. Lord Bingham of Cornhill observed that:

> The expression 'wrongful convictions' is not a legal term of art and has no settled meaning. Plainly the expression includes the conviction of those who are innocent of the crime of which they have been convicted. But in ordinary parlance the expression would, I think, be extended to those who, whether guilty or not, should clearly not have been convicted at their trials. It is impossible and unnecessary to identify the manifold reasons why a defendant may have been convicted when he should not have been. It may be because the evidence against him was fabricated or perjured. It may be because flawed expert evidence was relied on to secure conviction. It may be because evidence helpful to the defence was concealed or withheld. It may be because the jury was the subject of malicious interference. It may be because of judicial unfairness or misdirection. In cases of this kind, it may, or more often may not, be possible to say that he has been wrongly convicted. The common factor in such cases is that something has gone seriously wrong in the investigation of the offence or the conduct of the trial, resulting in the conviction of someone who should not have been convicted.

---

9. See *Allison v Her Majesty's Advocate* [2010] UKSC 6.
10. *R v Secretary of State for the Home Department (Appellant) ex parte Mullen (Respondent)* [2004] UKHL 18.

Lord Steyn interpreted the words 'miscarriage of justice' in section 133 Criminal Justice Act 1988 (dealing with the right to compensation for wrongful conviction) as extending only to those acquitted who were 'clearly innocent'. Since the case of *Mullen* involved an abuse of executive power in breaching the principles of extradition, and hence was a factor external to the trial process in that the defendant had incontestably been convicted of terrorist offences, there was no conceivable basis for statutory compensation. All five Law Lords agreed that the case could not, in any event, fall within either meaning of 'miscarriage of justice'; the difference of approach taken by Lord Bingham and Lord Steyn remains unresolved.

We think that some regard should be paid to the popular (non-legal) view that an acquittal might be equated with innocence. There is a need to underscore public confidence in the working of the criminal justice system for there to be a clear indication of why the conviction has been set aside. Thus, on a conviction being quashed, the Court of Appeal should make clear whether in that case the successful applicant can properly claim that his acquittal is proof of his innocence for all purposes. Alternatively, it should indicate how some defect makes it necessary for the conviction to be set aside. Lord Bingham's list is comprehensive enough to provide a template for such statements. Lord Goddard's direct, if exasperated, language in addressing the appellant in *Algar* is no doubt indicative of his awareness of the problem half a century ago. The problem persists.

It would not be desirable, or even practicable, for a jury in acquitting an accused to state publicly why it had done so, even if it was required only to state briefly the grounds. The only possible amendment to the law would be for the appellate court to adopt the equivalent of the Scottish verdict of 'not proven', which we do not think would suffice to meet the clear distinction between complete innocence and a failed conviction. But the Court of Appeal is quite capable of articulating the precise reasons for quashing a conviction. It should start to do so, without being prompted by the legislature.

All the judges who staff the Court of Appeal (Criminal Division) would readily testify to the inordinate amount of time spent—both in and out of court—in pursuit of fine distinctions between murder and manslaughter, not to mention the problems associated with the partial defences of provocation (now los of self-control) and diminished responsibility. The cost in terms of judicial manpower and associated legal services at the Royal Courts of Justice is immense. That is not to overlook similarly needless exercises in the Crown Court up and down the country where judges, lawyers and jurors wrestle with like problems at trial. The precise expenditure of public funds, whatever it may be, has never been quantified. But whatever the magnitude of the cost, the expenditure could be better deployed elsewhere in improving the efficiency and effectiveness of criminal justice. At the stroke of the legislative pen, our proposals would produce a huge saving in costs.

CHAPTER 16

WHAT AND HOW LONG IS 'LIFE'?

Historical Perspective

When in 1965 Parliament came to legislate for the alternative to the death penalty for murder, it is reasonable to assume that: (a) the sponsors of the Private Members Bill (Mr Sydney Silverman MP and Lady Wootton of Abinger); (b) the Labour Government (which orchestrated the Parliamentary process, having included in its election manifesto in 1964 a commitment to abolish capital punishment for murder); and (c) the parliamentarians who voted on the Bill at various stages, were all aware of the background to the sentence of life imprisonment. Long before abolition, the mandatory sentence of life imprisonment had included a system for the release of life sentence prisoners and recall to prison by executive action, together with a developing practice that life sentence prisoners should be released on licence after serving a finite term of years.

What was that awareness? At least since the Homicide Act 1957, with the introduction of non-capital murder, the mandatory sentence of life imprisonment had included a system for the release of life sentence prisoners and their recall to prison, together with a developing practice that life sentence prisoners should be released on licence after serving a finite term of years. Officials in the Home Office had operated until 1967 an exclusively administrative regime for determining how long prisoners remained in custody. (It was in practice a liberally-administered system. In 1965 a life sentence prisoner could expect on average (strictly, a mean) to serve nine years; today it would be 16 years.)

The death penalty for murder was statutorily declared by the Offences Against the Person Act 1861. Just as the Royal Prerogative of Mercy had been used during the early part of the 19th century to commute the death sentence to one of life imprisonment in respect of a wide range of crimes which were labelled felonies, for which capital punishment remained by law the fixed penalty, so too section 1 of the 1861 Act provided that the mandatory penalty for murder was sentence of death; the process of reprieve was used to mitigate the harshness of the penal law. But the prerogative power was not deployed by the Secretaries of State inflexibly: the historical cadastral indicates that the period of imprisonment was occasionally stated in terms of years as the substitution for the death penalty. In the famous case of *Dudley and Stephens*,[1] Sir William Harcourt, as Home Secretary, commuted the sentence of the two shipwrecked crew members who cannibalised the cabin boy just before being rescued to a term of six months' imprisonment. Before 1965 there had always been an identifiable group of lifers within the prison system who were subject to the release and recall system. The system was re-affirmed in the Homicide Act 1957, which in section 9(1) provided that 'when the court … is precluded from passing sentence of death [as in the case of non-capital murders, created under the Act as a species of murder] the death sentence shall be one of imprisonment for life'. Prior to partial abolition of the death penalty in 1957, and likewise from 1957 to 1965, the experience had been that the sentence of life imprisonment had never been carried out literally, although there were cases of lifers dying in prison. Sir Ernest Gowers, the chairman of the Royal Commission on Capital Punishment, 1949-1953, wrote in 1968 that

> a life sentence is never carried out literally. Convicts have died in prison, but there is no recorded case in which it has been decided that a prisoner shall be kept in prison until he dies.[2] [surely a negation of 'whole life']

That endorses the view that the life sentence was never equated with life-long incarceration, or imprisonment for an indefinite period; it always contemplated potential release on licence after a term of years determined by executive Government. That the system has invariably drawn a distinction between the automatic sentence by the court of life imprisonment and the

---

1. *R v Dudley and Stephens* [1884] 14 QBD 273.
2. *A Life for a Life?* (1968), p.125.

period of actual incarceration could be discerned from the wording of section 1(2) Murder (Abolition of the Death Penalty) Act 1965 (repealed under the Criminal Justice Act 2003). The subsection provided for a highly restrictive judicial involvement on how long the individual murderer should spend in custody. The judge was given a power to declare in open court the minimum period that he or she thought should elapse before release on licence could be effected by the prison authorities. Livingstone, Owen and Macdonald in their work *Prison Law*[3] commented that section 1(2) 'would have been meaningless if "life" meant lifelong detention in custody'. It is true that judges occasionally did state publicly that, in passing the mandatory sentence of life imprisonment, the convicted murderer (and presumably the public in court) must understand that 'life' meant literally what it said. Clearly, such pronouncements could not have formed part of a minimum recommendation under section 1(2), but were made extra-judicially by a trial judge. A lifelong imprisonment did not accord with the system pre-1965 and was not intended by Parliament so to provide thereafter. Apart from unauthorised judicial observations, there had been no statement judicially on the construction of section 1(1) of the 1965 Act until the challenge by Myra Hindley of her continued detention in prison beyond the period recommended by the Parole Board, with the Home Secretary retaining the power, other than in exceptional circumstances, to impose a 'whole-life' tariff on the convicted murderer. Her challenge failed to establish any unlawfulness in the Home Secretary's exercise of his statutory power to determine how long the prisoner should remain in custody.

When the judicial review came before the Divisional Court (Lord Bingham of Cornhill CJ, Hooper and Astill JJ) the Lord Chief Justice said:

> One can readily accept that in requiring a sentence of imprisonment for life on all those convicted of murder Parliament did not intend 'sentence' to mean what it said in all or even a majority of cases, but there is nothing to suggest that Parliament intended that it should never (even leaving considerations of risk aside) mean what it said.[4]

---

3. (4rd ed., OUP, 2008) para 14.12. p.568.
4. [1998] QB 751, at 769 B-C.

Hooper and Astill JJ did not demur. When the case came before the Court of Appeal (before Lord Woolf MR, Hutchinson and Judge LJJ) the Divisional Court was upheld, and Judge LJ specifically agreed with the Lord Chief Justice on the potential for 'life' including a whole life. Judge LJ said:

> There is no value in further elaboration. The language of the statute is clear…the *sentence* [present author's italics] is life imprisonment. In my judgment the possibility remains that for the purposes of deterrence and punishment alone, the criminal culpability involved in some cases of murder may lawfully permit imprisonment for life in accordance with the actual sentence pronounced by the trial judge.[5]

Earlier in his judgment Judge LJ (now Lord Judge CJ), when alluding to the Parliamentary debates in 1965 that engaged the attention of abolitionists and retentionists on the issue of the death penalty, considered that 'the analysis adds nothing to the language of the section which is simple and clear'.[6] There is simplicity in the phraseology of the Parliamentary draftsman's language, but clarity is provided only as and when the historical background is understood and Parliamentary appreciation is properly assessed. By the use of the phrase, 'shall be sentenced to imprisonment for life', Parliament intended to impose only an interference with the convicted murderer's liberty (whether that liberty was restricted to the time in prison or in the community on licence) for the rest of his or her natural life. Parliament did not intend that the mandatory sentence of life imprisonment at the time of its pronouncement should ever involve a lifetime in prison, although the sentence might very well contemplate that the tariff (or the minimum recommended period before release) would be of such a length that the convicted person might die in prison. On a statutory construction, the 'sentence' is distinguishable both conceptually and in practice from time spent in custody. As Lord Wilberforce said in *Kennedy v Spratt*,[7] there is a clear distinction between passing a sentence of imprisonment and ordering that the sentence shall not take effect, 'a distinction recognised in England and reflected in the language of Parker LCJ in *O'Keefe*'. The former is now

---

5.   [2000] QB 152, at 154.
6.   *Ibid*, at 182.
7.   [1971] 2 WLR 667 at 678.

exclusively a judicial function: only the trial judge can pass sentence. How long the 'lifer' spends in custody is a matter for decision, post-conviction and post-sentence.

Apart from reliance on the minimum recommendation in section 1(2) of the 1965 Act as an aid to statutory construction, and taking full account of the historical background to the life sentence system, there are other pointers to interpretation that preclude a 'whole-life' sentence being statutorily authorised, such as the parallel situation in the mental health legislation.

Under sections 60 and 65 Mental Health Act 1959 (replicated in sections 37 and 40 Mental Health Act 1983) the Crown Court may make a hospital order if it finds that the person convicted before it is suffering from a mental disorder which is of a nature or degree rendering it appropriate for treatment in hospital; and, for present purposes, the court may place a restriction order on any discharge of the patient. Having regard to the nature of the criminal offence, the offender's antecedents and the risk of further offences being committed if the patient is at large, the court may impose a restriction order, *either without limit of time* or during such period 'specified in the restriction order'. Many defendants to charges of murder who after 1957 successfully pleaded diminished responsibility were made the subject of hospital orders with restriction on discharge 'without limit of time'. If Parliament in 1965 — only a clutch of years after the 1959 Mental Health Act — had intended to ensure that life sentence prisoners could face on conviction a lifelong incarceration, the mental health system pointed the way to provide for such a situation; legislative replication was clearly at hand. Parliament in 1965 plainly did not adopt that solution.

To those now assessing retrospectively what Parliament intended by way of replacement of the death penalty by life imprisonment might take note of contemporary policy relating to the release of prisoners from custody. When Parliament introduced, for the first time, a statutory scheme of parole, there was not a hint of any emulation of the American notion of a life sentence without benefit of parole. Indeed, life sentence prisoners were entitled to the same benefit of parole as were prisoners serving long determinate sentences of imprisonment. Had Parliament intended in 1965 to contemplate 'whole-life' tariffs for some of the most serious murderers (Ian Brady and Myra Hindley, convicted in 1966, must have been foremost in the minds of policy-makers and legislators) it could easily have provided for them in the Criminal Justice Act 1967. At no time has the 'whole-life' tariff been statutorily authorised, until the Criminal Justice Act 2003. But even then, the applicability of a 'whole-life' tariff is introduced only as a part of the guidelines set out in Schedule 21 to the Act in the graduated list of categories of murder. The Act repeats in section 269 that the penalty for murder is the mandatory sentence of life imprisonment, as envisaged in the 1965 legislation.

In essence, the meaning of life imprisonment in the 1965 Act imported, by implication, the system of release on licence and potential recall of prisoners serving the indeterminate sentence, if only because at the time that system had been employed in relation to commuted sentences from 1861 onwards; it was assimilated into the non-capital cases from 1957 to 1965. The system of licensing life sentence prisoners, both pre-Criminal Justice Act 1967 and post that Act, was legislatively bolted on to the penalty structure: it was not an element of the penalty, but a discrete parole system.

'Whole Life' Today

What must surely concern us most is that the Act of 2003 gives legitimacy to the expression of a view that ought to be repugnant in any civilised society: the view that it is acceptable to sentence a person to what constitutes entombment for life, a literal immuring within prison walls, on the ground, not of credible public danger, but of imputed moral desert. No matter that the offender may have the capacity for change or may in fact change, no matter that the passage of years and physical degeneration may render the offender's condition no different from that of any other elderly person who is in need of long-term personal and nursing care: for that offender the prison door is as surely shut as if it had been bricked up, leaving no more than an aperture through which a coffin might pass.

Is it not inhumane treatment to say of anyone that he or she will never leave prison alive? Civil death is the prescription of populist politics. The reformer's plea, though it may at times be drowned in the clamour of those who would, one suspects, be not averse to the return of the gallows, must be for a straightforward penalty for murder, determined appropriately by the judge, with a maximum of life imprisonment, the sentence to be subject to review on appeal to which offender and prosecutor would have equal and unfettered access.

R v Bieber [8] raised the very issue directly of whether a whole life tariff violated Article 3 (and possibly Article 5) of the European Convention on Human Rights. Is the 'whole life' sentence disproportionate and arbitrary? The question is resolved by answering a further question: does one test the matter at the moment of the court passing sentence, or is it the consequent detention that is alone susceptible to an Article 3 or 5 challenge? If it is the latter, violation takes place only if the period of detention is irreducible — that is to say, there is no means for effecting a discharge from custody during the prisoner's lifetime. In *Bieber* the court found that the Secretary of State possessed a limited power to release a life prisoner, and so there was no violation. But the court was, we think, wrong to proceed on the footing that it was the consequent detention of a life sentence that attracted the provisions of Article 3. It is the impact of the judicially-pronounced sentence that counts. To be told that the prisoner will never be allowed his liberty — in modern terminology, life without benefit of parole — is inhumane treatment. The argument for asserting disproportionality in the whole life sentence was never more powerfully advanced than by Lord Justice Laws in *R (Ralston Wellington) v Secretary of State for the Home Department.* [9] He stated:

> The abolition of the death penalty has been lauded, and justified, in many ways; but it must have been founded at least on the premise that the life of every person, however depraved, has an inalienable value. The destruction of a life may be accepted in some special circumstances, such as self-defence or just war; but retributive punishment is never enough to justify it. Yet a prisoner's incarceration without hope of release is in many respects in like case to a sentence of death. He can never atone for his offence. However he may use his incarceration as time for amendment of life, his punishment is only exhausted by his last breath. Like the death sentence the whole-life tariff is *lex talionis.* But its notional or actual symmetry with the crime for which it is visited on the prisoner (the only virtue of the *lex talionis*) is a poor guarantee of proportion-

---

8.   [2008] EWCA Crim 1601.

9.   [2007] EWHC 1109 (Admin). It was cited, approvingly, by Lord Bingham in the Privy Council case of *De Boucherville v The State of Mauritius* [2008] UKPC 37.

ate punishment, for the whole-life tariff is arbitrary: it may be measured in days or decades according to how long the prisoner has to live. It is therefore liable to be disproportionate—the very vice which is condemned on Article 3 grounds—unless, of course, the death penalty's logic applies: the crime is so heinous it can never be atoned for. But in that case the supposed inalienable value of the prisoner's life is reduced, merely, to his survival: to nothing more than his drawing breath and being kept, no doubt, confined in decent circumstances. That is to pay lip-service to the value of life; not to vouchsafe it.

Proportionality outweighs any desire to inflict human suffering. That point was made unerringly by Mr Justice Wendell Holmes in his classic book, *The Common Law.*[10] He wrote:

There is a mystic bond between wrong and punishment...Hegel puts it in his quasi-mathematical form, that wrong being the negation of right, punishment is the negation of that negation, or retribution. Thus the punishment must be equal, in the sense of proportionate to the crime, because its only function is to destroy it. Others, without this logical apparatus, are content to rely upon a felt necessity that suffering should follow wrong-doing.

It is only the popular reliance on revenge that can sustain the ultimate sanction of the death penalty, or its equivalent, the sentence of life imprisonment without benefit of parole (to use the American terminology of no hope of release from custody short of death itself).

Lord Justice Laws was criticised by Lord Hoffmann when the case was heard in the House of Lords. Lord Hoffmann said (present authors' italics):

[The] passage was quoted with *apparent* approval by Lord Bingham of Cornhill in *De Boucherville v State of Mauritius* but in my respectful opinion the argument breaks down at the very first step. It is not the case that the abolition of the death penalty *must* have been founded upon the premise that the life of every person has such inalienable value that its forfeiture cannot be justified on the ground of retributive punishment. A perfectly respectable case for the abolition of the death penalty can

10. 1881.

368

be constructed without subscribing to the view that the lives of Streicher, Eichmann, Saddam Hussein or Myra Hindley had such inalienable value that their executions could not be morally justified.[11] Opposition to the death penalty may be based upon the more pragmatic grounds that it is irreversible when justice has miscarried, that there is little evidence that its deterrent effect is greater than that of other forms of punishment and that the ghastly ceremony of execution is degrading to the participants and the society on whose behalf it is performed. For people who hold such views, who must include many opposed to the death penalty, the parallels between the death penalty and life imprisonment without parole, to which Laws LJ draws attention, are the very reasons why they think that in some cases the latter sentence is appropriate. The preservation of a whole life sentence for the extreme cases which would previously have attracted the death penalty is for such people part of the price of agreeing to its abolition.[12] The Member States of the European Union [clearly

---

11. Julius Streicher, a Nazi Party member hanged at Nuremburg in 1946, was convicted of 'crimes against humanity' by a tribunal that was essentially *sui generis*. As a civilian he had played an enormous part in disseminating anti-semitic propaganda, but had no involvement in the planning or execution of the so-called 'Final Solution'. In contrast, Adolf Eichmann, the senior SS officer who was the bureaucratic architect of that mass extermination of European Jewry, had escaped in 1945 to Argentina, but was abducted to Israel (wholly outwith the normal internationally accepted procedures for extradition) where he stood trial in 1962 under Israeli law for his homicidal crimes committed in Europe before the State of Israel existed. Hanged, his remains were specially cremated and deposited in the Mediterranean beyond Israeli territorial waters. Myra Hindley (alone of those cited who was *not* executed) was convicted of murder under the English common law, but *after* the abolition of capital punishment. She died in prison of natural causes whilst subject to an executively imposed 'whole life' tariff. By suggesting that the case for abolition does not require subscription to the view that their lives had 'such inalienable value that their executions could not be morally justified' Lord Hoffmann would appear to accept that the 'sanctity of life' (a concept frequently cited as justification for the mandatory life sentence) is not, therefore, a generally applicable concept. This, of course, runs completely counter to what is the fundamental precept of Christian theology; namely that no one is beyond redemption. Even the Apostle Paul, it might be noted, had been a participant in the (possibly joint) enterprise that resulted in the killing of Stephen, the first Christian martyr! Theology aside, the point might be made that given that none of the signatories to the Convention are states which retain lawful executions the exceptions to Article 2, which otherwise enshrines a right to life, are effectively redundant, and the right to life it thereby guarantees is now comprehensively applicable even to those guilty of the most repellent crimes of homicide. If that be the case, then one might not unreasonably expect some future development of the jurisprudence regarding Article 3.

12. The identity of 'such people' is unhelpfully obscure. At the time of abolition of the death penalty in 1965 the debates in Parliament clearly indicate that among the most entrenched opponents of abolition there was strong support for judicial discretion in sentencing and

a slip of the pen as Lord Hoffman must have meant the Council of Europe] are in principle democracies and the views of such people must be taken into account by the courts which are invited to extend the reach of Article 3.

Lord Hoffmann uses the term 'whole life sentence': this causes us some perplexity, since it refers not to the mandatory nature of the penalty of life imprisonment, but to the temporal meaning of 'life'. The 1965 Act referred to imprisonment for life, and no more. As we have been at pains to point out throughout this book, we construe the meaning of the life sentence to be a liability to suffer imprisonment determinable upon the life of the person convicted for murder. The provision in 1965 for a judicial recommendation as to the minimum time to be served before consideration of licence clearly indicated that the term 'life imprisonment' was not to be interpreted as 'life-long incarceration', any more than it precluded the possibility of the offender actually spending the rest of his natural life in custody, for whatever reason.[13] The explanation for this, we would argue, was that at the time of abolition the release of life sentence prisoners was a matter governed by conventions within the Home Office, very much as an exercise along the lines of that of the Royal Prerogative. It was not until October 1983 when the Home Secretary Mr (as he then was) Leon Brittan announced to the Conservative Party Conference a new policy, whereby life sentence prisoners would in future serve a 'tariff' period to satisfy the requirement for retribution and deterrence before any release on licence. This novel doctrine was unsuccessfully challenged in *Findlay and others* in 1984,[14] in which the House of Lords held this to be a legitimate exercise of executive authority, and was not abandoned until November 2002 following *Anderson and Taylor*.[15]

No support whatsoever for the concept of 'whole life' imprisonment (or life imprisonment without the benefit of parole) is to be found in the pen-

---

certainly no evidence for the kind of *quid pro quo* to which Lord Hoffman refers (See *Chapter 7* of this volume).

13. 'Whole life' detention to protect the public from dangerous offenders showing no signs of change is both pragmatic and, we would argue, ethically acceptable as a necessity. 'Whole life', without reference to possible subsequent rehabilitation, raises serious moral issues about the making of permanent judgments that determine an unknown future.

14. [1985] AC 318.

15. *R (Anderson) v Secretary of State for the Home Department* [2003] 1 AC 837.

alties and discharge from custody of those convicted of war crimes by the International Criminal Court, set up under the Rome Statute—surely among the most heinous of crimes. Article 77 of the Statute provides for either a determinate sentence not exceeding 30 years, or a term of life imprisonment (if justified by the extreme gravity of the crime and the circumstances of the individual convicted person). The convicted person cannot be released before the expiry of the sentence pronounced by the court. Review of a determinate sentence must be undertaken by the court when two-thirds of the sentence has been served, and not before. In the case of a sentence of life imprisonment, review will be undertaken after 25 years. If, on the initial review, it is considered by the court inappropriate to reduce the sentence, any later question of reduction of the sentence shall be reviewed 'at such intervals and applying such criteria' as provided for in the rules of procedure and evidence of the court. War criminals thus can never be denied the prospect of discharge from custody.

The Way Forward

Over four decades the long-running saga of the penalty for murder, and the manner in which it has been administered under successive Governments, has run its tortuous path towards its hopefully final, orderly course. The domestic courts, the institutions at Strasbourg, the specialist interest groups, and expert opinion in various official and unofficial committees have in their various ways chipped away at that part of a structure of sentencing policy that is fundamentally unsound. Standing alongside the mandatory penalty for murder there have always stood the unfettered discretionary life sentences for other homicide offences (and some other serious non-homicidal offences). Little or no discernible dissatisfaction has accompanied the sentencing of those convicted of manslaughter, frequently indistinguishable in their degrees of moral culpability from many murderers. The defects of duality in the punishment of unlawful killers have pointed sharply to the lack of logic in the reasoning of obscurantist, if blinkered, politicians. Logic and ratiocination, that so blindly dictate a single maximum penalty of life imprisonment for all those convicted of murder or manslaughter (sensibly, in future to be merged into a uniform offence of criminal homicide), have been swamped by a tide of devotion to populism, even though there is an absence of any hard evidence that the populace supports the obduracy of Government ministers. Our experience in the study of homicide and our limited knowledge of groups of victims is that the families and friends of the victims of murder would be quite content with a rational sentencing system explicitly and exclusively performed by the judiciary, together with a more structured and legally-controlled system of discharge from custody of convicted murderers back into society. Safeguarding the community and the safety of the citizenry can be as readily assured as can the assured effects of any heightened sense of undiluted punitiveness. Retribution and revenge are safely relegated to a base level, as reflecting, obnoxiously, a felt necessity of instinctive punishment.

Vox Populi, Vox Legis

The character of law and its relationship to social and political institutions will vary from one society to another, both in the course of history and between societies at a given time. The England and Wales of the 21st century that is governed under the common law is much changed by comparison with its early 17th century counterpart when Sir Edward Coke was setting down his definition of murder. But far from having remained immutable in the succeeding centuries, the common law has been worked over by generations of judges and modified by statute such that, were Coke now, transported in some time warp, to be prosecuting Robert Carr, Earl of Somerset, and his wife for the murder of Sir Thomas Overbury, he would not only find himself in a very different sort of court,[16] but with a law much changed. Not only would he find that the capital sentence had been long abolished, but provisions on the Statute Book that allow for partial defences that would have been unknown to him, such as diminished responsibility and loss of self-control. He would be mystified by much case law relating to joint enterprise and would discover that unlawful killings by the drunken or dangerous driver

---

16. One much less likely to tolerate his frequently appalling courtroom behaviour: see *Chapter 2 supra.*

of horseless carriages were treated as if they were torts that had unfortunate consequences rather than homicidal events.

'It just can't be done'

All too often, when a new idea is promoted to deal with the problems that crime persistently presents to a society that is not only democratic, but also sensible of a need to proceed with caution before embarking upon abandoning concepts and practices hallowed by centuries of use, it is greeted with a scepticism that ensures its likelihood of sinking like a stone.

Thus it is today with the substantive law and penalties for homicide. Over three years from 2003 to 2006 the Law Commission laboured long and hard in considering and deliberating upon changes in the law in England and Wales, having been so charged by the Home Secretary. But none should be deluded into thinking that the Commission was allowed to indulge in free and untrammelled thinking. Such innovation as it might be pleased to recommend to the Government had to maintain the murder/manslaughter dichotomy and could not extend to any consideration of the mandatory penalty of life imprisonment for the crime of murder, no matter the symbiotic nature of the relationship between the substantive crime and the penalty. That the penalty for the crime of murder is now qualitatively affected by the relevant tariffs provided by Schedule 21 to the Criminal Justice Act 2003 is a further complicating factor. Far from any possibility of 'blue sky' thinking, the Law Commission's horizons have been dominated by the lowering clouds of negative constriction.

Both aspects of the penalty for murder—the mandatory element and 'whole life'—are more susceptible to legal challenge in the courts than at any time before. Any reform of the substantive law of murder seems even more remote, now that the Coroners and Justice Act 2009 contains only the very limited reform of section 2 and the replacement of section 3 of the Homicide Act 1957. The urgent problem is the mandatory life sentence, a penalty that is discordant with notions of individualised justice. A recent proposal from Professor John Spencer QC (from the Faculty of Law at the University of Cambridge) deserved and got instant consideration by the politicians, and was floated by Lord Lloyd of Berwick in the course of the debates on the Coroners and Justice Bill in the House of Lords. The proposal was that, in convicting individuals of murder, juries should be empowered in exceptional circumstances to declare the existence of 'mitigating circumstances' (which after all is at the root of the partial defences). The effect of the declaration would be that the judge would no longer be obliged to impose imprisonment for life, but would have a discretion as to the appropriate sentence. The idea is not novel. It was proposed by the Royal Commission on Capital Punishment in 1953 but fell foul of an outraged Lord Chief Justice, Lord Goddard, a pronounced proponent of the death penalty and not notably a penal reformer. He even announced extra-judicially (in the House of Lords[17]) that if there was any such change in the law, he would resign from being Lord Chief Justice, doubtlessly intended as a threat, but which sounded to his detractors more like an unfulfillable promise. The Criminal Law Revision Committee in its Fourteenth Report on Offences Against the Person in 1980 toyed with the idea, but was apprehensive of its consequences. The committee stated:

> While most judges would no doubt sentence the worst murderers to life imprisonment, some would be likely to pass very long determinate sentences of 30 to 40 years, or even more, in an effort to ensure that the prisoner would not be released too soon.[18] [hardly excessive by the standards of today!]

And the committee, rejecting a fully discretionary life sentence, added that 'both types of discrepancy [too high and too low] in sentences would be likely to lead to public disquiet, the more so as they could not be fully rectified by the Court of Appeal'. Those considerations no longer pertain, since the Court of Appeal can both curb any inordinately lengthy sentence and interfere with an unusually lenient one, at the instance of a reference to the court by the Attorney-General. Perhaps the simpler solution would be to give the prosecution and the defence alike the right of appeal against sentences for murder. Consistency in sentencing would thus be readily applied. If it be objected that it is not the function of juries to pass sentence, the answer

---

17. *Hansard* HL Vol 185 Cols 137-188.
18. Cmnd 7844, para 47.

374

is that the sentence will remain with the judge, the jury merely releasing the judge from the statutory bondage of the mandatory penalty. During the days of capital punishment it was not uncommon for juries, in delivering guilty verdicts, to add a rider recommending mercy. Such recommendations were judicially discouraged,[19] but only for the reason that as such they could not alter the death sentence of the court, and it was thought improper forensically if the purpose was to persuade the executive to reprieve the convicted murderer, that being a socio-political matter, and not a proper pronouncement from courts of law.

The Spencer proposal was debated in the House of Lords on 26 October 2009 as an amendment to the Coroners and Justice Bill. Despite considerable support from individual peers, it failed, the Government's intransigent attitude to the mandatory penalty finding a supportive echo among the political parties.[20] The opposition to any modification (however slight) of the penalty for murder adopted two lines of argument. First, the proposal would in effect abolish the mandatory sentence: support for this proposition — surprisingly, we think — came from an independent source. Professor Jeremy Horder, the Law Commissioner who headed the team which produced the comprehensive review of the law of murder by the Law Commission in 2006, proclaimed that the amendment 'rips the heart out of the mandatory sentence'. Contrariwise, the likely application of juries finding 'extenuating circumstances', after invitations from trial judges to consider such a recommendation, would be so minimal as to leave largely intact the concept of the fixed penalty for murder. Indeed, since the proposal would helpfully remove only the 'mercy killings', the acceptance of this limited reform might in fact make it more difficult to launch any all-out attack to abolish the mandatory penalty. The amendment might prove counter-productive to sensible reform.

The second line of argument from the Government spokesman, Lord Bach, was even more worrying in its lack of historical fact. There had been, he said, 'no consultation with the wide range of interested stakeholders who have been involved in the development'[21] of proposals for the reform of the

---

19. *R v Larkin* [1943] 1 KB 174; *R v Black* (1963) 48 Cr App R 52.
20. *Hansard* HL Vol 713 Cols 1008-1029. The vote was 113 in favour of the proposal, and 155 against.
21. *Ibid*, Col 1026.

375

law of homicide. Not merely has abolition of the mandatory penalty been the subject of intensive scrutiny over four decades, the overwhelming view of those involved in the administration of criminal justice has long favoured its demise. If only the opponents to this modest incursion into the reform efforts would have regard to past activity, the answer would be very different. By only a whisker of Parliamentary time in October 1965, the mandatory penalty for murder survived the legislative axe! History will record the continuous attempts to do what politicians indicated was, 45 years ago, a wise and sensible step in penal reform.

CHAPTER 17

SENTENCING ADRIFT AND PAROLE

The fundamental principle of sentencing offenders was stated with unqualified authority in a rare instance of a case in the House of Lords involving sentences for crime, over forty years ago. Rejecting an argument by the Attorney-General, appearing for the Crown, that 'an extended term of imprisonment means extended beyond the normal sentence for the type of crime', Lord Reid, the senior Law Lord and a giant figure in the legal world, said this:

> Offenders of a particular kind vary so vastly in gravity that there *cannot and should not be* any 'normal' sentence and there is no workable standard by which to judge whether any particular standard is extended beyond what is normal.[1]

This judicial warning to avoid tariff sentencing was ignored when Parliament introduced the concept of classified starting points to guide (if not to steer) trial judges in determining the minimum period convicted murderers should spend in custody under the mandatory sentence of life imprisonment. Defiance of that principle by executive Government, and endorsed by Parliament in Schedule 21 to the Criminal Justice Act 2003, lies at the heart of the current flawed system of the penalty for murder. It will experience its quietus if (or, expectantly, when) the proposals in the Green Paper of 7 December 2010 are enacted.

The notion of a 'tariff' as an element of the life sentence is traceable to the early administration of the sentence by the Home Office, both before and after the abolition of the death penalty in 1965; it was given political sanctification in the statement of Leon Brittan as Home Secretary at the Conservative Party Conference in the summer of 1983. Thereafter it figured in the tussle between the executive and judiciary. It found no legislative

---

1.   *DPP v Ottewell* [1970] AC 642 (italics supplied).

support until, following the final loss of the government's executive powers to determine the tariff to the judiciary, the then Home Secretary, Mr David Blunkett, produced the Criminal Justice Act 2003. Although Schedule 21 of that Act appeared to place considerable restriction upon the independence of the judiciary in this respect, it has by no means reduced the judges to *automata*.

Ending the 'Executive' Tariff: the Legislative Response

On 25 November 2002, the Home Secretary, as a result of court decisions,[2] was finally stripped of his power to fix the minimum term—the 'tariff'—of a mandatory sentence of life imprisonment which a convicted murderer should serve before he or she could be released from prison on licence. The Government response was a combative—some considered minatory—retort of Parliamentary action. It seemed as if, frustrated yet again, the Home Secretary was determined to retain the *status quo*, or perhaps go one better, by legislation that would consign the outcome of that litigation into the long grass. Parliament would deal with things.

The vehicle for this supposed triumph of the democratically-elected executive over the unelected judiciary was to be the Criminal Justice Act 2003, which would, in addition to many other matters affecting other parts of the criminal justice system, address the effect of the life sentence.[3] The assumption that was widely made in advance of the publication of the relevant parts of the Bill was that they would result in a substantial reduction in judicial autonomy. In the 'worst case scenario' the judiciary would, where the life sentence was concerned, be reduced to little more than automata, identifying the relevant legal prescriptions that Parliament had determined, and translating them into sentences.

The insertion, late in the day (too late for any extensive scrutiny by Members of Parliament) of Schedule 21 into the Criminal Justice Act 2003 in practice surprisingly confirms the judiciary's practice of exclusive tariff-fixing, while at the same time denying to the judges the power to pass

---

2.   *R v Secretary of State for the Home Department ex parte Anderson and Taylor* [2003] 1 AC 387.

3.   Criminal Justice Act 2003, especially section 269 and Schedule 21 to the Act.

determinate sentences of any length as an alternative to a maximum life sentence, or to impose non-custodial penalties, including hospital orders. The mandatory life sentence, established in 1965, remained firmly embedded in the sentencing structure—section 269 of the Act. Tariff-fixing was relegated to a schedule to the Act.

A Noisy Bark, But a Bite Less Mordant than Expected

The executive threat to judicial independence has thus proved to be less draconian than expected, and with the notable exception of 'whole life' orders (which we have dealt with in *Chapter 16*), the exercise appears at first blush to be European Convention-compliant; on closer examination the exercise is vulnerable to challenge in the courts. Section 269: *Effect of Life Sentence* indicates, *inter alia*, how the minimum term (the 'tariff') is to be determined. The court must consider the seriousness of the offence and in so doing have regard to both the principles set out in Schedule 21 and any guidelines relating to offences in general which are relevant to the case and not incompatible with the provisions of Schedule 21. The court must also give reasons, in open court and in 'ordinary language' (whatever that means) for having decided upon the order made and, in particular, indicate which of the 'starting points' in Schedule 21 it has chosen and its reasons for doing so, as well as reasons for any departure from the starting point. We set out the 'starting points' below.

4(1) If –

  (a) the court considers the seriousness of the offence (or the combination of the offence and one or more offences associated with it) is *exceptionally high*,[4] and

  (b) the offender was aged 21 or over when he committed the offence, the appropriate starting point is a whole life order.

---

4. Italics supplied.

(2) Cases that would normally fall within sub-paragraph (1)(a) include:

(a) the murder of two or more persons, where each murder involves any of the following:

    (i) a substantial degree of premeditation or planning,

    (ii) the abduction of the victim, or

    (iii) sexual or sadistic conduct,

(b) the murder of a child if involving the abduction of the child or sexual or sadistic motivation,

(c) a murder done for the purpose of advancing a political, religious or ideological cause, or

(d) a murder by an offender previously convicted of murder.

If the case does not fall within paragraph 4(1) but the court considers that the seriousness of the offence (or the combination of the offence with one or more offences associated with it) is *particularly high* and the offender was 18 or over at the time of the offence, the appropriate starting point in determining the minimum term is 30 years. Cases which would normally fall within this category are identified as including: (a) the murder of a police or prison officer in the course of his duty, (b) murder using a firearm or explosive, (c) murder done for gain (such as murder done in the course or furtherance of robbery or burglary, done for payment or done in the expectation of gain in the event of death), (d) a murder intended to obstruct or interfere with the course of justice, (e) a murder involving sexual or sadistic conduct, (f) the murder of two or more persons, (g) a murder that is racially or religiously aggravated by sexual orientation, or (h) a murder falling within paragraph 4(2) committed by an offender who was under 21 at the time of the offence, the appropriate starting point in determining the minimum is 15 years. If the offender was aged under 18 at the time of the offence the starting point is 12 years.

Having identified those various 'starting points', Schedule 21 continues, in prose embodying elephantine precision, the aggravating and mitigating factors which trial judges should take into account, to the extent that allowance has not been made for them in the choice of the 'starting point'. *Detailed consideration of these aggravating or mitigating factors may result in a minimum term of any length (whatever the starting point),*[5] or in the making of a whole life order.

Aggravating Factors

These are listed as follows: (a) a significant degree of planning or premeditation,[6] (b) the fact that the victim was particularly vulnerable because of age or disability, (c) mental or physical suffering inflicted on the victim before death, (d) the abuse of a position of trust, (e) the use of duress or threats against another person to facilitate the commission of the offence, (f) the fact that the victim was providing a public service or performing a public duty, and (g) concealment, destruction or dismemberment of the body.

Mitigating Factors

These are identified as: (a) an intention to cause serious bodily harm rather than to kill, (b) lack of premeditation, (c) the fact that the offender suffered from mental disorder or mental disability which (although not falling within the partial defence of diminished responsibility) lowered his degree of culpability, (d) the fact that the offender was provoked (for example by prolonged stress) in a way not amounting to a defence of provocation, (e) the fact that the offender acted to any extent in self-defence, (f) a belief by the offender that the murder was an act of mercy, and (g) the age of the offender.

---

5. Italics supplied.
6. For how this could be reconciled with the provision to take into account the mitigating factor that the offender believed that the murder was an act of mercy, see *R v Inglis* [2010] EWCA Crim 2637.

One might be forgiven for thinking that, as far as these criteria of aggravation and mitigation are concerned, the most that they do is to introduce an element of consistency into what is an essential component of the life sentence, namely, the determination of the tariff for the purpose of retribution and deterrence. They are unlikely to present many surprises to those experienced judges who conduct trials for murder. What, however, the list does contain is a recognition, albeit oblique, of what is perhaps the most patent absurdity in the substantive law of murder.[7] The first of seven mitigating factors is the murderer's *intention to cause serious bodily harm rather than to kill.*[8] Since a high percentage, perhaps as great as 80%, of those convicted of murder do not exhibit any intention to kill, presumably those whose intention was no greater than to cause serious harm will, at a stroke of the penological pen, have departed from whatever starting point has been judicially chosen. Hey-presto, for the run-of-the-mill murderer, the tariff is at large. Will, incidentally, judges seek a special verdict from the jury on finding the accused guilty of murder, in the form of asking what the jury thought the accused's intention to have been? Or will the task of answering this question be left to the judge, who alone is responsible for sentencing? And that is not all. Mitigating factors include any mental disorder or mental disability that 'lowered (the offender's) degree of culpability', though outwith the statutory defence of diminished responsibility. Likewise, loss of self-control (the substitute for the partial defence of provocation), even if not amounting to provocation, is also identified as a mitigating factor. Self-defence and the age of the offender are on the list. So too is 'a belief by the offender that the murder was an act of mercy'. Since the mercy killer intends to kill, this humane provision sits uneasily in a scheme designed to create clear water between the two classes of specific intent. The area of discretionary tariff-fixing may not be unfettered, but it is sufficiently ample to rectify some at least of the present defects in this aspect of sentencing, placing the matter squarely in the lap of the judiciary.

---

7. That is that to prove murder it is only necessary to prove an intention to do serious harm, in contrast to proof of attempted murder where the prosecution must demonstrate an intention to kill.

8. Italics supplied.

But the end result remains still well short of the satisfactory solution of leaving the judges to decide on sentences for murder, as they do with every other crime (including manslaughter, which is often indistinguishable from murder in terms of the degree of culpability). Schedule 21 had necessarily to fix a point of departure on its penal journey, because to have alighted upon a fixed point, without judicial adjustment to suit the individual case, would have fallen foul of the European Convention on Human Rights. What the Home Secretary has been able to do is to retain his or her power, in conjunction with the Parole Board (to which we allude hereafter), to engage in the other part of the life sentence — namely, an assessment of risk, if and when the prisoner is to be released back into the community. Dangerousness, however, is itself a dangerous concept. Even the opprobrious starting-point of 'whole life' for an exceptionally serious murder cannot be guaranteed to apply to those convicted of the most heinous murders, since the judges need not even open the door to that iron cage of vengeance.

The Experience of Operating Schedule 21

The judicial experience of the imposition, post-2005, of recommended starting points has been quite dramatically and worryingly to swell the daily average prison population to an all-time high of 85,000, of whom 12,000 are serving indeterminate sentences — a major contribution to overcrowding in prisons. The starting point for a deliberate ('normal') murder that possesses no aggravating factors is a minimum term of 15 years — the equivalent of a 30 year determinate sentence. Specified aggravating factors can double that starting point. If, for example, the murder involved the use of a gun, or was carried out for gain, then 30 years (or its equivalent of a 60 year determinate sentence) will be imposed. This formulaic structure conflicts with established sentencing principles, the effect of which is to constrain judges to impose tariff sentences which they would ordinarily consider unjust. Murderers in the 21st century are being sentenced to serve terms twice as long as they would have been at any time from 1965 until the Criminal Justice Act 2003.

In *Atkins v R*[9] the Court noted that the new statutory starting points had effected a 'major uplift in sentencing'. In *R v Bieber*,[10] Lord Phillips of Worth Matravers CJ said that the Court of Appeal (Criminal Division) 'has often deprecated the mechanistic use of Schedule 21'; and, extra-judicially, he has pointedly observed that the country is facing a prison system of geriatrics. His successor as Lord Chief Justice, Lord Judge, softened the full impact of Schedule 21, to the effect that the statutory guidelines in Schedule 21 are just that, guidelines, and must not be read literally so as to cause injustice.[11]

In *R v M*,[12] Lord Judge repeated the courts' view of Schedule 21, saying that the ultimate responsibility of the sentencing judge is not to place the offence within a particular paragraph of Schedule 21, but to make a judicial assessment of the facts of the case and its seriousness. The Ministry of Justice, however, persists in restricting the ambit of judicial discretion in fixing the tariff. If and when a commencement order is made under the Criminal Justice Act 2003 (Mandatory Life Sentence: Determination of Minimum Term) Order 2010 — amending paragraph 5(1) to fix 25 years as the starting point for 'knife murder' — the mechanistic approach to the sentencing of murder, so strongly deprecated by the judiciary, is thereby underlined. The tug-of-war between judiciary and executive continues, to the detriment of a sound sentencing policy. It is little wonder that one of the first reviews by the Coalition Government of May 2010 is of sentencing policy and has resulted in proposals to scrap the classification system in Schedule 21. The Government Green Paper of December 2010[13] describes the schedule as 'based on ill-thought out and overly prescriptive policy' and 'badly in need of reform'.

Parole

Any proposal for reform of the mandatory sentence of life imprisonment for murder must be viewed in the context of the present regime for the

---

9.   [2009] EWCA Crim 1876.
10. [2008] EWCA Crim 1601.
11. *R v Height and Anderson* [2008] EWCA Crim 2500, 29 October 2008.
12. [2010] Crim LR 243.
13. Cm. 7972/2010.

release of all prisoners serving an indeterminate sentence, both mandatory and discretionary. There has been a massive growth in the number of such prisoners. Approximately one in five prisoners is now serving either a life sentence or a sentence of imprisonment for public protection. More than 12,500 sentenced prisoners are currently unaware of the moment when they are going to be released, and may even not have any clear idea of how they might reach that goal. Extensive delays in the hearings of the panels of the Parole Board simply add to the ever-growing pressures on the 'lifer' system within the prison population, quite apart from the intolerable burden for the Parole Board and on prisoners awaiting the hearings of their cases for discharge. The decision to discharge is focused on the risk to the public of releasing prisoners identified as potentially dangerous. The Parole Board decreasingly functions as the arbiter of release of prisoners with determinate sentences. That is in stark contrast to the original purpose of the Parole Board which was, in seeking to reduce the prison population, aiming to balance the probable advantages of a phased and controlled rehabilitation back into the community against the risks in any particular case.

The establishment of the Parole Board in April 1968, under the provisions of the Criminal Justice Act 1967, was a major innovation of the penal system. Release of prisoners on various forms of licence had always existed, but it was at the discretion of the Home Secretary and largely limited to prisoners serving life sentences and juveniles detained during the Sovereign's pleasure. The principal exception was borstal training from which young offenders could be released on licence, which could be revoked for the outstanding period of a 3-year sentence. This function was performed by Local Review Committees (now defunct) at the establishment where the offender was detained. A similar system had applied to those serving sentences under the comparatively short-lived system of corrective training introduced by the Criminal Justice Act 1948, but abolished by the Criminal Justice Act 1967. Thus, until 1967, the paroling of prisoners was exclusively an act of executive Government (the Home Secretary's power to release lifers on licence to recall was put on a statutory basis only in section 57 Criminal Justice Act 1948). But the new statutory scheme was focused on carefully-selected inmates who could be let out of prison in advance of their expected date of release, but on condition that they accepted supervision by a probation officer and were liable to recall. The Act provided that discharge could not be recommended to the Home Secretary until the prisoner had served at least one third of his sentence, or one year, whichever was the longer. The extant lifer system operated alongside the new paroling of determinate-sentenced prisoners.

The Parole Board was from the outset exclusively an advisory body, and still is, although it has acquired some decision-making powers over its 40 years of existence. The Ministry of Justice at the end of 2009 considered whether in the future the Parole Board should be housed within the Court Service or the new Tribunal Service; the resultant reference in 2010 was inconclusive. Where to place the Board has now become irrelevant, since the Ministry is hard at work on merging the Court Service with the tribunal system. The need to review the Parole Board's jurisdiction, functions and powers is compelling. Under the chairmanship of Sir David Latham, almost the only judge or lawyer to chair the board over 45 years, it has been skilfully steered towards a judicial approach, far removed from its roots as a part of public administration. The revision of the board can only be conducted alongside a review of sentencing generally — which is now promised. The simple — and therefore unlikely — recipe is to abolish the Parole Board and restore determinate sentencing, to the point where the sentence passed by the court is what the prisoner has to serve — no more, no less. Once determinacy no longer requires a system of discretionary discharge before the lapse of the term of imprisonment, there is left only the prison population of indeterminate sentenced offenders, together with any recall procedure. Parole, as conceived by Roy Jenkins in 1967, has run its full course. Its confused role within the penal system is beyond simple revision. It needs replacement. An independent body to determine the risk involved in releasing a life sentence prisoner from custody, with the concomitant system of recalling back into custody those who demonstrate a revival of risk, will always be needed. Such a commission's task of risk assessment is primarily not a judicial one, and should not be dominated by panel members who are judicially qualified.

CHAPTER 18

ENVOI

Over 50 years ago—on 28 July 1960, to be more precise—the judicial House of Lords delivered its judgment in *DPP v Smith* which evoked a wave of hostile opinion and critical writings from legal practitioners and academic lawyers. If Parliament, seven years later, had to come to the rescue, simply to reverse the decision of the five Law Lords on an evidential procedure, the case was not just a judicial aberration; the English law of murder remained in, as the Law Commission described it in its 2006 report, a 'mess'. The famous decision in *DPP v Smith* was the first in a series of cases from the final court of appeal spread over the next five decades that has tinkered with the law and signalled loudly to Parliament to modernise the law of homicide. Apart from marginal changes to the partial defences of provocation and diminished responsibility in the Coroners and Justice Act 2009, we await reform. Who will do it, and when?

When Lord Mustill referred to the rule of English law, that a person can be guilty of murder if he or she merely intended to cause grievous bodily harm, as a 'conspicuous anomaly', and said that the law of homicide was 'permeated by anomaly, fiction, misnomer and obsolete reasoning',[1] he was adamant in asserting that the House of Lords at the end of the 20th century was in no position to abolish the four-century-old rule. He said:

> My Lords, in a system based on binding precedent there could be no ground for doubting a long course of existing law, and certainly none which could now permit this House even to contemplate such a fundamental change as to abolish the grievous harm rule; and counsel rightly hinted at no such idea.[2]

---

1.   *Attorney-General's Reference (No 3 of 1994)* [1998] AC 245 at p 250.

2.   *Ibid*, at p 258.

Lord Mustill added later in his judgment: 'I am willing to follow old laws until they are overturned, but not to make a new law on a basis for which there is no principle'.[3]

Given that, in the *Practice Statement* of July 1966, the House of Lords arrogated to itself the power to reconsider its previous decisions and, if appropriate, overrule any earlier decision which was either erroneous or on the ground of changed public policy, the homicide law could, in theory at least, be refashioned. Their Lordships were clearly inviting governmental review of the law of murder with a view to Parliamentary action. But if legislation is not forthcoming, what then? Should the judiciary not be prepared, creatively, to modernise the country's law of homicide? The story since Lord Mustill's forthright statement in 1998 needs telling.

In *R v Powell*[4] in 1999, two defendants appealed against their convictions for murder on the basis that they were secondary parties to events where deaths had occurred in the course of joint enterprises which were in themselves criminal. The House of Lords ruled that a secondary party might kill with intent so to do or with intent to cause grievous bodily harm, except that if the primary party's lethal act was fundamentally different from that foreseen by the secondary party, the latter would not be guilty of murder (or of manslaughter). Lord Hutton gave the single, reasoned judgment.[5] Lord Mustill concurred, but said that he had proffered a judgment coming to a different conclusion and withdrew it only because he did not want future trial judges, who had to direct juries as simply as possible, being confused by conflicting theories propounded by different Law Lords. Both Lord Mustill and Lord Steyn[6] made heartfelt pleas for Parliamentary intervention; they were entirely persuaded that the House of Lords in its judicial capacity could not effect change in this area of the criminal law. Lord Mustill reaffirmed his earlier statement:

Once again, an appeal to this House has shown how badly our country needs a law

---

3. *Ibid*, at p 262.
4. [1999] 1 AC 1.
5. Ten years later in *R v Rahman* [2008] UKHL 45, Lord Bingham elaborated on the reasoning established in *Powell*.
6. [1999] 1 AC 1 at p.15.

of homicide, or a new law of punishment of homicide, or preferably both. The judges can do nothing about this, being held fast by binding authorities on the one hand and a mandatory statute [the mandatory penalty of life imprisonment for murder, after the passing of the Murder (Abolition of Death Penalty) Act 1965] on the other. Only Parliament has the powers, if it will choose to exercise them. It may not be a popular choice, but surely it is justice that counts.¯

If the recent spate of appellate litigation around the basic ingredients of the crimes of murder and manslaughter, however unsatisfactory, have produced at least a measure of certainty to the law, the homicide law was rudely interrupted on another front: the partial defence of provocation to a charge of murder. In *R v Smith (Morgan)*[8] the issue was whether a jury was entitled to take into account the defendant's personal characteristics (severe depressive illness) when deciding if the defendant had exercised the standard of control to be expected by someone who was being provoked. The majority—Lords Slynn, Hoffmann and Clyde—held that the jury was so entitled, while the minority—Lords Hobhouse and Millett—dissented. The case attracted severe criticism in the academic world. In coming to their conclusion the majority refused to follow a contrary line favoured a few years earlier in the Privy Council in an appeal from Hong Kong.[9] The scene was set for a headlong conflict of judicial opinion about the proper approach to the defence of provocation—should the accused be judged by his own reduced powers of self-control, which would eliminate the objective element and remove the only standard external to the accused by which the jury could judge the sufficiency of the provocation relied on? An appeal from the Court of Appeal of Jersey[10] supplied the forum for the judicial split. A nine-judge Privy Council (all of them serving Law Lords) held by six to three to uphold the minority view in *R v Smith (Morgan)*.

The uncertainty was in a sense resolved when the matter came before the Court of Appeal (Criminal Division) in *R v James*[11] when a five-judge court

---

7.   *Ibid*, at p.12.
8.   [2001] 1 AC 146.
9.   *Luc Thiet Thuan v R* [1997] AC 131.
10. *R v Holley* [2005] 2 AC 580.
11. [2006] 1 All ER 759.

decided to follow the Privy Council decision rather than that of the House of Lords. Using their power, in effect, to reverse an earlier decision — namely, *R v Smith (Morgan)* — the Appeal Committee refused to entertain an application for leave to appeal. The interpretation of section 3 Homicide Act 1957 (the section on provocation) reverted to its pristine state of maintaining a strictly objective approach to the issue of self-control in response to the victim's provocative behaviour. Professor Brice Dickson summed up the record of the Law Lords in the area of homicide law since 1995 as 'disunited and unambitious'.[12] He might have added that the Law Lords did nothing effective to clear up the mess of the law of murder.

Possibly as a result of the controversy over the case of *R v Smith (Morgan)* in cases involving provocation in domestic violence, the Government decided to refer the question of the two partial defences — provocation and diminished responsibility — to the Law Commission. The story shifts from the court setting to the process preliminary to Parliamentary action, a move doubtlessly applauded by the judiciary. Its wishes were at last being met, if less than whole-heartedly. While recommending, in two consultation documents,[13] changes to both section 2 (on diminished responsibility) and section 3 (provocation) the Law Commission indicated that the partial defences could only properly be reviewed in the context of the substantive law of murder. And so it recommended that Government should make such a referral to the Law Commission. After some political hesitancy to comply with the Law Commission's request, the Home Secretary did make a limited reference, restricting the review to the established distinction between murder and manslaughter and putting the mandatory penalty of life imprisonment out of bounds. At the same time, the Home Secretary indicated that the Law Commission's review would be part of a two-stage process. The Home Office (its functions soon to be re-defined by the creation of a Department of Constitutional Affairs and the final emergence of a Ministry of Justice) would complete the exercise with a view to legislation in 2009. The Law Commission duly reported in November 2006 recommending the three-tier

---

12. See Chapter 9 of *Judicial Activism in the House of Lords 1995–2007*, Brice Dickson (ed.) (OUP, 2007).

13. *Partial Defences to Murder* (Law Com CP No 173, 2003) and *Provisional Conclusions on Consultation Paper* (Law Com CP No 173A, 2004).

system of Murder 1, Murder 2 and Manslaughter, with an updated version of its suggested amendments to the partial defences to murder.[14]

In December 2007 the Government changed tack. Officials were asked to report on four specific aspects of the law of homicide that seemed to be presenting peculiar difficulties. The four topics were: (a) diminished responsibility; (b) provocation; (c) infanticide; and (d) complicity of participants in unlawful killings. There was no indication of what was to happen with the wider scope of the substantive law of murder. That, at best, appeared to be consigned to the back burner. The report on the four topics was reflected in legislation scheduled for the new session in Parliament in November 2008.

In respect of homicide, the Coroners and Justice Act 2009 effected not the long overdue reform of the substantive law, but addressed only certain aspects of the partial defences to murder, notably diminished responsibility and what was previously termed provocation but now appeared in a new guise as 'loss of self-control'. If the Law Commission had laboured under the restrictions imposed upon it to produce at least some improvement in homicide law, the reaction of Government appears to have been to shy away from any substantial change, preferring to produce no more than a mouse; one which was, in some respects, an unwelcome rodent. For the rest there has been a legislative silence.

The general election of May 2010, being focused upon what were primarily issues in the economy, featured no reference to any change in the law. In the ensuing months the issue of the Law Commission's proposals for reform remained dormant. Lord Lloyd of Berwick, however, raised the matter by way of a Parliamentary Question put down on 12 July.[15]

Given the current situation of what would appear to be governmental reluctance to tackle by legislation what is widely acknowledged to be the highly unsatisfactory state of the common law of murder, the judiciary might echo Lord Mustill's plea that if Parliament declines to exercise its sovereign power to make law, 'surely it is justice that counts' and as such warrants the exercise of the judiciary's law-making powers. The judiciary could be reminded of Lord Devlin's distinction between 'activist law-making' (which means 'keeping pace with change in the consensus') and 'dynamic or creative

---

14. *Murder, Manslaughter and Infanticide* (Law Com No 304).
15. *Hansard* HL vol 720 cols 512-514 (12 July 2010).

law-making' (which is 'the use of law to *generate* change in the consensus').[16] And in his lecture on *Judges and Lawmakers* he wrote:[17]

> The strongest argument for judicial activism is not that it is the best method of law reform but that, as things stand, it is in a large area of the law the only method. The judges who made the common law must not abrogate altogether their responsibility for keeping it abreast of the times. Of course they can protest, as they frequently do, that it is for Parliament to change the law. But these protestations ring hollow when Parliament has said, as loudly as total silence can say it, that it intends to do nothing at all.

Longevity in a rule of law is no bar to the exercise of the power in the House of Lords to reverse an earlier decision. Quite the contrary: antiquated laws need to be modernised, and can be, though it took the House of Lords 30 years to reverse the decision in *Rondel v Worsley*[18] which had affirmed a rule of law which had established the immunity of barristers from action for professional negligence; a law that had subsisted for at least 300 years. Admittedly, the task of reconsidering the case law of murder over a period of 400 years might be daunting, but not as impossible as it might seem, given that the default position of the judiciary for most of those years has been rarely to innovate but predominantly to follow precedent. There is nothing to suggest that the contemporary judiciary is other than fully equal to the task, given that so many among them are only too aware of the shortcomings of the present law. But if there is no political will on the part of Government or Parliament to carry out the task, judicial notice must be given that, in the interests of justice, the courts will be invoked to do the legislature's duty. If the courts do not possess any direct mandate from the sovereign legislature to change the law, the legislative vacuum must be filled at the will of the people; thus the courts are mandated democratically. Is there any lesson to

---

16. *The Judge* (OUP, 1979). at p.2.
17. At page 12.
18. [1969] 1 AC 191, reversed in *Arthur J S Hall Ltd v Simons* [2002] 1 AC 615. See also the dissenting judgments of Lord Hope and Lady Hale in the seven-judge Supreme Court in *Jones v Kaney* [2011] UKSC 13, where the majority reversed the long-established rule of immunity of expert witnesses from action for professional negligence.

be learnt from the manner in which the House of Lords changed the law in *Woolmington*?[19]

Woolmington's appeal against his conviction at a second trial was dismissed by the Court of Criminal Appeal. That court, presided over by Mr Justice Avory, said that there was 'no question…that the learned judge laid down the law applicable to a case of murder in the way in which it is to be found in the old authorities', that law being the requirement that the onus of proving that the shooting was accidental was on the defence. Rosemary Pattenden in her work *English Criminal Appeals 1844-1994*[20] did not overstate the conclusion that the 14-page judgment of the Lord Chancellor, Lord Sankey, in the House of Lords 'contains on of the most definitive pronouncements ever made on any aspect of criminal evidence'.

Lord Sankey's opening remarks bear close scrutiny. He began by observing that the Court of Criminal Appeal was at a distinct disadvantage to the House of Lords in that 'it is true, as stated by the Court of Appeal, that there is apparent [he might even have used the adjective 'abundant'] authority for the law as laid down by the learned judge'.

What then prompted a distinct change in direction of a fundamental principle of criminal procedure? Lord Sankey's riposte to judicial precedents is instructive today. He noted that

> … your Lordships' House has had the advantage of prolonged and exhaustive inquiry dealing with the matter in debate from the earliest times, an advantage which was not shared by either of the Courts below. Over a number of days counsel were able to trace the law of murder from pre-Conquest times to the present day, through cases, textbooks and treatises.[21]

Today the Supreme Court of the United Kingdom, untrammelled by the Parliamentary constraints of its immediate predecessor, the Appellate Committee of the House of Lords, is in an ideal situation (as and when the occasion should arise in a murder appeal) to engage in a similar exercise of academic historical research to underpin Lord Mustill's assertion concern-

---

19. This is discussed in detail in *Chapter 6* of this work.
20. Oxford (The Clarendon Press, 1996) at p.337.
21. (1935) 25 Cr App R 72 at 87.

ing the obsolete reasoning of the case law in contemporary homicides. More particularly, relying on the defective reasoning of Lord Kilmuir in *DPP v Smith* (see *Chapter 5* of this work) *a propos* the writings of Oliver Wendell Holmes Jr in 1881, the Supreme Court could usefully canvass the rival arguments advanced in the late 19th century by Fitzjames Stephen and his judicial supporters who rejected the Holmes formula and endorsed the decisions of the judges who laid down the English law of homicide, so definitively rejected in *Woolmington* on the burden of proof in murder trials. From *Woolmington* to *Smith*, there is moreover a golden thread in English law that procedural values in criminal justice must in principle, on occasion, prevail over the substantive criminal law—even more so when due process conforms to a sensible, substantive law for unlawful killings.

In the course of the continuous development of the common law since the early 17th century, and substantially unchanged by the legislature, the judges have created, given increase to and perpetuated 'the mess'. If Parliament is unable, unwilling or incapable of clearing up the mess, the judges must do it themselves. It is no longer tolerable that the administration of criminal justice should be dictated by the archaic vision of Sir Edward Coke.

What then, if anything, can the Supreme Court do about the law of murder, given the inevitable constraints upon judicial law-making and some legislative handicapping?

First, the judges could do nothing about the mandatory penalty for murder: only Parliament can amend section 1 Murder (Abolition of Death Penalty) Act 1965. It is the substantive law that is the creature of the common law for which the judges must accept responsibility. Nor can the judges do anything about the two partial defences in the Coroners and Justice Act 2009. On that the legislature has spoken, even if the results are hopelessly defective. As and when the judiciary seeks to unravel the hopeless jumble of the new partial defence of loss of self-control the legislature will be likely to respond and amend the provision—in at least two or three years' time!

But there are two features of the substantive law that are untouched statutorily and could be put under judicial scrutiny. The judges could usefully pick up the theme of those 'fine lines and technical distinctions' pointedly castigated by Lord Parker in 1965 and echoed by Lord Kilbrandon in *Hyam v DPP* in 1974, and elsewhere in the general criticisms by Lord Mustill. It is entirely feasible for common law judges in the 21ˢᵗ century to declare that, with the ending of capital punishment, the distinction between murder and manslaughter is no longer a fundamental necessity. The judges would need to consider the recommendations of the Law Commission, but would not be similarly constrained by the terms of reference imposed politically on the Law Commission. And, above all, the Justices of the Supreme Court could usefully review exactly what is involved in the doctrine of *mens rea*. A study of the judgments in *Sweet v Parsley* discloses no judicial unanimity about the interpretation of that Latin phrase. Does it encompass knowledge and gross recklessness or is it exclusively tied to intention? A consideration of the 19ᵗʰ century debate between Holmes and Stephen would not be out of place in a 21ˢᵗ century court of final appeal.

GLOSSARY

Of Some Terms Used in this Book

Criminal event A contextual definition of the action or actions, including the circumstances antecedent and subsequent to them, which constitute an infringement of the criminal law. A criminal event cannot be allocated to any category of crime in advance of a legal verdict of conviction. For example, a violent death cannot be described as a 'murder' in advance of such a verdict but remains a homicide.

Criminal guilt A term effectively synonymous with criminal liability, being the term used to describe the condition of a person[1] having been convicted of an offence and thereby liable to the sanctions provided by the criminal law. The term guilt in this context is merely descriptive and is by this definition morally neutral.

Criminal liability The liability of the individual held to be responsible for a criminal offence and to such punishments or other sanctions for which the criminal law makes provision.

Criminal responsibility The overall notion whereby the individual citizen may be held to be responsible for acts prohibited by the criminal law and for omissions in respect of conduct defined as mandatory by it. Criminal responsibility is predicated upon the assumption that the defendant to a criminal charge is not handicapped in his actions or perception by any mental illness or condition.

Diminished responsibility A term introduced by the Homicide Act 1957, section 2(1). It is a partial defence to a charge of murder on the grounds of

---

1. Or where applicable a corporate body.

the abnormal mental condition of the offender: strictly speaking, the concept embodies diminished culpability, since the offence of murder is reduced to that of manslaughter and the convicted defendant is not thereby absolved from criminal liability.

Strict liability Offences where there is declared by statute to be no need for *mens rea*. A person may be convicted, not merely if he or she did not intend the prohibited consequence, but even though the conduct that led to them was not negligent. Strict liability is largely confined to conduct subject to statutory regulation, such as the sale of medicines and foodstuffs and certain offences relating to motor vehicles. It does not apply to the overwhelming majority of criminal offences in which proof of both *mens rea* and an *actus reus* is necessary for conviction.

Mens rea A term often — and misleadingly — translated as 'guilty mind'. For the purpose of establishing criminal guilt the prosecution must identify a state of mind in the offender contemporaneous with the unlawful act indicative of intention, recklessness or negligence. The much criticised judgment in *DPP v Smith* [1961] AC 290, which affirmed an irrebuttable presumption that a person foresees and intends the natural consequences of his actions was overridden by the Criminal Justice Act 1967, section 8.

Moral culpability The degree of blameworthiness attaching to an offender for a particular criminal event or events for the purpose of assessing the appropriate penal sanction for the individual offender. Moral culpability, though it may appear to make reference to an objective standard of conduct, is essentially the outcome of the way in which the sentencing process interprets the prevailing mores and standards of propriety in society. For example, until the 19th century it was not uncommon for offenders who were seriously mentally-ill to be subjected to capital punishment. To be distinguished from criminal liability and criminal guilt.

Objective liability The establishment of criminal liability on the basis that a person of reasonable prudence would have foresight of the potential consequences of his actions, irrespective of any intention on his part as to outcome.

APPENDIX 1

LAW LORDS VOTING FOR THE PARKER AMENDMENT ON 27 JULY 1965

The Lord Chief Justice, Lord Parker of Waddington, described the object of his amendment as very simple:

> to abolish once and for all a fixed penalty for murder; in other words, to prevent life imprisonment from being the only sentence which can be passed. If it is passed, subsection (1) will read: '…a person convicted of murder shall be liable at the discretion of the court to imprisonment for life'.[1]

The Lord Chancellor, Lord Gardiner, was opposed. While recognising that it was a debatable matter, he argued that the amendment was

> seeking, it may be rightly, to take for the judiciary a power which in murder cases they have never had.

> Murder, I suggest, is a crime apart…because there is no other crime which is so largely a product of the disordered mind.[2]

In his view, the life sentence provided the element of indeterminacy that was essential if murderers, who manifested so often this degree of abnormality, were to be safely released at some future date.

But perhaps the most important point was to emerge in Lord Parker's summing up at the end of the debate.

> The noble Lord, Lord Stonham, held up his hands in horror at the fact that I was tending and intending to merge manslaughter and murder. Let me make it clear. Of course, as a matter of law murder is a separate offence, and it is also perhaps the most serious offence. But…I dislike fine lines and technical distinctions. I think

---

1. *Hansard* HL Vol 268 Cols 1211-1212.
2. *Ibid*, Col 1239.

that there is one offence of homicide, varying infinitely from the lowest degree of manslaughter up to the most intentional, deliberate and calculated true murder. Therefore, I think that my argument...is based on the anomaly which has been produced by the abolition of the death penalty.[3]

Apart from the Lord Chancellor, Lord Gardiner, every other Law Lord voted for the Amendment, the list being as follows:[4]

Denning *[Teller]*
Dilhorne
Guest
Hodson
Morris of Borth-y-Gest
Parker of Waddington
Pearson
Reid *[Teller]*
Wilberforce

---

3. *Ibid*, Col 1241.
4. *Ibid*, Cols 1243-1244.

APPENDIX 2

EXTRACTS FROM THE MURDER (ABOLITION OF DEATH PENALTY) ACT 1965

Chapter 71

An Act to abolish capital punishment in the case of persons convicted in Great Britain of murder or convicted of murder or a corresponding offence by court-martial and, in connection therewith, to make further provision for the punishment of persons so convicted [8ᵗʰ November 1965]

(1) No person shall suffer death for murder, and a person convicted of murder shall, subject to subsection (5) below,[1] be sentenced to imprisonment for life.

(2) On sentencing any person convicted of murder to imprisonment for life the Court may at the same time declare the minimum period which in its view should elapse before the Secretary of State orders the release of that person on licence under section 27 of the Prison Act 1952 or section 21 of the Prisons (Scotland) Act 1952.

No person convicted of murder shall be released by the Secretary of State on licence under section 27 of the Prison Act 1952 or section 21 of the Prisons (Scotland) act 1952 unless the Secretary of State has consulted the Lord Chief Justice of England or the Lord Justice General as the case may be together with the trial judge if available.

Section 4 of the Act provided that it should continue in force until the 31ˢᵗ of July 1970 and should then expire unless Parliament by affirmative resolutions of both Houses should otherwise determine. That is what happened in 1969, and capital punishment for murder was finally abolished.

---

1. This relates to section 53 Children and Young Persons Act 1933 and the corresponding legislation for Scotland whereby those under 18 who are convicted of murder are subject to be detained during Her Majesty's pleasure and are not subject to the sentence of life imprisonment.

APPENDIX 3

LIFE SENTENCES FOR MURDER

The Views of Mr Jack Straw When Secretary of State for the Home Department

When the Lane Committee reported in 1993, the response of the then Home Secretary, Mr Michael Howard was unambiguous. He was not prepared to entertain any change respecting the mandatory nature of the life sentence for murder. On 30th May 2000 *The Times* published an article by one of the present authors[1] who shortly beforehand wrote to Jack Straw seeking his views. His substantially argued and extensive reply came to the same conclusion. He did not persuade us to abandon our position. In line with our view that it is important that the matter be resolved by reasoned argument, which includes considering opposing arguments, we publish, with his agreement, the text of his reply.

It must be borne in mind that the letter was written before the question of the Home Secretary's role in tariff setting had been considered in the case of *Anderson and Taylor*[2] and before even the conception of the Criminal Justice Act 2003 by which Jack Straw's successor in office, David Blunkett, sought to re-establish the status quo ante.

23 June 2000

Dear Louis

Thank you for your letter of 24 May 2000 seeking my views on the mandatory nature of the penalty for murder.

---

1. Louis Blom-Cooper.
2. [2003] 1 AC 387.

I read your article in *The Times* (Tuesday 30 May) on this subject with interest but, although many of the arguments are well made, they are insufficient to persuade me that the mandatory penalty for murder should be removed.

You ask to what extent I advance the arguments set out by Michael Howard in his response to the Lane Committee's report of 1993. I agree entirely with the view that murder occupies a very special place in our criminal law. The special status of the offence arises not only from the tragedy of the loss of life but also from the murderer's intention that the victim should die or at least suffer serious harm. These characteristics of the offence obtain whatever the circumstances in which it occurred. The sentence of mandatory life imprisonment reflects this unique nature of the offence and the fact that the public rightly regards it as a particularly abhorrent crime. In my view the arguments advanced by Mr Howard comprised all of the major points that need to be made in favour of retention of the mandatory penalty and the setting of tariffs by the Home Secretary. There are, however, a few points I would like to add.

There is a clear distinction between the mandatory life imprisonment for murder by adults and discretionary life. The former is characterised as a mandatory sentence automatically imposed by law as a punishment for life reflecting the unique gravity of the offence. The discretionary life sentences, on the other hand, are justified primarily by considerations of the offender's character, mental state or age, and their resulting dangerousness and consequently are not complete until the court has determined the relevant part. This distinction between the mandatory and discretionary sentences has been recognised and confirmed in a number of cases by the Commission and European Court of Human Rights notably in the cases of Wynne; Ryan; Thynne, Wilson and Gunnell; and most recently in Thompson and Venables. The distinction raises issues about the role of the discretionary life sentence if the mandatory life sentence was removed. Would the discretionary life sentence continue to have the same role when applied to murder or would judges simply use it as a substitute for long-term determinate sentences? What would be the relationship of the discretionary life sentence to the determinate sentence of imprisonment? An element of uncertainty would be introduced which I believe would undermine public confidence in the criminal justice system's ability to deal effectively with murderers. One could legislate to provide some kind of safeguard, as your article suggests, but such a course concedes the special place murder occupies.

The Human Rights Act, when it comes into force, will require our courts to take into account the reasoning in the decisions referred to above and, whilst it is true that they do not have to be followed, I believe that they are persuasive evidence that the current arrangements do not amount to a breach of the Convention. Moreover, the House of Lords in the judgment in the Hindley case on 30 March stressed the unique position of murder and the mandatory sentence in our criminal justice system and unanimously endorsed as both lawful and proportionate the decision of successive Home Secretaries to set a whole life tariff in that case.

The current arrangements work well in practice and have a number of advantages for victims' families, the public, judiciary and offenders. The mandatory life sentence for murder provides vital safeguards against re-offending by ensuring that murderers are released after only the most careful thought. It would be wrong to abolish such a sentence if we were not sure that an alternative would meet all of these important requirements. The mandatory life sentence ensures that a thorough assessment of the risk involved in releasing a prisoner occurs over a suitably long period and is finally determined only when a possible release date approaches. In the absence of a mandatory sentence this important safeguard would be lost. A court would be required to assess this risk at the time of sentencing. A prisoner sentenced to a determinate sentence would have to be released at a certain date even though there were concerns about the risk of re-offending. Even the extended licence period of an extended sentence under the Crime and Disorder Act 1998 is finite. Moreover, the mandatory penalty also ensures that those convicted of murder are released on a life licence. These provisions are a necessary and powerful tool for the supervision of lifers. They provide the powerful and immediate sanction of recall to prison for the lifer whose behaviour gives cause for concern, reassurance for the families of victims, and an important element in maintaining public confidence in the arrangements for the conditional release of convicted murderers. The risk of re-offending by released determinate prisoners currently causes concern; the stakes are likely to be unacceptably high in the case of murder.

You refer in the letter and the article to my view that removal of the mandatory element in the penalty would result in short sentences for murderers. It seems to me that the view that in the absence of mandatory life imprisonment judges may sentence murderers to determinate sentences under which they would spend less time in custody than they would have done if they had been subject to an appropriate tariff is entirely supportable. The role of the discretionary life sentence, as I suggest above, is an issue in itself but it must be that some of those convicted of murder would in the absence of the mandatory penalty receive determinate sentences. Judges may be reluctant to impose a determinate sentence of the length that would be required to ensure a prisoner spends the same time as he or she would spend in custody under a tariff. Such a sentence may appear to be disproportionately long. A prisoner who would have been subject to an eight year tariff, for example, would, under current release arrangements, have to receive a sentence of sixteen years imprisonment in order to ensure that he or she would spend the same period in custody.

The present system has the benefit of finality and clarity. Imposition of the mandatory life sentence immediately on conviction meets in most cases the needs of the family of the victim and public to see justice done straight away at the end of what has often been a harrowing ordeal. That feeling of relief is commonly expressed through the media in the aftermath of a trial. The arrangements allow the trial judge to reflect on the whole circumstances of the offence including any mitigating or aggravating circumstances before making a recommendation on tariff through the Lord Chief Justice. It is striking how few judges avail themselves of the statutory power to make a recommendation for a minimum period when they pass sentence (only 5 out of more than 200 in a recent 12 month period). There is no need to reconvene the Court some weeks later, with consequent further distress and inconvenience to the victim's family (and considerable extra cost), to consider reports and set publicly a determinate tariff which in many cases will not satisfy the family and will be open to lengthy appeal procedures.

The current tariff setting system is open and seen to be fair so far as the prisoner is concerned. Tariff recommendations are all seen by the LCJ who applies a common judicial approach. They are disclosed to the prisoner who can make representations before the tariff is set. The consideration of all cases by a single senior official and Minister ensures a high degree of consistency in tariff setting. Unlike 'relevant parts' set by the courts Ministerial tariffs can be reviewed at any time and can be reduced on grounds of exceptional circumstances including exceptional progress in prison (5 have been so reduced since the 10 November 1997 statement). This wide discretion enables the punitive periods to be reviewed and, exceptionally, reduced, long after the judiciary and Ministers concerned may have left the scene.

For all these reasons the current mandatory sentence for murder and the tariff setting arrangements attract public and Parliamentary support. The Secretary of State's role in tariff setting in murder cases is perceived by many as falling within the Government's responsibility to provide adequate public protection and does, in some good measure, contribute to public confidence in the criminal justice system.

Accordingly, I remain unconvinced that change to the current system is either necessary or appropriate.

Yours ever

(Sgd) Jack

JACK STRAW

APPENDIX 4

PRACTICE DIRECTION (CRIME: MANDATORY LIFE SENTENCES) (NO 2)

29 July 2004

It should not be assumed that Parliament, in enacting the Criminal Justice Act 2003, intended to raise to 15 years all mandatory life sentence minimum terms that would previously have had a lower starting point. Lord Woolf CJ so stated in the Supreme Court when handing down an amendment to *Practice Direction (Criminal Proceedings: Consolidation)* [2002] 1 WLR 2870 ('the consolidated criminal practice direction'). Lord Woolf said that this *Practice Direction* amends the consolidated criminal practice direction handed down by his Lordship on 8 July 2002.

IV.49 Life Sentences

IV.49.1 This direction replaces *Practice Direction (Crime: Mandatory Life Sentences)* [2004] 1 WLR 1874 handed down on 18 May 2004 (previously inserted at paragraphs IV.49.1-IV.49.25 of the consolidated criminal practice direction). Its purpose is to give practical guidance as to the procedure for passing a mandatory life sentence under section 269 of and Schedule 21 to the Criminal Justice Act 2003 ("the Act"). The direction also gives guidance as to the transitional arrangements under section 276 of and Schedule 22 to the Act. It clarifies the correct approach to looking at the practice of the Secretary of State prior to December 2002 for the purposes of Schedule 22 to the Act, in the light of the judgment in *R v Sullivan* [2004] EWCA Crim 1762; *The Times* 14 July 2004.

IV.49.2 Section 269 of the Act came into force on 18 December 2003. Under section 269 all courts passing a mandatory life sentence must either announce in open court the minimum term the prisoner must serve before the Parole Board can consider release on licence under the provisions of section 28 of the Crime (Sentences)

Act 1997 (as amended by section 275 of the Act) or announce that the seriousness of the offence is so exceptionally high that the early release provisions should not apply at all (a "whole life order").

IV.49.3 In setting the minimum term the court must set the term it considers appropriate taking into account the seriousness of the offence. In considering the seriousness of the offence the court must have regard to the general principles set out in Schedule 21 to the Act and any other guidelines issued by the Sentencing Guidelines Council which are relevant to the case and not incompatible with the provisions of Schedule 21. Although it is necessary to have regard to the guidance, it is always permissible not to apply the guidance if a judge considers there are reasons for not following it. It is always necessary to have regard to the need to do justice in the particular case. However, if a court departs from any of the starting points given in Schedule 21 the court is under a duty to state its reasons for doing so.

IV.49.4 The guidance states that where the offender is 21 or over, the first step is to choose one of three starting points: "whole life", 30 years or 15 years. Where the 15-year starting point has been chosen, judges should have in mind that this starting point encompasses a very broad range of murders. In *R v Sullivan*, at para 35, the court found that it should not be assumed that Parliament intended to raise all minimum terms that would previously have had a lower starting point to 15 years.

IV.49.5 Where the offender was 21 or over at the time of the offence, and the court takes the view that the murder is so grave that the offender ought to spend the rest of his life in prison, the appropriate starting point is a "whole life order". The effect of such an order is that the early release provisions in section 28 of the Crime (Sentences) Act 1997 will not apply. Such an order should only be specified where the court considers that the seriousness of the offence (or the combination of the offence and one or more other offences associated with it) is exceptionally high. Paragraph 4(2) of Schedule 21 to the Act sets out examples of cases where it would normally be appropriate to take the "whole life order" as the appropriate starting point.

IV.49.6 Where the offender is aged 18 to 20 and commits a murder that is so serious that it would require a whole life order if committed by an offender aged 21 or over, the appropriate starting point will be 30 years.

IV.49.7 Where a case is not so serious as to require a "whole life order" but where the seriousness of the offence is particularly high and the offender was aged 18 or over when he committed the offence, the appropriate starting point is 30 years. Paragraph 5(2) of Schedule 21 to the Act sets out examples of cases where a 30-year starting point would normally be appropriate (if they do not require a "whole life order").

IV.49.8 Where the offender was aged 18 or over when he committed the offence and the case does not fall within paragraph 4(1) or 5(1) of Schedule 21 the appropriate starting point is 15 years.

IV.49.9 18- to 20-year-olds are only the subject of the 30-year and 15-year starting points.

IV.49.10 The appropriate starting point when setting a sentence of detention during Her Majesty's pleasure for offenders aged under 18 when they committed the offence is always 12 years.

IV.49.11 The second step after choosing a starting point is to take account of any aggravating or mitigating factors which would justify a departure from the starting point. Additional aggravating factors (other than those specified in paragraphs 4(1) and 5(1)) are listed at paragraph 10 of Schedule 21. Examples of mitigating factors are listed at paragraph 11 of Schedule 21. Taking into account the aggravating and mitigating features the court may add to or subtract from the starting point to arrive at the appropriate punitive period.

IV.49.12 The third step is that the court should consider the effect of section 151(1) of the Powers of Criminal Courts (Sentencing) Act 2000 (or, when it is in force, section 143(2) of the Act) in relation to previous convictions and section 151(2) Powers of Criminal Courts (Sentencing) Act 2000 (or, when it is in force, section 143(3) of the Act) where the offence was committed whilst the offender was on bail. The court should also consider the effect of section 152 of the Powers of Criminal Courts (Sentencing) Act 2000 (or, when it is in force, section 144 of the Act) where the offender has pleaded guilty. The court should then to take into account what credit the offender would have received for a remand in custody under section 240 of the Act, but for the fact that the mandatory sentence is one of life imprisonment.

Where the offender has been remanded in custody in connection with the offence or a related offence, the court should have in mind that no credit will otherwise be given for this time when the prisoner will be considered for early release. The appropriate time to take it into account is when setting the minimum term. The court should normally subtract the time for which the offender was remanded in custody in connection with the offence or a related offence from the punitive period it would otherwise impose in order to reach the minimum term.

IV.49.13 Following these calculations the court should have arrived at the appropriate minimum term to be announced in open court. As paragraph 9 of Schedule 21 makes clear, the judge retains ultimate discretion and the court may arrive at any minimum term from any starting point. The minimum term is subject to appeal by the offender under section 271 of the Act and subject to review on a reference by the Attorney-General under section 272 of the Act.

Transitional Arrangements for New Sentences Where the Offence Was Committed Before 18 December 2003

IV.49.14 Where the court is passing a sentence of mandatory life imprisonment for an offence committed before 18 December 2003, the court should take a fourth step in determining the minimum term in accordance with section 276 of and Schedule 22 to the Act.

IV.49.15 The purpose of these provisions is to ensure that the sentence does not breach the principle of non-retroactivity by ensuring that a lower minimum term would not have been imposed for the offence when it was committed. Before setting the minimum term the court must check whether the proposed term is greater than that which the Secretary of State would probably have notified under the practice followed by the Secretary of State before December 2002.

IV.49.16 The decision in *R v Sullivan* gives detailed guidance as to the correct approach to this practice and judges passing mandatory life sentences where the murder was committed prior to 18 December 2003 are well advised to read that judgment before proceeding.

IV.49.17 The practical result of that judgment is that in sentences where the muder was committed before 31 May 2002, the best guide to what would have been the practice of the Secretary of State is the letter sent to judges by Lord Bingham of Cornhill CJ on 10 February 1997, the relevant parts of which are set out in paras IV.49.18-IV.49.21 below.

IV.49.18 The practice of Lord Bingham of Cornhill CJ, as set out in his letter of 10 February 1997, was to take 14 years as the period actually to be served for the "average", "normal" or "unexceptional" murder. Examples of factors he outlined as capable, in appropriate cases, of mitigating the normal penalty were: (1) youth; (2) age (where relevant to physical capacity on release or the likelihood of the defendant dying in prison); (3) subnormality or mental abnormality; (4) provocation (in a non-technical sense), or an excessive response to a personal threat; (5) the absence of an intention to kill: (6) spontaneity and lack of premeditation (beyond that necessary to constitute the offence: e g a sudden response to family pressure or to prolonged and eventually insupportable stress); (7) mercy killing; (8) a plea of guilty, or hard evidence of remorse or contrition.

IV.49.19 Lord Bingham of Cornhill CJ then listed the following factors as likely to call for a sentence more severe than the norm: (1) evidence of a planned, professional, revenge or contract killing; (2) the killing of a child or a very old or otherwise vulnerable victim; (3) evidence of sadism, gratuitous violence, or sexual maltreatment, humiliation or degradation before the killing; (4) killing for gain (in the course of burglary, robbery, blackmail, insurance fraud, etc.); (5) multiple killings; (6) the killing of a witness or potential witness to defeat the ends of justice; (7) the killing of those doing their public duty (policemen, prison officers, postmasters, firemen, judges, etc); (8) terrorist or politically motivated killings; (9) the use of firearms or other dangerous weapons, whether carried for defensive or offensive reasons; (10) a substantial record of serious violence; (11) macabre attempts to dismember or conceal the body.

IV.49.20 Lord Bingham of Cornhill CJ further stated that the fact that a defendant was under the influence of drink or drugs at the time of the killing is so common he would be inclined to treat it as neutral. But in the not unfamiliar case in which a married couple, or two derelicts, or two homosexuals, inflamed by drink, indulge

413

in a violent quarrel in which one dies, often against a background of longstanding drunken violence, then he would tend to recommend a term somewhat below the norm.

IV.49.21 Lord Bingham of Cornhill CJ went on to say that given the intent necessary for proof of murder, the consequences of taking life and the understandable reaction of relatives of the deceased, a substantial term will almost always be called for, save perhaps in a truly venial case of mercy killing. While a recommendation of a punitive term longer than, say, 30 years will be very rare indeed, there should not be any upper limit. Some crimes will certainly call for terms very well in excess of the norm.

IV.49.22 For the purposes of sentences where the murder was committed after 31 May 2002 and before 18 December 2003, the judge should apply *Practice Statement (Crime: Life Sentences)* [2002] 1 WLR 1789, 1790-1792, paras 9-19 handed down on 31 May 2002 and reproduced at paras IV.49.23-IV.49.33 below.

IV.49.23 This statement replaces the previous single normal tariff of 14 years by substituting a higher and a normal starting point of respectively 16 (comparable to 32 years) and 12 years (comparable to 24 years). These starting points have then to be increased or reduced because of aggravating or mitigating factors such as those referred to below. It is emphasised that they are no more than starting points.

The Normal Starting Point of 12 Years

IV.49.24 Cases falling within this starting point will normally involve the killing of an adult victim, arising from a quarrel or loss of temper between two people known to each other. It will not have the characteristics referred to in para IV.49.26. Exceptionally, the starting point may be reduced because of the sort of circumstances described in the next paragraph.

IV.49.25 The normal starting point can be reduced because the murder is one where the offender's culpability is significantly reduced, for example, because: (a) the case came close to the borderline between murder and manslaughter; or (b) the offender suffered from mental disorder, or from a mental disability which lowered the degree of his criminal responsibility for the killing, although not affording a defence of diminished responsibility; or (c) the offender was provoked (in a non-technical sense), such as by prolonged and eventually unsupportable stress; or (d) the case involved an overreaction in self-defence; or (e) the offence was a mercy killing. These factors could justify a reduction to 8/9 years (equivalent to 16/18 years).

The Higher Starting Point of 15/16 Years

IV.49.26 The higher starting point will apply to cases where the offender's culpability was exceptionally high or the victim was in a particularly vulnerable position. Such cases will be characterised by a feature which makes the crime especially serious, such as: (a) the killing was "professional" or a contract killing; (b) the killing was politically motivated; (c) the killing was done for gain (in the course of a burglary, robbery etc.); (d) the killing was intended to defeat the ends of justice (as in the killing of a witness or potential witness); (e) the victim was providing a public service; (f) the victim was a child or was otherwise vulnerable; (g) the killing was racially aggravated; (h) the victim was deliberately targeted because of his or her religion or sexual orientation; (i) there was evidence of sadism, gratuitous violence or sexual maltreatment, humiliation or degradation of the victim before the killing; (j) extensive and/or multiple injuries were inflicted on the victim before death; (k) the offender committed multiple murders.

Variation of the Starting Point

IV.49.27 Whichever starting point is selected in a particular case, it may be appropriate for the trial judge to vary the starting point upwards or downwards, to take account of aggravating or mitigating factors, which relate to either the offence or the offender, in the particular case.

IV.49.28 Aggravating factors relating to the offence can include: (a) the fact that the killing was planned; (b) the use of a firearm; (c) arming with a weapon in advance; (d) concealment of the body, destruction of the crime scene and/or dismemberment of the body; (e) particularly in domestic violence cases, the fact that the murder was the culmination of cruel and violent behaviour by the offender over a period of time.

IV.49.29 Aggravating factors relating to the offender will include the offender's previous record and failures to respond to previous sentences, to the extent that this is relevant to culpability rather than to risk.

IV.49.30 Mitigating factors relating to the offence will include: (a) an intention to cause grievous bodily harm, rather than to kill; (b) spontaneity and lack of premeditation.

IV.49.31 Mitigating factors relating to the offender may include: (a) the offender's age; (b) clear evidence of remorse or contrition; (c) a timely plea of guilty.

Very Serious Cases

IV.49.32 A substantial upward adjustment may be appropriate in the most serious cases, for example, those involving a substantial number of murders, or if there are several factors identified as attracting the higher starting point present. In suitable cases, the result might even be a minimum term of 30 years (equivalent to 60 years) which would offer little or no hope of the offender's eventual release. In cases of exceptional gravity, the judge, rather than setting a whole life minimum term, can state that there is no minimum period which could properly be set in that particular case.

IV.49.33 Among the categories of case referred to in para IV.49.26, some offences may be especially grave. These include cases in which the victim was performing his duties as a prison officer at the time of the crime or the offence was a terrorist or sexual or sadistic murder or involved a young child. In such a case, a term of 20 years and upwards could be appropriate.

IV.49.34 In following this guidance, judges should bear in mind the conclusion of the court in *R v Sullivan* that the general effect of both these statements is the same. While Lord Bingham of Cornhill CJ does not identify as many starting points, it is open to the judge to come to exactly the same decision irrespective of which was followed. Both pieces of guidance give the judge a considerable degree of discretion.

Procedure for Announcing the Minimum Term in Open Court

IV.49.35 Having gone through the three or four steps outlined above, the court is then under a duty, under section 270 of the Act, to state in open court, in ordinary language, its reasons for deciding on the minimum term or for passing a whole life order.

IV.49.36 In order to comply with this duty the court should state clearly the minimum term it has determined. In doing so, it should state which of the starting points it has chosen and its reasons for doing so. Where the court has departed from that starting point due to mitigating or aggravating features it must state the reasons for that departure and any aggravating or mitigating features which have led to that departure. At that point the court should also declare how much, if any, time is being deducted for time spent in custody. The court must then explain that the minimum term is the minimum amount of time the prisoner will spend in prison, from the date of sentence, before the Parole Board can order early release. If it remains necessary for the protection of the public, the prisoner will continue to be detained after that date. The court should also state that where the prisoner has served the minimum term and the Parole Board has decided to direct release the prisoner will remain on licence for the rest of his life and may be recalled to prison at any time.

IV.49.37 Where the offender was 21 or over when he committed the offence and the court considers that the seriousness of the offence is so exceptionally high that a "whole life order" is appropriate, the court should state clearly its reasons for reaching this conclusion. It should also explain that the early release provisions will not apply.

APPENDIX 5

MEMORANDUM: COMMENTS OF THE LAW COMMISSION ON THE CRIMINAL LAW REVISION COMMITTEE'S WORKING PAPER ON OFFENCES AGAINST THE PERSON[1]

Introduction

1. The Law Commission have considered the Working Paper on Offences against the Person which the Criminal Law Revision Committee published in August 1976. At the same time we have considered the twelfth Report of the Committee on the Penalty for Murder[2] which was presented to Parliament in January 1973 and which is also a consultative document containing the Committee's provisional views. We have taken into account in the comments we make the Report of the Butler Committee on Mentally Abnormal Offenders[3] which contains recommendations for changes in the law relevant to the matters contained in the Committee's two consultative documents.

2. We think that the most important and probably the most controversial of the Committee's provisional proposals are those relating to homicide and we deal with these first in this memorandum.

3. The twelfth Report of the committee dealing with the penalty for murder was made on the assumption that murder would, however defined, remain a separate offence.[4] This was then the view of the Committee and that view was repeated and fully argued in the Working Paper.[5] We deal with this question first but,

---

1. We have the authority of Etherington LJ, Chairman of the Law Commission, to reproduce this hitherto unpublished document which was subsequently uncovered at the National Archives, Kew.
2. Cmnd 5184.
3. (1975) Cmnd 6244.
4. Twelfth Report, para 6.
5. Working Paper, paras 3-11.

before doing so, we would wish to make one point which we think important. We do not think that the answer to the question whether there should be a separate offence of murder greatly affects what to us seems the more important question of what the penalty for murder should be. We entirely agree with the opinion expressed by the Butler Committee on this point.[6]

Murder a Separate Offence?

4. In the twelfth Report the Committee argues in favour of there being a separate offence of murder:

> We believe that the stigma which, in the public's mind, attaches to a conviction of murder rightly emphasises the seriousness of the offence and may have a significant deterrent value.[7]

And this is again one of the arguments given in favour of the retention of murder as a separate offence in paragraphs 3-11 of the Working Paper.

5. Whatever may or may not be the view of the public we think that it is difficult to argue that murder, however narrowly defined, is always the most serious criminal offence. Because it has to be defined in terms of the actual result of conduct, namely death, it ranges over an extremely wide spectrum of criminality from intentional mass murder to 'family' killings and 'mercy' killings. It is committed by people with the most wicked of motives and also by people with the most merciful of motives. Some murderers are extremely dangerous people, others are almost certain never to commit another offence in their lives. And even the most terrible of murders is arguably less socially undesirable than the activities of the heroin pusher. It also seems to us that the fact that death actually has to occur before murder can be committed leads to a distinction difficult to justify between the 'most serious offence' and other offences equally serious. The bomber who blows up a building intending to kill its occupants but fails because, though terri-

---

6. Butler Committee Report, para 19.15.
7. Twelfth Report, para 6.

bly injured, they escape death surely commits as serious a criminal offence, judged by any rational standards, as any murderer, no matter how heinous his crime.

6. The second reason given for retaining murder as a separate offence is that 'to have a single offence of homicide, combining murder with a lesser offence of manslaughter, would mean that the jury's verdict would leave the judge with no guidance as to the gravity of the offence'.[8] We do not ourselves think that this is a strong argument. In the case of all other crimes, especially where there is a plea of guilty, the judge has to exercise his discretion in sentencing and we do not think that this causes difficulty. The decision in regard to provocation where the issue is whether a man was provoked into committing an offence of intentionally inflicting grievous bodily harm is the same decision as the judge would have to make in like circumstances if provocation in murder was no longer a jury question. It is said that 'the offence of homicide would apply to a very wide range of circumstances, varying in their degree of gravity, and the judge would be left to determine the true nature of the offence without the assistance of the jury',[9] but this is already the case where manslaughter is charged or a verdict of manslaughter returned and we do not believe it causes judges any greater difficulties than those inevitably involved in sentencing.

7. The other arguments for and against the retention of murder as a separate offence which are mentioned in the Working Paper would seem to be equally relevant to the question whether there should be a mandatory sentence for murder and we deal with them when we come to consider that question. And there are, we think. other arguments which, though relevant to this question, are also relevant to the question of the mandatory sentence and we defer consideration of these also.

8. We would agree with the arguments briefly stated in paragraph 10 of the Working Paper which have been advanced to the Committee against retaining murder as a separate offence. We are not, however, able to follow the argument that there should be a 'change in practice in homicide cases so that evidence in mitigation after plea could be introduced and considered with the same formality and care as if it were being given before verdict'. If there were no separate offence of murder there

---

8. Working Paper, para 5.
9. *Ibid.*

could be no mandatory sentence and matters of mitigation would automatically be considered after plea or verdict. If matters are advanced in mitigation which are either disputed by the prosecution or do not accord with the depositions the judge can and should hear sworn evidence in support of and, if necessary, in rebuttal of the matters so advanced. No 'change in practice' would surely be necessary.

9. We do not think that the arguments in favour of retaining murder as a separate type of unlawful homicide are convincing and, for ourselves, we think that the distinction between murder and other forms of homicide should be abolished. We agree with Lord Kilbrandon that 'there does not appear to be any good reason why the crimes of murder and manslaughter should not both be abolished and the single crime of unlawful homicide substituted'.[10] However, we appreciate that public opinion might not be prepared to accept something which looks like a weakening of the criminal law and of respect for human life. We realise that the word 'murder' has emotive connotations which would militate against its excision from the vocabulary of the criminal law. We think that nearly all the great advantages[11] which would stem from subsuming murder under a general heading of unlawful homicide could also be achieved by the abolition of the mandatory sentence. We, therefore, go on to consider the question whether there should be a mandatory sentence for murder.

A Mandatory Sentence?

10. The only argument which is advanced in the twelfth Report as a positive argument in favour of retaining the mandatory life sentence for murder is contained in paragraph 22. It seems to us that the arguments contained in that paragraph are directed to the advantages of a life sentence not of a mandatory life sentence. Clearly a life sentence would have to be available either for murder as a separate offence or for a more extended homicide offence; the paragraph does not seem to us to deal with the question whether the sentence should be a mandatory one or not.

---

10. *Hyam v DPP* [1975] AC 55, 98.
11. See para 22 below for the main additional advantage which would result from there being no separate offence of murder.

11. Other arguments in favour of the mandatory life sentence appear in the report as answers to criticisms of the sentence. In paragraphs 10-12 are set out and answered what seem to us again to be criticisms of the life sentence as such and to be irrelevant for a discussion of the question whether the sentence should be mandatory. Paragraph 13 states the argument advanced by Professor Glanville Williams that a mandatory life sentence is wrong because it takes away the judge's discretion in sentencing. We agree with Professor Glanville Williams' view and we do not think that it is answered by showing that the judiciary takes an active part in deciding the term which individuals sentenced to life imprisonment in fact serve. The involvement of the judiciary in the deliberations of the Parole Board would be an equally good argument for having more mandatory sentences for other offences.

12. In paragraph 16 it is said that 'a fundamental objection to the suggestion that there should be a determinate sentence for murder in place of the present mandatory life sentence is the difficulty that the trial judge would have sentencing a person convicted of murder to a fixed term of years'. We do not think that murder presents any greater difficulty in sentencing than do other crimes. It is said to be 'particularly difficult in cases of murder to predict at the time of sentence whether the murderer in question will have to be detained indefinitely or not, or at what stage of his sentence he will become unlikely to kill again'. We would agree that this is, in *some* cases of murder, a difficulty but the difficulty applies equally to *all* dangerous criminals whether they have committed murder or some other serious offence against the person. For many murderers, particularly 'family' murders, the problems of prediction are peculiarly easy. And, as the point out, the judge has and exercises a discretion in the case of the defendant found guilty of manslaughter on the ground of diminished responsibility. We agree that 'if judges may be trusted with discretion with regard to disordered killers who are the most unpredictable kind, then, *a fortiori*, they can be trusted to sentence normal persons who may have killed only in exceptional circumstances of great stress'.[12]

13. We have considered and agree with the arguments and conclusions contained in paragraphs 19.8 to 19.16 of the Butler Committee and do not repeat them. The

---

12. Butler Committee Report, para 19.11(c).

Butler Committee's remit only covered mentally disordered offenders and their recommendation as to the mandatory life sentence was made in the context of their recommendation for the abolition of the partial defence of diminished responsibility and the crime of infanticide. We think that there are other strong arguments in principle which can in a broader context be made against the mandatory life sentence.

14. Minimum sentences are, we believe, contrary to the whole philosophy of English criminal justice and the mandatory life sentence is, in effect, a very high minimum sentence which only the Executive or the Parole Board can palliate. We think that this reduction of the Court's discretion in sentencing is wrong in principle. It was, we think, understandable that a judge should not have been asked to decide whether a sentence of death should be passed but no such argument applies to a sentence of life imprisonment. For offences other than murder judges are daily deciding whether to impose a sentence of life imprisonment or some less severe penalty.

15. In paragraphs 24-39 of their Twelfth Report the Committee considers and recommends the retention of the power of judges to make recommendations under section 1(2) of the Murder (Abolition of Death Penalty) Act 1965. We think that the necessity of retaining this power underlines the disadvantages implicit in a mandatory sentence. The power is at present used to indicate that the sentence passed is to be treated as more severe than a normal life sentence. This is only necessary if the life sentence is not the most severe sentence. We think that it should be. In general we think that it is unfortunate that the sentence of life imprisonment has come to be used as a euphemism for an indeterminate sentence reviewable by the executive. In some cases it is arguable that an indeterminate sentence should be available and a strong case is made out by the Butler Committee for a new form of reviewable sentence designed primarily for the dangerous 'psychopath'. We think that this approach is preferable to using the life sentence as a means whereby the judiciary are able to place the responsibility for deciding on the length of sentence upon the executive. The provision of the recommending

power is motivated by the reluctance of the judiciary to surrender their responsibility in the most serious cases; we approve the reluctance. But, if a measure of discretion is to be allowed to the judiciary in the most serious cases, why should it not also be given in the least serious cases? We think that the view of the Scottish Committee[13] is logical but we appreciate that to require the trial judge to decide on a recommendation which might vary from one day (for mercy killings) through a year or two (for some family killings) up to thirty years would demonstrate conclusively the irrationality of a mandatory sentence. We think that a sentence of life imprisonment should be restored to its place as *the* most severe sentence open to the Court, but this can only be done if its mandatory application to murder is abolished. For the dangerous criminal for whom prediction is extremely difficult, typically the young dangerous 'psychopath', we would favour a new reviewable sentence on the lines of the Butler Committee recommendation.

16. We think also that the mandatory life sentence applying only to murder causes great and irrational complications in the law of homicide. Because of the wide spectrum of guilt which must be comprehended by the offence of murder, however defined, there is a continual pressure to provide means to take conduct coming clearly within the definition out of the offence. The Working Paper recognises this difficulty in dealing with provocation. 'Provocation', it is said 'is a defence to murder because of the mandatory life sentence which that offence carries',[14] and the detailed consideration given to this special partial defence in the Working Paper demonstrates clearly the conceptual difficulties and difficulties of definition involved. In respect of all other offences provocation is a matter for consideration at the time of disposal and we think that this is the proper time to take it into account in homicide also.

17. The same sort of reasoning has led the Committee to suggest yet another new sort of homicide, mercy killing.[15] Here we think that the sacrifice of principle in an effort to mitigate the severity of the life sentence is especially manifest. The provisional proposal is that the new offence should contain as one of its ingredients the motive of the defendant for intentionally killing another person. We deal

---

13. Twelfth Report, para 26.
14. Working Paper, para 48.
15. Working Paper, paras 79-87.

in greater detail with this suggested new offence later in this memorandum. For present purposes we merely point out that, were it not for the mandatory life sentence, this new and extremely complicated offence would be quite unnecessary.

18. In paragraph 167 the Committee make the suggestion for discussion that there should be a new partial defence to murder reducing the crime to manslaughter where death was caused by the exercise of excessive force in self defence. This further possible complication of the law stems, we believe, once again from the wish to relieve some of the less heinous murders of the mandatory sentence.

19. If all the ameliorations suggested in the Working Paper were adopted there would be no less than five different ways in which a person coming within the definition of murder could have his crime reduced to some lesser offence; provocation, diminished responsibility and excessive self-defence would reduce the crime to manslaughter; in addition, there would be the old offence of infanticide and the new offence of mercy killing to cover other examples of intentional killing. But there would still remain beneath the umbrella of murder with its inevitable life sentence many of the least heinous killings, particularly those killings which happen within the stressful family environment. We think that the very natural impulse to relieve people who come within the definition of murder, but are thought to have some excuse for their conduct, from the inevitability of a life sentence is itself one of the strongest arguments against the mandatory sentence.

20. And because of the doctrine that murder is the most serious offence the Committee has, we think, been led into making another provisional proposal which we would not support. It is the opposite of those already considered. Having, in our opinion correctly, decided that risk taking should not be sufficient for murder, the Committee then recommends that one particular form of risk taking should be called murder. The reasoning is explicit that the new sort of murder 'causing death — by an act intended to cause fear (of death or serious injury) and known to the defendant to involve a risk of causing death' is put forward for comment 'in order to include such cases within the offence of murder'.[16] That such conduct should lay the defendant open to the most serious penalty known to the law no

---

16. Working Paper, para 42.

one would dispute but to complicate the law in such a way merely because of the stigma attached to the word 'murder' and the mandatory sentence it carries seems to us to be wrong. The heroin pusher intends (in the extended sense of having no substantial doubt that he will) to cause terrible distress and injury and knows that his acts involve a risk of causing death: should he be stigmatised as a murderer? Or something worse?

21. We would not suggest that the mandatory sentence should be abolished merely because the law could thereby be greatly simplified but that it would be simplified is, we think, an additional strong argument in favour of its abolition. Whether or not a separate offence of murder remained the abolition of the mandatory sentence would make it possible to abolish the partial defences of diminished responsibility and provocation; the offence of infanticide could go; it would be unnecessary to devise a new offence of mercy killing or killing following on risk taking intended to cause fear; it would likewise render unnecessary the suggested new partial defence of 'excessive self-defence'.[17]

22. The only disadvantage which it might be thought would follow from this very great simplification of the law is that mentioned in paragraph 19.16 of the Butler Report in respect of the proposed abolition of the partial defence of diminished responsibility. If a separate offence of murder is retained (although with no mandatory sentence) a person who would now be found guilty of manslaughter on the ground of provocation or diminished responsibility would suffer the stigma of a conviction for murder. We agree with the Butler Committee that this objection could be met by empowering the jury to return a verdict of murder with extenuating circumstances. And such a verdict would no doubt be of some assistance to the court in determining sentence.

23. We summarise our views on the preliminary questions raised in any consideration of homicide thus:—

---

17. Working Paper, para 167.

(a) We agree with Lord Kilbrandon that 'there does not appear to be any good reason why the crimes of murder and manslaughter should not both be abolished and the single crime of unlawful homicide substituted'.[18]

(b) If a separate offence of murder is retained we think that it should no longer carry a mandatory sentence.

(c) If our views on either (a) or (b) are accepted:-

    (i) We think that the special defences of diminished responsibility and provocation should be abolished.

    (ii) We think that the offence of infanticide should be abolished.

    (iii) We do not think that a new offence of mercy killing should be created.[19]

    (iv) do not think that a new partial defence of excessive self-defence should be devised.

    (v) We think that the jury should be empowered to bring in a verdict of murder (or unlawful homicide) with mitigating circumstance which could include all the fact situations in sub-paragraphs (i) to (iv) above, as well as other cases of mitigating circumstances such as 'family' killings.

    (vi) We do not think that there should be any new category of murder involving aggravated risk taking.

Consideration of Provisional Views on Assumption Murder Remains a Separate Offence

24. We now turn to consider in detail the provisional views of the Committee on the assumption that the crime of murder is going to remain as a distinct type of homicide. We begin by considering what should be the definition of murder.

---

18. Cited, Working Paper, para 4.
19. We deal specifically with mercy killings in paragraphs 35-44 below.

Definition of Murder

25. In our report on Imputed Criminal Intent we recommended that 'A killing should not amount to murder unless there is an intent to kill. But it should be made clear that, where a man does not have the purpose to kill in any event, he may nevertheless have the intent to kill if, at the time when he takes the act in fact resulting in death, he is willing by that action to kill in accomplishing some purpose other than killing'.[20] The test of willingness to kill has not met with approval and is criticised in the Working Paper as being 'uncertain and ambiguous' and 'too difficult and subtle for a jury to understand'.[21] We would not now make this proposal.

26. We do, however, think that if there is to be a separate offence of murder it should be narrowly confined. And we would, therefore, adhere to our earlier recommendation that it should be limited to cases of intentional killing. We think that, if there is a justification for the retention of murder as a separate offence, it lies in the abhorrence felt at the intentional taking of a human life. In our projected report on the mental element in crime we have proposed the following provision dealing with intention:-

> Where by virtue of any provision contained in any relevant instrument defining an offence a person's liability for the offence depends on whether he intends any particular result of his actions or omissions, a person who does not intend that result in the ordinary sense shall be taken for the purposes of that provision to intend that result if, but only if, he has no substantial doubt that his actions or omissions will have that result.

We think that this slight extension of the normal meaning of intention would be sufficient to include in the definition those cases which we think should be included.

27. We, therefore, agree with the arguments which appear in paragraph 26 of the Working Paper and disagree with those in paragraph 27. The argument in paragraph 28 would largely disappear if the mandatory sentence for murder were to

---

20. Law Com No 10, para 22(c).
21. Working Paper, para 22.

go. If it is to remain it would make even stronger our view that murder should be restricted to intentional killing. We think that the discretion of the court in sentencing should be as little fettered as possible.

28. If, contrary to our views, it is decided to retain as murder a killing with intent to cause serious injury, we prefer of the variations set out in paragraphs 29-36 of the Working Paper the one summarised in paragraph (2)(bb) of the Summary at the end of the Working Paper: 'If a person causes death by an unlawful act intended to cause serious injury and known to the defendant to involve a risk of death'.

29. We do not think that it should be murder 'to cause death by an unlawful act intended to cause fear (of death or serious injury) and known to the defendant to involve a risk of causing death'. We think that the intention to cause fear is an unsound way of distinguishing one sort of risk taking from another and, in particular, we think that the test of an intention to cause fear would bring into the definition an element of motive which is undesirable. One can easily imagine very serious risk takings where there is no intention to cause fear.

Provocation

30. Only if the mandatory sentence for murder remains would we support the proposal to retain provocation as a partial defence. We think that the mandatory sentence is the only justification for treating provocation as a substantive defence. We would not support its extension to attempted murder and the new 'section 18' offence which is suggested for consideration in paragraph 109. We think it would immensely and unnecessarily complicate trials. We believe that, essentially, provocation is something best taken into account by the judge in sentencing. It is at this stage that it is best dealt with and we know of no public criticism of the exercise of judicial discretion in sentencing where serious offences short of homicide have been committed under provocation. If, because the mandatory sentence remains, complicated provisions have to be made for defining provocation, we are in agreement with the provisional proposals made in the Working Paper. We pre-

fer 'reasonable explanation of the loss of self-control' to 'reasonable excuse for the loss of self-control'.[22]

Diminished Responsibility

31. Once again, it is only if the mandatory sentence for murder remains that we would support the retention of the partial defence of diminished responsibility. We think that the recommendation of the Butler Committee,[23] (alternative to their preferred solution of abolishing the mandatory sentence) for a new definition of diminished responsibility would effect a great improvement in the law.

32. We think that another disadvantage of having a mandatory sentence for murder arises out of the provisions for a defence of diminished responsibility. We think that the criticism of the mandatory sentence made in paragraph 19.11(f) of the Butler Committee Report is a good one —

> Because of the role of the jury in considering the medical evidence the diminished responsibility provision is not available to the man who has a mental disorder within the terms of the section but denies that he committed the act alleged against him. If his defence fails the sentence must be one of life imprisonment, notwithstanding that evidence of diminished responsibility could be given; he has ruled himself out of psychiatric disposal.

It is true that there are provisions for transferring from prison to hospital persons suffering from mental disorder but the report of the Butler Committee makes it clear that reliance upon the relevant provisions of the Mental Health Act 1959 is by no means a satisfactory substitute for a proper exercise of the judge's decision at the disposal stage. The number transferred is very small indeed compared with the number of prisoners who are mentally disordered: conditions in prisons are unfavourable for identifying the mentally disordered and those who are only slightly disordered are easily absorbed into the prison population.[24]

---

22. As suggested by one member in footnote 3 on p.21.
23. Butler Committee Report, paras 19.17-19.19.
24. See generally Chapter 3. In particular 3.20, 3.21 and 3.37-49.

Infanticide

33. We do not comment further[25] on the offence of infanticide in view of the Butler Committee's recommendations.[26] The New Zealand Crimes Act 1961[27] seems to recognise as a separate category of homicide one particular sort of 'family' murder. We have already commented on the irrationality of reducing to manslaughter the homicide of the dangerous psychopath and leaving as murder the 'family' killing[28] and we have made clear our preferred solution of the dilemma namely the abolition of murder as a separate offence or, at the least, the abolition of the mandatory sentence.

Killing by Consent and Suicide Pacts

34. Our views on killing by consent and suicide pacts depend upon whether murder remains a separate offence. If murder ceases to be a separate offence section 4 of the Homicide Act 1957 could be repealed. If it remains a separate offence the provisions as to suicide should remain in the law. However, in no circumstances do we agree with the view expressed that there should be a separate offence of killing by consent nor do we think that killing in pursuance of a suicide pact should cease to be a criminal offence at all.

Aiding and Abetting Suicide. Mercy killing

35. In considering the question of 'aiding and abetting suicide'[29] the Working Paper concludes that 'having regard to the present legal position in relation to euthanasia, we think (with one dissentient) that assisting a person to commit suicide should continue to be an offence'. But, neither at this point nor elsewhere in the Working Paper is there any consideration of what the present legal position in

---

25. See paras 19 and 21 above.
26. Butler Committee Report, paras 19.22-19.26. It is there made clear that there is no scientific basis for this crime.
27. Section 178.
28. See para 19 above.
29. See para 77.

relation to euthanasia in fact is. The Working Paper then goes on to discuss the suggested new offence of mercy killing and, in paragraph 80, it is said that the Committee has 'not discussed the question of legalising mercy killing, because this is a matter on which opinion is deeply divided and we do not regard an exercise in law reform as a suitable occasion for the solution of this controversial issue'. We are not clear whether the Committee intends to draw a distinction between mercy killing and euthanasia; for ourselves, we see none. And, whilst we do not disagree with the view that 'an exercise in law reform is not a suitable occasion for a solution of whether euthanasia should in any circumstances be legalised', we think that, in fact, the Committee has, in putting forward its provisional views on the definition of murder and the new offence of mercy killing, provided a solution to the problem. It is not one with which we agree.

Euthanasia, the Present Legal Position

36. Smith and Hogan, in considering 'The problem of causation', state: —

> The administration of pain-saving drugs presents difficult problems. In the case of *Adams* Devlin J directed the jury that there is no special defence justifying a doctor in giving drugs which would shorten life in the case of severe pain: 'If life were cut short by weeks or months it was just as much murder as if it were cut short by years'. He went on:-

> 'But that does not mean that a doctor aiding the sick or dying has to calculate in minutes or hours, or perhaps in days or weeks, the effect on a patient's life of the medicines which he administers. If the first purpose of medicine — the restoration of health — can no longer be achieved, there is still much for the doctor to do, and he is entitled to do all that is proper and necessary to relieve pain and suffering even if measures he takes may incidentally shorten life'.

> These passages are not easy to reconcile. If a doctor gives drugs with the object of relieving the pain and suffering of a dying man knowing that the drugs will

certainly shorten life, then he intends to shorten life. If, as Devlin J held, and as must surely be the case, the doctor has a defence, it cannot be because his act has not caused death nor because he did not intend so to do. Perhaps this is a case in which motive affords an excuse. Would not a legatee, who administered the same drugs with the object of hastening his inheritance, be guilty of murder if his actions accelerated the death to any appreciable extent?

Alternatively, it may be that there is a defence in these cases only where the drugs are not a 'substantial' cause of death; for, if the doctor is entitled to shorten life at all to save pain, presumably he may do this only where death is inevitable within a short time; hence the contrast made by the learned judge between 'weeks or months' and 'minutes or hours'.[30]

37. If Devlin J's direction is good law then, either looked at as an importation of motive into the criminal law as a part of the mental element or as a modification of the doctrine of causation, it would seem to be quite novel. And surely, in a codification, the ingredients of the defence (if any) should be stated with precision.

38. In our consultation on Working Paper No 55, Defences of General Application, Dr Finnis[31] has suggested that we should exclude the defence of necessity where the charge is murder. His reasoning is set out thus: —

> 4. Now the situation in which the question, whether or not to take such a decision [that is 'kill-in-order-to-avert-harm'], regularly arises is that of the treatment of incurable illness. It seems to be universally accepted that at present the law firmly forbids any decision to kill or to shorten life as a means of ending or abbreviating suffering or disability. It seems equally clear that it is generally accepted that the law does not forbid a decision to alleviate suffering by means which have as their foreseen 'side effect' the abbreviation of life where such means are necessary (ie are the only available means) for the alleviation of suffering. As Devlin J said in his direction to the jury in *R v Adams* (1957) quoted by Glanville Williams, *The Sanctity of Life and the Criminal Law* (1958), p. 289

---

30. Smith and Hogan *Criminal Law*, (3 edn.), p.214.
31. Reader in law at the University of Oxford, Fellow of University College, Oxford.

'a doctor ... is entitled to do all that is proper and necessary to relieve pain and suffering, even if the measures he takes may incidentally shorten life'. As the Report of the Special Panel of the British Medical Association (*The Problem of Euthanasia* (1971), reprinted in Hugh Trowell, *The Unfinished Debate on Euthanasia* (1973), Appendix A) says: 'Under existing law it is illegal to terminate the life of anyone deliberately ... Control of pain and alleviation of distress must be the object and not termination of life' (Trowell, *op. cit.* pp. 152, 153).

5. It is, of course, important to notice that this generally accepted notion of lawful but death-dealing treatment, of a kind of homicide by 'side' or 'incidental' effect, where death is not 'deliberate' in the sense that death is not the 'object' is difficult if not impossible to reconcile with the general theory or conceptual structure of English criminal law, which analyses murder as killing with intention to kill, and 'intention' as including consequences or effects foreseen as certain or probable. Devlin J's attempt in *Adams* to handle the problem in terms of causation can hardly be considered successful. Lord Hailsham's extensive dicta concerning the difference between 'intention' and 'foresight of probable consequences' are important as indicating an awareness of the difficulties occasioned by the tendency of English criminal law theory to conflate intention and foresight for the sake of conceptual economy: but again Lord Hailsham's suggested solution, relying as it does on an unelaborated notion of 'lawful excuse', is not a complete one: see *Hyam v DPP* [1974] 2 All ER 41 at 51-55. There is no doubt that a codification of the criminal law will have to devise a solution to the problem which is coherent not only with commonsense, common morality and medical ethics (as the present law, as expounded in the dictum of Devlin J quoted above, is) but also with the conceptual framework of the criminal law (as the present law is not).

We agree with Dr Finnis that in codifying the criminal law a solution will have to be found to this problem.

39. The partial solution offered in the Working Paper is the creation of a new offence of mercy killing,[32] (punishable with a maximum of two years' imprisonment)

---

32. Working Paper, paras 78-87.

which 'would apply to a person who, from compassion, kills another person who is or is believed to be (1) permanently subject to great bodily pain or suffering, or (2) permanently helpless from bodily or mental incapacity, or (3) subject to rapid and incurable bodily or mental degeneration'. Presumably there would also be provision, as in section 1(2) of the Infanticide Act 1938, for a finding of 'mercy killing', on a trial for murder (or manslaughter?).

40. This new offence would comprehend the shortening of life by the administration of pain-killing drugs. It would, therefore, make criminal some conduct which, under the ruling of Devlin J, would now be lawful.[33] If such an offence were created it would be very important indeed to decide whether some special defence should be available to anyone charged with it. If no defence were to be available we think that there would be a serious danger that the mere existence of the offence would lead to the prosecution of doctors or nurses for it in circumstances where no-one would, at present, think of preferring a charge of murder. But, of course, the provision of such a special defence would, in effect, be a pre-emption of the discussion as to whether euthanasia should ever be lawful.

41. We think it is at least arguable that the conceptually correct way in which to view euthanasia is as a form of necessity defence, the shortening of life being justified (on the balance of harm test) by the greater harm of continuing pain. We do not however think that the examination of the *general* defences which we are now completing is the correct place in which to consider the very special problems raised by euthanasia. Questions as to whether and to what extent the patient's prior consent should be obtained and whether the justification should be open to anyone outside the medical profession will have to be decided.

42. It is, however, we think clear that codification of the criminal law will have to deal with the question. If the mandatory sentence for murder remains we think that the problem must be tackled in any new legislation dealing with offences against the person. The narrowest possible definition of murder is bound prima facie to include mercy killing. If, however, the mandatory sentence for murder is abolished we would not be opposed to leaving the question of euthanasia in

---

33. See para 34 above.

temporary abeyance pending a resolution of the continuing public debate on the matter. A judicial discretion in sentencing would provide a safeguard against socially unacceptable charges of murder (or homicide).

43. On the question whether aiding and abetting suicide should continue to be an offence under section 2 of the Suicide Act 1961 we agree that the first type of case mentioned in paragraph 77 of the Working Paper, persuading another to commit suicide, should continue to be an offence. The second type of case, merely assisting someone to commit suicide, seems to us to be very closely connected with the whole question of euthanasia and mercy killing. We cannot ourselves distinguish between the doctor who provides an overdose of drugs at the specific request of a patient intent on committing suicide because of a painful terminal illness (whom a minority of the Committee would exempt from criminal liability),[34] and the same doctor who actually administers an overdose by hypodermic syringe (whom the same minority would apparently be content to see guilty of committing a criminal offence).[35] We think that the law as to aiding and abetting suicide should remain as it is, until the whole question of euthanasia is decided.

Involuntary Manslaughter

44. We have already made clear our preference for having an offence of homicide which should obviously comprehend within its definition reckless killing. If, however, there are going to be two or more separate homicide offences we would agree that one of them should be the new offence suggested of causing death recklessly. We would entirely agree that, in any event, involuntary manslaughter should be abolished. We do not favour the retention of the distinction between offences requiring a specific intent and others requiring only a general mens rea or mental element upon which the decision in *DPP v Majewski*[36] is based. We would support the Butler Committee's recommendation for the creation of a new offence of

---

34. See Working Paper, para 77.
35. The provisional conclusion as to mercy killing seems to be that of the whole Committee.
36. [1976] 2 WLR 623.

'dangerous intoxication'.[37] And we think that, if this new offence were created the decision in *Majewski* should be overruled.

Causing Death by Dangerous Driving

45. We agree with the provisional conclusion that section 1 of the Road Traffic Act 1972 should be repealed. Nor do we think that there is any need to retain section 35 of the Offences Against the Person Act 1861. We think that anyone who injures someone by the 'wanton or furious' driving of any vehicle will come within one of the offences of causing injury which the eventual codification will contain.

---

37. Butler Committee Report, paras 18.51-18.59.

APPENDIX 6

EXTRACT FROM LAW COMMISSION CONSULTATION PAPER NO 177

The Argument of Sir Louis Blom-Cooper and Professor Terence Morris

2.32 Sir Louis Blom-Cooper and Professor Terence Morris have recently argued in favour of the abolition of the crime of murder.[1] The importance of their argument, and the influence that it has had, warrants special attention here. In their view, there should be a single offence of "criminal homicide". Matters such as provocation, diminished responsibility, and other mitigating factors, should be dealt with through the nature and degree of severity of the sentence given, not through a rigid structure of grades of offence and discrete (partial) defences, with all their complex restricting conditions.

2.33 There is powerful force in this argument. An argument for a single offence of unlawful homicide is also put forward by Victim Support.[2] They see virtue in ridding the law of the adversarial dimension to trials generated by the natural desire of defendants to see their crime reduced from murder to manslaughter. This, says Victim Support, often entails blaming the victim as part of the defence to the murder charge, a feature of trials they would like to reduce or eliminate. It may be, however, that reform of the doctrine of provocation as a partial defence to murder will address these concerns to some degree.[3]

---

1. L Blom-Cooper and T Morris, *With Malice Aforethought: A Study of the Crime and Punishment for Homicide* (2004).
2. Response to Partial Defences to Murder (2003) Consultation Paper No 173.
3. See Partial Defences to Murder (2004) Law Com No 290; see also Part 6. The incoming Coalition government of 2010 has, at the time of writing, indicated that the mandatory penalty would be given consideration in the context of the forthcoming review of sentencing policy in general. On 12 July 2010 in the House of Lords the Minister of State at the Ministry of Justice, Lord McNally, indicated that, as part of his department's commitment to a review of sentencing, the reviewing team in his Ministry was 'mindful of the recommendation of the Law Commission's Report' of 28 November 2006. Such consideration ought not to be spurned even if the likelihood of a fundamental change by way of replacing the mandatory

2.34 Even if it were within our terms of reference to consider it, however, we do not agree that it is the right course to recommend the creation of a single offence of unlawful killing. If, for Blom-Cooper and Morris, fault is merely a factor to reflect in sentence, then that could logically be said to be true of the outcome (the victim's death) as well. Why single out unlawful *killing* for separate treatment, when it may purely have been chance that the victim died, and the result could have been more or less serious bodily harm done?[4] Let us consider this point further.

2.35 Professor Paul Robinson, has argued that causing death can, like the more culpable of the mental elements (intention/recklessness), be regarded as simply a matter of grading.[5] On his account, the rule one violates in homicide cases can be said to be a rule prohibiting unjustifiably harming someone *simpliciter*. On this view, the fact that one caused death is simply an aggravating factor, a possible ground for increasing the sentence.[6] It is not the basis for a separate offence.

2.36 We take it that Blom-Cooper and Morris would *not* wish to endorse this line of argument, if it led to the conclusion that there should be no separate offence focused on the fact that the defendant has committed "homicide".[7] In our view,

penalty is by no means certain. It is at least a welcome alternative to the implacable refusal of the previous administrations (from 1979 to 2010) even to give the matter a hearing. The Law Commission, prohibited from even considering it in the context of a new homicide law for England and Wales, cannot be held to account for looking at what might be done by way of reforming the law of homicide without taking the penalty into account. The Law Commission's three-tier formulation of homicide law will do no more than create an unsatisfactory state of affairs, different in substance but similar in effect to the Homicide Act 1957, and produce yet more by way of anomaly and irrationality. The provisions of the Coroners and Justice Act 2009, by which the partial defences were amended, are, in our view, an example of the kind of legislation that is reflexive to the mood of particular opinion. At best it is piecemeal legislation, which is never very satisfactory. Though the law may often give the impression of being unalterably set in stone, the reality is otherwise. Nothing is immutable.

4. This point seems especially pertinent in the light of the fact that in Blom-Cooper and Morris's definition of 'criminal homicide' a distinction is drawn between simply causing serious physical harm to another person, to which the various fault elements — such as intention and recklessness — are relevant, and the crucial fatal result, to which they are not: L Blom-Cooper and T Morris, *With Malice Aforethought: A Study of the Crime and Punishment for Homicide* (2004) 175.

5. See P Robinson, 'Should the Criminal Law Abandon the Actus Reus-Mens Rea Distinction?' in S Shute, J Gardner and J Horder (eds), *Action and Value in Criminal Law* (1993) 211.

6. See, in the driving context, *Boswell* (1984) 6 Cr App R (S) 257.

7. It should be noted that this is not Robinson's conclusion: P Robinson, 'Should the Criminal

though, if the fact that death has been caused can provide sufficient justification for the creation of a distinct offence worthy of special categorisation, so can the mental element with which it was caused.

2.37 All Consultation Papers must have some fixed points, if consultation is to be focused and meaningful. Virtually all jurisdictions have a special category of homicide approximating to murder, whether or not they impose the mandatory life sentence for that offence. Accordingly, it is not proposed that such a category should cease to be a part of the law of England and Wales.

2.38 Further, our provisional proposal is that to maintain a firm and clear connection between the sanctity of life and the structure of the law of homicide, intentional killing should be made into a unique offence: "first degree murder". Intended killing is rightly regarded as specially grave species of wrong, because it involves a successful attack on the most basic of values, life, through the deliberate destruction of human being born alive.

Law Abandon the Actus Reus-Mens Rea Distinction?' in S Shute, J Gardner and J Horder (eds), *Action and Value in Criminal Law* (1993) 211.

INDEX

'Every student entering law school should have a copy and read it':
Criminal Law and Justice Weekly

A History of Criminal Justice in England and Wales
by John Hostettler

An ideal introduction, charting all the main developments of
criminal justice, from Anglo-Saxon dooms to the Common
Law, struggles for political, legislative and judicial ascendency
and the formation of the modern-day Criminal Justice System.

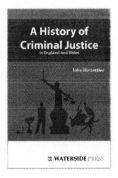

Among a wealth of topics the book looks at the Rule of
Law, the development of the criminal courts, police forces,
jury, justices of the peace and individual crimes and punishments. It locates all the iconic events of criminal justice
history and law reform within a wider background and
context - demonstrating a wealth and depth of knowledge.

'A captivating book that will have readers, who are interested in the subject matter and/or students studying any element of criminal justice
absorbed ... a thoroughly enjoyable read': *Internet Law Book Reviews*

'Highly recommended': *Choice*

'This is a good book from a well-respected publishing house. [It] could helpfully form part of the required reading on the programmes which develop
the criminal justice system's senior managers, as well as occupying a place
on the bookshelves of many other people': *Prison Service Journal*

ISBN 978-1-904380-51-1 (Paperback) **978-1-906534-79-0** (Ebook)
January 2009 | 352 pages

Whose Criminal Justice?

State or Community?

Editors Katherine Doolin, John Child, John Raine and Anthony Beech

The editors and contributors to this book are all members of The
University of Birmingham's 'Community and Criminal Justice
Group' (BCCJ Group). Drawing on the different disciplines of
law, criminology, forensic psychology, social work and public
management, they expertly explore the shifts and progress made
in criminal justice in England and Wales over the past two
decades and highlight the possibilities and pitfalls for the future.

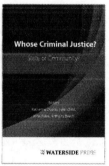

The overarching theme of the book is the balance between
the role of central government in creating and shap-
ing the regulatory framework of criminal justice and the
potential for 'localism', i.e. for communities at local level
to become more involved and to exercise more respon-
sibility for themselves in responding to crime and anti-social behaviour in their
midst. These twin dynamics are explored in the two main sections of the book:

Part I: The Regulatory State.
Part II: Empowered Communities as Stakeholders in Criminal Justice.

ISBN 978-1-904380-62-7 (Paperback) 978-1-906534-90-5 (Ebook)
February 2011 | 288 pages

WatersidePress.co.uk